FV

WITHDRAWN

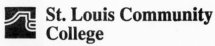

NINETEENTH-CENTURY
Piano Music

STUDIES IN MUSICAL GENRES AND REPERTORIES
R. Larry Todd, General Editor

Published:

Nineteenth-Century Piano Music
R. Larry Todd, Editor
Duke University

Twentieth-Century Piano Music
David Burge
Eastman School of Music

In Preparation:

Keyboard Music before 1700
Alexander Silbiger, Editor
Duke University

Eighteenth-Century Keyboard Music
Robert L. Marshall, Editor
Brandeis University

Lieder: Composers, Forms, and Styles
Rufus Hallmark, Editor
Queens College, CUNY

NINETEENTH-CENTURY

Piano Music

Edited by R. Larry Todd
Duke University

Schirmer Books

A DIVISION OF MACMILLAN, INC.
New York

COLLIER MACMILLAN CANADA
Toronto

MAXWELL MACMILLAN INTERNATIONAL
New York   Oxford   Singapore   Sydney

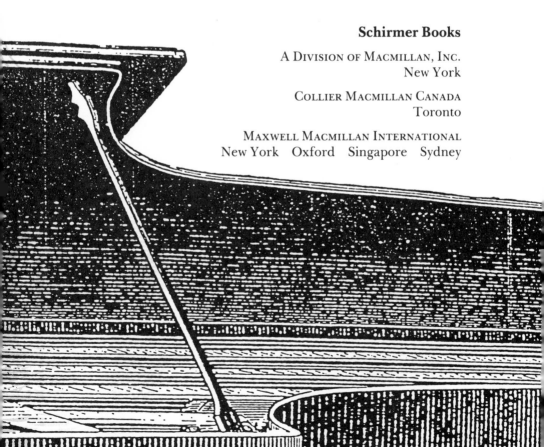

Schirmer Books
A Division of Macmillan, Inc.
866 Third Avenue, New York, N.Y. 10022

Collier Macmillan Canada, Inc.
1200 Eglinton Avenue East, Suite 200
Don Mills, Ontario M3C 3N1

Library of Congress Catalog Card Number: 90-8681

Printed in the United States of America

printing number
1 2 3 4 5 6 7 8 9 10

Library of Congress Cataloging-in-Publication Data
Nineteenth-century piano music / edited by R. Larry Todd.
    p.   cm. — (Studies in musical genres and repertories)
    Includes bibliographical references and index.
    ISBN 0-02-872551-4
    1. Piano music—19th century—History and criticism.   I. Todd, R.
    Larry.   II. Title: 19th-century piano music.   III. Series.
    ML706.N56   1990
    786.2'09'034—dc20   90-8681
                                                CIP
                                                MN

Contents

Preface

The piano—that most familiar of modern instruments—acquired its prominence during the nineteenth century, when it became essentially the instrument of choice. Its complex and accelerating development from the eighteenth-century fortepiano was prompted by a network of interdependent factors, including, of course, the technological innovations of the Industrial Revolution, which facilitated its mass production; the vogue of the romantic virtuoso, which found its most complete and versatile expression at the keyboard; and the new, irrepressible musical consumerism, which demanded a constantly "improving" instrument responsive to the ever-changing needs of composers, virtuosos, and musical amateurs alike. Not surprisingly, in nineteenth-century arts and letters the piano emerged as a veritable cultural symbol—for example, as an object associated with romantic subjectivity and Victorian sentimentality; as a conveyor of a special emotional language that transcended the mere play of words; as a symbol of Biedermeier respectability and domesticity in post-Napoleonic Germany and Austria; and as a sturdy article of furniture in middle-class drawing rooms.

Especially vivid impressions of the instrument's role in nineteenth-century life and manners are recorded in William Makepeace Thackeray's trenchant "novel without a hero," *Vanity Fair,* which appeared in serial form in 1847 and 1848 as "pen and pencil sketches of English society" during the Regency and the 1820s. The piano makes its entrance as early as the third chapter, where it appears as a powerfully emotive agent used by respectable ladies engaged in the art of "husband-hunting": "What causes them to labour at pianoforte sonatas, and to learn four songs from a fashionable master at a guinea a lesson, . . . but that they may bring down some 'desirable' young man with those killing bows and arrows of theirs?" In the next chapter, the idealized "heroine" Amelia Sedley, upon whom any number of misfortunes are visited during the course of the novel, falls in love with the wayward, undependable George Osborne, and the two go "off to the piano, which was situated, as pianos usually are, in the back drawing-room; and as it was rather dark, Miss Amelia, in the most unaffected way in the world, put her hand into Mr. Osborne's, who, of course, could see the way among the chairs and ottomans a great deal better than she could." In the twelfth chapter, titled "Sentimental and Otherwise," a different drawing room is the scene of another, this time unsuccessful, attempt by Amelia to attract George: "Amelia hoped George would soon join them there. She began playing some of his favourite waltzes (then newly imported) at the great carved-legged, leather-cased grand piano in the drawing room overhead." Here the piano is used to accompany a waltz, the then *risqué* dance that was, of course, the rage of Vienna during the Congress of 1815.

Elsewhere in *Vanity Fair* Thackeray affords us more intimate views of the preferred nineteenth-century instrument. In contrast to the ornate, powerful, drawing-room grand, Amelia possessed for her own use a "little square piano" from "the upper regions of the house," one specially chosen for her when she was a child "at Broadwood's." But she loses the square piano when, as a result of Napoleon's surprise landing at Cannes in 1815, her father, John Sedley, suffers financial ruin so that the entire household furnishings have to be sold to satisfy his creditors. Notwithstanding this reverse, Captain William Dobbin, secretly in love with Amelia, purchases the piano at the auction block and has it sent to her. But Amelia mistakenly imagines that her beloved George was the one who secretly interceded on her behalf. Only much later, years after George's death at Waterloo, is the error corrected. In chapter 59 we again encounter "that little old piano which had now passed into a plaintive jingling old age, but which she loved for reasons of her own. She was a child when first she played on it: and her parents gave it her." And, thinking that it had been George's gift, "the only one which she had received from her lover," it became "the thing she had cherished beyond all others, her dearest relic and prize. She had . . . played his favourite airs upon it: sat for long evening hours, touching, to the best of her simple art, melancholy harmonies on the keys, and weeping over them in silence." Amelia now recognizes the identity of her benefactor, and, as she expresses her gratitude, Dobbin, who "could hold no more," breaks down and professes his love for her. It is the piano that prompts this emotional outburst.

The special role of the piano in nineteenth-century European culture helps to explain, perhaps, the profusion of extraordinary music written for the instrument during the century, and, indeed, the preoccupation of many of the leading composers with the instrument. George Bernard Shaw wrote in 1876 that "the great majority of us receive our musical education almost entirely through the pianoforte,"[1] an assertion, of course, that remained valid for generations of music lovers who followed. In "The Religion of the Pianoforte," an especially witty and forceful piece written for *The Fortnightly Review* in 1894, Shaw expounded at length on the nineteenth-century phenomenon of "culture from the piano," indulging in a bit of autobiography to drive home his point:

> This musical starvation it was that drove me to disregard the rights of my fellow lodgers and go to the piano. I learnt the alphabet of musical notation from a primer, and the keyboard

from a diagram. Then, without troubling Czerny or Plaidy, I opened *Don Giovanni* and began. It took ten minutes to get my fingers arranged on the chord of D minor with which the overture commences; but when it sounded right at last, it was worth all the trouble it cost. . . . I soon acquired a terrible power of stumbling through pianoforte arrangements and vocal scores; and my reward was that I gained penetrating experiences of Victor Hugo and Schiller from Donizetti, Verdi, and Beethoven; of the Bible from Handel; of Goethe from Schumann; of Beaumarchais and Molière from Mozart; and of Mérimée from Bizet, besides finding in Berlioz an unconscious interpreter of Edgar Allan Poe. . . .

Now, in this fragment of autobiography, what is it that stands as the one indispensable external condition of my musical culture? Obviously, the pianoforte. Without it, no harmony, no interweaving of rhythms and motives, no musical structure, and consequently no opera or music-drama. But on the other hand, with it nothing else was needed, except the printed score and a foreknowledge of the power of music to bring romance and poetry to an enchanting intimacy of realization.[2]

In short, for Shaw and many nineteenth-century contemporaries, the piano was the primary medium through which musical culture was expressed and disseminated.

As familiar as the piano and its nineteenth-century repertoire have remained for twentieth-century listeners, scholarship from recent decades has paradoxically suggested just the opposite: that the nineteenth-century piano and its music have become strikingly unfamiliar to present-day musical culture. This unfamiliarity is perhaps most evident when we consider the great variety of instruments nineteenth-century composers had at their disposal. The piano as we know it did not become standardized until well into the second half of the century, decades after Beethoven, Schubert, and Weber, but also after Mendelssohn and Chopin had died; after Schumann had composed his most substantial and experimental works for the instrument; and, indeed, after Liszt's *Glanzzeit,* when he reigned supreme as unexcelled virtuoso during the 1830s and 1840s.

Even Brahms's contributions to the piano must be reconsidered in view of the instrument's evolution during his lifetime. George Bozarth has summarized the issue in this way: "When the young Johannes Brahms began his career as a pianist and composer in Hamburg in the 1840s, the keyboard instruments on which he would have played were essentially the same as the early romantic fortepianos of Beethoven and Schubert. By the time he wrote his final compositions half a century later, the piano had evolved to a state virtually identical with the modern instrument."[3] Two of the pianos Brahms is known to have possessed—an 1839 Viennese Graf formerly owned by the Schumanns and an 1868 Viennese Streicher—

were, Bozarth notes, "conservative," even "anachronistic" for their times. The fact is, the letters and memoirs of nearly all the great nineteenth-century pianist-*cum*-composers are filled with ever-varying comments about contemporary instruments—their mercurial coloristic properties, the quality of their actions and pedal mechanisms, their technical limitations, and the like. One is impressed, in short, by the dynamic, changing qualities of pianos and piano construction during the nineteenth century. This reality, in turn, fundamentally affected the way in which composers approached and wrote for the instrument and influenced in no small way the development of their compositional styles.

Research of the past few decades has emphasized, too, our considerable ignorance about the great body of nineteenth-century piano music. To appreciate fully the significance of, say, Beethoven's magisterial series of piano sonatas, Schubert's improvisatory sketches, Mendelssohn's studied fugues, or Schumann's flights of literary-musical fantasy, we must consider, in the larger context, the contributions of their contemporaries—for example, the abundant, if largely epigonic, efforts of Clementi's, Hummel's, or Dussek's sonatas; Voříšek's or Tomášek's character pieces; Czerny's or Antoine Reicha's fugue collections; or Sterndale Bennett's romantically effusive larger piano works. A staggering mass of piano music was published during the century—already in 1835 Robert Schumann could predict that pianists would collapse under the sheer weight of études in print alone.[4] Great quantities of this output enjoyed only brief currencies before falling into oblivion, so that to twentieth-century ears much of it is, in effect, "new music."

The encyclopedic approach of William S. Newman's *The Sonata since Beethoven* did much to broaden our awareness of the scope of nineteenth-century piano music.[5] Similarly, the recent efforts of Nicholas Temperley to investigate the so-called London Pianoforte School, which centered on Clementi, Dussek, and Cramer but extended well into the nineteenth century with Moscheles, Field, Sterndale Bennett, and others, have compelled us to reconsider the overall development of the more familiar canon of nineteenth-century piano music.[6] And recent studies of the role of women composer-pianists in nineteenth-century European culture—figures such as Clara Schumann, Fanny Mendelssohn Hensel, Louise Farrenc, and, later in the century, Cécile Chaminade—have revealed that an especially productive new line of inquiry remains to be pursued. Regrettably, much of this music is now forgotten, if not virtually unknown; indeed, its intrinsic musical value for the most part still awaits judgment. In the remarkable case of Fanny Mendelssohn Hensel, for example, we encounter a prodigy who in many ways was the equal of her celebrated brother, but who, because of societal pressures, was discouraged from publishing her music until the last year or two of her life. Much of her piano music survives in manuscript; little has been critically evaluated. Her music, and that of other nineteenth-century women, takes on added significance when we recall that in the nineteenth century (and before) women of social standing were encouraged or expected to show some measure of artistic accomplishment as performers at the keyboard.[7]

In what follows we seek both to summarize and to explore some of the current critical approaches to nineteenth-century solo piano music—to the instrument and its principal composers. Two introductory chapters provide the contextual basis for the volume. In the first, Leon Plantinga considers the instrument, a "familiar, fixed object," as the disseminator of nineteenth-century musical culture. In the second, Robert S. Winter underscores our present-day unfamiliarity with nineteenth-century pianos and argues cogently that, in order to recapture something of their wonderful variety, we need to reconsider our approach to the nineteenth-century piano repertoire "from the ground up."

The remaining eight chapters are devoted to a selection of the most significant nineteenth-century composers for the instrument. As odd as it may seem at this time to focus chiefly on the piano works of Beethoven, Schubert, Weber, Mendelssohn, Chopin, Robert Schumann, Brahms, and Liszt—all composers whose music won early recognition and admission to the pianist's staple repertoire—nonetheless the ever-accelerating pace of new research about these familiar figures and the sheer limitations of space lead, as if inevitably, to this organization. Nearly every year, little-known autographs of Liszt's piano music surface (most recently the torso of a substantial, unknown work, his third piano concerto), and a complete edition of Mendelssohn's piano music remains a significant desideratum. The manuscripts and composing methods of Robert Schumann have suggested new ways of approaching his piano music; Chopin's figure as a Polish emigré has prompted a fresh consideration of nationalism as a musical-cultural determinant in European culture; and Brahms's relation to both the classical tradition and modernism has encouraged a reevaluation of his status as a composer of autonomous instrumental music. In short, in recent decades every major nineteenth-century composer has endured increasingly painstaking and critical scrutiny, and the results of this research have begun to challenge some of the prevalent conceptions and interpretations of their piano music.

In this volume readers will encounter a variety of approaches—analytical, sociocultural, and historical—to the piano music of these composers. Michael Tusa and R. Larry Todd present the first extended studies in English of the piano music of, respectively, Carl Maria von Weber and Felix Mendelssohn. William Kinderman examines Beethoven's sonatas, variations, and bagatelles in an attempt to reveal their progressive tendency toward juxtaposition of severe contrasts, a process that emerged in Beethoven's late music to test the boundaries of irony, humor, and tragedy. Eva Badura-Skoda treats in detail Schubert's extensive series of piano sonatas, in which he eventually found his own voice as a composer. Jeffrey Kallberg, reminding us that "we know Chopin in many ways," examines the role that genre played in communicating nationalist ideas and sentiments. Anthony Newcomb proposes a new classification of Robert Schumann's piano music into three groups and shows how the first group, containing the most experimental efforts up to 1839, gave way to a more marketable and accessible type of *Hausmusik*, though the judgment of history, in effect, later ignored that progression. Walter Frisch traces the progress of classic-romantic and romantic-modern dialectics in Brahms's piano oeuvre, which spanned some forty years. And, finally, Dolores Pesce examines the ever-present tension between form and content in the piano music of Franz Liszt's long career.

As common an object as the piano became in nineteenth-century Europe, it remained a symbol of the evolutionary nature and changing fashion of musical life. Its appeal and popularity remained broad; as the century progressed, its indispensable role became increasingly evident. Indeed, no less than Shaw was encouraged to prophesy, "in the end the pianos will make most people musical."[8]

R. Larry Todd

Notes

1. George Bernard Shaw, *Shaw's Music: The Complete Musical Criticism*, ed. Dan H. Laurence, 3 vols. (London, 1981), 1:70.

2. *Ibid.*, 3:111–13.

3. George Bozarth, "Brahms's Pianos," *The American Brahms Society Newsletter* 6 (1988): 1.

4. See *Neue Zeitschrift für Musik* 4 (1836): 45–46.

5. William S. Newman, *The Sonata since Beethoven*, 3d ed. (New York, 1983).

6. See Nicholas Temperley, "Piano Music: 1800–1870," in *Music in Britain: The Romantic Age 1800–1914*, ed. Nicholas Temperley (London, 1981), 400--423, and Temperley's multivolume series, *The London Pianoforte School* (New York, 1984–1988).

7. As early as 1770 Carl Philipp Emanuel Bach had published his *Six sonatas . . . à l'usage des dames*; in the 1830s and 1840s, most of Mendelssohn's *Lieder ohne Worte* appeared in collections dedicated to women.

8. *Shaw's Music*, 3:115.

Acknowledgments

The appearance of *Nineteenth-Century Piano Music* has benefitted considerably from the expertise and assistance of many individuals. The genesis of the volume and of the series it inaugurates, *Studies in Musical Genres and Repertories,* is owing in considerable part to the editorial vision and acumen of Maribeth Anderson Payne, editor-in-chief of Schirmer Books. Anne Adams and Robert Axelrod, also of Schirmer Books, have helped in any number of ways to smooth the progress of the volume through the press. A superb staff at A-R Editions, including Becky Chapman-Winter and James Zychowicz, has managed all phases of production in a most timely fashion. In addition, several individuals who assisted with the preparation of the manuscript should be acknowledged, including Isabelle Bélance, Professor Bryan Gilliam of Duke University, Professor Jenny Kallick of Amherst College, Barbara Norton, Phyllis Sutherland, and Stephen Zank. A special acknowledgment is due Professor Alexander Keyssar of Duke University for technical assistance of various kinds.

Several libraries and institutions have kindly provided illustrative material for this volume. These include: Yale University Libraries; McPherson Library, University of Victoria; Bibliothèque nationale, Paris; Österreichische Nationalbibliothek, Vienna; The Curtis Institute of Music, Philadelphia; The Pierpont Morgan Library, New York; Huntington Library, San Marino, California; Stanford University Library; Biblioteca Jagiellońska, Kraków; University of Pennsylvania Libraries; British Library, London; Gesellschaft der Musikfreunde, Vienna; Library of Congress, Washington, D.C.; B. Schott's Söhne, Mainz; and Belmont Music Publishers.

Contributors

Eva Badura-Skoda has served on the faculty of the University of Wisconsin and has taught at several institutions in the United States and Europe. Among her publications are editions and studies of Mozart, Schubert, and Clementi; a monograph on Mozart's Piano Concerto K. 491; and with her husband, the distinguished pianist Paul Badura-Skoda, *Interpreting Mozart on the Keyboard.*

Walter Frisch, Associate Professor of Music at Columbia University, is the author of *Brahms and the Principle of Developing Variation,* editor of *Brahms and His World,* and editor of the journal *19th Century Music.* He is presently completing a book about the early music of Arnold Schoenberg.

Jeffrey Kallberg is Associate Professor of Music at the University of Pennsylvania. He has recently completed a book about Chopin's Nocturnes and has written frequently about Chopin's piano music and the treatment of musical genres in the nineteenth century. His contribution to this volume was awarded the Stefan and Wanda Wilks Prize for Research in Polish Music.

William Kinderman, Professor of Music at the University of Victoria, has published several studies of Mozart, Beethoven, Schubert, and Wagner. He is the author of *Beethoven's Diabelli Variations* and is currently preparing a volume of essays about nineteenth-century tonality.

Anthony Newcomb is Professor of Music at the University of California at Berkeley. The author of *The Madrigal at Ferrara: 1579–1597,* he has written extensively about Schubert, Schumann, and the problem of programmatic music in the nineteenth century, and has served as editor of the *Journal of the American Musicological Society.*

Dolores Pesce, Associate Professor of Music at Washington University, is the author of *The Affinities and Medieval Transposition* and has written articles about the thirteenth-century motet, Edward MacDowell, and Franz Liszt.

Leon Plantinga, Professor of Music at Yale University, is the author of three books, including *Schumann as Critic, Clementi: His Life and Music,* and, most recently, *Romantic Music: A History of Musical Style in Nineteenth-Century Europe.*

R. LARRY TODD, Professor of Music at Duke University, has recently taught at Amherst College. The author of *Mendelssohn's Musical Education* and co-editor of *Mendelssohn and Schumann Essays,* he has contributed other studies about Obrecht, Liszt, and Webern.

MICHAEL C. TUSA, Associate Professor of Music at the University of Texas, has contributed several studies of Beethoven, Schubert, and Weber and has recently completed a book about Weber's opera *Euryanthe.*

ROBERT S. WINTER, Professor of Music at the University of California, Los Angeles, has written widely on issues in nineteenth-century performance practice and on Beethoven. He is the author of *Compositional Origins of Beethoven's Opus 131* and a co-author, with Douglas Johnson and Alan Tyson, of *The Beethoven Sketchbooks: History, Reconstruction, Inventory.*

NINETEENTH-CENTURY
Piano Music

CHAPTER ONE

The Piano and the Nineteenth Century

Leon Plantinga

In chapter 26 of Jane Austen's *Emma* (1815), the heroine attends a high tea at the home of neighbors. At some point, "a little bustle in the room showed them that tea was over, and the instrument in preparation." Emma presently acceded to the "very pressing entreaties" of the others and sat at the pianoforte to sing and play: "She knew the limitations of her own powers too well to attempt more than she could perform with credit; she wanted neither taste nor spirit in the little things which are generally acceptable, and could accompany her own voice well." At a later gathering (chapter 28) young Frank Churchill begs the more able pianist Jane Fairfax to continue playing:

> "If you are very kind," said he, "it will be one of the waltzes we danced last night; let me live them over again." . . .
> She played.
> "What felicity it is to hear a tune again which *has* made one happy! If I mistake not, that was danced at Weymouth."
> She looked up at him for a moment, coloured deeply, and played something else.

Here, in the second decade of the nineteenth century, the instrument is understood to mean the piano. And the piano was indeed, in a variety of ways, the instrument of the century. In Austen's novel we see it in its most usual context, serving in a genteel domestic setting as both a solo and accompanying instrument for amateur music making. The performers are mainly women, as piano playing—at not too advanced a level—was one of the most desired feminine accomplishments. The levels of expertise expected of women even vary with stations in life. Emma, "handsome, clever, and rich," and therefore having every prospect of a good marriage, is quite content to play less well than Jane Fairfax, whose circumstances suggest a future as a teacher or governess. The latter is caught up, however, in the poignant extramusical social forces at work in the second passage just cited. Otherwise the very soul of probity, Miss Fairfax is led at the piano to collaborate with her admirer in reliving a scene where they had evidently danced the waltz—that daring entertainment, recently imported from the Continent, which with its close-clasping contact was barely acceptable to upper-level English sensibilities. Just as the dance itself (no doubt originally accompanied on the piano) provided an occasion for intimacies usually forbidden, its music, re-created at the piano, allowed reference to them that would have been out of the question in proper conversation.

Wilkie Collins's *The Woman in White* of almost half a century later (1860) has a similar scene. Laura Fairlie is in love with her resident drawing teacher, Walter Hartright; but through an arranged marriage she has been promised to another man. Hartright accordingly makes plans to move away. He later recounts the events of his last evening at the Fairlie estate (chapter 14):

> "Shall I play some of those little melodies of Mozart's which you used to like so much?" she asked, opening the music nervously, and looking down at it while she spoke.
>
> Before I could thank her she hastened to the piano. . . . She kept her attention riveted on the music—music which she knew by memory, which she had played over and over again, in former times, without the book. . . . I only knew that she was aware of my being close to her, by seeing the red spot on the cheek that was nearest to me fade out, and the face grow pale all over.
>
> "I am very sorry you are going," she said, her voice almost sinking to a whisper, her eyes looking more and more intently at the music, her fingers flying over the keys of the piano with a strange feverish energy which I had never noticed in her before. "I shall remember those kind words, Miss Fairlie, long after tomorrow has come and gone."
>
> The paleness grew whiter on her face, and she turned it farther away from me.
>
> "Don't speak of tomorrow," she said. "Let the music speak to us of tonight, in a happier language than ours."

Here, too, piano playing is an evening entertainment provided by a young unmarried woman. And again it is more than an entertainment; in an adaptation of the nineteenth-century conceit of music as speaker of that which cannot be spoken, Miss Fairlie's playing intimates to Mr. Hartright her feelings for him—in circumstances governed by social convention that does not permit them even to address each other by first name. Nineteenth-century novels and plays, in England and Germany in particular, suggest that such little dramas were often played out in bourgeois drawing rooms (see Illustration 1.1). In France, Stendhal wrote as early as 1801 that "in our century it is absolutely essential that a girl know music;

otherwise one would think her quite uneducated" (Guichard, 71). But music, on whatever level, was not simply a trifling amusement or a meaningless way of filling the idle hours of unmarried daughters (whose very idleness was a desirable sign of gentility). Music was woven into the very fabric of social interaction; it was part of the system of signs by which people communicated with each other. And for the entire century this occurred routinely around that familiar fixed object, symbol of both success and sensibility: the piano.

ILLUSTRATION 1.1. Engraving from *The Ladies' Companion and Monthly Magazine* (1859).

How hugely the piano dominated the world of amateur music can be suggested by a few dry (and near-random) data from music publishing—an enterprise overwhelmingly directed toward the home-music market. Of the twenty-two musical publications of Artaria & Comp. (some in collaboration with Tranquillo Mollo) of Vienna in 1800, all but two required participation of the piano (Weinmann, 51–56). In the same year some seventy-three publications of new music were reviewed in the *Recensionen* columns of the fledgling *Allgemeine musikalische Zeitung*; sixty-three of them involved (explicitly or implicitly) the piano.[1] A similar tally of "revues critiques" in the *Revue et Gazette musicale* of 1835 shows use of the piano in forty-eight of fifty-five new releases. The exhaustive listings of musical publications in the Hofmeister *Handbuch* reveal similar figures later in the century. Of the many hundreds of instrumental offerings listed for the years 1844–51, about eighty-four percent involved the piano, as did the vast majority of vocal publications (Hofmeister, 1852: 1–219). The proportions were still much the same in the period 1892–97 (Hofmeister, 1900: 1–189). In the 1770s the London publisher Novello put out a catalog of its mammoth "Universal Circulating Music Library." Of the thousands of Continental and English musical publications listed—from full scores (in many cases with parts) of operas, oratorios, and symphonies down to flute solos—more than three-quarters require piano. The kind of music Europeans heard most often in the nineteenth century seems to have been generated largely by a single social practice, that of amateur music performed around a piano at home.

But the piano was also an intensely public instrument. Its development in the eighteenth century coincided exactly with the growth of a bourgeois "public," and from its first known appearance in a solo role at a public concert in mid–1768,[2] it grew steadily in favor to become in a few decades the only musical instrument that routinely was played alone before an audience. This burgeoning popularity of solo piano playing was a main ingredient in the rise of that new breed of musician, the international concert virtuoso. The first wave of virtuosi, from about 1780 to 1820, issued largely from those twin hothouses of pianistic activity, London and Vienna. Participants were Muzio Clementi, Johann Baptist Cramer, Jan Ladislav Dussek, John Field, the young Ludwig van Beethoven (to a limited degree), Johann Nepomuk Hummel, and Ignaz Moscheles. These musicians made their initial reputations as players—they composed, it was often assumed, mainly to fuel their performances—and together they blazed a kind of "concert circuit" whose principal loci were London, Paris, Vienna, Berlin, and St. Petersburg.

But it was Paris alone where political and cultural conditions were exactly right for the distinctive virtuoso of the 1830s and 1840s. Paris of the 1830s retained the prestige it had acquired in the days of the Sun King as the dictator of fashion in almost every sphere, from literature and theater to couture and cuisine (some noted chefs of the old nobility, having lost their jobs in the revolutions, operated expensive restaurants in the city). The revolutions of 1830 had effectively split Europe into two political entities: East of the Rhine the old Holy Alliance was still able to intervene in the affairs of individual nations; in France and the other western countries the hold of the reactionary powers was broken for good. Under the July monarchy, Paris became a place of unparalleled liberalism and liberty. Nonconformity of almost any kind was tolerated, and virtually all careers were open to talent, or, as the historian E. J. Hobsbawm puts it, "at any rate to energy, shrewdness, hard work, and greed" (Hobsbawm, 189). The ascendant bourgeoisie of Paris deified the individual achiever, whether the achievement took place at the Bourse or in the concert hall. And artists of all sorts probably enjoyed a greater degree of social acceptability than in any other European city.

The virtuosi of Paris all came from somewhere to the east, having joined a steady procession of intellectuals, artists, and fortune seekers who arrived in the 1820s and 1830s to seize opportunities scarcely available anywhere else. The greatest of them, of course, were Frédéric Chopin and Franz Liszt. We tend to remember two others mainly in connection with these: Frédéric Kalkbrenner was for a time Chopin's teacher, and Sigismond Thalberg (see Illustration 1.2) was Liszt's most threaten-

ILLUSTRATION 1.2. "The Pianist Sigismond Thalberg," French engraving, ca. 1835.

ing competitor. Some, like Johann Peter Pixis, Henri Herz, Franz Hün-ten, and Alexander Dreyschock, are now little but names. But together this group virtually redefined the art of piano playing. And though first inspired at least partly by the example of Paganini, they—and their instrument—gained in the public imagination proprietary rights to the name and notion "virtuoso."

Part of the distinctive character of the virtuosi is their membership in the recently evolved species of artists who addressed their efforts al-most exclusively to the new public audience. Cut loose from the demands for varied fare that noble or churchly patrons had always placed upon musicians, they were free to specialize to an unprecedented degree in their own instrument. Liszt's daily regime (reported in a letter from 1832) of "four to five hours of trills, sixths, octaves, tremolos, repeated notes, cadenzas and the like" was a luxury possible only for the unbeholden. A spectacular explosion of new keyboard techniques followed. The virtuosi treated their audiences to inventive new figurations played at unheard-of velocity and to a thorough exploitation of the extremes of the piano's range. Novel keyboard textures proliferated; two that became standard were a figuration featuring rapid-fire repeated octaves and chords di-vided between the hands, and Thalberg's sonorous midrange melody with arpeggios above and below. Contemporary reviewers noted a new resonance and fullness in piano sound, particularly in Thalberg's playing; Henri Blanchard wrote in 1836, "No one has ever *sung* at the piano like Thalberg. The sound is sustained with nuances added through *rinfor-zando,* such that you believe you are hearing the expressive bow of [Alex-andre] Batta, gliding gracefully over the strings of his cello, or the sweet horn tones of [Jacques-François] Gallay, penetrating your being with a gentle melancholy."[3]

The imagination and industry of the virtuosi were one major factor in the emergence of a new brand of pianism during this period; changes in the instrument itself (which the pianists encouraged) were another. Liszt and Thalberg made their reputations just as the modern piano (roughly speaking) appeared on the scene. There would have been little point for Liszt to spend his hours on "repeated notes" (and the "repeated octave" texture and related figurations would have been a near impossi-bility) before the repetition action was perfected by the Erards in the 1820s. And the grand piano with metal braces, introduced by English and French makers in the 1820s to accommodate increases in range and ten-sion, literally made a new style of playing possible. Pianists could now em-ploy the weight of their arms and shoulders for added intensity and reso-nance. Before this time, a "weight technique" was out of the question—as any modern pianist learns when he tries out even the sturdiest Erard or Broadwood from before about 1820. Thalberg's piano method and con-temporary reports imply that the new fullness of sound heard from the piano was indebted to this technique.

The virtuosi of Paris and their instrument were easily assimilated into the popular culture of the city. Parisians of the time showed a strong taste for every stripe of sensationalism in art and life, but they seemed especially to favor the macabre or diabolical. The trial of the multiple murderer Lacenaire in 1835 and his public execution in 1836 (referred to in Hugo's *Les Misérables*) were the most talked-of events of the time—stiff competition, surely, for the strong drama along similar lines that Scribe and Meyerbeer were just then offering on the stage of the Opéra.[4] Since Paganini, the idea of the virtuoso had taken on a special coloring that appealed to this taste for the terrifying. The violinist's implausible technical feats seemed, in a kind of inversion of the old notion of supernatural inspiration, to hint at sinister otherworldly connections; "his dark and penetrating eye, together with the sardonic smile which occasionally played upon his lips, appeared to the vulgar, and to certain diseased minds, unmistakable evidences of a Satanic origin" (Fétis, 59). Liszt was not quick to discourage similar suspicions about the sources of his own extraordinary powers; his mistress, the Countess d'Agoult, wrote of his "distracted air, unquiet and like that of a phantom about to be summoned back to the shades" (Perényi, 80). And he and the other pianists regularly attempted to capture something of the special chill and excitement of the current opera in their countless fantasies and variations on its music. Under the hands of the sorcerer-virtuoso, the piano became a miniature stage where distinctive moments of the drama were again and again reenacted.

The heady public world of the piano virtuoso existed in a kind of symbiotic relationship with the private one of domestic music making. The two were connected by the double umbilical chord of piano manufacture and music publishing—those two indispensable service industries of amateur music. The clear pioneer in establishing such a connection had been Clementi, who made his reputation before 1800 as a cosmopolitan virtuoso and composer for piano, a reputation that in the new century reaped profits for Clementi & Co., piano manufacturers and music publishers of London (Plantinga, 293–95). Here we see the birth of that Janus-like practice of the nineteenth century that marries music with commerce: a famous pianist attaches his name to a certain make of instrument or line of musical publications and shares in the profits from sales to the domestic music market. Many of the best-known piano virtuosi of the following generation participated in some such plan. Kalkbrenner promoted the pianos manufactured by the firm of (the former composer) Ignace Pleyel; Herz entered into partnership with the Parisian piano maker Klepfer and subsequently sold instruments under his own name. Piano manufacturers early in the century inaugurated the modern practice of providing free instruments to noted musicians (Beethoven received two such, from Erard of Paris in 1803 and Broadwood of London in 1818). Larger establishments like Pleyel and Erard even maintained recital halls where both player and piano could be applauded. In much the same spirit music publishers entered into business arrangements with famous pianists. Maurice Schlesinger of Paris, for example, together with the pianist Thalberg held transcription rights to the music of current hits at the Opéra. Thalberg would produce the piano arrangements and elaborations; Schlesinger did the printing and advertising—and stimulated further sales by orchestrating high praise for their joint effort in the columns of his firm's house organ, the *Revue et Gazette musicale*.[5]

Some contemporaries were quick to deplore the abuses of this compact between music and mammon. Schumann's excoriations of the virtuosi and their repertory are well known. (And Heine occasionally applied the edge of his wit to the situation, as when he likened Kalkbrenner to "a bon-bon that has fallen in the mud"[6]). All the grandiloquent fantasies and glittering variations, the vacuous *morceaux de salon* and *souvenirs de . . .* of the virtuosi were particularly galling to Schumann and like-minded musicians, who saw the piano and its music as belonging to the essence of a "new poetic era" in music that had its beginnings in Beethoven. And whether or not we wish to quarrel with the music historiography of Schumann's "new era," there is no disputing the centrality of the piano in serious composition from Beethoven's time to his own. Surely there has not been another period in Western musical history when a single instrument has been so dominant in the work of leading composers. The young Beethoven's musical imagination was firmly rooted in the piano, and until the time of the last quartets the trajectory of his style is most clearly traced in his music for (or with) it. The piano was Schubert's instrument, and it figures in most of his best music. Chopin and the young Liszt wrote for it almost exclusively, as did Schumann during his first decade as a composer. In the oeuvre of Weber and Mendelssohn the piano is a less tyrannical force, but yet a very solid presence. And of course the number of the period's *Kleinmeister* (so judged by posterity) who devoted themselves mainly to the piano is legion. In addition to the aforementioned Dussek, Field, Hummel, Moscheles, and the entire crew of Parisian virtuosi, we might cite only the beginning of an easily assembled list: Ludwig Berger, Henri Bertini, J. B. Cramer, Carl Czerny, I. F. Dobrzyński, and Heinrich Enckhausen.

As the piano soared to a position of dominance in the late eighteenth and early nineteenth centuries, it left in its wake a number of new musical genres. Earliest of these was the accompanied keyboard sonata, whose rise to prominence starting in the 1770s closely paralleled that of the new instrument. While the accompanied keyboard sonata arose from a demand for easy music for amateurs, its offspring in the nineteenth century are all the species of chamber music with piano—sonatas for piano and one other instrument, piano trios, quartets, and the like. How persistently the patrimony of these pieces asserted itself can be gathered from a remark Schumann made in 1836 while reviewing some new piano trios by minor composers; the sort of ensemble needed to perform them, he said, is "a fiery player at the keyboard, and two understanding friends who accompany softly" (*Neue Zeitschrift für Musik* [hereafter *NZM*] 5 [1836]: 4). And vestiges of that ancestry can still be felt in the leading role the piano plays in chamber music as late as that of Brahms and Dvořák.

The life of another genre associated with the piano, the Lied with keyboard accompaniment, followed a somewhat similar trajectory. It too started in the eighteenth century as music written explicitly for amateurs. The necessary ease of performance was in this case made into a virtue as north-German theorists pointed to the Lied as the very embodiment of the hallowed ideal of "folklikeness."[7] Most often accompanying the Lied until the 1780s or so was that favorite German household instrument, the clavichord. But during the 1790s in South Germany there arose within the genre a new subtype, the dramatic ballad, whose style strongly suggests the presence of the ascendant pianoforte. Vivid programmatic effects in the accompaniments and keyboard interludes to Johann Rudolf Zumsteeg's *Colma* or *Lenore*—depicting such things as waterfalls, storms, and galloping horses—seem like a veritable celebration of the capabilities of the new instrument. Beginning about two decades later the humble Lied was transformed into high art at the hands of Franz Schubert. In all the rich new variety of style and expression effected by that transformation—whether purely lyrical, dramatic, or narrative—the centrality of the sound of the piano remained a constant.

In the nineteenth century, the piano became the "utility" instrument par excellence it remains today. It inherited the mantle of the ubiquitous continuo instrument of the previous two centuries, accompanying almost any sort of music sung or played on other instruments.[8] And keyboard instruments had always been invaluable for teaching music; they lay out before the student a graphic display of the tonal system, and they make acceptable sounds at the touch of an unpracticed finger. During the nineteenth century studying music became synonymous in many quarters with studying the piano; as early as the 1820s the "music masters" retained by English boarding schools were simply understood to be piano teachers.

Pianos have always been used, too, for "trying things out," or "showing how a piece goes." The nineteenth century leaves us countless vignettes illustrating this. One might think, for example, of the scene from late 1805 in which Beethoven's friends, gathered at the home of Prince Lichnowsky, tried to persuade the recalcitrant composer to shorten the first act of *Fidelio*; the tenor Joseph August Röckel recalled (in a conversation with Thayer in 1861), "As the whole opera was to be gone through, we went directly to work. Princess L. played on the grand piano the great score of the opera and Clement, sitting in a corner of the room, accompanied with his violin the whole opera by heart . . ." (Forbes, 389). Wagner, as we know, habitually played his new music at the piano for his friends, and (to leap ahead a bit) Debussy first heard Stravinsky's *Le Sacre du printemps* when he played it with the composer as a four-hand piano duet

(Lockspeiser, 2:181). The practice among nineteenth-century composers of making short scores, or "particells," of music for large forces is surely related to this habit of playing things over at the piano; Brahms's routine production of two-piano versions of his orchestral music represents a kind of formalized extension of the habit.

Thus far we have been speaking of the nineteenth century as a single chronological entity, as an integral stretch of time within which one can point out certain fairly coherent musical and cultural developments having to do with the piano. The question as to how well the century in fact coheres—and how well our observations may be coordinated with its musical-cultural topography—is of course a vexed one. Perhaps we may indulge in a brief excursus in order to examine this point.

In his essay "Neuromantik"[9] of 1974 Carl Dahlhaus muses about various ways of partitioning the century from a music-historical perspective. Should 1830, the time of the July Revolution, be seen as a historical caesura in music as well as in politics? Berlioz and Meyerbeer, he feels, seem sufficiently different from Beethoven and Rossini to justify such a procedure, but "in Germany, on the other hand, the relationship between Weber and the young Wagner (the composer of romantic operas, which it is willful to reinterpret as 'music dramas'), or that between Beethoven and Schubert on the one hand . . . and Schumann and Mendelssohn on the other, is too close to allow talk of two ages or the end of a musical era" (*19 CM* 3 [1979]: 104).

The year 1830 as a dividing line will vary in distinctness, Dahlhaus says (reasonably enough), according to where we place our emphasis. If we think of music mainly as one participant in a social and political nexus, that division is fairly convincing; it is much less so if music is considered in and of itself. And if our focus is on events in France (where musical developments seem closely related to social and political changes), a caesura around 1830 is easier to defend than it is in the Germanys where such a connection appears much more tenuous. Dahlhaus again distinguishes between music as an autonomous activity and as a participant in a culture or *Zeitgeist* when he surveys the century's midpoint (just after the next revolutions) as another possible line of division in music history. The continuity between Berlioz and Liszt, Schumann and Brahms, and the younger and older Wagner, he concludes, is sufficient to discredit any such caesura established on purely musical grounds. But the century seems rather neatly divided in half, he maintains (and this appears to be the main point of his essay), in respect to the coordination of music with its intellectual and cultural environment: "Early nineteenth-century music could be said to be romantic in an age of romanticism, which produced romantic poetry and painting and even romantic physics and chemistry, whereas the neoromanticism of the later part of the century was romantic in an unromantic age, dominated by positivism and realism" (*19 CM* 3 [1979]: 99).

In this essay Dahlhaus does not tell us very clearly which of the rich variety of intellectual currents that have been called "romanticism" he is putting forth as a dominant force of the earlier nineteenth century and as a congenial host to music.[10] But his citation of Hoffmann, Wackenroder, and Schopenhauer as its representatives—and the "positivism" and "realism" of the later century as its antipodes—suggests that he has in mind the transcendental idealism and the belief in the primacy of a noumenal world that these writers share. If this is the case, surely he should have made use of the other distinction, having to do with national and regional differences, that he had applied to the problem of the century's subdivisions. This latter-day idealism, this grappling with the Kantian metaphysical legacy that we see during the first decades of the century in Schopenhauer, Schelling, and Fichte, and in literary guise in writers as diverse as Hoffmann and Kleist, was a powerful preoccupation in Germany. But it will hardly do to attribute the same to the French, English, and Italians, among whom metaphysics after the German model was little in favor. In about 1830 Auguste Comte described a developmental process operative in all branches of human knowledge in which a "metaphysical" stage has already been succeeded by a "positivist" one characteristic of the physical sciences. At the same time in England—where philosophy had shown a strong empiricial and practical bent since the days of Hume and Locke—leading thinkers like John Stuart Mill shared Comte's enthusiasm for bringing to social, political, and moral concerns something of the methodology and certainty of science.

But however skewed Dahlhaus's formulation may appear, there seems to be some rough justice in viewing European intellectual history of the nineteenth century as marked by a more than usually pronounced dualism. An idealist impulse, most popular in Germany in the earlier part of the century, aspired to levels of consciousness and knowledge inaccessible to the ordinary operations of human rationality; it distrusted the compilation and ordering of sense-data in science as superficial, and valued emotion, intuition, flights of imagination, and poetic sensibility—and art and music—as avenues to true understanding. The opposed "positivist" view, present from the first but gathering momentum as the century progressed, placed great faith in the ascendant science and technology of a burgeoning industrial age, in the forces that were transforming, seemingly overnight, the life of the continent: manufacture and travel powered by steam, outdoor lighting by gas and electricity, invention of astonishing machines to do things that had always been done by hand. Such triumphs in the later century suggested that the ways of thinking offered by science provided a model of certainty and demonstrated results that all branches of knowledge would do well to follow. And they contributed to an intellectual climate in which belief in a transcendental cognitive function of art, or a proposition such as Schopenhauer's, that music is an "immediate representation of the Will," was judged idle at best.

Nineteenth-century music and a belief in its importance always remained tied to the idealistic outlook. At various points around its periphery, as in the late-century scholarship of Friedrich Chrysander or the acoustical researches of Hermann von Helmholtz, musical concerns brushed shoulders with a new dominant scientism in European thought. But music itself, with its maddeningly elusive substance and its frequent lack of clear reference to anything else, remained the most immaterial and (in E. T. A. Hoffmann's formulation) "the most romantic of all the arts." Thus the serious cultivation of music in the later century could seem unresponsive to prevailing modes of thinking and feeling, a quaint and irrelevant activity in a world of science, technology, industry, machines, capitalism (with advertising), and empire.

The piano, however, as an instrument and as an institution, participated comfortably in both of these nineteenth-century worlds. On the one hand it inherited and expanded the role of the eighteenth-century German clavichord: it was the instrument of choice for private playing, for the celebration of sensibility and feeling in intimate settings. Whether it was the poignant, vaguely reedy sound of the Viennese piano (still used by Schumann in the 1830s), or the velvety, incandescent timbre of the English or French instrument (to become *the* piano sound of the second half of the century), the sonority of this instrument was inextricably bound up with the notion of "musical expression." This was true partly because it was what everyone played; in the nineteenth-century mind "music" and "music played on the piano" tended to merge. But the piano was also singularly well adapted for "expression." This percussion instrument apparently was not seen as seriously deficient in melodic capabilities; with a little coaxing, it was thought (even before Thalberg), the piano could fairly "sing."[11] And its enormous range and variability as to volume and texture permitted musical statements running the gamut from overpowering passion to the quietest lyricism.

But the piano was also a machine (surely it is the only machine from the nineteenth century in regular use toward the close of the twentieth). Especially in the earlier 1800s, its overall design and its hundreds of moving parts were a consistent object of that craze for technological innovation that characterized the century.[12] It also became something of a creature of the Industrial Revolution, participating fully in the gradual change that saw the efforts of individual craftsmen replaced by the specialized labor and high production of a factory (by the 1820s Broadwood of London produced more than 1,000 squares and 400 grands a year[13]). And of course the piano was a commodity, at once a highly complicated piece of equipment and a handsome item of furniture, one whose desirability could be enhanced by that inevitable companion of capitalist industry, public advertising. This musical instrument seemed to find its way well enough in a world of technology and commerce.

The role of the piano in the musical life of the century was not entirely uniform. In western Europe the cult of the keyboard virtuoso declined after midcentury—perhaps because there were so many other things to be amazed at. The tradition persisted longer in the eastern countries, especially in Russia and Poland (which have continued through the first half of the present century to produce more than their share of virtuosi). And there is no denying that a great deal more piano music of real consequence was written in the first half of the nineteenth century than in the second. The decline of the piano as a vehicle for the musical thoughts of the leading composers seems to have paralleled the general fall from grace of sonata-type pieces.[14] For the orchestra the void was filled with new types of large-scale works, such as the programmatic overture and symphonic poem, in which a musical experience was expected to be strongly shaped by extramusical associations. That nothing comparable appeared in piano music may have been due to a feeling that in this arena, after the shorter keyboard works of Schumann, Liszt, and many others, such associations were already an old story. The single role in which the piano enjoyed uncontested dominance from the beginning of the century to its end was in its use as a domestic musical instrument. And this formed the basis, surely, for much of its remarkable career overall. Most of the best musicians of the century were pianists, and most became so early in life, at home, where the instrument of the century held sway.

Notes

1. Lieder were sometimes published with no mention of an accompaniment in the title. The reviews in question, however, make it clear that all collections of Lieder under consideration that year had piano accompaniments.

2. In a concert at the Thatched House in London, played by J. C. Bach. It was announced in the *Public Advertiser,* 2 June 1768. What Bach seems to have played that evening was a square piano—a most unlikely instrument for public performance. Later in the same year the piano made its Paris debut in a solo role at the Concerts spirituels.

3. *Revue et Gazette musicale* 3 (1836): 178. "Singing at the piano" was a kind of trademark of Thalberg's. His piano method was entitled *L'Art du chant appliqué au piano.*

4. In the collective imagination, violent action in the streets and in the theater tended to mingle. Reflecting on the current preoccupation with crime in the city, the Vicomte de Launay wrote in 1843, "For the past month the sole topic of conversation has been the nightly assaults, holdups, daring robberies. . . . Evening parties all end like the beginning of the fourth act of *Les Huguenots,* with the blessing of the daggers. Friends and relatives are not allowed to go home without a regular arms inspection" (Chevalier, 3).

5. The fullest account of the piano in its nineteenth-century social and commercial setting is still Arthur Loesser, *Men, Women and Pianos* (New York, 1954).

6. Heinrich Heine, *Sämtliche Werke* (Leipzig, 1915), 9:280.

7. Among the earliest to espouse this doctrine of the Lied was Christian Gottlieb Krause in *Von der musikalischen Poesie* (Berlin, 1753). Some of the stylistic traits prescribed there, such as avoidance of melisma and word repetition, adhered to the genre throughout the nineteenth century.

8. The piano was literally used as a continuo instrument in England from Haydn's second London sojourn of 1794–95, when he "conducted" his symphonies from the piano, until at least the mid-1820s, when Clementi did the same.

9. In *Zwischen Romantik*, 5–21. Whittall's translation of this essay also appears in *19th Century Music* (hereafter *19 CM*) 3 (1979): 97–105.

10. Is it an admiration for the "primitive" and the "simplicity of nature" such as we see in English writers of the 1740s and in some places in Rousseau? Or is it an allegiance to "universality of content" (hence to diversity and complexity), to that expression of the entire range of human experience widely attributed to Shakespeare and warmly endorsed by Friedrich Schlegel in his famous Fragment 116 of the *Athenaeum*? Does it have to do with a nostalgia for the past, especially the Middle Ages, a taste for knightly adventure and Gothic architecture? Or does it represent (as in Schlegel's characterization of "die romantische Poesie") "das eigenthümlich-Moderne"? Does it suggest a devotion to a specifically Christian tradition (as in Chateaubriand and the romantic adherents of Schleiermacher) wherein the position of mankind is assumed to be fallen and helpless? Or does it imply the primitivist trust in a basic goodness of "unspoiled human nature" espoused by other "romantics"? Seldom inattentive to methodological or historiographical puzzles, Dahlhaus offers in *Die Musik des 19. Jahrhunderts*, 13–21, some discussion of the difficulties of arriving at a unified conception of romanticism, at least in its application to music.

11. Beethoven wrote to the piano maker Streicher in an undated letter from ca. 1794–96, "You are one of the few who realize and perceive that, provided one can feel the music, one can also make the pianoforte sing" (Anderson, 1:26).

12. Rosamond Harding has listed about 1,290 patents relating to pianos issued between 1800 and 1855 (Harding, 317–58).

13. See Adlam and Ehrlich. The same firm in 1851 employed specialists in dampers, hammers, keys, strings, soundboards, metal plates, wrest pins, bent sides, brass bridges, and many other parts (see Loesser, 388–89).

14. In 1839 Schumann observed that the only composers writing sonatas were young unknowns for whom the genre was merely a formal exercise, and that most contemporary symphonies were imitative of early Beethoven or even of Haydn and Mozart (*NZM* 10 [1839]: 134 and 11 [1839]: 1). Hofmeister's *Handbuch der musikalischen Litteratur* for 1892–97 lists virtually no new piano sonatas or symphonies.

Selected Bibliography

Adlam, Derek, and Ehrlich, Cyril. "Broadwood." *The New Grove Dictionary of Music and Musicians*. London, 1980.

Anderson, Emily, ed. *The Letters of Beethoven*. London, 1961.

Chevalier, Louis. *Laboring Classes and Dangerous Classes in Paris during the First Half of the Nineteenth Century*. Translated by F. Jellinek. Princeton, 1973.

Dahlhaus, Carl. *Zwischen Romantik und Moderne: vier Studien zur Musikgeschichte des späteren 19. Jahrhunderts*. Munich, 1974. Translated by Mary Whittall, *Between Romanticism and Modernism: Four Studies in the Music of the Later Nineteenth Century*. Berkeley, 1980. "Neo-Romanticism," *19 CM* 3 (1979): 97–105.

———. *Die Musik des 19. Jahrhunderts.* Wiesbaden, 1980.

Fétis, François-Joseph. *Biographical Notice of Nicolo [sic] Paganini.* London, n.d.

Forbes, Elliot, ed. *Thayer's Life of Beethoven.* Princeton, 1964.

Guichard, Léon. *La Musique et les lettres au temps du romantisme.* Paris, 1955.

Harding, Rosamond. *The Piano-forte: Its History Traced to the Great Exhibition of 1851.* Cambridge, 1933.

Hobsbawm, E. J. *The Age of Revolution: Europe 1798–1848.* Cleveland, 1962.

Hofmeister, Adolf. *Handbuch der musikalischen Litteratur.* Leipzig, 1852–1900.

Krause, Christopher Gottfried. *Von der musikalischen Poesie.* Berlin, 1753.

Lockspeiser, Edward. *Debussy: His Life and Mind.* London, 1965.

Loesser, Arthur. *Men, Women and Pianos.* New York, 1954.

Perényi, Eleanor Spencer. *Liszt: The Artist as Romantic Hero.* Boston, 1974.

Plantinga, Leon. *Clementi: His Life and Music.* London, 1977.

Weinmann, Alexander. *Vollständiges Verlagsverzeichnis, Artaria & Comp.* Vienna, 1952.

CHAPTER TWO

Orthodoxies, Paradoxes, and Contradictions: Performance Practices in Nineteenth-Century Piano Music

Robert S. Winter

The study of "performance practice"[1] is today a musical orthodoxy. One would be hard pressed to find an American institution of higher education—whether conservatory, school of music, or university—without at least one course offered under the rubric of performance practice. Institutions now offer degrees in performance practice or degrees in which the study of performance practice plays a prominent role. This avenue of inquiry is no longer sustained solely by devotees of early music or of period instruments; finding a mainline conductor under fifty who will scoff publicly at the enterprise of performance practice—however broadly defined—becomes more difficult each year.[2]

Like patriotism, performance practice has many definitions. For too many academics it has gone little further than determining the number of singers to a part, though change is brewing. A few decades ago, professional performers looked upon the elements of period performance with generalized contempt or patronizing dismissal. Today they are likely to acknowledge the advisability of reliable editions, the benefits of knowing period styles, and the viability of period-instrument performances—though often adding in the same breath that it does not matter which edition is used, which period practices are incorporated, or which instrument is played, as long as the performance has that ill-defined quality of inspiration.

There are encouraging signs that the traditional chasm between the study of music in academia (the source of most writings about performance practice) and the professional music world (where actions necessarily speak louder than words) is shrinking. There have always been a few persons who straddle both worlds—professional performers who teach in universities, scholars who are called upon to advise professional organizations—but the level of interaction has never lived up to its potential. In the concert world, the recent inroads by period-instrument performers into the standard repertoire—and the performance-practice claims often advanced by those performers or their recording companies—have produced rejoicing in some quarters, bewilderment and dismay in others, and angry rejoinders from still others.[3]

The issue of performance practice comes into sharp focus when we consider nineteenth-century piano music.[4] The nineteenth-century piano was a self-sufficient, all-conquering machine; about the union of human and machine Liszt wrote in 1838: "[The piano] embraces the range of an orchestra; the ten fingers of a single man suffice to render the harmonies produced by the combined forces of more than 100 concerted instruments. . . . We make arpeggios like the harp, prolonged notes like wind instruments, staccatos and a thousand other effects which once seemed the special prerogative of such and such an instrument."[5] On no other instrument except the organ (where issues of portability and repertoire limited the possibilities) could one person impose his or her will more completely on the music. Nineteenth-century piano music is the repertoire where personal styles and approaches have traditionally been viewed as most legitimate—and indeed, most necessary. Paganini, true, was a violinist, but it is no surprise that virtually all of those who responded to his wizardry—Chopin, Schumann, Liszt, Brahms, Rachmaninoff, and others—were pianists.

The common thread uniting almost all performance-practice studies over the last century in both Europe and America is their eminent practicality. The issues are largely those of immediate execution: Should I play this passage connected or detached? Is it appropriate to use the damper pedal here? What is the ideal tempo? Certainly this approach characterizes the two most recent and comprehensive studies of keyboard music in the classical era. Sandra Rosenblum's *Performance Practices in Classic Piano Music* gathers together a wealth of information regarding dynamics, pedaling, articulation, fingering, ornamentation, and tempo in the keyboard music of Haydn, Mozart, Clementi, and Beethoven. William S. Newman's unfortunately titled *Beethoven on Beethoven: Playing His Piano Music His Way* examines much of the same material as it applies to Beethoven's music, while giving weight to secondary studies such as those of Hermann Beck on Beethoven's tempos.

Both of these rich studies contain much that is valuable, indeed essential, for any performer of these repertoires, yet both are examples of what anthropologist Mary Douglas has called "member's accounts" (Douglas, 276–318). In Douglas's analysis, any expert or insider within a particular discipline will almost always frame its issues from a perspective that includes a series of unarticulated assumptions. These assumptions, argues Douglas, will inevitably color the conclusions reached by that "member."

Rosenblum and Newman write from a perspective that rests upon two contradictory assumptions. The first is the assumption that period instruments are valuable resources—a view widely held in academic and early music circles. Both studies devote about five percent of their text to a description of the fortepiano and its early evolution. Both authors regard period instruments appreciatively and sympathetically; Newman observes that the few people who have had the opportunity to "live" with period pianos agree that "differences between past and modern pianos can profoundly affect the music played on them" (Newman, 46). For Rosenblum, "the early instruments . . . afford us the best way of penetrating the spirit of the contemporary repertoire" (Rosenblum 54).

But undermining these glowing endorsements is a second assumption—that pianists play (and will continue to play) this repertoire almost exclusively on modern pianos and that it is therefore not feasible (or necessary) to pay much heed to period instruments. This is the only conclusion both studies allow. One could lift the sections on the fortepiano from their surroundings, scrap them, and find that they were barely missed in the other ninety-five percent. There is nary a mention of period instruments in the lengthy discussions of tempo, articulation, and ornamentation, and only pro forma mention under pedaling and dynamics. Young pianists coming for the first time to the Beethoven sonatas and looking to either study for guidance in the most fundamental decision they must make—their choice of instrument—will find a curious dissonance between the virtues accorded the fortepiano and their irrelevance to virtually all of the discussion that follows.

What produces this contradiction is that neither Rosenblum nor Newman addresses the fundamental issue of identifying the late twentieth-century audience. We can be sure the audience is different from the ones before which Haydn, Mozart, and Beethoven played. It is a different audience from that in the nineteenth century, when the piano was still evolving. It is a different audience from that in the first half of our century, when an aristocratic layer of European (and, in America, transplanted European) society bred on "high culture" viewed the Beethoven sonatas as the pianist's (and the listener's) bible. Today that audience no longer exists. The last survivors of the old European culture are slowly dying off, just as surely as Rosenthal, Hofmann, Cortot, Gieseking, Rubinstein, and now Horowitz have died off. Outside a few cities like New York, London, and Vienna one would be hard pressed to assemble a sizable group of listeners under forty for whom the Beethoven sonatas are in any way central to their listening experience.[6]

Both Rosenblum and Newman are, I would argue, writing about performance practice for that vanishing "high culture" audience with which they grew up. Even if we acknowledge that this audience can no longer be counted on, why, we might ask, should the audience have any bearing on the issues of pedaling or *non legato*? The answer is that issues of interpretation cannot ultimately be separated from the issue of *for* whom one is interpreting. The audience supplies not only the support system for any performing tradition but also the framework in which that performing tradition is defined. Ignoring the audience leads to the kind of contradiction outlined above.

Rather than offering another essay in the practical-survey genre—at best, incomplete, and at worst, misleading—I propose instead to frame the issues surrounding performance practice in nineteenth-century piano music more broadly than has hitherto been the case. Until these broader issues are aired, foreground discussions of practical problems have limited value. Once these issues have been understood, the practical problems begin to sort themselves out.

The Shift in Performance Traditions

My principal argument is straightforward: The nineteenth century was an era that valued color, contrast, and variety above all else. Yet, most of the developments over the last hundred years in the piano as an instrument, as well as in the performance of its remarkably rich repertoire, have served to diminish the very color, contrast, and variety so central to the style itself. For the kind of variety we profess to cherish, we have to look back to the nineteenth century itself. To recapture this variety, we will need to rethink our approach to this repertoire from the ground up.

The fleshing out of this argument requires, to begin with, a brief consideration of how performance practice developed. Performance practice sprang up as a separate discipline in the second half of the nineteenth century when a repertory of unknown music (largely from the Middle Ages and Renaissance) necessitated the rediscovery of performance techniques that had lain dormant for centuries. Those who would perform this repertory had no choice but to be practical. They had first of all to rediscover the instruments that were used—or, more often, to create reasonable facsimiles. Then they had to learn what they could about singing styles; how to decipher the music, especially its incompletely notated rhythms; how to "orchestrate" works whose instrumentation was by definition unspecified; how to lay the text under the music; and about the central role of improvisation.

Those who led the way in these endeavors had at least one consolation: They began at the same place as their audience. While this might not appear to be much of an advantage, the fact that the audience was learning to hear this music at the same time that performers were learning to play it gave performers the freedom to experiment. It made audiences more tolerant of technical lapses. There were no virtuosos or recordings (with their artificial perfection) against which to compare. The performers grew with their audiences—just what we can presume happened when Beethoven, Chopin, Liszt, or Brahms introduced a new work. The ancient music being revived by the pioneers of performance practice was, in essence, new music.

The result of this approach to the rediscovery of an extinct repertoire was that performance practice codified itself as an "applied" science. The German term *Aufführungspraxis* is routinely translated as "performance practice." But the Germans, who invented the field as a subdiscipline of *Musikwissenschaft,* used the German word *Praxis* in the same way as its literal English equivalent—that is, the "practical application or exercise of a branch of learning," a connotation lacking in the common English translation of "practice." From the beginning the relationship of *Aufführungspraxis* to *Musikwissenschaft* was approximately the same as the relationship between the clinical physician and the research biologist. The one discovers the important ideas that the other applies.

For most of the last century, then, writers and musicians assumed two things about the youthful discipline of performance practice: first, that it was a practical field requiring no larger perspective on function; and, second, that it was needed only for those repertoires where a decisive break in the performing tradition had occurred. The first of these perspectives still holds sway. The second has undergone long-overdue modification in recent years. To begin with, as Howard Mayer Brown has pointed out, "We have all surely exaggerated the extent to which musicians before the late nineteenth century performed and studied only the music of their own time."[7] Although only in the nineteenth century did interest in early music become large enough to generate a scholarly subdiscipline, lively interest in "old" music dates back to at least the seventeenth century.

But the major shift has been in our view of the "uninterrupted" performance tradition said to have begun in the early years of the nineteenth century.[8] The orthodox view held that, beginning with Mozart, virtually all music worth hearing has remained in the concert repertoire; consequently, the study of performance practice is unnecessary. As in many non-Western cultures, oral transmission was supposed to insure a stable performing tradition. The more we learn about such "traditions" in the West, however, the more we realize that they are marked by evolution and change rather than by continuity and stability.

Views on Interpretation

Both of these points of view, I believe, point up the need for a much broader definition of performance practice, especially as it applies in the late twentieth century to music by composers long dead. *Performance practice is the study of the worlds—musical, cultural and social—in which a work ex-*

isted and the relating of those worlds, through interpretation, to that work in the present. Both past and present are essential. The goal of performance practice is *not* the literal re-creation of an irretrievable past. Even in the visual arts, where the object "stands still," this is not the case. For example, great knowledge and skill are required to restore a painting by a Renaissance master to its original pristine condition. But all the knowledge and skill in the world cannot bring back the age in which the painting was created. To the extent that re-creation and contextualization take place, they occur in the imagination of the viewer, one who is able to reconcile—better, to marry—past and present.

This mediation between past and present is considerably more critical in the re-creative, or performing, arts, where the analogies with the visual arts largely break down. Whereas a painting or sculpture can be taken in without the participation of others, a performing art demands the intervention of a human being whose background and experiences will necessarily differ from those of a work's creator or any of his contemporaries. Without that intervention the work cannot be experienced at all. This represents both a dilemma for, and one of the principal attractions of, the performing arts.

A further dimension to music as a re-creative art makes its interpretation considerably more thorny than that of its sister art, theater. By and large controversies over "authenticity" that are raging in musical circles have not arisen in the theater. It is not expected that a new production of Shakespeare's *Hamlet* will attempt to re-create the environment of the Globe Theater, the original staging or costumes, or the characteristics of stage movement, elocution, and delivery that prevailed in the sixteenth century. The grounding of a dramatic work in words—regardless of how those words might differ from current habits of speech—gives that work an intrinsic contemporaneity that purely instrumental music cannot attain. One can play Hamlet as a protagonist who struggles to control his own fate; one can play him as a victim of that fate; or one can play him as a fatalist who passively accepts his fate. Each of these interpretations will be grounded in Shakespeare's words, and those words will provide the scaffolding from which the arguments are hung. But everyone assumes that, whatever interpretation is chosen, the character Hamlet must speak to a contemporary audience via the rhetorical styles of our own day. This interpretive freedom sometimes results in profound historical dislocations (Hamlet in a motorcycle jacket), but even the most outspoken critics of such dislocation would not argue that the solution is to outfit Hamlet in a copy of the costume worn at the premiere.

The performance of music—and especially of instrumental music—cannot be grounded to nearly the same extent in words or ideas. Performers of Liszt's *Dante* Sonata can immerse themselves in the literary milieu of Paris in the 1830s and 1840s, in Dante's *Divine Comedy,* or in the poem by Victor Hugo that conjures up a Romantic vision of Dante, but in the end connecting this context to an actual performance will require a great leap of imagination. The praise or criticism heaped on this performance will relate much less to the performer's view of either Dante or Hugo than will the praise or criticism of a performance of *Hamlet* to the Shakespearean's view of Hamlet as a character.

Instrumental music, we must conclude, is the most culture-bound of the arts. In most cases it cannot be said to have meaning beyond itself. Inversely, meaning resides *within* the work. While evocative titles (*Carnaval, Faschingsschwank aus Wien, Nocturne, Lieder ohne Worte, Liebestraum, Intermezzo,* etc.) may provide clues, interpretations are erected on foundations that cannot be defended on the basis of external ideas. This observation suggests two distinct approaches to meaning, individualist and historic. In the first, interpretation is a private matter in which one reading is inherently no better or worse than another. In this scenario we might judge a performance on how well the interpretation was carried out, but not on the validity of the interpretation itself. In the historic approach, circumstances surrounding performance of a work—the kind of instrument that was used, the size of the hall, the social setting in which the work was heard—assume more significance than usual for the simple reason that we have few other bases for judgment.

Each of these approaches would appear to have a natural constituency. The ostensible defenders of individual interpretation in the piano world are those who see themselves as heirs to an individualist tradition extending from Beethoven to Liszt to Rosenthal. Artists' managers scour reviews looking for scraps that will set their clients apart from the hundreds of others seeking the same imprimatur of individuality. Almost without exception this group remains loyal to modern instruments. The ostensible defenders of historical context are those whose faith in tradition has been supplanted by a new emphasis on historical performance practices via period instruments.

I would submit that neither of these constituencies does what it professes to do. Individual performance styles today are more a product of marketing campaigns than of individual conceptions. The sanctity afforded individual interpretation in our own century has by and large exercised a great leveling effect, where differences among performances are matters of detail rather than conception. And the achievements to date of the period-instrument movement do not begin to live up to the claims of its most intemperate advocates.[9] We are just beginning to hear performances that go beyond novel sounds.

The Decline of Color

If we look at the piano, at pianists, and at their repertoire over the last century, we get a picture of a field in which evolution has for all practical purposes ceased. No direct pupils of such pivotal figures as Liszt survive. (Bartók was undeniably a great composer for the piano, but both his repertoire and his influence were considerably narrower than Liszt's.) In the last fifty years, we have lost all direct contact with the Romantic tradition in music. One's teacher may be someone whose teacher studied with Liszt (or Busoni or Sauer), but he or she is no longer someone who studied with Liszt.

Most of the Romantic virtuosi were also composers, at least to the extent of arranging operatic paraphrases and other kinds of potpourris for their own use in live concerts. In terms of exploiting the resources of the Romantic piano, Liszt's paraphrases—of Verdi and Wagner operas, of Schubert, Schumann, and Chopin songs—must be counted as his most important pianistic legacy. In a remarkable early biography of Liszt published in 1844, two thirds of the more than fifty works "known to the author" are paraphrases and transcriptions. (Schilling, 257–59). Transcriptions and arrangements by De Greef, Busoni, Godowsky, Rosenthal, and others kept this tradition alive through the first decades of the twentieth century, assuring at least a modicum of individual style. With the death in 1989 of Vladimir Horowitz, this practice, long since regarded as a curiosity, lost its last important practitioner. We ought not to long for a wholesale revival of this potpourri repertoire (though the best of it, such as Godowsky's *Fledermaus,* can still inspire wonder and awe), but we can lament the passing of the kind of active music making that such practices represented.

But by far the most graphic illustration of the shrinking Romantic world is painted by looking at the pianos. Throughout the nineteenth century there were dozens of major piano manufacturers—among them Graf, Streicher, Bösendorfer, [Johann Andreas] Stein, Erard, Pleyel, Pape, Clementi, Broadwood, Chickering, Bechstein, Grotrian, Feuerich, Mason & Hamlin, and Steinway—each of whom counted a loyal following. From our modern vantage point we too easily view the evolution of the piano as the steady progress toward a Steinway, but this is not how the nineteenth century viewed itself. There was scarcely a major manufacturer who could not boast that he had received Liszt's endorsement of his instrument.[10] Liszt was doubtless sincere in each of his endorsements; each instrument possessed qualities that Liszt admired, and no one expected all of these to be present in the same instrument. The Romantic keyboard style was built on color and variety.[11]

Consider, for example, these remarks attributed to Chopin:

"When I feel out of sorts, I play on an Erard piano where I easily find a ready-made tone. But when I feel in good form and strong enough to find my own individual sound, then I need a Pleyel piano."

> [On the Erard]: "You can thump it and bash it, it makes no difference: the sound is always beautiful and the ear doesn't ask for anything more since it hears a full, resonant tone."

> "Broadwood, [who is the] real [London] Pleyel." (Eigeldinger, 26)

It would be a mistake to conclude from Chopin's remarks that he wished for Erard to be put out of business and for the Pleyel to be installed as the dominant instrument in Parisian musical life. Though he had his preferences, Chopin assumed, like every other artist of the time, that his preference represented only one of many.

If the description is his own, Liszt compared Chopin's Pleyel to a glass harmonica: "It permitted him to draw therefrom sounds that might recall one of those harmonicas of which romantic Germany held the monopoly and which her ancient masters so ingeniously constructed by joining water and crystal."[12] The tone of such an instrument is sweet but penetrating, with overtones outweighing the fundamental. It was also a highly idiosyncratic sound, invoked by Liszt without a trace of criticism.

Elsewhere I have outlined the evolution of the Romantic piano (Winter, 1989). Here it will be instructive to look more closely at the differences between the two individual manufacturers alluded to so pointedly by Chopin and Liszt. A full-size Erard concert grand from this period was generally about 253 cm. long. In a catalog published in 1878 Erard was still producing instruments of this size (see Illustration 2.1). The total tension on the massive wooden frame was about 11,000 kgs., or in excess of twelve tons.

Almost without exception, the Pleyel grands of this period were between 200 and 230 cms. in length; hence the bass strings were 25–50 cms. shorter (see Illustration 2.2).[13] Moreover, the total tension ranged somewhere between 6,500 and 9,000 kgs., as much as forty percent less than an Erard. In practical terms the Pleyel was a drawing-room instrument, while the Erard was designed for a concert stage. No one in the nineteenth century would have viewed the more intimate Pleyel as inherently inferior to the more robust Erard.

An Erard and a Pleyel differed significantly in the striking points.[14] Whereas the Pleyel varied from $8^{1}/_{2}$ to just over 9 in the bass, a typical Erard might range from $9^{1}/_{2}$ to almost 10. This difference afforded the Erard a more brilliant, penetrating bass, heard to good advantage, for example, in the coda of Liszt's transcription of Schumann's *Widmung* (Illustration 2.3 shows the original Kistner edition). Although lasting only a few moments (I assume the octave to be pedaled through the end of the measure), the thunderous *fff* octave in measure 66 is the climax of the entire transcription. In performance it functions quite literally as a lightning rod, absorbing all of the work's accumulated passion (*con somma passione*). Since it enters alone, clarity is essential; on a modern instrument the effect is thick and muffled.

ILLUSTRATION 2.1. "Concert Grand Piano No. 3—7¹/₄ octaves from A to c, / with Erard double escapement action, harmonic bar, new system of agraffes and metal frame; / an instrument exceptional for the power and roundness of its tone. / Length: 2 meters 53 [cm.]—Width 1 meter [46 cm.]." Reprinted in *Dossier Erard* (Geneva, 1980), which includes the Erard sales catalog of 1878.

ILLUSTRATION 2.2. Chopin's Pleyel grand of ca. 1845 in the Warsaw Conservatory.

ILLUSTRATION 2.3. The final page from Liszt's transcription of *Widmung*, published by Kistner, Leipzig, 1848.

In the treble the Pleyel began a rise in striking ratio from 8 at about f^2 that then continued to almost 14 in the highest treble. This dramatic increase is the major contributor to the silvery, ethereal treble of a mid-century Pleyel. The Erard, by contrast, rises later and less precipitously, peaking at just over 11. Overall, then, the striking points on the Erard presuppose a more powerful and brilliant tone, those on the Pleyel a more intimate but varied tone.

EXAMPLE 2.1. Liszt, Transcription of Robert Schumann's *Widmung* (mm. 65–67)

The hammer shapes and coverings reinforce these differences. To begin with, the Pleyel hammers were smaller than those of an Erard, but decreased in size much more dramatically in the treble. Pleyel employed a striking needle-shaped hammer core (Illustration 2.4) designed to emphasize the delicate upper partials of this range. A single layer of hard felt was covered—presumably even in Chopin's day—by an outer layer of buckskin.[15] By contrast, Erard went to inordinate lengths to create a resilient hammer that would provide as much fundamental as possible. To this end the Erard factory went through a time-consuming and costly process of alternating layers of felt and buckskin—sometimes as many as four of

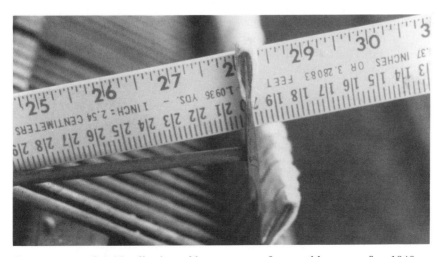

ILLUSTRATION 2.4. Needle-shaped hammer core from treble range of an 1840s Pleyel piano.

each in a single hammer (Illustration 2.5). Erard's "underdamping" system was spring-loaded to suppress the tone more quickly. Pleyel's overdampers were extremely light and narrow and relied only on gravity, leaving behind a discreet veil of sound even in passages where no sustaining pedal was used.

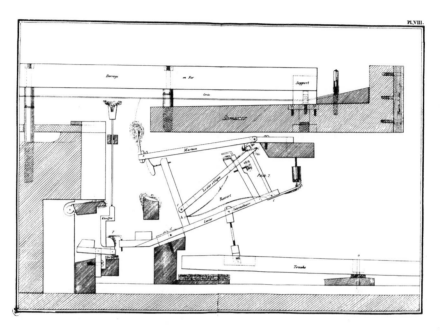

ILLUSTRATION 2.5. Erard's double-escapement action.

The Erard double-escapement action provided more leverage, and hence power, than the traditional single-escapement action of the English grand. The Pleyel firm could easily have converted to a double-escapement system, with its additional *levier oblique* on the whippen assembly. Although such a shift would have produced more power, it would have sacrificed the more direct connection between player and sound in the single-escapement action. This is doubtless what Chopin was referring to when he spoke of Erard's "ready-made tone" as opposed to the "more individual tone" of a Pleyel.

Finally, Pleyel constructed his grand with a slightly smaller octave span (16.15 to 16.35 cm.) than the 16.5 cm. span customary on mid-century Erards. Though insignificant in most passages, pieces like the Etude op. 10 no. 1 are substantially easier to negotiate on the Pleyel.

These comparisons by no means exhaust the catalog of differences between the two designs. Both firms well understood the differences between their instruments, and both chose to maintain these differences until the end of the century.[16] In this regard Pleyel and Erard acted no differently than did dozens of other European piano manufacturers.

The kinds of coloristic distinctions between an Erard and a Pleyel grand at mid-century do not exist between any two makes of instruments today. Since the peak of piano manufacturing toward the end of the nineteenth century, the trend has been unremittingly and irreversibly in the direction of increasing homogenization of design. By World War I, the number of important piano manufacturers had decreased dramatically, from hundreds to perhaps a few dozen. Pre-eminent among these were American Steinway, Hamburg Steinway, Bechstein, Blüthner, and Bösendorfer (who produced models with Viennese actions until 1905). Yet these firms still offered a residue of the variety taken for granted during the nineteenth century.

American Steinway excelled in a powerful, even tone, richest in fundamental (Hamburg Steinway mediated between the warmer European sound and the more brilliant American sound). Bechstein of Berlin offered the instrument with the clearest tone and the most precise articulation. It is no surprise that Artur Schnabel, preeminent as a Mozart, Beethoven, and Schubert player, maintained a lifelong preference for Bechsteins, where crisp passage work was still a part of the instrument's natural speech. Blüthner offered sweetness, aided by a stringing system that included extra strings that vibrated sympathetically. Bösendorfer sought a warm, mellow tone rich in overtones. Even in America there were still choices; one could opt for the richer, creamier, but less booming tone of a Mason & Hamlin.

If we look around today, and especially if we listen, we find that virtually all of the remnants of this variety have vanished. Though Bechsteins and Mason & Hamlins are still manufactured, the ownership of these firms has long since passed from their founders, and little of the earlier individuality remains. The American Steinway sound (perhaps the sound from 1920 through 1950 rather than the less satisfactory sound from 1960 through 1980) has achieved worldwide dominance. Proof lies in a comparison of the actions, scaling, and other design features of newer firms, especially those of the Pacific Rim (including Yamaha and Kawai from Japan, and now Young-Chang in Korea). All these firms have taken over wholesale the design features of the American Steinway.

In recent years Steinway and Bösendorfer have engaged in a small-scale but spirited public relations war, with the tiny Austrian firm (now a subsidiary of Kimball of Jasper, Indiana) winning a few rounds by signing such artists as Garrick Ohlsson. The Bösendorfer Imperial, with its additional lower range (down to CCC) and extra six inches of length, has been touted as a genuine alternative to Steinway. For most of this century Bösendorfer has manufactured its own double-escapement action. Yet in the late 1980s it appeared that even Bösendorfer capitulated by quietly adopting a Steinway-type action. Hence not only are far fewer pianos manufactured today, but almost all are manufactured against a single sound ideal. How, we must ask ourselves, can we celebrate the varieties of color in nineteenth-century piano music when the instruments themselves have been purged of so much of that color?

The Nature of Romantic Color

Regardless of how varied the sound qualities of earlier instruments, all shared certain features that separate them from the sound ideal of our modern instruments. Chief among these was registral variety. When Andreas Streicher suggested in his 1801 guide to the firm's fortepianos that the "tuning fork should be at exactly the same pitch as the wind instruments at any given place," he was acting on the clear understanding that the fortepiano replicated a wind band on the keyboard. Viennese music abounds with passages in which the rapid ascent or descent through registers is the point of the phrase. A typical example is the opening of Beethoven's Piano Sonata in B-flat op. 22 (Example 2.2a). The opening gesture in measures 1–2 lies in the fullest register of the Viennese instrument. The rapid climb in measures 3–4 is of little direct musical interest, but on a fortepiano the color grows more brilliant with each successive quarter note. In measures 10–11 (Example 2.2b) Beethoven makes an

EXAMPLE 2.2a. Beethoven, Piano Sonata in B♭ major, Op. 22/I (mm. 1–4)

EXAMPLE 2.2b. Beethoven, Piano Sonata in B♭ major, Op. 22/I (mm. 10–11)

even more dramatic ascent, at the top of which he plummets precipitously to the bottom of the instrument's range. The first two beats of measure 11 encompass both the highest and lowest notes on Beethoven's instrument (f³ and FF). The brilliance bordering on brittleness at the top of this passage contrasts sharply with the power and clarity in the bass and tenor. The dramatic effect on a contemporary Walter or Stein is diminished on a modern piano built with the goal of registral homogeneity.

These kinds of effects are built into the very grammar of Viennese keyboard music. When Robert Schumann wrote the highly charged opening movement of his *Kreisleriana* op. 16 in 1838 (Example 2.3), he replicated in Romantic terms what Beethoven had done almost four decades earlier.

EXAMPLE 2.3. Robert Schumann, *Kreisleriana*, Op. 16/1 (mm. 1–8)

Kreisleriana fits well on a 6½-octave Viennese instrument little different from those for which Beethoven wrote after 1815. The d^4 at the top of the phrase is a minor third from the top of the range. Its crisp, short-lived tone sounds like the breathless conclusion to a steep climb; on a modern instrument the sound never really leaves the ground. These distinctions are clear from two recordings made almost twenty-five years apart, the first a justly popular 1964 reading on a modern Steinway by Artur Rubinstein for RCA (re-released on CD as 6258-2-RC), and the second a 1988 recording by Edmund Battersby for Musical Heritage Society (MHS 512249Z) on a replica by Rodney Regier of a grand built by Conrad Graf in 1824 (see Illustration 2.6). Not only does Battersby sound as if he has played Viennese instruments all his life, but for the first time of which I am aware, we can glean from a recording why Graf enjoyed such an enviable reputation. The Graf's tone is variously warm, rich, powerful, veiled, and explosive. Most important, its tone color has a seemingly infinite range of shadings.

The *äusserst bewegt* movement cited above shows how two splendid artists react to their instruments. Clara Schumann's suggested marking of quarter note = 104 feels rushed on the more resonant Steinway, so Rubinstein begins several notches below at 92. Minus the tonal resources of the Graf, Rubinstein compensates instinctively by making a subtle but clearly articulated *accelerando* (from 92 to almost 100) to the top of the phrase. Though projecting considerable spontaneity throughout, Bat-

ILLUSTRATION 2.6. Grand piano by Conrad Graf, ca. 1820.

tersby locks right in to Clara's 104 and lets the tonal shading do the work for him.

In the last movement (no. 8) Battersby combines *schnell und spielend* ("quickly and playfully") with *die Bässe durchaus leicht und frei* ("the basses light and free throughout") at the prescribed *pianissimo* (and, in the final dissolve, *ppp*) dynamic. By comparison, Rubinstein sounds like a race-car driver trying to negotiate a winding mountain road in a truck. Once we appreciate how ill-suited his homogeneous, big-toned instrument is to Schumann's intimate but vivid fantasy world, Rubinstein's success in even suggesting Schumann's expressive range comes across as a great achievement.

Not only registral characteristics are telling in nineteenth-century piano music where the music calls for rapid sweeps across a wide range. Schubert, in the first of his six Ecossaises, D 421 (Example 2.4) expresses his instrument as well as a musical idea. The imitation between the soprano/alto in measures 1–2 and the tenor/bass in measures 5–6 grows naturally out of the disposition of the Viennese instrument. On a modern instrument the pianist will play the response as an "echo." On a Viennese instrument the effect is one not of an echo but rather of a powerful interruption that propels the phrase to the cadence in measure 8.[17]

EXAMPLE 2.4. Schubert, Ecossaise in A♭, D 421 no. 1

Though his career extended to the end of the nineteenth century, Brahms wrote consistently to the characteristics of Viennese pianos. The *Paganini* Variations of 1866 (Examples 2.5a–b) are a showcase for instruments by Streicher and Bösendorfer, whether their registral variety and clarity, or the sweetness and expressiveness of the extreme treble. The clarity of the octave doubling in this instance is a welcome byproduct of the registral variety. Convincing performances of many of the late character pieces face serious obstacles on our modern instrument, for example, the opening of one of the most atmospheric, Brahms's Intermezzo in E-flat Minor op. 118 no. 6 (Example 2.6). No modern pianist can hope to replicate Brahms's distant, disembodied (but clear!) bass response to the plaintive solo opening—not to mention the *una corda* at measures 5 ff.[18]

Although their sound was generally larger, registral variety was no less important on French and English instruments. Consider, for example, the rapid shifts in color that characterize Chopin's Etude in F op. 10

EXAMPLE 2.5a. Brahms, *Variations on a Theme of Paganini*, Op. 35, Book I, Var. 7

EXAMPLE 2.5b. Brahms, *Variations on a Theme of Paganini*, Op. 35, Book I, Var. 11

no. 8 (Example 2.7), only one of many examples that could be adduced from his works. To the extent that our modern piano is designed to minimize tonal variation across the entire range, it operates at cross-purposes with such music. No modern builder has yet dared to replicate a period Pleyel grand, but I have little doubt that eventually we will be treated to op. 10 no. 8 in a warm, unforced tenor melody counterpoised to a light, silvery treble.

The issue of registral variety and clarity is no different in the tenor and bass. The quite literal descent—into Purgatory? Hell?—at the opening of Liszt's *Dante* Sonata (published 1858; Example 2.8) presumes an instrument with both of these virtues. The deepest bass register of our modern piano is rich and sonorous, but what is needed here is a bass that will snarl and growl.

EXAMPLE 2.6. Brahms, Intermezzo in E♭ minor, Op. 118 no. 6

In addition to timbral variety, there are other ways in which the virtues of the modern piano mitigate against the effect a nineteenth-century composer has striven for. Contemplate, for example, the modern piano's unparalleled ability to sustain individual tones. Schubert's *Wanderer* Fantasy, D 760 (Example 2.9) includes a remarkable passage in a *pianissimo* dynamic with recurring off-beat accents.

Faced with a gurgling accompaniment in the fat tenor register, most modern pianists opt for a general dynamic of at least *mezzo piano*. It is then impractical to pay any credence to the weak-beat accents that occur for these ten consecutive bars. The sustaining power of a modern piano makes any accent here sound like a *crescendo* instead. So modern pianists, from Richter to Perahia,[19] wisely ignore the directive. It is the very inability of the Viennese piano to sustain tone to this degree that enables it to

EXAMPLE 2.7. Chopin, Etude in F major, Op. 10 no. 8 (mm. 1–5)

EXAMPLE 2.8. Liszt, *Après une Lecture de Dante, Fantasia quasi Sonata* (mm. 1–7)

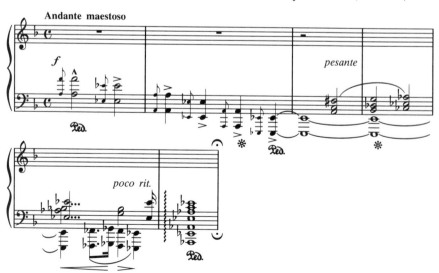

EXAMPLE 2.9. Schubert, *Wanderer* Fantasy D 760 (mm. 112–21)

project Schubert's markings (not to mention the shift in color that occurs when the melody is doubled in measures 116 ff.).

The introduction of cross- or overstringing in the 1850s led to characteristics of the piano bass that are equally at cross-purposes with Romantic piano literature. It is often stated that "overstringing" was introduced to lengthen bass strings. As employed by Steinway and the manufacturers who soon followed suit, however, the overstrung strings are generally no longer than those on equivalent straight-strung instruments.

The reason was to increase the piano's sustaining power, and the method was based on the trampoline principle. If you jump on a trampoline, the springiest, most responsive portion is that nearest the middle. You get less elasticity and lift near the rim. A soundboard works the same way. Any single tone will be fuller and last longer if it activates the soundboard at a point nearest the center. By moving all the bridges as close to the middle of the soundboard as spacing of the strings permitted, Steinway and those who followed suit achieved a remarkably sustained sound that is the glory of the modern piano. At the same time, however, they altered another equation—the clarity of individual tones. Imagine a trampoline with many persons jumping on it. If all of them try to jump at the center, the profile of any single jumper becomes blurred. On a piano, where many tones generally sound at once, the distinctness of individual tones is the tradeoff for greater sustaining power. On straight-strung instruments the sound is distributed more equally across the entire soundboard. The bass notes will have less sustaining power but they will be correspondingly more distinct. The development of the piano, then, can be best understood as a series of tradeoffs rather than as a series of linear improvements, as most accounts presume.[20]

This is why Brahms's straight-strung Viennese pianos could negotiate the low-slung passage from the first set of the *Paganini* Variations (Example 2.10). The execution of an *fpp* and sustained tremolo at this dynamic and in this register is inconceivable on a modern instrument.

EXAMPLE 2.10. Brahms, *Variations on a Theme of Paganini*, Book I, Var. 9

Many pianists believe that the greatest source of color on the modern instrument is pedaling. Since so many of the original sources of color have been removed from our modern instrument, this may well be true. The literature on pedalings is abundant, and much has solid practical value.[21] The concerns that apply to other dimensions of tone color in the nineteenth-century piano also apply to pedaling. Through the 1820s Viennese makers such as Georg Haschka and Joseph Dohnal included, apart from the standard damper, shift, and moderator (which placed a strip—and sometimes two—of felt between the hammer and the string, muting and muffling the sound), two optional pedal-operated stops: a Janissary stop, which, with each depressing of the pedal, struck a small bell (and sometimes a mallet to the bottom of the soundboard), imitating the triangle (and bass drum) of the popular Turkish bands; and a bassoon stop, which allowed a piece of parchment (sometimes encasing a few pieces of buckshot) to rest lightly on the bass strings, producing a raspy, buzzing sound. Although only a few of the battle pieces then in vogue include any instructions for using these stops, those whose instruments were fitted with them probably used them.[22] After about 1830 the Janissary and bassoon stops disappeared, though the moderator remained on Viennese instruments almost until mid-century.

We should not assume that, once the exotic pedals had been dropped from nineteenth-century instruments, the remaining damper and shift pedals behaved like those of modern instruments.[23] The construction and operation of these pedals were as varied as the instruments themselves. The amount of lateral keyboard movement that occurred when the shift pedal was depressed, and the concomitant change in tone color, varied enormously. The *una corda* effect on an 1840s Pleyel makes the music sound as if it were coming from a kilometer away; the same pedal on an 1870s Bechstein produces an effect that is pointed and very much present. The damper pedal exhibited even more variety. Until mid-century Viennese and English instruments had dampers all the way to the top of their range, unlike the stop at ca. e^3 on modern instruments. There was no uniformity in the size, shape, weight, and scaling of the dampers themselves, or in the way they were activated. The dampers on most grands built before 1840 used adaptations of the harpsichord jack rail. For much of the nineteenth century Erard employed an underdamping system driven by springs. In the last half of the nineteenth century most Viennese makers employed a *Hebeldämpfung* or "lever damper" system, which permitted heavier dampers to be raised and lowered easily.

The result was that dampers on period instruments operated with varying speeds and at varying efficiencies over varying ranges. Light Viennese dampers often make a characteristic "oink" as they settle onto a string. English dampers were intentionally inefficient. Dampers in some ranges worked more quickly than those in others. Nineteenth-century dampers were in general lighter and damped more slowly than their modern counterparts. Whereas the dampers on a well-regulated modern grand will "kill" the entire sound almost instantly (and uniformly across the range), dampers on period instruments often leave a faint residue of sound that is heard as a pleasant haze. This haze is not sufficiently intrusive to interfere with crisp passage work (aided in any event by a rapid attack), but it is enough to obviate the dry textures that ensue without any help from intermittently raised dampers on modern instruments. When Chopin specified the pedaling in his A Major Prelude, as shown in Example 2.11, he knew that a contemporary French piano would subtly blur the chromatic neighbors on the first beat of each measure without undermining the essential sweetness, giving this hackneyed miniature a disembodied quality to which one can only allude on a modern instrument.

In simple terms, period pianos through at least 1840 are designed to function very satisfactorily without dampers. This characteristic helps ex-

EXAMPLE 2.11. Chopin, Prelude in A major, Op. 28 no. 7 (mm. 1–8)

plain the dearth of damper pedal markings in piano music before Schumann. A modern piano is designed with the understanding that the damper pedal will be in play almost all of the time. The widespread assumption that, armed with a little second-hand knowledge about the workings of the damping system on a period piano, one can approximate the same effect on a modern piano is valid only if one also believes that, with a little coaxing, a Volvo can emulate the handling characteristics of a Ferrari. This point of view persists because modern grands continue to dominate our conservatories and concert halls. We should welcome the attention now being given to period instruments in recent writings, but it is generally being offered by musicians with far more experience on superbly conditioned modern instruments than on generally poorly conditioned period instruments.

We are just beginning to hear the results of matching a nineteenth-century repertoire to an instrument appropriate to its sound ideals. Perhaps the most dramatic example to date is all the more dramatic because its repertoire—eight pieces of Louis Moreau Gottschalk (1829–1869)—is widely viewed as ephemeral. As performed dazzlingly by Lambert Orkis on a tolerably restored 1865 Chickering in the Smithsonian Institution, the left-hand etude *Manchega* and the *Union* paraphrase become glittering showers of color, with melodies and rhythms sharply drawn against a background of Romantic haze that never gives way to fog.[24]

The Diminishing of Interpretive Range

I have gone on at length about the relationship between nineteenth-century piano music and pianos partly because the gradual diminishing of color on our modern instrument has been accompanied by a corresponding diminishing in interpretive range. I realize that this assertion flies in the face of conventional wisdom, in which every pianist's goal is an individual interpretation that sets him or her apart from the crowd. But in practice, I believe that very much less of this goes on than is assumed.

It is relatively easy to lament the absence of colors over which few modern pianists have immediate control. The point that might be pondered among today's performers is whether those dimensions over which we do have control offer any more variety. Let us indulge in the momentary fantasy that interpretations of Beethoven and Schumann and Liszt can be separated from issues of color. The issues to which all performers of this repertoire must assign the highest priority are tempo and its corollary, flexibility within a given tempo. These issues are infrequently raised in discussions of performance practice, but they affect performance more profoundly than such secondary issues as ornamentation or pedaling, and influence such major issues as phrasing more than any other factor. Without discounting the importance of tone, articulation, and all of those foreground qualities by which we are prone to judge pianists, let us look at the decisions that form the bedrock of an interpretation.

Conventional wisdom has it that the late eighteenth century loosened the bonds of regularity that had been imposed by the late Baroque style and that the nineteenth century abolished metrical regularity altogether. It is hard to disagree with this orthodox view, but it is one that is far easier to grasp as a generality than in individual cases. I will again state a paradoxical premise: Despite the freedom that performers of nineteenth-century piano music purport to bring to such fundamental issues as tempo and tempo flexibility, we move within a remarkably restricted range. The weight of what I prefer to call the "silent [unacknowledged] tradition" in music governs our decisions far more than we care to admit. This tradition is fueled to a frightening extent today by sound recordings that take on a kind of "canonical" status. The nineteenth-century performer probably heard fewer performances in a year than any pianist today can hear in a week. But that same pianist probably heard more variety simply because it was not possible for a single performance style to dominate all the others.

Perhaps the most instructive support for this premise in all of nineteenth-century piano music is a comparison of performances of the *Arietta* that concludes Beethoven's last piano sonata. Among the sonatas, op. 111 is a cult figure, invested with all sorts of quasi-mythological lore, such as Beethoven's "No time!" in response to Schindler's purported inquiry about the absence of a third movement. This and many other apocrypha are taken up in Wendell Kretschmar's celebrated lecture that forms the core of chapter 7 of Thomas Mann's *Doktor Faustus*—a lecture that ought to be required reading for all pianists.[25]

Before turning to actual performances, we should review two factors that make this transcendent variation movement of particular interest with regard to tempo relationships. First is its use of unusual and complex meters, beginning with a theme and first variation in $\frac{9}{16}$, a second variation in $\frac{6}{16}$, a third variation in $\frac{12}{32}$, and, in the fourth variation, a return to $\frac{9}{16}$, which carries through the remainder of the movement.[26] Indeed, just this idiosyncratic use of meter exasperated a contemporary English reviewer:

> We have devoted a full hour to this enigma, and cannot solve it. But no sphinx ever imagined such a riddle as the $\frac{12}{32}$ time presents.... The general practice of writing notes apparently very short, then doubling their length by the word *Adagio,* is one of the abuses in music that loudly cries for reform; but the system of notation pursued in this *Arietta* is confusion worse confounded, and goes on . . . to the extent of thirteen pages.[27]

At the foreground level in which the reviewer was mired, confusion is indeed a possible outcome. How does the performer relate the sixteenth-note triplets of the theme and var. 1, for example, to the thirty-second-note duplets of var. 2 or to the sixty-fourth-note duplets of var. 3?

Had the overwrought reviewer taken note of the second factor, his burden would have been substantially lightened. For Beethoven devoted considerable care to the tempo relationships among the variations and within the movement as a whole. When the meter changes (between vars. 1 and 2 and vars. 2 and 3), Beethoven specifies *L'istesso tempo* ("the same tempo"). Since the note values change considerably between var. 1 and var. 2, we might ask what "tempo" is to be "the same." The issue is whether Beethoven was referring to the slower background pulse (in which case the three-sixteenth units of var. 1 correspond to the two-sixteenth units of var. 2) or to the foreground sixteenth note (in which case the background pulse of var. 2 will be one-third faster than the pulse of var. 1; Example 2.12).

EXAMPLE 2.12. Beethoven, Piano Sonata in C minor, Op. 111/II (mm. 33–34)

Assuming the pianist pays any heed to Beethoven's directive, the solution arrived at will profoundly influence the performance. The assumption of a regular background pulse suggests a unified tempo throughout. The assumption of a regular foreground pulse suggests a freer approach to the individual variations. Var. 2 will, in effect, be "faster" than var. 1, and some way will have to be found to reconcile the tempo of var. 4 with the separate tempos of the theme and var. 3.

Beethoven's notation, it seems to me, argues for the *L'istesso tempo* applying to the slower background pulse. In the autograph (Aut. 198, Berlin DSB) the marking is placed clearly above the entire four-note up-beat to the first $\frac{6}{16}$ bar. Moreover, the $\frac{9}{16}$ meter of the theme and var. 1 is first and foremost a background triple meter and secondarily a triple foreground (the same way $\frac{6}{8}$ is a duple meter with a triple foreground). It makes more sense to assume that a composer is referring to his background meter rather than to its subdivisions.

Other factors support the notion of a unified tempo. When the fourth variation returns abruptly to the $\frac{9}{16}$ meter of the opening (m. 65), there is no *Tempo primo*, as would be necessary had Beethoven meant a general increase in tempo in var. 2 (the alternative—that Beethoven intended the last half of the movement to unfold one-third faster than the opening—seems even more far-fetched). Second, the entire movement has only one specific tempo indication, the *Adagio* at its head. The *molto semplice e cantabile* appended to *Adagio* is one more indication that Beethoven did not foresee a great many tempo shifts within the individual variations themselves.[28] He does not label the variations separately, underscoring their continuity. There is not a single *ritard* or *accelerando* within the movement. The only two directions that could possibly be construed as tempo-modifying are the *leggiermente* at measures 72 and 89 in the double fourth variation and the *espressivo* at measure 120 (the bridge to the reconstituted theme). Although modern performers often treat these terms as tempo-modifying (*espressivo* as broadening the tempo, *leggiermente* as pushing it), there is no evidence in tutors from Beethoven's time or in his music that either term mandated a noticeable tempo modification.

We have, then, a paradoxical combination of highly complex rhythms and a serenely regular pulse—just the kind of paradox that turns up regularly in late Beethoven. Given the transcendent environment in which this movement unfolds—on the heels of a stormy opening movement and disappearing into the ether rather than reaching a traditional climax—we might justifiably refer to this underlying regularity as a kind of "cosmic pulse" that brings order to all the chaos (rhythm) that accompanies life. Whether or not one accepts this characterization, Beethoven's intention seems to have been to weld highly diverse musical ideas together with a common pulse, harmonies, and phrase structure. Care, of course, must be given to the realization of this underlying pulse. The general tempo will ideally do justice to the most animated version, var. 3. The junctures between variations must be made smoothly so that the continuity of the pulse is maintained. Within the *semplice* directive, variations in tempo ought to reinforce rather than undercut the sense of pulse.

I will not argue that this interpretation excludes the possibility of others. But it seems reasonable to expect that twentieth-century performances of this movement would address the crucial issue of tempo relationships.[29] Alas, for the most part they do not. The fifteen recordings surveyed (summarized in Table 2.1) claim only to be representative of "modern" Beethoven performance. By design they include pianists with international careers (Arrau, Ashkenazy, Pollini, Barenboim), Beethoven specialists (Schnabel, Fischer, Lateiner, Badura-Skoda, Rosen, Goode), mavericks (Michelangeli, Pogorelich), "intellectuals" (Buchbinder), and period-instrument specialists (Badura-Skoda and Binns). The most remarkable composite feature of these performances is the extent to which they all echo performances of Artur Schnabel, captured permanently in his 1932 recording for EMI.[30]

It was apparently Schnabel who sanctified playing the theme extremely slowly and freely, applying Adagio to the sixteenth note rather than to the slower triplet pulse. Whether Schnabel introduced this eccentricity I cannot say, but it is strongly at variance with the markings for the *Arietta* given in several nineteenth-century editions, such as those by Carl Haslinger and Carl Czerny, both of whom specify dotted-eighth = 63;[31] Schnabel begins at a tempo closer to half of this speed. Was it also Schnabel who introduced the practice of drastically speeding up the first and second variations? By the middle of the second variation his tempo has almost doubled over the theme (approaching the Haslinger/Czerny marking). Var. 3 marks the beginning of an erratic slowing in the pulse. From var. 3 to 4 the sixteenth note remains constant. In the double fourth variation, Schnabel treats the varied repeat as a separate variation with its own, markedly faster tempo. From the trills in measure 106 through the end of the reprise the tempo accelerates once again, sometimes abruptly, sometimes smoothly. The coda returns to the slow opening tempo of the theme. In the course of the movement the pulse changes markedly a dozen times.

Schnabel's interpretation—while highly charged—seems to be considerably at odds with Beethoven's more serene directives. It is, moreover, strikingly at odds with Schnabel's own 1949 edition (also shown in Table 2.1), where the tempo fluctuations are considerably narrower. But Schnabel's recorded (and presumably live) performance has exercised a much greater influence than his edition. Consider the practice of speeding up in vars. 1 and 2; eleven of the fourteen performances do this. Or consider Schnabel's treatment of var. 4 as two separate variations with their own tempos; ten of the performances do this. Or consider the *accelerando* starting at measure 131 and continuing throughout the reprise; ten of the performances do this. Or consider the great slowing in the coda; eleven performances do this. Performances such as Ashkenazy's betray the direct and overriding influence of Schnabel. In caricatured imitations of Schna-

TABLE 2.1.
Tempo Variations in Recordings of Beethoven, Piano Sonata op. 111, Second Movement

Op. 111/II	Theme	Var. 1	Var. 2	Var. 3	Var. 4	Trills	Reprise	Coda
	m. 1	m. 17	m. 33	m. 49	m. 65	m. 106	m. 131	m. 162
	(E.T.)	(E.T.)	(E.T.)	(E.T.)	m. 72	m. 120		m. 176
Schnabel	*33–37* /	*48–52* /	*59–63* *	*51–55* †	35–37 /	31–33	*40–50*	*36–31*
(1932)	(2:54)	(1:59)	(1:41)	(1:55)	48–50	*39–42*		(10)
Schnabel	48–50	[48–50]	50–52	46–48	44–46	46	48–50	42–44
(1949 edition)					48–50	[46]	52–54	
Fischer	*48–52* /	58–59	64–66	51–54 †	34–33 /	44–45	45–64	36–38
(1954)	(1:53)	(1:41)	(1:38)	(2:03)	54–56	61–59		(25)
Arrau	36–38 /	43–45 /	59–56	52–48	38–40	32–33	40–50	36–37
(1964)	(3:05)	(2:21)	(1:50)	(2:07)	40–42	37		(18)
Michelangeli	40–38 /	46–45 /	*43–47*	51–52	42–43	35–36	*42–50*	43–41
(1965)	(2:34)	(2:13)	(2:14)	(1:51)	48–47	*43–41*		(30)
Lateiner	*40–35* ‡	39–38	*45–41*	50–48	40–39	32–34	37–39	‡ *38–34*
(1968)	(2:42)	(2:40)	(2:22)	(1:55)	43–41	41–38		(29)
Badura-Skoda	*44–48*	50–52	58–55	52–51	36–37 /	39–42	43–52	40–42
(1973	(2:12)	(2:00)	(1:50)	(2:00)	48–50	45–43		(17)
Rosen	*35–40* ‡	39–42 ‡	39–37	45–44	35–34 /	*38–36*	31–42	38–36
(ca. 1974)	(2:34)	(2:23)	(2:29)	(2:17)	43	31–29		(18)
Ashkenazy	*42–38* /	48–50 /	60–64 *	*51–55* †	37–38	38–40	*40–50*	38–39
(1974)	(2:25)	(1:58)	(1:33)	(1:56)	40–41	40		(25)
Pollini	37–39 /	50–51	54–58	48–49	38–40 /	37–39	*40–50*	37–38
(1975)	(2:40)	(1:59)	(1:45)	(2:01)	50–52	39		(18)
§ Badura-Skoda	45–47	52–55	58–55	52–55	39–42 /	40–41 /	*47–57*	42–41
(1980)	(2:14)	(1:57)	(1:46)	(1:52)	54–55	51–48		(16)
§ Binns	39–38	43–44	54–53	49	36–35 /	40–38	38–41	35–36
(1981)	(2:22)	(2:14)	(1:57)	(2:06)	43–44	40–38		(20)
Buchbinder	34–36 ‡	37–36	55–57	50–51	42–43	43	36–39	39–40
(1981)	(2:44)	(2:43)	(1:45)	(2:00)	46–45	35		(28)
Pogorelich	33–34	39–41 /	60–64 /	49–48	30–31 /	33–31	33–36	31–29
(1982)	(2:51)	(2:28)	(1:32)	(2:04)	40	36–35		(30)
Barenboim	28–30 /	39–38 /	56–57	53–51 /	27 /	33–31	32–40	33–31
(1984)	(3:22)	(2:24)	(1:49)	(2:03)	35–36	35		(14)
Goode	36–38 /	45–47 /	56–54	51–50	39–40 /	33–31	37–50	33–36
(1987)	(2:41)	(2:06)	(1:51)	(1:58)	46–45	37–35		(25)

NOTE: E.T. stands for "elapsed time" in vars. 1–3.

Italic type means that the passage in question is played freely. Since all performances involve a degree of rhythmic freedom, only those passages performed very freely are in italic.

/ indicates a marked change of tempo between variations.

* indicates a small-scale linking of pulse between variations, usually via a ritard.

† indicates a large-scale linking of the sixteenth-note pulse.

‡ indicates a large-scale linking of the slower triplet pulse. Where no sign appears, the linkage is neither strong nor weak.

§ before the artist's name indicates a performance on a period instrument.

bel, like that of Barenboim, we can almost imagine Schnabel's ghost wringing his hands. It seems to make no difference whether one plays on a period instrument or a modern piano.

Only the performances of Edwin Fischer and, to a slightly lesser extent, of his pupil Paul Badura-Skoda even approach the tempo prescribed by Haslinger or Czerny. What is most noteworthy, however, is that—regardless of tempo—not a single one of these performances projects a unified pulse throughout. Even had Beethoven left no indications about the tempo relationships among variations, the idea ought to have occurred to someone as simply an experiment. In the performances by Jacob Lateiner, Charles Rosen, and Rudolf Buchbinder we get glimpses of the equilibrium that Beethoven may have in mind, and the effect, however temporary, is in each instance magical. In the end, however, the shared features of the tempo relationships in these performances are far more noteworthy than their differences.[32]

What, then, of works in which frequent changes of tempo are mandated? Would we not then find the interpretive variety whose lack in the *Arietta* of Beethoven's op. 111 I have documented at such lengths? An ideal test case is a work composed in Beethoven's memory, Robert Schumann's Fantasy in C op. 17, published in 1839. The first movement of this quintessentially Romantic work contains more than thirty changes or modifications of tempo in eleven minutes of music—more than three per minute. Few works even at century's end rival it for variety of tempos.

The movement, marked *Durchaus phantastisch und leidenschaftlich vorzutragen* ("To be performed fancifully and passionately throughout"), is more than a collection of tempo changes. It consists of a web of themes that are varied, developed, and transformed in altogether remarkable ways. In the first 125 measures, the opening motto is heard no fewer than six times, each time in a different guise. Material of explosive passion (mm. 1ff.) alternates with music of a reflective nature (m. 62ff.). Despite the frequent tempo modifications, the parallel outer sections of the movement are governed by a single metronome marking of half note = 80. This marking must be taken seriously because it is not only the one Robert prescribed for the first edition but also the same one Clara advocated in her subsequent edition. On the modern piano it is an admittedly fast tempo, and no one to my knowledge has recorded the first movement with this tempo governing more than the first few bars.

We can safely assume that post–World War II performers of this work will pay attention to Schumann's frequent ritards and less frequent tempo changes. But despite the density of such directives, more than three quarters of the movement is governed by—depending on one's point of view—the opening metronome marking or (if one believes it affects only the first few measures) by no tempo marking. The sameness with which modern performers present this three-quarters is the most eye-opening aspect of the movement's performance history. Given the range of prescribed tempo modifications, we would expect that, in those areas where the precise tempo is left up to the performer, a great variety of tempo relationships would spring forth from different interpreters. If the five recordings surveyed in Table 2.2 are representative, such is not the case.

Table 2.2.
Tempo Variations in Recordings of Schumann, Fantasy in C, op. 17, mvt. 1, mm. 1–124

	Artur Rubinstein (1965) M.M.	Abbey Simon (ca. 1969) M.M.	Maurizio Pollini (1973) M.M.	Richard Goode (1981) M.M.	Murray Perahia (1986) M.M.
mm. 1–10 (ff)	69–68	74–76	80	77–76	76–73
mm. 10–16 (p)	63–61	72–70	74–73	75–70	73–70
mm. 19–25 (p)	55–53	68–66	74–75	62–64	69–66
mm. 29–33 (f)	55–60	70–72	72–73	70	68
mm. 33–38	61–63	72	72–70	69–71	73
mm. 41–46	59–56	70–63	60–61	72–71	68–63
mm. 49–52	56–54	61–62 /	63	68	62
mm. 53–58	63	73	71–72	73–72	70–73
mm. 62–70	59–60	59–58	57–58	60	59–57
mm. 82–93	65–68	79–80	79–81	78–82	75–77
mm. 97–103 (p)	56–53	61–62	72–74	60–61	60–61
mm. 106–17 *Im lebhaften Tempo*	75–78	93–94	94	96	94–93
mm. 119–24 (ff)	58	65–64	76	64	64–65

NOTE: Only measures not affected by ritards or tempo changes have been calibrated. *Italic* measures are statements of the descending motto theme. The *Im lebhaften Tempo* ("In a lively tempo") has been included to see how tempo change without a metronome marking is treated.

We might be tempted to read into Rubinstein's broad tempos a disdain on the part of an older generation for metronome markings that a new generation takes more seriously. This may be true, but the younger generation backs off from Schumann's marking after the briefest of skirmishes. All five performances slow down the motto theme after its initial statement, as if agreed that "softer is slower." Four of five slow down for the descent in measures 49–52, and all without exception speed up in the ascending continuation. All five recordings pick nearly identical tempos for the pensive derivative of the motto theme at measures 62ff. Four out of five pick virtually identical tempos for the *Im lebhaften Tempo*. The performances by Simon and Goode are largely indistinguishable with regard to tempo. Only Pollini grabs the bull by the horns at the outset, but as the movement progresses his interpretation blends increasingly with the others.

Each of the performances surveyed is by a major artist with a well-deserved reputation. What their performances of the Fantasy's first movement suggest, however, is that pianists "know" how the Schumann Fantasy "goes." They agree far more on tempo relationships that are not prescribed by the composer than on following what the composer and his best-known interpreter requested. Without discounting the importance of details and nuances, the primary influence seems again to be a "silent performing tradition"—one doubtless underwritten generously by the recording industry.

Lest I be accused of a myopic preoccupation with large-scale design, I would like to conclude with an example that addresses briefly the issue of phrase articulation, perhaps the least cultivated source of Romantic color. In our zeal to raise *legato* to divine status, we often forget that nineteenth-century piano music celebrated *legato* alongside many other touches and that rests were means of expression. Every pianist would benefit from close study of two recordings of the finale of Schubert's most dramatic piano sonata, the D major op. 53 (D 850, Example 2.13), by the preeminent

EXAMPLE 2.13. Schubert, Piano Sonata in D major, D 850/IV (mm. 1–10)

interpreters of their day, Artur Schnabel and Alfred Brendel.[33] The theme of this simple yet elaborate Rondo is a study in musical declamation.

In this disguised eight-bar theme, Schubert creates an impression of asymmetry by placing off-beat rests in measures 2 and 7.[34] The first, third, and fifth bars of the theme establish a regular pattern of two staccato quarters that is broken by the seventh bar. Bars 4, 6, and 8—but not bar 2—begin with half notes. The "antecedent" triplets of measure 6 lead to a short downbeat in measure 7, while the "consequent" triplets of measure 7 lead to a half note in measure 8. The observance of these carefully marked articulations is essential to expressing the theme's delicate equilibrium. The gestures set up in these first ten bars resonate many times in the last two-thirds of the theme and throughout the movement.

Limited only by the finite tonal resources of his instrument, Schnabel grasped the importance of these rhetorical devices from the outset. His recording reveals a playfulness and spontaneity at odds with his sober, intellectual image. He uses Schubert's well-articulated speed to press the phrase forward ever so slightly in the second half of measure 3, and to relax it at the first half note in measure 4—with corresponding inflections to the half notes across measures 5–6 and 7–8. The short downbeat of measure 7 enables Schnabel to linger for just an instant on the second quarter note, which sets up the only cadence in the phrase.

Mr. Brendel is quite another matter. After six token staccato beats in the curtain, he articulates the first phrase of the theme—and the movement (with the capricious exception of six beats in the left hand from the second half of measure 12 through measure 13)—as if it were Wagner's *Tristan*. Indeed, one would never guess that Schubert had written anything except one long slur over each major section of this Rondo. Hence Brendel's accent on the second beat of measure 6 (left hand) of the theme and his prolongation of the first beat of measure 7—perhaps intended to compensate for the overall lack of articulation—seem arbitrary and mannerist. These wholesale dismissals of unambiguous directions are especially remarkable from an artist who is marketed as a "thinking" pianist (typically, the cover art to this recording shows Mr. Brendel not in performance but poring over a score).

Few pianists can create as consistently beautiful a sound on the modern piano as Mr. Brendel, few have his control over nuance and shading, and few have written more thoughtfully and illuminatingly about its music (Brendel, 1975). This makes Brendel's dismissal of Schubert's language all the more disheartening. Were he to argue that the modern instrument is utterly incapable of reproducing the nuances of Schubert's delivery, then at least we would know where he was coming from. The absence of commentary or discussion is entirely typical of our age, and also most typical of our homogenized late twentieth-century performing style.

Given the strongly personal tradition within which nineteenth-century piano music evolved, I am going to conclude with what may seem a contradictory position. For the very reason that personal interpretation plays such a vital role, the performance of nineteenth-century piano music demands the widest possible knowledge of performance practices. The notion that, in forging an interpretation, the performer of any repertoire relies first and foremost on innate creativity is one of the most seductive fictions in the music business. Those performers of nineteenth-century piano music who cling to this view today sound more like all those who share that view than like the individual interpreters they aspire to be—a conclusion strongly supported not just by the recordings we have surveyed but also by the output of an entire industry.

Regardless of the degree of talent with which any individual performer is blessed, the musical environment in which he or she is nurtured has a powerful impact on individual performance styles. The development of an individual style depends to a great extent on performers' realization and understanding of what has shaped and molded them. Inspired performances result from choices that are conscious and deliberate as well as instinctive and intuitive. Youthful artists by and large have these choices made for them; mature artists have identified what influences underlie their approaches, and they accept responsibility for these as well as for those of their own making.

There has never been a better time for us to rethink our performances of repertoire that has become so familiar it almost plays itself. Our audience is increasingly one that is coming to Beethoven, Chopin, and Liszt as young adults, without having been weaned from a "high culture" tradition. That tradition, which so many of us revere, can no longer be counted on to deliver a fresh generation of listeners. This new breed of listener is not satisfied watching reenactments of ritualized performances, however perfectly carried out. Modern culture offers too many consumer options for us to rest on a belief—regardless of how sincere—in the self-evident worth, much less superiority, of this repertoire. The new audience may not have the sophistication upon which musicians in previous generations relied, but it has a nose that can smell the difference between an adventure and a rerun.

The strength of the period-instrument movement to date lies not in its largely spurious claims to authenticity, but precisely in its spirit of adventure. This adventurism has too frequently permitted period-instrument performers to get away with standards that would attract only scorn in the modern instrument world. The great majority of recordings on nineteenth-century pianos to date have simply transplanted well-worn interpretations from a previous era onto well-worn instruments from an even earlier era. In the long run that orientation will sustain neither the old nor the new audience. Modern performers are equally guilty in their claim to have a corner on inspiration. The momentum of previous generations becomes the inertia of the present generation, and too many of the recordings we issue today offer eloquent testimony to the staleness of our vision.

Perhaps the most difficult part in rethinking pieces that we know so well is acknowledging the degree to which we have settled for playing by rote. It may be impossible to banish the smothering effect of countless recordings from our collective memory, but we can retrain ourselves to look at scores with an open and unbiased mind. We can regain a sense of experimentation (dare one say improvisation?) that lay at the basis of so many individual performance styles in the nineteenth century. There is absolutely no reason why modern instrument performers cannot regain ground they feel they have lost by forging interpretations from scratch and by exposing the posturing of much of the period-instrument movement.[35] We need passionate defenders of the modern piano's fitness for expressing the Romantic repertoire, armed not just with slogans but with specifics.[36] The shibboleths that both sides have applied to the other have long since lost their force. Performance practice belongs to every pianist willing to take seriously the claims of a Chopin mazurka or Brahms intermezzo, of their times, and of ours.

Notes

1. "Performing practice" in Great Britain, where gerunds are still commonly used.

2. The current fashionableness of performance practice was illustrated by a PBS broadcast in July 1989 of the New York *Mostly Mozart Festival*. Following a performance of Mozart's *Linz* Symphony, K. 425, host Martin Bookspan commented approvingly and at length on conductor Gerard Schwarz's use of the prescribed Andante tempo in the Siciliano slow movement rather than the Poco Adagio tempo that prevailed under numerous unnamed conductors from "the past." Probably few listeners had any idea of what Bookspan was talking about, but the message was clear: Mr. Schwarz is hip to performance practice.

3. For one view of the current relationship between performance practice and period instruments, see Winter, "Debunking."

4. This essay focuses on the nineteenth-century repertoire for the virtuoso pianist. It does not explore the domestic piano-music market that sprang up during the 1840s and 1850s. By mid-century, the amateur pianist had replaced the amateur string player who had been the paradigm during the era of Haydn, Mozart, and Beethoven. This shift was significant, for the amateur pianist did not need to have any sense of intonation, of how to blend pitches with other instruments, or of how to tune—all prerequisites for the string player.

5. Letter to Adolphe Pictet first published in *Revue et Gazette musicale de Paris* 6 (1838): 58.

6. Some will argue that this old European constituency is being replaced by an Asian or Asian/American audience, but—whatever the validity of this claim—this repertoire is new music for the Asian audience rather than part of its traditional "high culture."

7. Howard Mayer Brown, "Pedantry or Liberation?" in Kenyon, 30.

8. See Winter, 1984 ("Performing"): 53.

9. See, among others, Winter, "The Emperor's New Clothes," and Taruskin, "The New Antiquity."

10. The piano makers whose instruments Liszt is known to have used or played in concerts include Erard, Pape, Dietz, Petzold, Pleyel, Herz, and Klepfer in Paris; Boisselot in southern France, Spain, and Portugal; Graf and Streicher in Austria; Eck (Cologne), Breitkopf & Härtel (Leipzig), Kaps (Dresden); Volkening (Bielefeld), Biber (Munich), Heek (Frankfurt), Rachals (Hamburg), Berndt, Bessalie, Leicht (all three in Breslau, today Wrocław, Poland), Kisting, Stöcker, Schönemann, and Perau (all four in Berlin) in Germany; Broadwood, Erard, Bechstein, Boisselot, Beregszaszy, Streicher, Bösendorfer, and Steinway at the Altenburg in Weimar; Bechstein, Erard, Bösendorfer, and Chickering. These twenty-nine types probably represent an incomplete list of the instruments Liszt must have known. I am indebted to Geraldine Keeling, who is preparing a full-length study of Liszt's pianos, for details concerning Liszt's use of pianos.

11. Reliance on color is far less true of such periods as the Baroque. It is no accident that an early album of electronic music was "Switched-on Bach." Bach's music exists in large measure independently of any particular color, which also explains the popularity of transcriptions in the first half of the eighteenth century. "Switched-on Chopin" is inconceivable.

12. Liszt, trans. 1963: 90. The kind of glass harmonica with which Liszt would most likely have been familiar was the pedal-operated type introduced by Benjamin Franklin in 1761 and popular in Europe to about 1830. The passage is often quoted without identifying the allusion, as in Maurice Hinson, "Pedaling the Piano Works of Chopin," in Banowetz, 180.

13. The only exception I have encountered in the study of more than two dozen Pleyels from the first half of the century is a privately owned instrument in Brentwood, California, from the mid-1840s and measuring about 245 cm.

14. For a fresh look at this design element, see Winter, 1988 ("Striking"): 286–87.

15. The evidence for this construction is usually obscured on surviving instruments because the hammers have invariably been recovered in straight felt.

16. Erard closed down his London factory in 1890 rather than surrender to the homogenization of taste.

17. Richard Burnett—who understands exactly how to handle the phrase—performs Schubert's D 421, no. 1 on an 1826 Viennese fortepiano by Conrad Graf (Amon Ra CD-SAR 7). This original instrument shows its age, especially in the treble, but enough of its earlier beauty remains for us to imagine how it might once have sounded.

18. Not all Viennese instruments were capable of a true *una corda* effect, but all of them moved to at least two strings, and all of them altered the tone color significantly. Many pianists do not realize that using the shift on most modern grands only moves the hammer to a different location on all three strings.

19. Richter can be heard on Angel RL-32078; Perahia, on CBS MK42124.

20. See, for example, Harding and Ehrlich.

21. For the most up-to-date bibliography, see Banowetz. The most illuminating article on the subject of Romantic pedaling to date is Rosen.

22. Colorful examples of their application can be heard on two recordings by Richard Burnett (Amon Ra SAR 6 and Amon Ra SAR 7).

23. The middle, or "sostenuto," pedal was introduced by the Marseille maker Boisselot as early as the Paris Exposition of 1844. After improvements in 1862 by Claude Montal, Steinway patented its own version in 1875. This pedal sustains notes being held at the moment the pedal is depressed. Many firms, such as Bechstein, never adopted the sostenuto pedal.

24. Smithsonian ND 033.

25. Translated into English as *Doctor Faustus* by H. T. Lowe-Porter and published by Alfred A. Knopf (New York, 1948). Mann's account of the lecture is on pp. 51–56 of the paperback edition.

26. To stress the movement's seamlessness, Beethoven does not label the variations separately; the nomenclature is used here for convenience.

27. This review from *The Harmonicon* (London, August 1823) is quoted in Nicholas Slonimsky's *Lexicon of Musical Invective* (Seattle, 1969; reprint of 1953 edition), 43.

28. This marking is more significant for having been added *after* the Adagio was entered.

29. Passing reference to tempo relationships in the *Arietta*—and large-scale ignoring of their consequences—can be found in Goldstein, 266.

30. Angel GRM 4005 (COLH 63). The fourteen other recordings surveyed are Edwin Fischer (HUNT CD 514), Claudio Arrau (Philips 835 382 2Y), Arturo Benedetti Michelangeli (London CS 6446), Jacob Lateiner (RCA LSC-3016), Paul Badura-Skoda (Music & Arts CD-241), Charles Rosen (Columbia M3X 30938), Vladimir Ashkenazy (London 417 150-2), Maurizio Pollini (DGG 419 199-2), Paul Badura-Skoda (playing a fortepiano built by Conrad Graf in the 1820s, Astrée AS 49), Malcolm Binns (playing a fortepiano built by Conrad Graf ca. 1835, L'Oiseau-Lyre D185D3), Rudolf Buchbinder (TELDEC 8.43027), Ivo Pogorelich (DGG 410 520-2), Daniel Barenboim (DGG 423 371-2), and Richard Goode (Elektra/Nonesuch 9 79211-2).

31. A thorough tabulation of metronome markings in these and other nineteenth-century Beethoven editions can be found in Rosenblum, 354–61.

32. For similar conclusions drawn from performances of Beethoven's Piano Concerto No. 1, see Winter, 1988 ("Performing").

33. Schnabel's performance is on Arabesque Z6573 and Brendel's is on Philips 422 063-2.

34. Measure numbers in this discussion refer to the thematic structure and hence omit the two-bar "curtain."

35. David Zinman of the Baltimore Symphony has successfully introduced period-instrument techniques and fresh interpretations (taking seriously Beethoven's metronome markings, for example) into his modern-instrument performances of Beethoven symphonies, reinvigorating this repertoire for players and audience alike. Some might argue that Zinman's next step ought to be the introduction of period instruments, but all agree that he has kindled the kind of debate that brings old repertoires back to life.

36. The only example I know of an articulate defense of the modern piano for older repertoire is Richard Taruskin's "Bach on Cello and Piano," *Opus*, April 1987, 25. Though many may disagree with either the essay's premises or its con-

clusions, its arguments are fashioned so clearly that all who read them are forced to rethink their own positions.

Selected Bibliography

Banowetz, Joseph. *The Pianist's Guide to Pedaling.* Bloomington, 1985.

Brendel, Alfred. *Musical Thoughts and Afterthoughts.* Princeton, 1976.

Douglas, Mary. "Self-Evidence." In *Implicit Meanings: Essays in Anthropology.* London, 1975. Pp. 276–318.

Ehrlich, Cyril. *The Piano: A History.* London, 1976.

Eigeldinger, Jean-Jacques. *Chopin, Pianist and Teacher: As Seen by His Pupils.* Translated by Naomi Shohet. Cambridge, 1988.

Goldstein, Joanna. *A Beethoven Enigma: Performance Practice and the Piano Sonata, Opus 111.* New York, 1988.

Harding, Rosamond. *The Piano-Forte: Its History Traced to the Great Exhibition of 1851.* Cambridge, 1933; reprinted New York, 1973.

Kenyon, Nicholas, ed. *Authenticity and Early Music.* Oxford, 1988.

Liszt, Franz. *Frédéric Chopin.* Paris, 1852. Translated by Edward N. Waters. Glencoe, Ill., 1963.

Newman, William S. *Beethoven on Beethoven: Playing His Piano Music His Way.* New York, 1988.

Rosen, Charles. "The Romantic Pedal." In *The Book of the Piano,* edited by Dominic Gill. Ithaca, 1981. Pp. 106–13.

Rosenblum, Sandra. *Performance Practices in Classic Piano Music.* Bloomington, 1988.

Schilling, Gustav. *Franz Liszt: Sein Leben und Wirken.* Stuttgart, 1844.

Streicher, Andreas. *Kurze Bemerkungen über das Spielen, Stimmen und Erhalten der Fortepiano welche von Nannette Streicher geborne* [sic] *Stein verfertigt werden.* Translated by Preethi de Silva. Ann Arbor, 1983.

Taruskin, Richard. "The New Antiquity." *Opus,* October 1987: 31–41, 43, 63.

Winter, Robert. "The Emperor's New Clothes: Nineteenth-Century Instruments Revisited." *19th-Century Music* 7 (1984): 251–65.

———. "Performing Practice after 1750." *New Grove Dictionary of Musical Instruments.* London, 1984. Pp. 53–61.

———. "Performing Beethoven's Early Piano Concertos." *Early Music* 16 (1988): 214–30.

———. "Striking It Rich: The Significance of Striking Points in the Evolution of the Romantic Piano." *Journal of Musicology* 6 (1988): 267–92.

———. "Keyboards." In *Performance Practice: Music after 1600,* ed. Howard Mayer Brown and Stanlie Sadie. The New Grove Handbooks in Music. London, 1989. Pp. 346–73.

———. "Debunking the Debunkers: The 'Great Performance Practice Muddle' Reconsidered." *19th-Century Music* (forthcoming).

CHAPTER THREE

Beethoven

William Kinderman

The piano works of Beethoven comprise a vast musical legacy from all periods of his career and include a number of pathbreaking compositions that anticipated his most outstanding achievements in other genres. Following his arrival at Vienna in 1792, Beethoven composed primarily for solo piano or combinations of instruments including piano. By the time he finished his First Symphony and the String Quartets op. 18 in 1800, Beethoven had completed thirteen piano sonatas (up to and including op. 22 and the two sonatas op. 49), the first two concertos, and more than a dozen sets of independent piano variations. Contemporary reports described his extraordinary abilities in improvisation. In view of his formidable mastery of the instrument, we need hardly marvel that Beethoven's piano music remained a vehicle for his most advanced ideas, from the op. 31 Sonatas and opp. 34 and 35 Variations of 1802, at the threshold of his "second period," to the last three sonatas, opp. 109–111, *Diabelli* Variations, and late bagatelles from the 1820s, when many of his most profound and original works were conceived. Our discussion will focus first on the sonatas, and then on the most important variation sets, bagatelles, and miscellaneous pieces.

The Early Sonatas

Beethoven's first published works dating from his Bonn period were the *Dressler* Variations for piano, issued in 1782, and the three piano sonatas WoO 47, which appeared the following year. Despite their considerable biographical interest, these works are of course juvenilia, and the first of his artistically important sonatas are those of op. 2 from more than a decade later, in which Beethoven's thorough assimilation of the Viennese classical sonata style is already evident. It would be a serious error to underestimate Beethoven's piano sonatas from the 1790s. Whereas his first published examples of the concerto, quartet, and symphony are generally inferior to the masterpieces in these genres by Haydn and Mozart, the same cannot be said of the early sonatas. In the piano sonata Beethoven first revealed the full expressive range and power of invention that he was to demonstrate only years later in some other musical forms. Ultimately,

Beethoven's sonatas not only demonstrated his mastery of the Viennese classical style but succeeded in considerable measure in defining the style itself. The influence of these works has been incalculable and has left an imprint not only on subsequent composition and performance traditions but on the development of serious musical criticism and analysis, shaping the very ways in which we think about musical art.

A good example of Beethoven's early but consummate mastery of this genre is the Sonata in D op. 10 no. 3, completed in 1798, when he was twenty-eight years old. Like its predecessors (the Sonata in E-flat op. 7 and the three Sonatas op. 2), op. 10 no. 3 contains four movements, with a Minuet and Trio in penultimate position.[1] At the time this four-movement framework, not yet conventional for the piano sonata, was normally used in symphonies and quartets. Beethoven's use here of the tonic major or minor in all four movements is unusual. One reason for this tonal plan is found in the expressive relationship between the inner movements: an extended *Largo e mesto* of tragic character in D minor, whose solemn darkness is broken by the beginning of the gentle minuet in the major, marked *dolce*. This wonderfully sensitive and gradual effect of light dispelling darkness depends crucially on the use of a common tonality. A different sort of complementary relationship holds between the bold and energetic first movement, marked Presto, and the meditative slow movement in minor.

The very opening of the sonata, in unharmonized octaves, presents material that in itself is not particularly distinctive: its initial descending fourth, D-A, and subsequent ascent through tonic triads of D major represent commonplace elements of classical tonality (Example 3.1). The

EXAMPLE 3.1. Piano Sonata in D major, Op. 10 no. 3/i (mm. 1–4)

sparse, elemental nature of this opening lends itself well to reinterpretation and reworking, however, as is soon evident in the exposition, where extended passages are given over to developmental processes. The sudden interruptions and contrasts characteristic of this movement are carefully coordinated with a logical, progressive unfolding and development of the basic thematic material.

Not far into the Presto, a varied restatement of the motive in octaves is extended to a climax on F-sharp (m. 22), which serves as a pivot to the key of B minor, and a new subject in that key (m. 23ff). A process of foreshortening[2] leads to an emphatic cadence in the dominant key, A major, and only here (m. 53) is the main part of the second subject group reached. (The passage beginning in B minor, heard in retrospect, has been treated much in the manner of a transition, and it concludes with conventional passagework leading to a cadential trill in the dominant.) This subject in A major audibly derives from the opening measure of the movement, now treated in rhythmic diminution, with the descending fourth D-A given three times in the major (mm. 53–56) and three times in the minor before it is interrupted by silence. As Jürgen Uhde has pointed out, the silence seems to become part of the thematic structure, which Beethoven extends by treating contrapuntally a phrase prominently utilizing the descending fourth (Uhde, 1970, 2:180–81). This phrase provides the basis for an extended developmental continuation of modulating sequences and persistent syncopations; the result is a large-scale metrical tension that looks ahead, in a way, to the famous syncopated passages in the first movement of the *Eroica* Symphony.[3] A series of cadential themes follows, clearly based on the initial phrase of the movement, and especially on the thematic motto of the descending fourth. The exposition of this Presto, as well as the remainder of the movement, shows an intense internal dynamism that strains the formal framework of the classical sonata and expands it from within—a hallmark of Beethoven's forceful early style.

In the following *Largo e mesto* in D minor, Beethoven exploits the contrast between thick, dark chords (with frequent stress on the sonority of the diminished-seventh) and a more transparent, plaintive, recitative-like voice in the upper register. (A similar expressive juxtaposition reappears, in heightened form, in the slow introduction of Beethoven's next sonata, the *Pathétique*, op. 13.) This slow movement is one of the great tragic utterances in early Beethoven, and it displays a sense of abortive struggle and resignation in Beethoven's treatment of the sonata form. The mood of brightness and hope at the beginning of the F-major development is negated by the fortissimo diminished-seventh chords of measure 35, which lead us forcefully back to the minor, while their register and motives remind us of the opening theme of the movement. Especially powerful is the coda, in which a statement of the principal theme in the lowest register leads to a dramatic, chromatic ascent through an entire octave in the bass. The movement ends with references to fragments from the opening theme and allusions to the registral disparities between its low chords and the extracted motive of a semitone in the highest register.

If the ensuing transparent Minuetto leaves behind the gloomy depths of the slow movement, the concluding rondo introduces yet another characteristic essential to Beethoven: whimsical and unpredictable humor. Here the dynamic stops and starts from the Presto become a game of hide-and-seek for the primary theme itself (Example 3.2). Indeed, is the theme ever found? It seems to suggest a process of seeking, doubting, and evasion. Its prominent deceptive cadence on B minor (m. 7) is later developed in an entire central episode built upon a more jarring deceptive cadence on B-flat (m. 33). This episode, in turn, leads to a false recapitulation in that key, and to a transition based on the crucial interval of the fourth—no less important in this movement than it had been in the Presto. The final episode (mm. 92–99) is like a quest for a more substantial but unattainable goal, and its sequences rise ecstatically into the highest register of the piano before falling back in a short cadenza. In a peculiar way, we seem not to have left the original ground: the opening motive returns yet again and even assumes the minor mode, reminding us of the tragic slow movement. A series of chords based on the rhythm of the initial motive follow, and the sonata ends with repetitions of the motive in the bass, heard beneath chromatic scales and arpeggios in the right hand.

EXAMPLE 3.2. Piano Sonata in D major, Op. 10 no. 3/iv (mm. 1–9)

The range of expression Beethoven explores here, in a series of movements derived from similar motivic relationships, is no less than prodigious and cannot be adequately described in technical terms alone. An emphasis on process, on ongoing development, informs the outer movements of this sonata, as we have seen, and this quality also contributes to the sense of openness at the close of the rondo finale. Other sonatas, like

the *Pathétique*, op. 13, display a more concentrated sense of summation. In
the coda of the finale of the *Pathétique*, at the last appearance of the head
of the rondo theme (m. 203), Beethoven moves into the key of the flat
sixth, A-flat major, recalling thereby the key of the slow movement and
the central episode of the rondo. (The register of this coda passage in
A-flat also corresponds precisely to the main theme of the *Adagio cantabile*.) Although this last-minute departure into a remote key might seem to
disturb seriously the formal equilibrium, in fact, Beethoven uses the technique as a means of formal integration and resolution of tensions. Not
only has the key of A-flat assumed importance (as in so many of
Beethoven's C-minor works), but the sonority of the German augmented-
sixth chord built on A-flat has appeared conspicuously in the accompaniment to the rondo theme.

In the final bars, this sonority serves as the pivot for the return to C
minor, while the final cadence, with its powerful descending scale in triplets from high F, assumes a structural significance evidently overlooked in
the analytical literature. A cardinal principle of classical sonata procedure
entails the ultimate resolution to the tonic of material originally heard in
secondary keys. In this instance, the downward-rushing triplets recall earlier musical gestures, for example, descents from high F above the
dominant-seventh chord of C minor (mm. 58–60, 117–120), or in the
coda, above the dominant-seventh of A-flat (mm. 198–201). The trick of
delaying resolution of such a gesture until the final bar was a specialty of
Haydn, but never before Beethoven did it assume such dramatic force
and significance.[4]

The Middle-Period Sonatas

The terrible recognition of the loss of his hearing precipitated an
inward crisis in Beethoven, the nature of which is most clearly revealed in
the *Heiligenstadt Testament* of 1802, with its references to suicide contemplated and then rejected in favor of stoical acceptance of his condition. "It
was only my art that held me back," Beethoven wrote, referring to his sui-
cidal thoughts. It seems inescapable that the remarkable evolution in his
musical style at this time was connected to his personal confrontation with
adversity. A sense of deepened conflict is in fact characteristic of many of
Beethoven's most celebrated works, though in other masterpieces a humorous or comic spirit prevails, as in the op. 31 sonatas no. 1 and no. 3, op.
54, and the *Diabelli* Variations.

A series of sonatas completed by Beethoven in 1801 and 1802 shows
a variety of innovative approaches to the genre and specifically to the
problem of welding the successive movements into a unity. The Sonata in
A-flat op. 26 begins with a variation movement (as had Mozart's A-major
Sonata, K. 331) and dispenses entirely with movements in sonata form,
whereas the two works of op. 27 are each specifically described by

Beethoven as "Sonata quasi una fantasia." The C-sharp-minor Sonata op. 27 no. 2 is one of Beethoven's few works in which the finale is of unremittingly tragic character, and the epithet "Moonlight" is quite inappropriate for the work understood as a whole.[5] A central idea of this sonata concerns the transformation of the gently ascending arpeggios of the opening *Adagio sostenuto* in the *Presto agitato* finale, where surging arpeggios lead to emphatic syncopated chords in the highest register, supported by a descending bass progression similar to that at the beginning of the first movement (Examples 3.3a–b).[6] The second subject of the finale also recalls the principal theme of the opening movement in its use of dotted rhythms, while still other passages of the finale, such as the end of the development and the elaborate cadenza in the coda, bear marked thematic and textural similarities to the *Adagio sostenuto*. The middle movement, a Minuet and Trio in D-flat major, represents a kind of interlude that connects the almost static opening movement with the rapid, agitated finale. Some twenty-five years later, in his great String Quartet op. 131 in the same key, Beethoven returned to this conception of a series of interconnected movements leading, in the finale, to a fully developed sonata form; and in op. 131, as in op. 27 no. 2, the clear return of thematic material from the opening movement helps to confirm the role of the finale as a culmination to the entire work.

EXAMPLE 3.3a. Piano Sonata in C♯ minor, Op. 27 no. 2/i (mm. 1–3)

EXAMPLE 3.3b. Beethoven, Piano Sonata in C♯ minor, Op. 27 no. 2/iii (mm. 1–2)

The next sonata, op. 28 in D, was titled *Pastorale* by the publisher Cranz of Hamburg.[7] The title is not unfitting: one may find pedal points at the beginning of the first and last movements and occasional bagpipe fifths; and the cadential theme in the first movement and internal episode of the slow movement are rustic in character. Nevertheless, this is not a genre piece, and it has little in common with the *Pastoral* Symphony. Its broad lyric warmth leaves much room for motivic development, as is perhaps most evident in the development of the opening Allegro, which is dominated even more than usual by Beethoven's favorite device of foreshortening, whereby segments from the opening theme are progressively compressed into smaller units, here comprising four, two, and one measure(s), respectively, before Beethoven achieves a further intensification by means of syncopation and a contrapuntal overlapping of voices.

The first of the three op. 31 sonatas, in G, remains a somewhat neglected and misunderstood—if not maligned—work.[8] Like the finale of op. 10 no. 3, or the first movement of Beethoven's earlier F-major sonata op. 10 no. 2, the opening *Allegro vivace* of op. 31 no. 1 represents *komische Musik,* comic music abounding in sudden contrasts and surprising turns. As Tovey pointed out, the harmonic boldness and unusual tonal plan of this movement foreshadow the *Waldstein* Sonata (Tovey, 1931: 115). As early as the twelfth bar, Beethoven restates the opening theme, which moves from the tonic to dominant, on the lowered seventh degree, F major, so that the restatement closes a fifth higher, on the subdominant. Such treatment of the nearer keys "as if they were mere local chords" renders the dominant ineffective as the tonality of the second subject group, and Beethoven modulates instead to the major mediant (just as in the *Waldstein* Sonata op. 53).

A striking feature of the outer movements is the manner in which Beethoven prepares the turn figure of the finale in the first-movement coda, while the last bars of the finale coda recall in turn the *first* movement. The coda of the finale, too, is comic in character, unlike the finale of Schubert's great posthumous A-major Sonata, which was very closely modeled on the finale of Beethoven's op. 31 no. 1 (Cone, 1970: 779–93; Rosen, 1972: 456–58). Like the original slow movement of the *Waldstein* Sonata (*Andante favori*), the *Adagio grazioso* of this sonata indulges in ornate and decorative melodic lines and assumes at times an operatic character.

The Sonata op. 31 no. 2, the so-called *Tempest,* is Beethoven's only sonata in the key of D minor. A major innovation of this work is its use of an opening that embraces two diametrically opposed tempi and characters: a hovering, ambiguous unfolding of dominant arpeggios in first inversion, marked Largo; and a turbulent continuation stressing a rising bass and expressive two-note sigh figures or appoggiaturas, marked Allegro. The harmonically ambiguous opening allows Beethoven to delay the first strong cadence in D minor until the beginning of the apparent bridge (m. 21), where the initial rising arpeggiated motive is embodied in the driven, propulsive Allegro, and repeated in a long series of ascending sequences in the bass. From a variant of this passage Beethoven derives much of the development section, leading toward the climax of the movement at the beginning of the recapitulation. Here the mysterious arpeggios return, a kind of temporal oasis removed from the strife of the Allegro, and their expressive implications are now made explicit through passages of unaccompanied recitative.

Significantly, this was the passage that influenced Beethoven, consciously or unconsciously, when he conceived the famous baritone recitative "O Freunde, nicht diese Töne!" in the choral finale of the Ninth Symphony, written twenty years later (Examples 3.4a–b). In both works, the ascending sixth G-E precedes the descending fourth B♭-F (in the symphony in a different, lower register). This close thematic similarity invites comparison, but the analogous expressive function of the two recitative passages does so as well. Even the "Terror Fanfare" (*Schreckensfanfare*) against which the baritone recitative is pitted bears a similarity to the music near the beginning of the Allegro in the *Tempest* Sonata, like the symphony, in the key of D minor. The celebrated transition to the choral finale of the Ninth, and the emergence in it of a utopian vision of brotherhood posited against despair (*Verzweiflung*, which, according to a sketch, Beethoven associated with the first movement) is already prepared, in latent form, in the remarkable rhetorical contrasts of this sonata.

EXAMPLE 3.4a. Piano Sonata in D minor, Op. 31 no. 2/i (mm. 143–148)

EXAMPLE 3.4b. Symphony No. 9 in D minor, Op. 125/iv (mm. 216–221)

We have referred above to the parallels between op. 31 no. 1 and the *Waldstein* Sonata op. 53, the first of three sonatas composed by Beethoven between 1804 and 1806. The scale of conception of the *Waldstein* and its companion, the *Appassionata*, op. 57, reminds us of such contemporaneous works as the *Eroica* Symphony and the op. 59 Quartets, to say nothing of the original three-act version of Beethoven's opera *Fidelio,* first performed in the fall of 1805. Yet Beethoven substantially reduced the length of the *Waldstein* when he resolved to cut the original slow movement, a luxurious rondo in F major, and have it published separately, while substituting a brief but profound *Introduzione* to the finale. In a number of works after the *Waldstein,* Beethoven experiments with linking slow movements directly to the finale (for example, the Fourth and Fifth Piano Concertos, and the Sonatas opp. 57 and 81a). In the *Waldstein,* an intense inwardness of expression, enhanced by bold harmonies above a chromatically descending bass, sets into sharp relief the brilliant pianistic textures of the outer movements in C major. In the last bars of the *Introduzione,* the bass progression converges onto the dominant, G, poised before the cadence in C major, while the high G in the treble is reinterpreted as the beginning of the broad rondo theme of the finale, heard three octaves above a sustained tonic pedal in the bass.

The first movement of the next sonata, op. 54 in F, is above all a study in contrasts. Richard Rosenberg dubbed it "La Belle et la Bête," and Alfred Brendel has described how its two contrasting themes—a gracious, dignified, "feminine" theme resembling a minuet; and a stamping, assertive, "masculine" theme employing accented octave triplets—gradually influence one another in the course of the movement, until they become thoroughly integrated and combined in the final passages (Brendel, 1976: 47–50). Here the music resembles the conventional form of Minuet and Trio only superficially, and the point of the dissonant outburst immediately preceding the final cadence is to remind us—through the diminished-seventh harmonies, triplet rhythm, and the use of register—of the contrasting thematic complex that has gradually become absorbed into the Minuet while transforming it. In this movement Beethoven thus explores a directional process and an ongoing synthesis of experience—qualities he further developed in some of his last sonatas, such as in the Arietta of op. 111.

Tovey pointed out that the Sonata in F minor op. 57 is Beethoven's only work to maintain a tragic solemnity throughout all its movements (Tovey, 1931: 169). The title *Appassionata,* though not from Beethoven, is not inappropriate. In its poetic power and richness of allusion, and in the gigantic simplicity of its structural foundation, this sonata represents a profound achievement, outstanding even for Beethoven. We shall examine this work in some detail, concentrating above all on the large-scale structural plan and its expressive significance.

Of special importance are the parallels in character and musical structure between the opening *Allegro assai* and the finale, *Allegro non troppo.* These two sonata-form movements enclose a set of variations in D-flat major on a theme of almost static and hymnlike character. The course of these variations seems predetermined by the quietly reflective nature of the theme, which consists initially of stationary pedal tones on the dominant or tonic scale degrees, and which repeatedly closes harmonically on the tonic triad. The variations embellish the theme through a series of progressive rhythmic diminutions coordinated with a gradual ascent in register; yet the entire process is contemplative and dreamlike, to be abruptly shattered, as Tovey observed, by the first hint of action. That confrontation occurs at the harmonic substitution of an arpeggiated diminished-seventh beneath the cadential D-flat in the treble which might, under other circumstances, have closed the movement (Example 3.5). The arpeggiated chord returns an octave higher and then is reiterated thirteen times in the original register at the outset of the *Allegro non troppo,* now intensified rhythmically and dynamically. The "self-sufficiency" of the variation movement is thus annihilated, as D-flat, the tonic note of the slow movement, now becomes a crucial dissonance in the context of F minor, recalling a similar treatment in the first movement. Indeed, from those thirteen repeated staccato chords Beethoven derives the principal theme of the finale by composing out the diminished-seventh chord as a sinuous line in sixteenth-notes, which descends by thirds into the lowest register, before reaching a structural downbeat on low F in measure 20 of the *Allegro non troppo.* This structural downbeat marks the true beginning of the finale, after the *Schreckensfanfare* of the chords and the descending transitionary passagework, but it is from this passagework that the figuration of the finale proper is drawn.

According to Ferdinand Ries, Beethoven conceived this passage, and much that follows it, during and immediately after a long walk in the

EXAMPLE 3.5. Piano Sonata in F minor, Op. 57/ii, iii (mm. 93–97; 1–20)

countryside near Döbling, a small town outside Vienna where Beethoven spent part of the summer of 1804. Ries wrote that during the walk,

> in which we went so far astray that we did not get back to Döbling, where Beethoven lived, until nearly 8 o'clock, he had been all the time humming and sometimes howling, always up and down, without singing any definite notes. In answer to my question what it was he said: "A theme for the last movement of

the sonata has occurred to me" [in F minor, Op. 57]. When we entered the room he ran to the pianoforte without taking off his hat. I took a seat in the corner and he soon forgot all about me. Now he stormed for at least an hour with the beautiful finale of the sonata. Finally he got up, was surprised still to see me and said: "I cannot give you a lesson today, I must do some more work" (Forbes, 356).

The basic character and structure of the passage are, not surprisingly, prefigured in the first movement. The *Allegro assai* begins with a phrase of four measures, whose two halves embody contrary tendencies: the first two, unharmonized measures consist of a triadic figure in gapped octaves, with the bass reaching the lowest F—significantly, the same pitch as in measure 20 of the finale—in the first full measure (Example 3.6). The second half of the phrase, in contrast, presents an imploring, plaintive, harmonized gesture around an expressive trill. The tension implicit in this motivic juxtaposition is heightened in the second four-measure phrase, which is placed by Beethoven on the Neapolitan, so that it closes on the dominant harmony of the Neapolitan, D-flat.

EXAMPLE 3.6. Piano Sonata in F minor, Op. 57/i (mm. 1–4)

Subsequently, Beethoven follows his technique of foreshortening, compressing the four-measure phrases into units of two measures, beginning with the plaintive gesture of the trill. Now, however, we hear a terse, four-note motive in the bass—D♭-D♭-D♭-C—a motto that encapsulates the harmonic tension generated by the second phrase in the Neapolitan, beginning and ending on D-flat. This D♭-C conflict is stressed throughout the opening sixteen-measure thematic period and remains a primary structural element later in the movement, especially in the development and beginning of the recapitulation. A major event in the development is the arrival of the second theme from the exposition in D-flat major (m.

110), prepared by a prolonged pedal on A-flat. This theme is clearly based on a rhythm of the opening measures of the movement, but it is lyrical in character and thus stands apart from the surrounding music. Earlier in the exposition this lyrical theme trails off into a series of mysterious trills ascending into the highest register before a long, quiet, scalar descent leads to a sudden resumption and intensification of the tempestuous music in the minor. Now, when this lyrical theme appears in D-flat major in the development, its rising bass—which ascends through a fifth in the exposition—continues to rise, carrying the music through a series of modulations. After the ascent spans two octaves, the theme dissolves, and the music becomes, in Tovey's words, "inarticulate" (Tovey, 1944: 44). What remains is a further ascent through the diminished-seventh sonority beginning on D-flat, reaching the highest pitches of Beethoven's piano just as a final rhythmic diminution accelerates the upward movement of the bass in its drift to high D-flat. The texture of diminished-seventh arpeggios is all that remains of the thematic material, and the music now descends, in a free fall of four octaves, until impact is made on the low D-flat. In a brilliant stroke, Beethoven introduces at this point the four-note motto from the outset of the movement, the motive that so resembles the so-called fate motive of the Fifth Symphony. Initially confined to D-flat, this figure soon expands to its original form outlining the semitone conflict Db-C; and this gesture, prolonged through a sustained pedal of triplet eighths in the bass, marks the beginning of the recapitulation. In the sketches for this passage, Beethoven contemplated a resolution of the bass pedal to F, but later wisely rejected the idea in favor of the dominant pedal, which of course heightens the tonal tension and allows for further intensification of the fundamental semitone conflict when the pedal rises to D-flat in the following phrase.[9]

The rhythmic and motivic intensification of this passage is extraordinary, but perhaps most impressive is the vast scale of the passage beginning at the D-flat theme in the development and continuing up to the variant of the principal theme stated, with irony, in the tonic major (mm. 174–180). In effect, the lyrical theme in D-flat has proven unable to withstand the processes of musical development and to retain its identity; its essential fragility is exposed and confirmed by the goal-directed process leading to the recapitulation. Beethoven fittingly derives its rhythm and triadic contours from the principal theme, which assumes primacy and emphasis at the great gesture of recapitulation, where the accumulated energy of the development, and especially of the four-octave fall through the diminished sevenths, seems to be unleashed in the ostinato pedal in the bass. This kind of rhythmically enhanced recapitulation deeply impressed later Romantic composers, such as Chopin.[10]

The Sonatas op. 78 in F-sharp and op. 79 in G, both composed in 1809, are works on a smaller scale. Op. 78 returns to the two-movement plan of op. 54; its opening *Allegro ma non troppo* is introduced by a short but subtle slow introduction, which sets the tone for this intimately lyrical movement. The second group of the exposition contains a motive of three emphatic chords, the last marked *sforzando,* which are juxtaposed with more gentle figures marked piano. A variant of this motive is employed in the principal theme of the finale. The opening *Presto alla tedesca* of op. 79 has a rustic, dancelike character. Following a short slow movement in the minor, this work concludes with an energetic Vivace, whose opening theme—with its stepwise descending bass in thirds—bears a strong structural resemblance to the beginning of Beethoven's later Sonata in E op. 109.[11]

Beethoven's next sonata, op. 81a (1809–10), is closely associated with his royal patron, friend, and student, the Archduke Rudolph, who departed from Vienna on 4 May 1809, before the French invasion, and returned in January 1810. Beethoven honored Rudolph with the dedications of several other important works as well, including the largest of all the sonatas, the *Hammerklavier* op. 106, the Trio in B-flat op. 97, and the *Missa Solemnis.* None of these works is as specifically related to the person of the Archduke as is op. 81a; Beethoven entered the dates of his friend's departure and return to the city into his score and allowed the emotional progression of "farewell-absence-reunion" to determine the basic character of the three movements. He was irritated by the use, in the first edition, of French instead of German titles, probably not only because of the difference in meaning between "Les adieux" and "Das Lebewohl," but because of the relationship between the falling horn motive (G-F-Eb) in the first measures of the opening slow introduction and the words "Le-be wohl," which are written above these chords.

The initial harmonization of this "Lebewohl" motive in the slow introduction of the first movement does not affirm the tonic E-flat major, but leads first deceptively to the submediant C minor, and then, in the eighth measure, to a sustained harmony on the more remote flat sixth, C-flat major. The first strong cadential arrival at the tonic triad of E-flat is thus delayed until five measures into the following Allegro. The tonal ambiguity of the slow introduction thus contributes to its suspended, searching character, qualities that reappear in the music of the second movement, the "Absence." At the same time, the "Lebewohl" motto of a stepwise descending third assumes a central importance throughout the Allegro of the first movement, which begins with an energetic reinterpretation of the progression G-F-Eb above a chromatically falling bass. In the development, Beethoven further exploits the association of this motto with ambiguous harmonies, leading the music into remote key areas; but the harmonic boldness characteristic of this sonata is most of all evident in the coda, where the tonic and dominant are repeatedly sounded together. Here, the imitations of the original motto seem to recede into the distance, implying the departure has taken place. (In many passages of this Allegro, the "Lebewohl" motive appears written in whole notes, so that its actual duration in performance approximates its initial appearances in the Adagio, where it is notated in quarter notes.)

The "Absence" has a slow processional character and (like the *Introduzione* of the *Waldstein* Sonata) leads directly into the finale. Though its principal key is C minor, the music dwells not on the tonic triad but on a diminished-seventh chord in the opening measures; indeed, in a later restatement of the initial motive at the same pitch level (m. 11), the harmony is intensified through the use of a dissonant chord of the eleventh. Immediately following, the motive is foreshortened and stressed by accents above a descending bass; this poignant and expressive passage leads through a brief transition to a consoling, cantabile passage in the dominant key. The entire period embracing these two themes is then repeated, beginning in B minor; and we are given the sense that this cyclic repetition of grief and consolation could continue indefinitely. After six measures of a third period, in which the music ascends to the dominant-seventh chord of E-flat, the long-awaited event occurs in the form of a decisive and jubilant elaboration of this chord in a ten-measure transition to the finale, in sonata form. This is, of course, the moment of reunion. Beethoven apparently delayed the composition of this exuberant finale until the actual return of the Archduke gave him cause for celebration and a reason to immortalize their friendship through a work of art.

After the *Lebewohl* Sonata, several years passed before Beethoven finished his next sonata, op. 90 in E minor, in August 1814. The intervening years had seen the composition of the Seventh and Eighth Symphonies, the *Archduke* Trio, and the revision of *Fidelio*, but no other sonatas were written apart from the remarkable Violin Sonata in G op. 96. Beethoven's famous letter to the Eternal Beloved stems from 1812; by then, it seems, the composer was resigned to his increasingly solitary and isolated existence. He enjoyed his greatest public and financial successes shortly before and during the Congress of Vienna period of late 1814 and early 1815, however, and during this period the opportunity arose for a revival of *Fidelio*, which dated in its original form from nearly a decade earlier. The first sketches for the op. 90 Sonata survive alongside those for the revision of the opera and were evidently made during the spring of 1814. (In 1815 this sonata became the first work of Beethoven's printed by S. A. Steiner, a firm that published a substantial number of Beethoven's compositions in succeeding years. The title page of the first edition of op. 90 is shown in Illustration 3.1.)

The first movement of this work foreshadows aspects of Beethoven's late style, especially in its formal compression and in the astonishing canonic passage leading to the recapitulation. As in the next sonata, op. 101 (as well as in opp. 57 and 110), there is no repetition of the exposition. The development begins quietly in measure 82, on the pitch B drawn from the preceding dominant chords that close the exposition. The development is based almost entirely on the first theme, though the accompaniment in

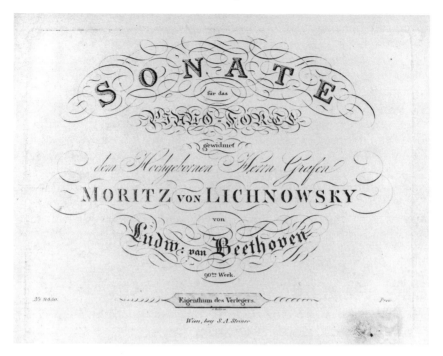

ILLUSTRATION 3.1. Title page of the first edition of Beethoven's Piano Sonata in E minor, Op. 90, published by S. A. Steiner at Vienna in 1815. Printed with permission of Special Collections, McPherson Library, University of Victoria, Victoria, Canada.

repeated notes and chords is drawn from the second group. The entire second half of the development (mm. 113ff.) employs a different accompanimental texture outlining broken chords in the right hand, while a figure drawn from the opening theme is intensified with *sforzandi* in the left hand. Especially fascinating is how the musical content of measure 130—where Beethoven makes the change in key signature to one sharp, indicating E minor—is treated in the succeeding measures to allow for the emergence of the recapitulation (Illustration 3.2 shows this passage in the first edition of the score). This measure already contains the essence of the recapitulation in its second and third beats, in particular in the descent of the third G-E in the high register. After three repetitions of this figure (m. 131), it is isolated and stressed dynamically in the next measure, with an imitation an octave lower. Then a series of canonic mutations elongate the figure in three successive augmentations of its rhythm, and its relationship to the principal theme gradually becomes clarified. The close stretto at the unison (mm. 138–141) stresses the pitch level of the imminent recapitulation; in performance, these measures are difficult to bring out effectively, on account of their dense texture, as the motive continues to turn onto itself. Finally, the stretto expands across other registers and yields to

ILLUSTRATION 3.2. This page from the first edition of Beethoven's Piano Sonata in E minor, Op. 90, published by Steiner in 1815, shows the end of the development and beginning of the recapitulation of the first movement. Printed with permission of Special Collections, McPherson Library, University of Victoria, Victoria, Canada.

the recapitulation (m. 144). There is no cadence; harmonically, this entire, static passage has remained on the tonic. The rapid sixteenth-note figuration of the development has proven against all expectations to be one with the head of the principal theme. Instead of defining a single structural moment, the recapitulation represents a process that extends over the eighteen measures preceding the literal recapitulation. As in the first movements of two of the last quartets, opp. 130 and 132, the tonal and thematic recapitulations do not coincide here.

The second, final movement in E major is the most Schubertian movement in Beethoven, a luxurious rondo dominated by many, almost unvaried, appearances of a spacious cantabile theme.[12] In this movement, and in the A-major Sonata op. 101, Beethoven comes closest to the emerging romantic style, yet there are elements in these works that point unmistakably toward the unique synthesis embodied in many compositions of his last decade. In the nineteenth century, opinion about Beethoven's later music was divided, and the last sonatas and quartets were often regarded as bewildering, if not incomprehensible. From the perspective of the late twentieth century, however, these works appear as Beethoven's most impressive achievements. To a remarkable extent, Beethoven's late style resists historical categorization; conventions appear transformed, and the textures and forms of music are pushed relentlessly toward new boundaries.

The Late Sonatas

As Alfred Brendel has suggested, Beethoven's late music involves a general expansion and synthesis of the means of expression, whereby opposites are often juxtaposed, with every new complexity of style seeming to parallel, as its antithesis, a childlike simplicity. Normal modes of analysis are inadequate to grasp the tremendous richness of this idiom, which "embraces equally the past, present, and future, the sublime and the profane."[13] This expansion in expressive range is often associated with new departures in the large-scale formal organization of these works, and especially with Beethoven's tendency to replace symmetrical forms with a central climax by a progression leading to a final, culminating experience. Not only does Beethoven avoid the enclosure of literal recapitulation within movements; he also tends to arrange the successive movements of these works into a directional sequence leading towards the finale, now usually the most weighty movement of the sonata cycle.

Beethoven also devises new, unique means of linking the movements of his sonatas. In the A-major Sonata op. 101, the crux of the work is contained not in the opening *Allegretto, ma non troppo,* despite its quiet, lyrical beginning *in medias res* on the dominant. Following this short movement of yearning character, and the brusque, angular, contrapuntal march in F major forming the second movement, a more fundamental level of feeling or state of being is uncovered in the slow introduction to the finale, marked *Langsam und sehnsuchtsvoll.* Here, the music is drawn progressively lower in pitch, falling through a series of diminished-seventh chords before it drops still further in register, collapsing onto a soft sustained chord that is to serve as a turning point and a new beginning (Example 3.7). This passage anticipates in striking fashion the *Praeludium* to the Benedictus of the *Missa Solemnis* op. 123, where a low chord reached through a similar descending progression is transposed upward several octaves to the solo violin and flutes, to symbolize, with astonishing effect, the divine presence.

In the case of the sonata, this soft chord, which represents the end of the descending progression and the termination of the Adagio, also embodies the *a priori* condition for the first movement, since it presents the exact sonority, in the precise register, out of which the opening of that movement has sprung. In view of this, the opening of the sonata *in medias res* assumes a new and deeper significance. The importance of this original sound—an E-major sonority marked by a fermata—is confirmed by its transformation, after a short cadenzalike passage, into the actual begin-

EXAMPLE 3.7. Piano Sonata in A major, Op. 101/iii (mm. 15–24)

ning of the opening movement (m. 21). This reminiscence lasts a few measures before it dissolves into the emphatic beginning of the finale, marked
by the first strong tonic cadence (in A major) that has yet been heard in the
sonata.

The finale is in sonata form, with its development assigned to a fugato, as in the first movements of opp. 106 and 111. The coda of this
movement contains remarkably subtle allusions to earlier passages from
the sonata and assumes thereby an important synthesizing function.
Thus, the *dolce* passage at the beginning of the coda is palpably close melodically and harmonically to the beginning of the slow introduction to the
finale, though the music is here in major, rather than minor. And, the
continuation of the coda corresponds to the beginning of the earlier fugal
development, which had been heard in A minor. In particular, the staccato octaves that had introduced the fugue reappear in the coda, at first
confidently and forcefully in the subdominant major, and then quietly
and doubtfully in the minor. The implication of D minor is not confirmed,
however, as the music instead prolongs the harmony of F major, the key
of the *Vivace alla Marcia*, which resolves to a dominant E-major chord in
measure 290. The spacing of this chord reminds us of the first movement,
while the many repetitions of the semitone F-E in the following bars
confirm the resolution of F major as flat sixth of the tonic A major.

In the final measures, furthermore, Beethoven brings back as a
pedal the low contra E previously used in the cadence to the recapitulation
of the finale, and adds above it a low, sustained trill on the leading tone,
both of which are emphatically resolved into the final ascending triadic
fanfare. The fanfare itself ultimately derives from the ascending chain of
dominant arpeggios heard at the climactic cadence to the recapitulation in
the finale. The depth of synthesis and the richness of allusion in passages
such as this present a special challenge to listener and interpreter alike.

In several of the late sonatas, Beethoven employs parenthetical
structures that enclose musical passages within contrasting sections. The
Hammerklavier Sonata op. 106, for example, contains three such parenthe-
ses in the slow introduction to the fugal finale. The main material of this
slow introduction presents a distillation of the intervallic basis for the
whole sonata: the descending third, which is prominent, and indeed almost omnipresent in the motivic, harmonic, and tonal structure of each of
the movements.[14] In this slow introduction, Beethoven reduces the music
to a fundamental, underlying level of content consisting of a chain of falling thirds outlined in the bass, accompanied by soft, hesitant chords in the
treble. This descending chain of thirds is interrupted three times by brief
visions of other music, and the last of these evocations (mm. 3–7) is obviously Bachian in character. As in the transition to the choral finale of the
Ninth Symphony, there is thus a search toward new compositional possibilities, with the clear implication here that baroque counterpoint is tran-

scended by the creation of a new contrapuntal idiom embodied in the revolutionary fugal finale of the sonata.

Beethoven's use of such parenthetical structures assumes more and more importance in the last sonatas and seems to have deepened as a result of his work on the Credo of the *Missa Solemnis* during the first half of 1820, when he devised an immense parenthetical structure separating the musical setting of the events on earth (from the "et Incarnatus est" to the "Resurrexit") from the remainder of the movement. Here, an abrupt interruption of the cadence at "descendit de coelis" prepares a later resumption of the music at "ascendit in coelum."[15] The first movement of op. 109 was composed at precisely this time, and its unique formal structure is evidently the product of similar techniques of parenthetical enclosure. The opening material in Vivace tempo is interrupted after only eight measures, as it reaches the threshold of a cadence in the dominant of E major. The cadence is not granted but evaded in the ensuing passage in Adagio tempo, which is fantasylike in character, and makes a striking contrast to the initial Vivace material, with its uniformity of rhythm and texture. Yet, when the music finally arrives firmly on a dominant cadence (m. 15), this event is timed to coincide with the resumption of the Vivace music in the very same register as before. The entire Adagio section is thus positioned at the moment of the interrupted cadence, and the resulting parenthetical structure gives the effect of a suspension of time in the contrasting section, or the enclosure of one time within another.

Awareness of this parenthetical structure is essential for a full understanding of the formal design of the movement, which has resisted the schematic categorization so often advanced by analysts. Charles Rosen and others have suggested that the "second subject" of this movement is found already in measure 9, at the beginning of the Adagio, but this explanation is partial and not entirely satisfactory (Rosen, 1980: 283–84). In fact, the firm arrival of a cadence in the dominant, which typically marks the beginning of a second subject group, is delayed here until the beginning of the development section based on the Vivace material. The central idea of the exposition consists precisely in the interdependence of the two contrasting thematic complexes, in which the parenthetical structure plays an essential role. The bold and unpredictable quality of this design is sustained by Beethoven's avoidance of literal recapitulation in later stages of the movement, such as at the recapitulation (m. 48), where the music penetrates the highest register, or the return of the Adagio (m. 58ff.), which is no mere transposition of the exposition but a reinterpretation of the earlier passage, carrying the music emphatically and climactically into the remote key of C major. It remains for the coda to synthesize the contrasting themes and bring them into a new and closer relationship. These elements of continuing development and reinterpretation represent a paradoxical assertion of Beethoven's fidelity to classical principles: since the initial material had involved an astonishing and abrupt contrast, a predictability of design involving literal transpositions in the recapitulation would be out of keeping with the unpredictable, exploratory character established at the outset of the movement.

In the final sonata, op. 111 in C minor, this technique of parenthetical enclosure assumes special significance as a means of linking its two movements, so antithetical in character. (A sketchleaf showing Beethoven's work on both movements is shown in Illustration 3.3.) The first movement of op. 111 is the last example of Beethoven's celebrated "C-minor mood," evidenced in a long line of works from the String Trio of op. 9 and *Pathétique* Sonata to the *Coriolanus* Overture and Fifth Symphony. As in these works, great stress is placed on diminished-seventh chords in a turbulent, dissonant idiom. The slow introduction opens with octaves outlining the diminished-seventh interval, E♭-F♯, and its opening phrases are based on the three possible diminished-seventh chords, emphasized by majestic double-dotted rhythms and trills. Subsequently, in the *Allegro con brio ed appassionato,* the diminished-seventh interval is incorporated into the principal subject, which is treated fugally. A major portion of the sonata exposition (mm. 35–50) consists of a fugal exposition employing a variant of this subject, combined with a countersubject in octaves. This material is coordinated to create a large-scale ascending progression, beginning on C and rising through an octave, before the bass brings the music climactically to D-flat, D-natural, and finally E-flat (mm. 48–50; Example 3.8). This extraordinary climax is underscored by the registral disparities of the sustained pitches, played in the right hand, F-D♭-D♮-C♭, which represent a variant, in rhythmic augmentation, of the principal fugal motive. The shift from this low D to the high C-flat traverses an ascent of almost five octaves, so that the motive appears enlarged, or gapped, over an immense tonal space. Then, suddenly, with the arrival of the bass at E-flat in measure 50, a lyrical voice is heard in the remote key of A-flat major. A three-measure phrase with expressive appoggiaturas fills measures 50–52, a fleeting lyrical moment that is extended by a decorated restatement in the following measures and by a gradual slowing in tempo to Adagio.

An effect of parenthetical enclosure is created through the sudden return of the original tempo and agitated musical character at the upbeat to measure 56, where Beethoven brings back the very same diminished-seventh sonority heard earlier, when the climactic progression had been broken off (also shown in Example 3.8). Here the high C-flat is stressed as the clear link back to the earlier passage, and the diminished seventh is elaborated by descending sequences through those pitch registers that had been spanned in the earlier gesture. Consequently, the intervening lyrical utterance in A-flat major is isolated, like "a soft glimpse of sunlight illuminating the dark, stormy heavens," in the imagery of Thomas Mann's character Kretzschmar in *Doktor Faustus.*[16]

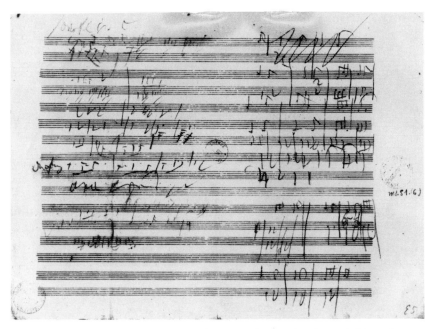

ILLUSTRATION 3.3 A pocket sketchleaf with entries for Beethoven's Piano Sonata in C minor, Op. 111, in the Paris 51 MS, part 6. The page was originally folded in the middle. In his later years, Beethoven often carried gatherings of such leaves with him during walks away from his lodgings. The left-hand side contains a sketch for the main subject of the first movement on the third stave, beneath Beethoven's inscription "Sonate," whereas the right-hand side is filled with sketches for the Arietta theme, which is sketched here in smaller note values than are used in the finished work. For an analysis and transcription of Beethoven's sketches for this sonata, see William Drabkin, *The Sketches for Beethoven's Piano Sonata in C minor, Opus 111,* 2 vols. Ph.D. dissertation, Princeton, 1977. The facsimile is printed with permission of the Bibliothèque nationale, Paris.

In the recapitulation, this lyrical material is not so easily swept aside; rather, Beethoven extends the passage and—beginning in measure 128—reshapes it to lead us back into the tempest. The lyrical passage has now reached C major—the key of the second movement—when it is restated here, and around measure 120 it seems to foreshadow the sublime atmosphere of the finale. A direct transition to the ensuing Arietta movement is built into the coda, when threefold phrases resolving plagally to the tonic major seem to resolve the tension and strife of those threefold phrases that had opened the slow introduction. The rhythm and register of the last bars of the coda allude unmistakably to the menacing diminished-seventh chords that interrupted the lyrical episode in the exposition (mm. 155–56; Example 3.9). Here, however, the diminished seventh is resolved, once and for all, into the C-major triad, whose high regis-

EXAMPLE 3.8. Piano Sonata in C minor, Op. 111/i (mm. 47–56)

ter and wide spacing foreshadow important features of the Arietta movement.

This slow Arietta movement is perhaps the most extraordinary example of a new type of variation set characteristic of Beethoven's later

EXAMPLE 3.9. Piano Sonata in C minor, Op. 111/i (mm. 155–158)

years. Formerly, variations were most often used in inner movements of the sonata cycle; but here, as in op. 109, they assume such weight and finality as to render any further movements superfluous, if not unthinkable. In a sense, the op. 111 variations are based structurally on the model provided by the final variation of op. 109: There, a reprise of the slow rhythmic values of the original theme is followed by a series of rhythmic diminutions culminating in protracted trills. Now, in the op. 111 Arietta movement, each variation brings diminutions in the rhythmic texture without affecting the basic tempo. Consequently, the theme seems to evolve from within through a rigorously controlled process. By the third variation, there is a resulting transformation in character, due to the great agitation and complexity of the rhythm, which Beethoven notates in a meter of $\frac{12}{32}$. To be sure, use of a series of progressive rhythmic diminutions was a venerable device in variation writing, but no composer before Beethoven uncovered the full expressive potential of the procedure. For Beethoven, a musical texture created by extreme subdivisions in rhythm can actually reapproach the suspended and almost static character of the original slow theme. Thus, in the fourth variation, the tremoli and arabesques of thirty-second-note triplets, together with the syncopated chords in the right hand and the striking registral contrasts, create an ethereal atmosphere, as if the music has entered a transfigured realm.

The outcome of this gradual process of rhythmic diminution is reached in the cadenza preceding the recapitulatory fifth variation. This cadenza and the following transition represent an extended parenthesis in the formal plan, for the cadence in C major is fully prepared before the cadenza is reached but is delayed by the lengthy, protracted trill on the supertonic. Moments later, this trill becomes part of a sustained triple trill above a B-flat pedal, and the tonality shifts for the first time, to E-flat major. Beethoven explores and contemplates the theme from within, as a gradual ascent into the highest register unfolds, expressed entirely by trills. Here, a phrase from near the end of the first half of the theme is heard in E-flat major, with a vast registral gap between treble and bass, a feature that fascinated Thomas Mann's Kretzschmar. As Rosen has observed, this episode of the movement seems to suspend the flow of time; it involves an intensely contemplative vision imbedded within the context of a variation series which is itself highly introspective.

Variation Five brings a synthesis and superimposition of the various rhythmic levels: the triplet thirty-second notes in the bass derive from the ethereal fourth variation, while the sixteenths in the inner part derive from the transition and from the first two variations. Here Beethoven recapitulates the original Arietta theme in a formal gesture of considerable weight and significance. This movement is the first important example of the aging Beethoven's preference for decorated recapitulatory variations preceded by episodes in foreign keys, a procedure at work in the slow variation movements of two of the late quartets, opp. 127 and 131, as well as in the third movement of the Ninth Symphony.[17] In the op. 111 Arietta movement, however, we move beyond this recapitulatory gesture in the coda, which presents a second and more ethereal synthesis of rhythmic levels: The theme is now heard in the high register, accompanied by the triplet sixteenths in the left hand, and the sustained trill, now on high G.

The Arietta theme itself is one of the most sublime examples among Beethoven's piano works of that hymnlike character that often inspired reflective slow movements surrounded by contrasting outer movements. Here, however, the inward vision is more sustained and far more affirmative and ecstatic than in earlier slow movements; yet, this variation framework is not incompatible with dynamic processes, such as the system of rhythmic diminutions and the modulating cadenza preceding the recapitulatory fifth variation. Being and Becoming are merged here into a unified structure. The uplifting and visionary quality of the second half of the Arietta movement derives not only from the transformation of the theme, and the culminating effect of synthesis and recapitulation, but also from the role of this movement as a transcendence of the strife-ridden Allegro movement and all that it implies. In many respects, the Arietta movement strives toward perfection, whereas the Allegro is obviously imperfect; even the progression from the duple meter of the opening movement to the triple meter of the Arietta movement—with its many subdivisions in groups of three—is significant in this connection. Various commentators have rightly perceived a philosophical and even religious dimension in this great work.[18]

Of all the late sonatas, perhaps op. 110 in A-flat (1821) reveals the most explicitly transcendental or religious characteristics. These features are concentrated in the unique finale, with its pairing of *Arioso dolente* and fugue, but the rising ascending fourths of the fugue subject (A♭-D♭; B♭-E♭; C-F) are already present in latent form at the very beginning of the sonata. The second movement (*Allegro molto*) is scherzolike in form and character, though it is unlabeled and written in $\frac{2}{4}$ meter. (Only one of the last sonatas, op. 106, includes a scherzo identified as such, but the second movements of both opp. 101 and 109 display some scherzolike traits.) The *Allegro molto* contains a trio and shows the humorous temper characteristic of Beethoven's scherzos, even though the tonic key is minor. A turn at the conclusion to the tonic major, F major, provides dominant preparation for the ensuing *Adagio ma non troppo*, beginning in B-flat minor.

As in the *Hammerklavier* Sonata and in the Ninth Symphony, Beethoven incorporates a transition here before reaching the finale proper; the music is notated partly without bar lines and with a profusion of tempo and expressive directions. An explicit recitative emerges in the fourth measure and carries us to A-flat minor, tonic minor of the sonata as a whole. For some moments, the music dwells contemplatively on a high A-natural; the recitative then falls in pitch, briefly affirming E major before returning to A-flat minor in the measures immediately preceding the beginning of the great lament. In a sense, the ensuing *Arioso dolente* is operatic in character, with a broadly extended but asymmetrical melody supported by poignant harmonies in the repeated chords of the left hand. The recitative already foreshadows the tragic passion of the lament and prefigures some of its motivic relationships. There is even a framing cadential gesture at the conclusion of the *Arioso dolente* that harks back to the end of the passage in recitative (cf. mm. 6–7 and 25–26).

The pairing of the *Arioso dolente* with the fugue in A-flat major has no precedent in Beethoven's earlier piano music; its closest affinity is with the Agnus Dei and Dona Nobis Pacem of the *Missa Solemnis,* the work that occupied him contemporaneously with the sonata (the Mass was begun in 1819 and finished in all but a few details by the summer of 1822; all three of the last sonatas represented interruptions in Beethoven's labors on this immense work). The Agnus Dei in B minor is burdened by an overwhelming awareness of the sins of mankind and the fallen state of earthly existence; by contrast, the Dona Nobis Pacem represents the promise of liberation from this endless cycle of suffering and injustice, symbolized by the recurring and ominous approach of bellicose music. Significantly, Beethoven's setting of the Dona Nobis Pacem in D major employs a prominent motive outlining ascending perfect fourths, which are filled in by conjunct motion. The fugue subject of op. 110 consists similarly of three ascending perfect fourths, with the last of these filled in by stepwise descending motion, while smooth conjunct motion is also characteristic of the countersubjects (Example 3.10a–b). The only parallel to this sublime fugal idiom in Beethoven's piano music is the wonderful *Fughetta* from the *Diabelli* Variations, written soon thereafter, in early 1823.

Beethoven's later fugues tend to make extensive and sometimes exhaustive use of the devices of inversion, stretto, diminution, and augmentation, and the fugue of the *Hammerklavier* also makes substantial use of

EXAMPLE 3.10a. Piano Sonata in A♭ major, Op. 110/iii (mm. 1–6)

EXAMPLE 3.10b. *Missa Solemnis*, Op. 123, Agnus Dei (mm. 107–110)

retrograde motion. These devices tend to be employed not for their own sake but as a means of expressive intensification, especially in the later stages of a work; in op. 110 they are concentrated in the second part of the fugue beginning in the remote key of G major. As we have seen, the central idea of this finale consists in the relationship between the earthly pain of the lament and the consolation and inward strength of the fugue. Initially, however, the fugue cannot be sustained; it is suddenly broken off on a dominant-seventh chord of A-flat major, which is interpreted as a German augmented-sixth chord, resolving to the triad of G minor, and this dark sonority is treated as tonic for the return of the *Arioso dolente.* The tonal relationship involved is bold and unprecedented in Beethoven: the entire lament is restated, in intensified and varied form, in G minor; and the framing cadential gesture brings a shift to the major, which assumes the character of a miraculous discovery. Nine increasingly intense repetitions of this G-major sonority follow, and a gradual arpeggiation of that sound leads upward to the inversion of the fugue subject, which now enters quietly and *una corda,* in G major.

The concluding fugue thus begins in the key of the leading tone, to reemerge only later into the tonic A-flat major, in the triumphant final passages. This unusual tonal relationship enhances the power of the conclusion; equally striking is Beethoven's masterful treatment of contrapuntal permutations in the transition from G major to A-flat major. Not only does the subject appear against itself in diminution and augmentation but it appears in double diminution, comprising a decorating motivic cell that surrounds the sustained note values of the inverted subject (mm. 170–74; Example 3.11). The entrance of the original subject in measure 174 is accompanied by sixteenth-note figuration continuing the texture of double diminution, giving the effect that the theme is glorified by its own substance. The transition from the darkness and pessimism of the *Arioso do-*

EXAMPLE 3.11. Piano Sonata in A♭ major, Op. 110/iii (mm. 170–175)

lente to the light and ecstasy of the fugue is now fully accomplished; and in the final moments Beethoven extends the fugal subject melodically into the high register before it is emphatically resolved, once and for all, into the A-flat major sonority five measures before the conclusion. This structural downbeat represents a goal toward which the whole work seems to have aspired.

Variations and Bagatelles

Of Beethoven's numerous early variation sets on borrowed themes, the set of twenty-four variations on *Venni amore* by Righini, WoO 65—a product of the last Bonn years, from 1790 to 1791—is perhaps the finest. The first major sets of variations by Beethoven, however, are two works written on original themes: the Six Variations in F op. 34 and the Fifteen Variations and Fugue in E-flat op. 35, composed as a pair in 1802. In a letter from October 1802, Beethoven described them as having been written in "quite a new style and each in an entirely different way." Both works introduce features that overcome the basically static and additive nature of the classical variation technique. The tonal plan of op. 34, for example, is innovative and wide-ranging. The successive variations do not remain in the expected tonic but appear in keys forming a chain of descending thirds leading from the tonic F major through D major, B-flat major, G major, E-flat major, and C minor; a short extension to the fifth variation elaborates the dominant seventh on C, preparing the F-major cadence at the beginning of the final variation, which closes the circle of falling thirds. This variation reminds us of the original theme in more compelling terms than the intervening ones (highly individualized and marked by strong contrasts, with frequent changes of meter); the set concludes with an ornately decorated reprise of the theme, marked *Adagio molto.*

The op. 35 Variations represent a larger and even more original conception than op. 34 and assume a special significance by serving as a model for the finale of the *Eroica* Symphony, the seminal movement of that great work, as Lewis Lockwood has shown.[19] In op. 35, as in the *Eroica* finale, the bass of the theme is first presented alone, and then in a series of introductory variations, with two, three, and four voices. The subsequent appearance of the actual theme, together with its bass, thus represents in a sense the fourth variation, but Beethoven's numbering begins only after this statement of the composite theme. (The theme in its fully harmonized form was used earlier as the seventh of the Contredances for Orchestra, WoO 16, and in the *Prometheus* Ballet op. 43.) Opening with the *basso del tema* enables Beethoven to highlight its comic aspects, particularly the three fortissimo B-flat octaves in its second half, which are surrounded by rests, creating a humor of expressive silences. In the ninth and especially thirteenth variations, this stress on B-flat is developed as a pedal throughout the first half, with amusing effect. The *Minore,* the fourteenth, and *Maggiore,* fifteenth—a majestic, decorated Largo—represent a new section in the overall formal progression, which culminates in the powerful fugal finale. In its structural grandeur and comprehensive range of expression from the comic to the sublime, this set anticipates the greatest of Beethoven's works in this genre, the Thirty-three Variations on a Waltz by Diabelli op. 120.

The Thirty-two Variations in C minor, WoO 80, from 1806, were seriously underrated by Beethoven himself, who referred to them disparagingly and failed to assign them an opus number. This work is strongly reminiscent of the baroque chaconne and employs a short, eight-measure theme with a chromatically descending ground bass. Beethoven effectively overcomes the terseness of the theme by often grouping the variations together, as in Variations 1–3, 7–8, 10–11, 12–14, 15–16, 19–22, 26–27, and 31–32. By no means do these groupings exhaust the many relationships between the individual variations, which are based on general rhythmic and textural features and on modal contrast (the *Maggiore* section, Variations 12–16, for example, embraces two of these groupings, and provides large-scale contrast after the agitated variation pair, nos. 10–11). Variation 31 provides a reprise of the original theme above an arpeggiated accompaniment, whereas in Variation 32 a rhythmic elaboration of the theme leads upward in register to the high C three full octaves above middle C, marking the beginning of the coda. (This high C occurs for the first time among the sonatas in op. 57, composed in 1804–05, and reflects the upward expansion of register in the pianos available to Beethoven; in works up to op. 31, from 1802, the range rarely exceeds high F, a fifth lower.)

Beethoven's abilities in keyboard improvisation are captured in two works from 1808, both of which make extensive use of variation: the *Choral* Fantasy op. 80 opens with an improvisatory piano introduction, leading to a set of variations for piano, orchestra, and chorus on a text in praise of art. This work impressively foreshadows the finale of the Ninth Symphony. The Fantasy for piano solo op. 77 also culminates in a set of variations, in B major, following a strikingly free opening section abounding in thematic contrasts and sudden modulations. The opening gesture of this work is a rapid descending scale, which seems torn, as it were, from the celestial ether; rather than support its key, G minor, Beethoven proceeds to the remote D-flat major, the key of the contrasting lyrical theme. The op. 77 Fantasy provides us a rare glimpse at Beethoven's considerable powers of invention outside the formal demands of the classical sonata style.

That the Thirty-three Variations on a Waltz by Diabelli op. 120 became Beethoven's longest and one of his most intellectually demanding works for piano may seem surprising when one considers the origins of the work. In 1819 the Viennese music publisher Anton Diabelli circulated a waltz of his own invention to fifty composers, each of whom he requested to contribute a variation to a collective work. Beethoven first disdained the theme as a "cobbler's patch" on account of its mechanical sequences, but then reacted to Diabelli's invitation by conceiving twenty-three variations. After setting aside his composition for several years, Beethoven finally expanded his draft in 1823, when he added ten more variations, nos. 1–2, 15, 23–26, 28–29, and 31, and greatly elaborated the conclusion.[20] (Illustration 3.4 shows Beethoven's draft from 1819 of the original first variation, Variation 3 of the finished work.)

No other work by Beethoven is as rich in allusion, humor, and parody. Trivial or repetitious features of the waltz, such as the C-major chords repeated tenfold in the right hand in the opening bars, can be mercilessly exaggerated, as in Variation 21, or dissolved into silence, as in Variation 13 (in its humor of expressive pauses, this variation is reminiscent of the *basso del tema* of op. 35). Such inconspicuous elements of the theme as the ornamental turn heard at the outset can assume astonishing importance, as in Variations 9 and 11, which are based throughout on the turn.

ILLUSTRATION 3.4. The beginning of Beethoven's 1819 draft of the *Diabelli* Variations, Op. 120, in the Paris 77A MS, fol. 1ʳ. The variation shown was originally planned as the first and is labeled "Var: 1" in Beethoven's hand at the top left, but it became Variation 3 after Beethoven's expansion of the work in 1823. Transcriptions of the superimposed layers of writing are provided in William Kinderman, *Beethoven's Diabelli Variations.* Oxford, 1987. Pp. 142–45. Printed with permission of the Bibliothèque nationale, Paris.

Certain variations allude to Mozart, J. S. Bach, and other composers. Most obvious among these is the reference, in the unison octaves of Variation 22, to "Notte e giorno faticar" from Act 1 of Mozart's *Don Giovanni.* This allusion is convincing not only because of the musical affinity of the themes—they share, for example, the same descending fourth and fifth (see Example 3.12a–b)—but through the reference to Mozart's Leporello. Beethoven's relationship to his theme, like Leporello's relationship to his master, is critical but faithful, inasmuch as he thoroughly exploits its motivic components. And like Leporello, the variations after this point gain the capacity for disguise. Variation 23 is an étudelike parody of pianistic virtuosity alluding to the *Pianoforte-Method* by J. B. Cramer, whereas Variation 24, the *Fughetta,* shows an affinity in its intensely sublimated atmosphere not only to the fugue of op. 110, but also to some organ pieces from the third part of J. S. Bach's *Clavierübung.*

The work as a whole consists of one large form with three distinct regions. The opening variations remain close to basic attributes of the theme (such as its meter) and show a gradually increasing freedom, which eventually turns into dissociation in Beethoven's juxtaposition of two con-

EXAMPLE 3.12a. Diabelli's Waltz (mm. 1–8)

EXAMPLE 3.12b. *Thirty-Three Variations on a Waltz by Diabelli,* Op. 120, Var. 22 (mm. 1–4)

trasting canonic variations (nos. 19 and 20), and in Variation 21, in which the structural parts of each variation half are themselves placed into opposition. In performance time, these variations represent the midpoint. A sense of overall formal coherence is created in part through unusually direct reference to the melodic shape of the original waltz in its original register in three variations inserted in 1823—nos. 1, 15, and 25. In Variation 25 the waltz is reincarnated as a humorous German dance, but this image is gradually obliterated in the series of interconnected fast variations culminating in no. 28, in which harsh dissonances dominate every strong beat throughout.

After Variation 28, we enter a transfigured realm in which Diabelli's waltz and the world it represents seem to be left behind. A group of three slow variations in the minor culminates in Variation 31, an elaborate aria reminiscent of the decorated minor variation of Bach's *Goldberg* set, but also foreshadowing the style of Chopin. The following energetic fugue in E-flat is initially Handelian in character; its second part builds to a tremendous climax with three subjects combined simultaneously before the fugue dissipates into a powerful dissonant chord. An impressive transition leads to C major and to the final and most subtle variation of all: a Mozartian minuet whose elaboration through rhythmic means leads, in the coda, to an ethereal texture unmistakably reminiscent of the fourth variation of the Arietta movement from Beethoven's own last sonata, op. 111, composed in 1822. The many parallels between op. 111 and the final *Diabelli* variation are structural in nature and extend to the thematic proportions and the use of an analogous series of rhythmic diminutions leading, in each case, to the suspended, ethereal texture; but the most obvious similarity surfaces in the concluding passages outlining the descending fourth C-G so crucial in both works (Example 3.13a–b). Herein lies the final surprise: the Arietta movement, itself influenced by the Diabelli project, became in turn Beethoven's model for the last of the *Diabelli* Variations. The final allusion thus became a self-reference, a final point of orientation within an artwork whose vast scope ranges from ironic caricature to sublime transformation of the commonplace waltz.

EXAMPLE 3.13a. Piano Sonata in C minor, Op. 111/ii (mm. 175–77)

EXAMPLE 3.13b. *Thirty-Three Variations on a Waltz by Diabelli*, Op. 120, Coda (mm. 42–43)

Beethoven produced only one important work for piano after the *Diabelli* Variations: the "Cycle of Bagatelles," op. 126 in 1824. He had long been interested in the genre of the bagatelle, a short, intimate piano piece making modest technical demands on the performer. The popular *Für Elise*, WoO 59 (1810), is an example,[21] and in his op. 33 from 1802,

Beethoven had already published a group of seven bagatelles. Several other unpublished bagatelles from earlier years were revised and included in the eleven bagatelles of op. 119, brought out in 1823, together with newly composed pieces, two of which were actually byproducts of the *Diabelli* Variations.[22] Even the first movement of the Sonata op. 109 may originally have been conceived as a bagatelle.[23]

Whereas opp. 33 and 119 are collections of individual pieces, op. 126 suggests an integrated cycle, as the sketches reveal; Beethoven took special pains in ordering this group of six pieces.[24] Lyrical pieces in slow or moderate tempi alternate with more rapid, agitated ones until no. 6, in which a short and furious Presto frames a reflective *Andante amabile e con moto*. The music is characterized by a directness of expression and use of three-part song form, yet its simplicity is deceptive: The reprise sections, for instance, almost invariably differ from the initial passages and represent a significant reinterpretation of the music already heard. In the middle section of no. 1, where the meter changes from $\frac{3}{4}$ to $\frac{2}{4}$ (measure 21), the music seems to turn inward, arresting the forward momentum through meditation on the motive from the preceding measure, now rhythmically elaborated to lead into a cadenza. In the ensuing recapitulation, Beethoven places the head of the opening theme in octaves in the bass against a new texture of chords in the treble, leading to an imitation of the theme in the highest register. The opening material of the bagatelle is compressed, and a cadential phrase with close motivic links to the theme appears in imitation in the final measures. Beethoven thus conspicuously avoids a literal restatement, and the transformation in texture, broadening in register, and many other changes in the reprise give us a sense that the theme is being explored from a new, heightened perspective. The effect is not unlike the enhanced recapitulatory techniques in the variation movements of Beethoven's later years.

The fifth bagatelle, a *quasi Allegretto* in G major, evokes an atmosphere of childlike naiveté, especially in its middle section beginning in C major. Here, as elsewhere, the effect of simplicity results from the utmost purity of the musical language: The parallel thirds in the treble (mm. 17ff.) derive from the bass of the first section, while the return to the C-major sonority in measure 20 is enhanced by means of the C-sharp in the tenor voice and the asymmetrical phrasing (Example 3.14). The pedal on C contributes to the static, idyllic quality of the passage and sets off the more active continuation in measures 25–30, with its crescendo, modulation to G major, and expansion in register. The yearning character of the ascent into the high register carries over into the ensuing reprise of the opening, now stated in the upper octave.

The framing device of the Presto in the final bagatelle seems to draw attention to the boundary separating inward, subjective feeling from external reality, or art from life. The relationship of his art to society was of course an important theme for Beethoven, one he addressed most explic-

EXAMPLE 3.14. Bagatelle in G major, Op. 126 no. 5 (mm. 17–32)

itly in *Fidelio,* the Ninth Symphony, and the *Missa Solemnis,* but one also present in his instrumental music. Beethoven's aesthetic convictions were far removed from the doctrine of *l'art pour l'art.* In the case of op. 126 no. 6, we are reminded of Czerny's account of Beethoven's practice, after moving his listeners to tears through his improvisations, of bursting into loud laughter and mocking his hearers on their emotion, saying "You are fools!"[25] The easy sentimentality that Beethoven scorned is indeed alien to his musical style, but depth of emotion essential to it. And although the framing gesture of the Presto in the last bagatelle effects a bold contrast in character almost ominously like a kick downstairs, the music so enclosed in the *Andante amabile e con moto* assumes an intensely meditative character while it transforms the material from the Presto.

The beginning of the *Andante amabile e con moto* clearly derives from the opening gesture: the bass pedal on E-flat and B-flat comes from the sustained tremoli of the Presto, whereas the register of the treble line and the harmonic texture in thirds are outlined in the rapid eighth-note figures of the Presto (Example 3.15). But in contrast to the Presto, the music of the Andante has taken on a contemplative quality, and in the course of the piece this material undergoes a further evolution. Beethoven places the reprise section in the subdominant, A-flat major, and arranges the pedal figure into a pattern of sixteenth-note triplets reminiscent of the Arietta of op. 111. The initial six-measure phrase now reappears in varied form, so that its disjunct intervals are filled in by conjunct motion, bringing the thematic profile closer still to the initial Presto. Then, after the repetition of the second section of the form, the music reaches a climax on high C (mm. 55–56), the registral ceiling of the bagatelle.

EXAMPLE 3.15. Bagatelle in E♭ major, Op. 126 no. 6, Beginning

In a sense, the descent from this climax embraces three levels of experience, as the adornments of art are progressively stripped away. In measure 64, the elaborate texture in sixteenth and sixteenth-note triplets is suddenly broken off to reveal the music from the beginning of the Andante, corresponding to measures 10–12 but with the pedal now placed

EXAMPLE 3.16. Bagatelle in E♭ major, Op. 126 no. 6, Conclusion

initially on the dominant instead of on the tonic (Example 3.16). A varied sequence of these measures carries the progression into the low register, leading to an exact restatement of the framing gesture in presto tempo. Previously the Presto had offered raw material, as it were, out of which the Andante had been shaped, but now Beethoven reverses the process: the Andante is dissipated into the frenetic activity of the Presto, whose fanfare of chords on the E-flat tonic concludes the bagatelle. A humorous or ironic quality arises here through Beethoven's juxtaposition of highly introspective music with a gesture much more evocative of the common daylight of outward events. And, inasmuch as this passage implies humble or low origins for the work of art, corresponding to Beethoven's use of Diabelli's waltz in op. 120, it also embodies that quality of universality and challenging breadth of experience so characteristic of Beethoven.

Notes

1. The Sonatas op. 10 nos. 1 and 2, op. 13, and op. 14 nos. 1 and 2 all contain three movements. Beethoven returned to a four-movement plan four times, in op. 22, op. 26, op. 31 no. 3, and op. 106.

2. Whereby phrases are divided into progressively smaller units. This process is a particularly important feature of Beethoven's style, to which Alfred Brendel has drawn special attention in his essays "Form and Psychology in Beethoven's Piano Sonatas" and "The Process of Foreshortening in the First Movement of Beethoven's Sonata Op. 2, No. 1," in *Musical Thoughts and Afterthoughts.*

3. Cf., for example, measures 248–80 in the development of the first movement of the *Eroica.*

4. For an example of this practice in Haydn, see the first movement of the String Quartet in C op. 33 no. 3, in which a last-minute adjustment enables Haydn to close the movement with its opening phrase.

5. The sonata is dedicated to Countess Giulietta Guicciardi, who was regarded in the nineteenth century as a likely intended recipient of Beethoven's letter to the "Eternal Beloved." In light of this, the opening slow movement of the sonata was sometimes misconstrued as a kind of love song without words. See Forbes, 296–97.

6. In the bass of the first movement Beethoven uses the diatonic descent C♯-B-A-F♯-G♯; in the finale, he employs the chromatic tetrachord: C♯-B♯-B♮-A-G♯, a figure loaded with pathos and emotion since the baroque.

7. In an edition that appeared during the 1830s. According to Georg Kinsky, the title may have appeared in English editions issued as early as 1805. See Kinsky and Halm, 70.

8. See, for instance, Blom, 125–26.

9. For a study of Beethoven's sketches for the *Appassionata,* see Martha Jane Frohlich, *Beethoven's Piano Sonatas Op. 57 and 54: A Study of the Manuscript Sources* (Ph.D. dissertation, Ramat-Gan University, 1988).

10. See, for example, the recapitulations of Chopin's C-minor Nocturne op. 48 no. 1 and *Polonaise-Fantaisie* op. 61.

11. Both of these themes, in turn, are based on a harmonic sequence employed by many composers during the "common practice" period.

12. This movement served as a model for Schubert's A-major Rondo for piano duet from 1828, as Brendel has pointed out ("Schubert's Piano Sonatas, 1822–28," in Brendel, 1976: 65); its influence is also felt in Mendelssohn's Sonata op. 6. See R. Larry Todd's chapter in this volume, pp. 185–87.

13. Alfred Brendel, "Der neue Stil," in *Nachdenken über Musik*, 76. This essay is not included in the English-language editions of Brendel's book.

14. See Rosen, 404–34; also, Ratz, 201–41.

15. This relationship is discussed in William Kinderman, "Beethoven's Symbol for the Deity in the *Missa Solemnis* and the Ninth Symphony," *19th-Century Music* 9 (1985): 102–118.

16. Thomas Mann, *Doktor Faustus: Das Leben des deutschen Tonsetzers Adrian Leverkühn, erzählt von einem Freunde* (Stockholm, 1947), 83.

17. See William Kinderman, "Tonality and Form in the Variation Movements of Beethoven's Late Quartets," *Beiträge zu Beethovens Kammermusik*, ed. Sieghard Brandenburg and Helmut Loos (Munich, 1987), 135–51.

18. As Brendel observes in "Der neue Stil," p. 85, the dichotomy embodied in the two movements of op. 111 has been variously described in terms of "Samsara and Nirwana" (von Bülow), the "Here and Beyond" (Edwin Fischer), and "Resistance and Submission" (Lenz); Brendel also mentions the dichotomy of "Male and Female Principles" (of which Beethoven sometimes spoke) and that of the real and the mystical world. Studies of a speculative cast treating op. 111 include Philip T. Barford, "Beethoven's Last Sonata," in *The Beethoven Companion*, eds. Thomas K. Sherman and Louis Biancolli (New York, 1972), 1040–50 (this essay originally appeared in *Music and Letters*); and Mellers, 254–84.

19. See Lewis Lockwood, "The Compositional Genesis of the *Eroica* Finale," in *Beethoven Studies I*, ed. William Kinderman (Lincoln and London: University of Nebraska Press, forthcoming in 1991).

20. See Kinderman, 1987, for a detailed study of the manuscript sources.

21. As Max Unger first pointed out, Nohl's reading of the inscription as *Für Elise* ("For Elise") is probably an error, since the manuscript was found among the possessions of Therese von Malfatti, and was apparently entitled "For Therese." See Forbes, 502.

22. The first five apparently have an earlier origin, and Gustav Nottebohm proposed on the basis of sketches that nos. 2–5 dated from the period 1800–04. Nos. 7–11 were sketched by Beethoven in the summer or fall of 1820 and first published as nos. 28–32 in Friedrich Starke's *Wiener Piano-Forte-Schule* in 1821. No. 6 was sketched on a leaf containing work on the Credo of the *Missa Solemnis* and probably dates from 1820. No. 7 bears similarity to the third and tenth *Diabelli* Variations, and no. 8 also shows a motivic relationship to the third *Diabelli* Variation.

23. See William Meredith, "The Origins of Beethoven's op. 109," *The Musical Times* 126 (1985): 713–16.

24. See the facsimile edition of the sketches for op. 126, with transcription, commentary, and a discussion of the sketches and drafts in Brandenburg, 2:60–62.

25. This anecdote is related in Forbes, 185.

Selected Bibliography

For an overview of the extensive literature on Beethoven's piano sonatas, see William S. Newman, *The Sonata in the Classic Era* (2nd ed.; New York, 1972). Newman counted more than fifty books devoted to the sonatas alone.

Blom, Eric. *Beethoven's Pianoforte Sonatas Discussed.* New York, 1938.

Brandenburg, Sieghard, ed. *Ludwig van Beethoven: Sechs Bagatellen für Klavier Op. 126.* 2 vols. Bonn, 1984. A facsimile edition of the musical sketches, autograph, and first edition, with transcriptions and commentary.

Brendel, Alfred. *Musical Thoughts and Afterthoughts.* Princeton, 1976.

———. *Nachdenken über Musik.* Munich, 1977.

Cone, Edward. "Schubert's Beethoven." *Musical Quarterly* 56 (1970): 779–93.

———. "The Late Bagatelles: Beethoven's Experiments in Composition." In *Beethoven Studies*, vol. 2, edited by Alan Tyson. London, 1977. Pp. 84–105.

Cooper, Martin. *Beethoven: The Last Decade 1817–1827.* London, 1970.

Czerny, Carl. *On the Proper Performance of All Beethoven's Works for the Piano.* Edited and with a commentary by Paul Badura-Skoda. Vienna, 1963.

Dahlhaus, Carl. *Ludwig van Beethoven und seine Zeit.* Laaber, 1987.

Forbes, Elliot, ed. *Thayer's Life of Beethoven.* Princeton, 1964.

Halm, August. *Beethoven.* Berlin, 1927. Includes an extended discussion of the *Diabelli* Variations.

Kinderman, William. *Beethoven's Diabelli Variations.* Oxford, 1987.

———. "Thematic Contrast and Parenthetical Enclosure in Beethoven's Piano Sonatas, Opp. 109 and 111." In *Zu Beethoven*, vol. 3, edited by Harry Goldschmidt and Georg Knepler. Berlin, 1988. Pp. 43–59.

Kinsky, Georg, and Halm, Hans. *Das Werk Beethovens: Thematisch-bibliographisches Verzeichnis seiner sämtlichen vollendeten Kompositionen.* Munich and Duisburg, 1955.

Mellers, Wilfrid. *Beethoven and the Voice of God.* New York and London, 1983. A highly speculative discussion of Beethoven's piano sonatas, *Diabelli* Variations, and late bagatelles.

Newman, William S. *Performance Practices in Beethoven's Piano Sonatas.* New York, 1971.

———. *Beethoven on Beethoven. Playing His Piano Music His Way.* New York, 1988.

Prod'homme, Jacques-Gabriel. *Les sonates pour piano de Beethoven.* Paris, 1937.

Ratz, Erwin. *Einführung in die musikalische Formenlehre.* Vienna, 1968. Includes an extended analysis of the *Hammerklavier* Sonata op. 106.

Reti, Rudolph. *Thematic Patterns in Sonatas of Beethoven.* London, 1967.

Riemann, Hugo. *L. van Beethovens sämtliche Klavier-Solosonaten.* 3 vols. Berlin, 1918–19.

Riezler, Walter. *Beethoven.* Berlin and Zurich, 1936.

Rosen, Charles. *The Classical Style.* New York, 1972. Contains a detailed analytical discussion of the third relationships in the *Hammerklavier* Sonata.

———. *Sonata Forms.* New York, 1980.

Rosenberg, Richard. *Die Klaviersonaten Ludwig van Beethovens.* Olten/Lausanne, 1957.

Schenker, Heinrich. *Die letzten Sonaten von Beethoven: Kritische Ausgabe mit Einführung und Erläuterung.* 4 vols. Vienna, 1913–21; new edition, 1971. Critical editions with analysis of all the last sonatas except the *Hammerklavier*.

Tovey, Donald Francis. *A Companion to Beethoven's Pianoforte Sonatas*. London, 1931.

————. *Essays in Musical Analysis: Chamber Music*. London, 1944. Pp. 124–34. (On the *Diabelli* Variations.)

————. *Beethoven*. London, 1944.

Uhde, Jürgen. *Beethovens Klaviermusik*. 3 vols. Stuttgart, 1968–74. A comprehensive discussion of all of the piano music, including the variations, bagatelles, and miscellaneous pieces.

————, and Wieland, Renate. *Denken und Spielen: Studien zu einer Theorie der musikalischen Darstellung*. Kassel and New York, 1988. Contains analytical discussions of a number of Beethoven's works and addresses issues related to performance.

Wolff, Konrad. *Schnabel's Interpretation of Piano Music*. New York, 1972. Includes many examples drawn from Beethoven's works.

CHAPTER FOUR

The Piano Works of Schubert

Eva Badura-Skoda

As a truly great composer of instrumental music Franz Schubert was surprisingly little known in his lifetime. It is also remarkable how slowly and reluctantly after his death the greatness of even his finest instrumental works was acknowledged. In this regard, examples can be found especially among Schubert's piano sonatas.

Shortly after World War II, a young Austrian pianist traveling through Latin American countries visited a music club. There he was asked to play unknown Austrian music. He immediately sat down and played early piano sonatas by Schubert. All musicians in the room had to agree that they never before had heard the sonatas and that these works, though unknown, were beautiful indeed. Such an event could still occur today, though the popularity of Schubert's piano music has grown tremendously during the last decades. Only half a century ago, the popular English music critic Hubert Parry did not hesitate to issue the verdict that "Schubert's movements [for piano] are in varying degrees diffuse in form, slipshod in craftmanship and unequal in content." Nowadays this criticism is rather unlikely to be expressed, and statements of this kind presumably will never be made again.

The change in the doctrinaire assessment of Schubert's piano music, common especially in English-speaking countries, began to manifest itself with the appearance in 1928 of Sir Donald Tovey's essay "Tonality," in which he observed that an important motivation in Schubert's sonatas was key relationship.[1] With this pronouncement, Tovey "in one stroke opened worlds of significance in these works: he suggested that the intellectual drive behind them need not be sought solely in theme manipulation, or in the Beethoven architectural schemes; it may be found equally in Schubert's patterns of modulation, in the juxtaposition and combination of the tonal colors implied by the key in which he was composing."[2]

In spite of Tovey's enthusiasm for Schubert and the increasing awareness of Schubert's greatness after 1928, the commemorative year of his death, several decades passed before Schubert's piano sonatas appeared regularly on concert programs. Though today many pianists and piano teachers throughout the world admire and sometimes also play

Schubert's piano music (though usually only the late masterpieces), the average pianist is still not accustomed to consider more than six or seven Schubert sonatas to be worth hearing frequently. Fortunately, pianists now may have at their disposal one of the reliable critical editions that were published during the last few decades, and they probably also own one or the other recording of Schubert sonatas. They even may have read through all sonatas in the Henle three-volume Urtext edition in a quiet hour or two. Rarely, however, do we come across a pianist who has performed all twenty Schubert sonatas in a concert cycle, and an even greater rarity is a complete recording of all the Schubert sonatas.

Because of the rather late acknowledgement of Schubert's great achievements as an instrumental composer, it may sound bold to state that Schubert's piano music somehow ranks in importance with that of Beethoven (for example, the *Hammerklavier* Sonata or the Sonata op. 111). If, however, we consider Beethoven's output as of 1802, when he reached the age of thirty-two (Schubert died two months short of thirty-two), the body of Beethoven's piano works might appear less significant than that of Schubert. Since Beethoven started at age twenty-six to give opus numbers only to those works that he found worthy of preservation, his list contains thirty-two masterpieces. On the other hand, Schubert never found himself in a position to make as careful a selection,[3] and his twenty (or twenty-one) sonatas that can be performed today include a number of unfinished works as well as some early sonatas with which he probably would not have been satisfied in later years. Still, even the earliest completed sonata, the one in E major D 157, deserves to be played much more frequently than before, since it already displays typically Schubertian stylistic features and beauties, especially in the second movement in E minor, with its lovely melancholic *siciliano* character and its mood of "tearful smiling." The first movement (it was his second attempt to master the problems of sonata form; the fragment D 154 survives as a kind of draft for this movement) may still be open to some criticism. However, the second movement makes up for that, and among the other seldom-heard early sonatas are other masterpieces worthy of being discovered by every music lover.

Apparently Schubert had managed in a totally independent way to develop, during his apprenticeship years prior to 1815, an idiomatic style of writing for voice *and* for piano. This process took place mainly in the accompaniments of his songs. His way of expressing feelings—evoked through texts that inspired him to compose a poem or a ballade—in the piano parts of his lieder soon became a signpost of his style, a far cry from the simple continuo accompaniment typical of earlier songs. Truthfully painting the contents of the poems by means of colorful harmonic progressions and carefully fashioned motives and melodies, early on Schubert composed for the piano in an advanced, newly developed pianistic idiom. His vocal parts, too, sounded more and more natural; the declamation of the words always seemed to guide his melodic invention; and the melodies found their way from the vocal parts into the piano parts. They are sometimes charming, sad, or melancholic, sometimes simply heart-warming; sometimes, too, there are highly dramatic outcries as in the celebrated early masterpieces "Gretchen am Spinnrade" and "Erlkönig." The narration of "Erlkönig" completely grips the listener, who can vividly "hear" or sense the galloping horse and the storm in the piano accompaniment, as well as the fear of the child, the shudder of the father and the dialogue—all of which becomes an organic unity. In a similar compelling manner, "Gretchen am Spinnrade" depicts in the accompaniment the incessant turning of the spinning wheel, which stops only when Gretchen is overwhelmed by her emotions. This song, too, would not be as convincing a masterpiece if Schubert had not given the accompaniment such a decisive role.

These two masterpieces were written in 1814 and 1815 respectively. In 1815, Schubert finally managed to escape from the schoolhouse and the teaching profession, which had been an unbearable burden for him. From this year onward Schubert composed piano sonatas in an idiomatic pianistic style that reveals how effectively and innovatively he could write for this instrument. Thus, at the age of eighteen Schubert was already frequently able to express musically his most personal feelings—often in such a direct and truthful way that no musical listener could or can remain untouched.

As recent research has shown,[4] Schubert's destiny to become a musician was decided in 1804, when at the age of seven he passed a preliminary examination held by Salieri for candidates for the position of choirboy in the Court Chapel in Vienna (not as hitherto believed as late as 1808, when at the age of eleven Schubert passed the final entrance examination). From that date in October 1804 onward, his father knew that by studying music seriously the child could receive an excellent education free of charge. He let the child learn not only singing and composition but also piano and violin playing, for all these abilities were expected of choirboys in the Imperial Court Chapel. Schubert's first piano teacher seems to have been his brother Ignaz (twelve years older and hunchbacked, deprived of the then considerable privileges of a legitimate child since he had been born only two months after the marriage of his parents—what a fate!) and Michael Holzer, the *Regens Chori* at the nearby Lichtenthal Church, who taught the child all he knew about singing and composition. He became probably the most influential teacher during Schubert's childhood years.

Schubert's very first *known* composition, dating from the year 1810, is a Fantasy for piano duet in G major D 1 (sometimes confused with the *Leichenfantasie* or *Fantasy of a Corpse*). This Fantasy is apparently not much more than a composition study but shows Schubert's interest in all kinds of chamber music. More interesting is the second Fantasy for piano duet in G minor D 9 from 1811, though this piece still seems to be not much more than a student's essay in composition. Extant short pieces for piano solo of these apprenticeship years include the Fantasy in C minor D 2E; among other works (D 19B, D 128, D 21, D 22, D 24A–D, D 25, mainly dances but also two variation sets and counterpoint exercises), are several that seem to be lost.

In 1811 Schubert entered the Imperial Court Chapel as a choirboy, thus gaining a free place in the *kaiserlich-königliches Stadtkonvikt*, an excellent boarding school where he received further musical instruction from the pianist Wenzel Ruziczka. Some fugal expositions and variation movements were written in the following years, but Schubert's pianistic style developed more clearly in his songs and "solo-cantatas": During these early adolescent years, mainly between 1811 and 1816, Schubert composed his longest monodic songs. Though we naturally also find some strophic settings among the songs composed in these years, most of the early lieder were ballades. And though some ballades remind music historians that in the *Konvict* Schubert encountered the songs and "solo cantatas" of a minor German composer named J. R. Zumsteeg, Schubert's ballades stand remarkably apart: The piano accompaniment is no longer a progression of simple chords but assumes a new musical significance; now the pianist acts as a real partner of the singer. In this way, Schubert's pianistic style reached its first level of excellence.

Schubert's works for piano solo can be grouped into four categories: sonatas, fantasies, shorter piano pieces, and dances. Of these, the sonatas are undoubtedly the most important and profound works of his pianistic output, while the dances, mostly *Ländler, Deutsche,* and waltzes, are somehow less significant, often bordering on popular music. Yet they should not be discounted: Their graceful charm antedates the symphonic waltzes of Johann Strauss Jr., and more than once they contain daring innovations that apparently served Schubert as "guinea pigs" for works of symphonic complexity. Thus, the Scherzo of the D-minor String Quartet can be traced back to the *Ländler* in G-sharp minor D 790/No. 6. Despite the charm and beauty of many of these dances, in the present essay we shall concentrate on the first three categories.

The Sonatas

A survey of Schubert's sonatas shows that they can be divided into three groups. The first group of ten sonatas was written between 1815 and 1818, when Schubert was aged eighteen to twenty-one. These early works are still widely and unjustly neglected. The Sonata in A Major D 664, composed in 1819, links the first and the second group of sonatas. The second group was written in the years between 1823 and 1826 and was preceded in 1822 by the famous *Wanderer* Fantasy, which is most important as a turning point in the development of Schubert's mature pianistic style (it will be discussed later with the other fantasies, though—with some justification—it was once described as a "sonata in four movements with no pauses in between"). The last group of three sonatas represents one of the greatest miracles of creativity in the history of Occidental music: The autographs of the gigantic three sonatas in C minor, A major, and B-flat major D 958–960 were written during September 1828. Though sketches for these sonatas dating from the beginning of 1828 survive, and though the compositional process thus required more time than previously thought, Schubert probably organized, remodeled, and wrote down the premeditated material of the sonatas in one month. The simple act of writing 130 pages during such a short period is staggering, more so in light of its accomplishment only a few weeks prior to Schubert's death.

The difficult question of how many sonatas Schubert actually left as his precious legacy to the musical world should be answered in a pragmatic rather than a philological way: There are twenty different sonatas of which a performance is meaningful, and not twenty-one, twenty-two, or twenty-three, as sometimes mentioned in the literature (see Table 4.1).[5] Some scholars (including Maurice Brown) count additional sonatas

TABLE 4.1. Schubert's Piano Sonatas

1. Sonata in E major, D 157	February 1815
2. Sonata in C major, D 279/346/277A	September 1815
3. Sonata in E major, D 459 (published as *Fünf Klavierstücke*)	August 1816
4. Sonata in A minor, D 537	March 1817
5. Sonata in A-flat major, D 557	May 1817
6. Sonata in E minor, D 566/D 506*	June 1817
7. Sonata in D-flat major and E-flat major, D 567/568 (the second transposed and enriched version of D 567 became D 568)	1817 (1818?)
8. Sonata in F-sharp minor, D 571/604 with Scherzo D 570	July 1817
9. Sonata in B major, D 575	August 1817
10. Sonata in C major, D 613/612	April 1818
11. Sonata in F minor, D 625/505	September 1818
12. Sonata in A major, D 664	Summer 1819
13. Sonata in A minor, D 784	February 1823
14. Sonata in C major, D 840, so-called *Reliquie* Sonata	April 1825
15. Sonata in A minor, D 845	April/May 1825
16. Sonata in D major, D 850, so-called *Gastein* Sonata	August 1825
17. Sonata in G major, D 894	October 1826
18. Sonata in C minor, D 958	September 1828
19. Sonata in A major, D 959	September 1828
20. Sonata in B-flat major, D 960	September 1828

*Some scholars reverse the order of the sonatas Nos. 6 and 7. However, the Sonata in E minor most probably was finished before the D-flat major sonata.

by including an E-minor fragment of 38 measures (D 769A = D 994) and another fragment in C-sharp minor of 73 measures (D 655). In these two fragments Schubert stopped composing at such an early stage that to complete them convincingly is impossible. Thus, they should not be counted as full sonatas.

The Allegro in E major D 154 is nothing more than a draft for the first movement of the Sonata in E major D 157. It contains 118 measures and is sometimes counted, too. There is also the tendency to number separately the first version of a (perhaps) completed sonata: An earlier and simpler version of the Sonata in E-flat major D 568 exists in D-flat major, numbered by Deutsch as D 567. In spite of minor differences it is certainly misleading and actually wrong to count the two versions as separate sonatas (otherwise, one would have to credit Beethoven with two operas and Bruckner with sixteen symphonies!).

The only "unfinished" sonatas that stand justifiably as sonatas are those for which three or four movements have survived. As a rule the inner movements of these works are complete, while the opening—and sometimes the closing—movements in sonata form break off at a late point (usually at the end of the development or the beginning of the recapitulation), suggesting that their completion remained a somewhat mechanical task for Schubert. Most likely, Schubert interrupted the writing process in these "fragments" only because he thought that they could easily be finished at another time. How he tackled this task can be seen in his B-major Sonata D 575 of which a draft with an incomplete first movement and two contemporary copies of the finished sonata exist.

The fact that movements of Schubert's sonatas were often published after his death as single piano pieces rather than coherent sonatas added considerably to the long-standing confusion about the actual number of sonatas. This confusion was resolved during the 1960s simultaneously by Maurice Brown and Paul Badura-Skoda. Their conclusions were validated and essentially confirmed by investigations of two Italian scholars, Fabio Bisogni and Gabriele Cervone. Paul Badura-Skoda completed those five sonatas that could be completed easily (by writing recapitulations closely based on the expositions and, if needed, adding a coda), edited the early sonatas of Schubert (Henle edition), and recorded all twenty sonatas for RCA Victor.

The Early Piano Sonatas

The question why Schubert's early piano sonatas have been neglected so long becomes more understandable when one considers that for many years no editions were on the market and only few scholars knew of their existence. Only in recent times did these sonatas become available to a wider public in an edition (the third volume of the Henle *Urtext* Edition, mentioned above), in which sonatas still in need of completion were included.

Pianists are understandably reluctant to perform unfinished works by any composer. But in Schubert's case, some of these sonatas are in fact not at all unfinished. The Sonata in A-flat major D 557 may serve as an example. It was a whim of Schubert to compose the last movement, a typical final movement comparable to that of Sonata D 664, not in A-flat major but in the "wrong" key of E-flat major. But why not? Beethoven's Fantasy op. 77, Chopin's Scherzo No. 2 op. 31, and Mahler's Second Symphony are works that end in another key than the one in which they started, yet they are not considered "incomplete." Why should Schubert not be allowed to have such an idea? But for a long time, scholars considered it impossible that this Allegro in E flat could be the finale of an A-flat sonata.

The two sonatas D 157 and D 279/346/277A are incomplete insofar as they lack final movements. Concerning Sonata D 279, Maurice Brown has written:

> That the composer took more pains than usual with this early work is clear from the fact that he rewrote the Menuetto, with an alternative Trio in F. But although his manuscript contains only three movements, with the finale missing, there is a strong probability that the music of the last movement was composed and is still extant. There is an Allegretto in C, undated, the manuscript of which is in the City Library, Vienna. It is cataloged by Deutsch as D 346. This Allegretto is a thoroughly characteristic work of the young Schubert, and since it was not his custom in those early years to write isolated movements when he was absorbed in the composition of complete sonatas, it is highly probable that it is a finale. And the key suggests that it belongs to the Sonata in C.[6]

One of several possible explanations why Schubert sometimes did not finish a sonata comes to mind: The wealth of ideas and the sheer force of inspiration must have haunted him very often. It is likely that, having barely set the essential parts of a sonata movement down on paper, Schubert immediately set out to write the next movement. Although he had a very quick pen, apparently his mind was far quicker. Paul Badura-Skoda, who completed the unfinished movements, commented on them in this way:

> It is to our advantage that Schubert was very systematic in writing down nearly all his unfinished sonata movements up to the point of recapitulation. As the complete compositions show, most of Schubert's recapitulations are literal or nearly literal transpositions of the exposition. Thus, completing an unfinished movement remained for him a somewhat mechanical task, which he laid aside for later moments. . . . All I had to do in completing the unfinished sonata movements was to follow Schubert's own example.[7]

After three "forerunners," two from 1815 (Sonatas D 157 and D 279) and one from 1816 (Sonata D 459), Schubert's involvement with the piano sonata intensified in 1817 and 1818, when he composed no fewer than eight sonatas. While it is true that Schubert "inherited" the sonata form from Haydn, Mozart, Beethoven, and a few others, it is equally true that he brought to it—and to piano technique—a new, fresh approach. His frequent use of melodies in octaves (often in a unison opening) accompanied by the left hand in open (wide) position clearly foreshadows Chopin and the late romantics. Little in these works suggests an anxious imitation of Mozart or Beethoven; more often than not we encounter bold passages as well as experiments that, admittedly, are not always successful.

A special formal feature in Schubert's sonatas, rarely mentioned in the literature, is his use of a first theme designed in the form of a two- or three-part song melody with a full cadential close at the end. Typical examples of this kind of main subject can be found in the openings of his F-sharp-minor Sonata D 571/604/570 and his A-major Sonata D 664 (Example 4.1). Such a full close could easily compromise the structure of a

EXAMPLE 4.1. Schubert, Sonata in A major, D 664, movt. 1 (mm. 1–20)

sonata-form movement. Why continue after such a beautiful lied with anything other than a variation movement? Yet, unlike his famous predecessors, Schubert dares the impossible and carries it off just by writing a simple "naive" continuation. Miriam Whaples has stated aptly that already in his early string quartets the young Schubert invented a new kind of sonata form

with such experiments as a one-key-exposition (D 94) and recapitulations beginning in the dominant (D 46, 74), the subtonic
(D 94), and the relative major (D 173). The subdominant recapitulation, which quite probably comes directly from Mozart's
C Major Piano Sonata K. 545, does not appear in Schubert until his second Piano Sonata (September, 1815), but then fairly
frequently through 1817. Like Mozart, Schubert generally
does not use this since-disdained "short-cut" to reproduce his
exposition in exact transposition, but with very few
exceptions—notably the B Major Piano Sonata, D 575—
rewrites, abbreviates, and otherwise rearranges his materials
leading back to the tonic key. And if the B Major Sonata looks
like a "short-cut"—*i.e.,* a way of avoiding renewed thought in
the recapitulation—it may be in a sense just the opposite: a
reflection of Schubert's absorption in the remarkably long way
he has taken in the exposition from I to V (*i.e.,* I-♭VI-IV-V, reproduced in the recapitulation as IV-♭II-♭VII-I). In view of
the fact that, as we shall see, he left no fewer than five recapitulations unwritten in the piano sonatas of these two years (all of
the unfinished movements are sonata allegros which break off
at the end of their developments), we may deduce from his
having bothered to complete here what was essentially only a
copying task that he took a more than perfunctory interest in
his seemingly perfunctory recapitulation.

Haydn's and Mozart's sonatas usually make their first move
to the dominant with great dispatch and directness. Schubert's
lifelong fascination with the multiform ways of moving from I
to V is a legacy from Beethoven, which the younger composer
carried to a much higher level of development. The four-key
scheme of D 575 above is the most elaborate: in subsequent
works he rarely introduces more than one, usually third-
related, intermediate key. Indeed, if any one aspect of the
1817–18 period assumed a predominant importance in Schubert's development as an instrumental composer, it is his discovery of the power of third-related keys within the tonal plan
of the sonata. His earlier experiments in transitional keys had
relied upon IV (String Quartet D 32, Overture to *Claudine von
Villa Bella* D 239, Second and Third Symphonies). From 1817
on, this key no longer appears in a transitional role in an exposition, except in the four-key plan of D 575. Instead the paths
from I to V now lead in turn through almost all the keys third-
related to I or V or both: III (finale of D 613), iii (Ninth Symphony), and the favorite ♭III (D 613, E Major Symphony
sketch D 729, String Quintet D 956, among others), ♭VI
("Grand Duo" for piano four-hands D 812), VI (C Major "Italian" Overture D 591, and finale of the Sixth Symphony), and
vii (C Major Piano Sonata D 840). Neapolitan key relations, on
the other hand, which were to assume great importance in the
last few years of his life, play little part in the 1817–18 period.
(Whaples, 35)

EXAMPLE 4.2. Schubert, Sonata in C major, D 279, movt. 1 (mm. 86–98)

Not only in the tonal/harmonic blue print but also in certain chord progressions Schubert proved himself a "modernist" or even a "futurist" who went far beyond the harmonic range of his immediate successors. A few examples might illustrate this: Already in the first movement of his second Sonata in C major D 279, Schubert starts the development section with a series of harmonic shocks (Example 4.2).

One Schubertian "invention" consists of a new treatment of the chord of the (dominant) ninth: While composers before or after him considered it a strict rule that the uppermost note had to descend to the octave (Example 4.3a), Schubert "discovered" that the resolution of the dissonance could also occur by allowing the bass note to ascend (Example 4.3b). This novelty he tested in the first movement of D 279, measures 105–106.

EXAMPLE 4.3a. Resolution
of Dissonance by Descent

EXAMPLE 4.3b. Schubert,
Sonata in C major, D 279, movt. 1

A similar resolution in which the bass ascends can be seen in the first theme of the A-minor Sonata D 537, measures 8–9. And as late as in his great A-major Sonata D 959 he used a similar pattern, this time with the major seventh—see Example 4.4. But the most striking and dramatic use of a new kind of resolving a dissonant chord is heard in the so-called *Reliquie* Sonata in C major D 840. At a crucial point the dominant minor ninth resolves "incorrectly" into a foreign key, so that instead of securing C minor we reach B minor! (See Example 4.5.)

EXAMPLE 4.4. Schubert, Sonata in A major, D 959, movt. 1 (mm. 28–31)

EXAMPLE 4.5. Schubert, Sonata in C major, D 840, movt. 1 (mm. 50–53)

SONATA NO. 1 IN E MAJOR D 157 (HENLE EDITION, VOL. III/1)

In classical fashion this youthful sonata starts with a typical "Mannheim rocket," a rising triad. "Conventional," one might say, were it not for the feature that Schubert's "rocket" rises through the range of three octaves! This kind of vitality is the hallmark of the first movement. As stated above, the second movement is a *siciliano*-like Andante in E minor in a melancholic mood. It is one of Schubert's earliest masterpieces for the piano (for the subject see Example 4.6). It is written in what became Schubert's favorite formal scheme for slow movements, a five-part rondo (Wilhelm Fischer called it "kleine Rondo-form") with subtle variations at the returns of the refrains. Pianists ought to be reminded that on a Viennese instrument of Schubert's time the *fortissimo* in measures 63ff. was not as thundering as it too easily sounds on a modern piano, especially a concert grand (particularly in the bass!).

The third movement, entitled "Menuetto," is in reality a scherzo. It is a fitting final movement—to which everybody would agree were it not for the "wrong" key of B major. The Trio section in G major foreshadows nearly note for note the Trio of the Scherzo in the D-major Sonata D 850, composed ten years later. Yet, here the Trio appears one octave higher than in D 850, sounding like a boy's soprano voice in comparison to the more manly register of the *Gastein* Sonata.

EXAMPLE 4.6. Schubert, Sonata in E major, D 157, Andante (mm. 1–8)

SONATA NO. 2 IN C MAJOR D 279/346/277A (HENLE EDITION III/2)

The opening movement, lively in character despite the tempo designation Allegro moderato, has symphonic proportions that draw freely on classical features in Mozart's and Beethoven's works (especially in the latter's *Waldstein* Sonata); yet, the *bel canto* subsidiary theme is typical Schubert. The harmonic surprises of the development section (see Example 4.3b) are supposed to shock the listener into recognizing that this is not just another imitation of a classical sonata movement. The gentle Andante movement has the effect of a soothing balm after the jolts of the first movement. The Menuetto in A minor (again, in character a Scherzo) with its delightful Trio in A major is a sublime masterpiece.

A stylistic feature shared by the Rondo D 346 and the opening movement of this sonata furnishes one more argument in favor of the theory that D 346 is the missing finale: In both movements there is a strong tendency toward contrapuntal play, a trait otherwise rare in Schubert's piano works. The imitating octaves in the Rondo (mm. 131–145) can be traced back to Haydn (cf. his C-major Sonata, Hob. XVI/48, final Presto).

Sonata No. 3 in E major D 459 (Henle Edition III/3)

This work appeared posthumously in an 1843 German edition by Klemm (Leipzig) as *Fünf Klavierstücke*. Even if Schubert would not have entitled the autograph fragment of the first two movements "Sonata," the formal layout leaves little doubt today that these five pieces belong together[8] and were in fact perceived by Schubert as a sonata. However, five movements for a sonata of 1816 are unusual, indeed. Though one might recall that the *Trout* Quintet also consists of five movements, there is perhaps a slight possibility that originally these five movements were not planned to belong together. One may well ask whether during the compositional process Schubert intended to replace the second movement, a lengthy Scherzo in sonata form (!), with the more concise second Scherzo in A major, presently placed as the fourth movement. Since autographs survive for only the first two movements, the riddle remains unsolved. In my opinion this appealing work would only gain by the omission of the first Scherzo.

The charming first movement is related in its layout and expressiveness to the opening Allegro of the violin-piano Duo in A major D 574; so, too, is the Adagio to the Andantino of the same work. Both share a mood that fluctuates between the elegiac and the lilt of a slow waltz. The two Scherzos that frame the Adagio differ not only in form but also in character. The last movement is less "pathetic" than its title, *Allegro patetico*, might suggest. It is a brilliant concert piece, a "pathetic" experience only for incompetent players who fail to perform it with virtuosity and the suitable temperament.

Sonata No. 4 in A minor D 537 (Henle Edition I/1)

This profound, tragic work was written in a new pianistic style, boldly original and certainly quite different from any previous piano composition. Like all Schubert piano sonatas up to the year 1823, D 537 is short and concise in form. A striking symphonic element in the first Allegro nearly cries out for an orchestral rendition. A passage like that shown in Example 4.7 is almost Brucknerian in style; note the progression from F major to the lower mediant D-flat major in measures 20–27 of Example 4.7. These harmonic blocks, later found not only in the works of Bruckner but also of Mahler, must have been considered a musical novelty in Schubert's time, though occasionally they appear also in Beethoven's works. The harmony assumes here a meaning for itself and is now of the greatest importance; it replaces somehow the thematic process in earlier sonatas. A performer must create a sense for the broad melodic line and should also give special attention to the beauty of sounds, should "indulge in sound."

EXAMPLE 4.7. Schubert, Sonata in A minor, D 537, movt. 1 (mm. 20–27)

In the second theme we encounter for the first time another feature typical of Schubert, the expression of what has been termed "death's cradle song" (Example 4.8). Had Schubert's deadly disease set in already as early as age seventeen or eighteen? Was this stylistic feature a foreboding of it? His numerous songs dealing with the many aspects of death often use similar musical ideas, particularly in settings of poems in which death

EXAMPLE 4.8. Schubert, Sonata in A minor, D 537, movt. 1 (mm. 27–31)

is considered a friend of man who liberates the soul from suffering. The second movement, based on the juxtaposition of a legato melody with staccato accompaniment, is a sublime march expressing serene resignation, with the wayfarer finally fading out of sight.

The third movement contrasts the anguished opening theme with an "innocent" dance melody. Remarkable is the virtuoso element in the codetta, a veritable reminiscence of Domenico Scarlatti. The mood of resignation prevails in the coda until a final *fortissimo* chord breaks the spell.

SONATA NO. 5 IN A-FLAT MAJOR D 557 (HENLE EDITION III/4)

This delightful, unproblematic sonata might be used to introduce Schubert to children, unless a teacher prefers Schubert's dances for that purpose, which also abound in delightful ideas. Schubert conceived this three-movement Sonata in the style of a *Sonata facile*, obviously with Mozart in mind for the outer movements. We find reminiscences of Haydn in the Andante, for instance, the characteristic horn imitations. Still, it is impossible to draw direct parallels to Mozart's or Haydn's piano works; one might discover such parallels more easily in their symphonies.

One wonders whether Schubert originally intended to write a fourth movement, since not only the Andante but also the fast third movement is in the dominant key. From the musical point of view, however, this Allegro movement turns out to be a perfectly satisfying finale and, thus, nothing is missing. After all, Schubert was an innovator like Joseph Haydn who also broke "schoolmaster rules," for example, when inserting into the Sonata in E-flat major (Hob. XVI/52) a middle movement in E major.

SONATA NO. 6 IN E-MINOR D 566/506 (HENLE EDITION III/5)

The Rondo finale of this sonata was published posthumously together with the (transposed and truncated) Adagio D 505 as op. 145. However, a manuscript copy of this movement in the library of the Gesellschaft der Musikfreunde in Vienna bears the title *Sonate von Franz Schubert* with *Rondo* underneath. Kathleen Dale was the first musicologist to combine this Rondo with the rest of the Sonata in E minor in a publication.[9]

The Rondo fits perfectly into the sonata in terms of tonality, compositional style, and pianistic technique. There can be no doubt that the movements belong together.

This sonata has all the characteristics of a typical Schubert work without being overly demanding technically and musically. The slow movement is not slow at all but is rather a charming Allegretto that sounds like a young brother of the second movement of Beethoven's Sonata in E minor op. 90. Here Beethoven appears Schubertian rather than vice versa, even though his sonata preceded Schubert's by three years. The last movement of D 566 is sparkling and seems at times to be a harbinger of the closing movement of Chopin's E-minor Piano Concerto.

Sonata No. 7 in D-flat major D 567, and in E-flat major D 568
(Henle Edition III/6 and I/2)

We now know that, despite the different keys of these two versions of the same sonata, the D-flat Sonata is essentially an earlier version of D 568. The two share the same thematic material, though D 568 treats it sometimes in a more elaborate way than D 567.

Why did Schubert transpose this sonata? Was it perhaps on the request of a publisher who considered a key of five flat signs to exceed the abilities of amateur sightreaders? As Hans Gál once pointed out, we may regret that Schubert did not retain the key of D flat for the final fair copy. The sonata would otherwise have been the only D-flat major Sonata of a great composer of the Viennese classic and the early romantic period.

The "missing" Scherzo of D 567 is undoubtedly the separately transmitted Scherzo in D flat D 593/2 from November 1817. It has the same Trio as the Minuet of the E-flat Sonata, though in a more primitive form. From this fact we may deduce that D 568 was finished not earlier than November 1817, probably even later. Thus, Maurice Brown rightly suggested reversing the old order of the E-minor Sonata and the D-flat major Sonata (see note to Table 4.1). Both works were composed during June 1817, but apparently the E-minor Sonata was finished first.

The D-flat Sonata is not completely invalidated by its later companion in E-flat, but it stands on its own as a youthful work, is easier to perform, and thus is useful for teaching purposes. But to count D 567 as a separate sonata because it differs somewhat from D 568 (it has shorter development sections in the outer movements) is certainly wrong.

The E-flat Sonata D 568 is perhaps the finest of Schubert's youthful sonatas, comparable in quality to the later "perfect" Sonata in A major D 664, which stands as a guidepost toward the works of the middle period. The first movement of this E-flat Sonata presents in the middle of the dominant theme group (m. 63) a new theme, first in D flat (prepared by B-flat minor) and immediately afterwards in C minor. In its complexity this harmonic scheme is of a kind with the exposition of the F-sharp minor Sonata D 571. According to Miriam Whaples (36), "the appearance at this point of both the relative major of the minor dominant and a Neapolitan key relationship (although D-flat and C minor are not here explicitly related as Neapolitan) is what connects the practice with Haydn. Schubert makes his indebtedness more obvious in the much simpler version of the device found in the finale of the A-flat Major Sonata (the movement is unaccountably in E-flat major). Playful here, as in Haydn, this passage (m. 35–43) nevertheless leads directly to the two anguished Neapolitan outbursts which serve the same articulating purpose in the C Major String Quintet of 1828 (m. 118–122)."

The wealth of musical ideas in the first movement of this E-flat sonata is balanced by an admirable use of such unifying motives as the ascending triad, which appears as a structural element of the main theme, in the transition (measures 28 onward), and in the closing theme (measures 88–98). The epilog theme, starting in measure 102, picks up the rhythm of the subsidiary theme, a *Ländler* in measures 41–58 (Example 4.9).

The second movement, a deeply moving lament, is based on a progression that Beethoven also repeatedly used (for example in the Adagio of his Sonata op. 10 no. 1; there, however, in the major key). Schubert sketched the first draft of this movement in D minor (and also the C-sharp minor Andante of the Sonata D 567) on the outer pages of a double sheet

EXAMPLE 4.9. Schubert, Sonata in E♭ major, D 568, movt. 1 (mm. 41–49)

containing a Beethoven autograph of his song "Adelaide." (Later Brahms acquired this valuable double autograph and added his signature, thus creating a unique document in music history: the writings of three great composers on the same sheet of paper.)

Today, scholars concur that in the agitated second section of this slow movement all dotted notes are meant as triplets. This has been justly pointed out by Howard Ferguson in his edition of Schubert's sonatas.[10] The engraver of the Henle edition (vol. I), however, unfortunately insists here on a "mathematical" arrangement which in measure 49 and measures 57–61 produces plain nonsense (Example 4.10). Even in the Menuetto—one of the few genuinely slower minuets in Schubert's output—most of the dotted rhythms should be rendered as triplets.

The last movement returns to the rising triadic motive of the opening Allegro and achieves miracles of beautiful sounds by combining it with the *perpetuum mobile* figure in sixteenth notes. The development of this movement introduces a new theme, a delightful Viennese waltz, and the sonata ends with a smile, as it were, fading away *pianissimo*. There is a strong resemblance to the ending of Beethoven's Sonata op. 7 in the same key. One is (anachronistically) inclined again to label Beethoven's closing "Schubertian" rather than to discover a Beethoven imitation in Schubert.

SONATA NO. 8 IN F-SHARP MINOR D 571/604/570 (HENLE EDITION III/7)

This sonata needs a truly "romantic" interpretation in order to convince and to move.

From the appearance of the autograph, the slow movement of the sonata would seem to be missing, but it is not. At the same time that Paul Badura-Skoda discovered that the movement D 604 belongs to this sonata, Maurice Brown wrote:

> Here knowledge of Schubert's methods in 1817 points to the fact that the missing movement is an Andante in A, D 604. For reasons of economy, the composer used the blank pages from earlier manuscripts for his sketches and fair copies; the Andante is written on the back of an empty leaf found in sketches for the Overture in B flat, D 470. The overture was composed in September 1816, and the Andante must be of a later date— presumably of the same period as the rest of the sonata, June 1817. In style and beauty the A-major Andante fits the other three movements like a glove; it is one of the loveliest inspirations of Schubert's early years, and I for one would willingly accept far flimsier reasons than these for its inclusion in the f-sharp minor Sonata, if thereby it can emerge from obscurity. Paul Badura-Skoda has completed the fragmentary first and last movements, which gives us the opportunity to hear this original and graceful example of an early Schubert sonata.[11]

The Andante D 604 fits "like a glove" because it starts with an interrupted cadence in F-sharp minor, a passage that by itself makes little sense. Schu-

EXAMPLE 4.10a. Schubert, Sonata in E♭ major, D 568, movt. 2 (m. 49),
Henle Edition: incorrect placement of notes

EXAMPLE 4.10b. Schubert, Sonata in E♭ major, D 568, movt. 2 (m. 49),
Associated Board Edition: correct placement of notes

EXAMPLE 4.10c. Schubert, Sonata in E♭ major, D 568, movt. 2 (mm. 55–60),
Henle Edition: incorrect placement of notes

bert used the same harmonic procedure to connect the last two movements of his Sonata in B-flat major for four hands D 617, a work also written in 1818.

In the history of the expansion of classical sonata form into its romantic sequel, Schubert's long harmonic routes to the dominant at the
end of the exposition occupy a crucial position. Miriam Whaples writes:

> But equally expansive, and equally important in the 1817–18
> sonatas, is the practice, derived this time from Haydn, of artic-
> ulating between the theme-groups *within* the dominant section
> by means of another tonal excursion. Nowhere is this more
> highly elaborated than in the F Minor Sonata, where, between
> the secondary and closing themes of the exposition, both in A-
> flat, appears a development—completely independent of the
> formal development section following the double bar—which
> introduces a strictly symmetrical arrangement of third-related
> keys as follows: C-flat, A-flat minor, F-flat (written as E). (Wha-
> ples, 35–36)

The F-sharp minor Sonata is Schubert's only solo piano sonata to begin
with a lied-like opening, prepared by four measures of accompaniment to
create "the atmosphere," as Schubert does so often in his songs. (A parallel can be found in Schubert's Sonata in A major for Violin and Piano D
574, dating from August 1817 and posthumously published as a "Duo"
instead of "Sonata.") The dreamlike opening of the F-sharp minor Sonata, though undoubtably idiomatic, seems to foreshadow Schumann.
The repeated C-sharp notes of the main theme reappear in the form of a
Leitmotiv in the final Rondo, but here the motive is transformed into a sort
of country dance.

The Scherzo is truly "Viennese." It was written (probably by error)
on the back page of a double sheet of music paper. Therefore, Schubert
had to write the final Allegro on the remaining pages 1–3, thus creating
the false impression that the Scherzo came after the Allegro.

SONATA NO. 9 IN B MAJOR D 575 (HENLE EDITION I/3)

For this sonata, first published in 1846 as op. 147, there survive a
first incomplete draft in Schubert's hand and two copies of the finished
version made by friends, one dated August 1817 (Vienna, Archive of the
Gesellschaft der Musikfreunde) and the other headed in Albert Stadler's
writing "Franz Schubert, 1818, August" (University Library, Lund, Sweden, Taussig Estate). The autograph of the finished version is lost. There
are quite a number of subtle differences between the first draft and the
finished sonata. For instance, in the first incomplete draft the recapitulation starts in the tonic key B major and not in the subdominant E major as
in the final version.

The first movement begins with a considerable impetus, with the widest (and wildest) leaps possible—and it ends with a gentle *pianissimo* murmur. In between are a serene march and a liedlike secondary theme. This diversity is matched by the unusual tonal scheme mentioned above. The first movement seems to re-create especially the various changing moods of adolescence that can be observed to a lesser degree also in the ensuing movements. Thus, the Andante in $\frac{3}{4}$ time changes to a $\frac{4}{4}$ time (mm. 77 onward) which is rather unusual in a "classic" sonata. The liedlike Scherzo is distinguished by its long rests and beautiful flowing Trio. The spirited last movement again has a Scherzo character, deepening the impression that this is an unusual sonata.

Sonata No. 10 in C Major D 613/612 (Henle Edition III/8)

There can hardly be any doubt that the Adagio D 612 belongs to this sonata. As in similar cases, this movement was published separately after Schubert's death, because the two outer movements had remained "unfinished"; in both, however, Schubert had written out nearly the complete exposition and development sections before stopping work at the beginning of the recapitulation.

This sonata is a truly experimental work, introducing fast chromatic runs, odd modulations, and difficult chords, features one might rather associate with Weber or Chopin than with Schubert. The second subject of the first movement shows a typical polonaise rhythm. One of the "odd" passages in the third movement is progressive, indeed, even "futuristic" (see Example 4.11). Some other ideas (for example, the romantic modulation from C major to E minor at mm. 5–8 of the final Rondo) are very attractive (Example 4.12). They make even this least successful sonata of Schubert worth hearing.

Sonata No. 11 in F Minor D 625/505 (Henle Edition III/9)

Even though the autograph of the Sonata D 625 is missing, the Adagio D 505 is listed as the second movement of this sonata in a thematic catalog of Schubert's works compiled after his death by his brother Ferdinand, thus confirming that D 505 belongs to D 625.

In his edition of this sonata (which contains his completion of the first movement), Paul Badura-Skoda suggests that the Adagio be played *after* the Scherzo as the third movement, notwithstanding the order given in Ferdinand's catalogue. He argues that otherwise a sequence of two quiet and two agitated movements would result, and he refers to the fact that Schubert himself had reversed the order of the inner movements in the two versions of his B-major sonata D 575. Also, in Schubert's "Duo" D 574 the Scherzo appears as the second movement.

This somber, tragic sonata is unique in many ways. The first and last movements seem to contain the germ of Chopin's Sonata in B-flat minor

EXAMPLE 4.11. Schubert, Sonata in C major, D 613, movt. 2 (mm. 73–80)

op. 35 (though, of course, Chopin could not possibly have known Schubert's sonata, which was not published until the end of the nineteenth century). Also, the *unisono* brooding beginning of the finale forecasts later romantic works; this time one is reminded of the last movement of Brahms's B-major Trio op. 8. The Scherzo, a wild piece in the unusual key of E major, goes up to the high G-sharp[4], a note not found on pianos before about 1850! The Adagio (related to the Andante of D 575) is perhaps the least inspired movement of this sonata; yet, its presence provides a needed point of respite.

SONATA NO. 12 IN A MAJOR D 664 (HENLE EDITION I/4)

According to a letter by Albert Stadler, this sonata was composed in 1819. Schindler, who obviously had no idea of Schubert's style, placed it in

EXAMPLE 4.12. Schubert, Sonata in C major, D 613, movt. 2 (mm. 5–8)

1825, a date that is quite impossible, for by that time Schubert had developed a completely different and more expansive piano style.

Gentle and unassuming, this A-major sonata is a masterpiece. Beneath its smooth surface lies a hidden depth that erupts occasionally in dramatic outbursts; nevertheless, it would be wrong to play the sonata in a "profound" manner with a heavy touch and too slow a tempo. (For the "innocent" Andante a proper tempo in Viennese style is ♩ = 63).

The singing liedlike opening theme of the Allegro moderato sets the mood for the entire first movement. In the development section, after a passage in canonic initiation, an ascending triplet figure from the exposition (measure 20) is dramatically enlarged into octave runs in both hands. Here Schubert uses a "modern" device, "splitting" the G sharp into its two neighboring half steps G and A, a procedure repeated later by Chopin and Bruckner.

The two closing notes of the first movement, B and A, lead in a most natural way to the beginning of the Andante with the same two notes one octave higher. Still one octave higher—and we have the opening notes of the concluding Allegro (see Example 4.13).

The gentle singing Andante, which starts with a seven-measure phrase, is one of Schubert's most inspired movements. It breathes the pious religious atmosphere often encountered in Schubert's instrumental

EXAMPLE 4.13. Schubert, Sonata in A major, D 664, movt. 1, Andante, Allegro (mm. 130–133, 1–4, 74–75, 1–2)

works, reminding us of the impression of Robert Schumann in his famous review of Schubert's C-major Symphony, in which he wrote of a "fine fragrance of incense" permeating the Austrian landscape with its many chapels. The Andante comes to a peaceful close after an outcry of anguish at the recapitulation of the theme.

The final Allegro is dancelike throughout, comparable in spirit to Mozart's finale movements in $\frac{6}{8}$ meter. However, the second theme is a genuine Viennese waltz for which one does not find a parallel in the earlier works of the master. Its exuberant outburst near the close foreshadows passages in Schumann's *Carnaval*.

Sonatas of the Middle Period

SONATA NO. 13 IN A MINOR D 784 (HENLE EDITION I/5)

Few words justly convey the tragedy expressed in this sonata, which well deserves the epithet "The Tragic." The opening theme reminds the Schubert lover of the song "Der Zwerg" D 771 (composed together with the song "Wehmut" D 772 during the winter of 1822–23, when Schubert must have realized that he would never be able to lead a healthy, normal life). The similarity—the song is also in the key of A minor—is better heard than described; it is the dark mood, the hopeless despair, that characterizes the song as well as the sonata. Schubert's own words written one year later to Leopold Kupelwieser (in a letter dated 31 March 1824) might perhaps depict best the suffering expressed in this work:

> In a word, I feel myself to be the most unhappy and wretched creature in the world. Imagine a man whose health will never be right again . . . to whom the felicity of love and friendship has nothing to offer but pain . . . *My peace is gone, my heart is sore, I shall find it never and nevermore.* I may well sing every day now, for each night, on retiring to bed, I hope I may not wake again.

Schubert pushes all conventions aside in this sonata and develops a pianistic texture that finds its counterpart perhaps only in certain works by Modest Mussorgksy, another "unhappy creature." Passages such as the one in Example 4.14 are unique in piano literature.

The first movement (one of the most densely constructed movements in the whole of piano literature) presents a succession and elaboration of sigh motives derived from measures 2 and 4 of the opening theme. A giant of a pianist with an iron rhythm is required to weld these innumerable sighs together into a whole. In contrast, the "orchestral" entry in E major leading to the second theme seems to express the words of the *Te Deum,* "Non confundar in aeternum" ("I shall not perish in eternity")—see measures 53–54 of Example 4.14.

The Andante movement that follows impresses as a vain attempt by friends or by nature to console "the wretched soul." An uncanny *pianissimo* motive marked *con sordini* continually interrupts (and disrupts) a "springtime" melody (Example 4.15). In measures 7 and 8 Schubert invented a harmonic progression that, fifty years later, became a "property" of Brahms.

The beginning of the last movement evokes the impression of snowflakes gently covering a flowery spring landscape. Technically this opening foreshadows Smetana's symphonic poem *Vltava (The Moldau).* But the soft beginning only precedes an all-devastating storm. The second subject, given three times, recalls the "Death's cradle song" ("Todeswiegen"), already encountered in the earlier A-minor Sonata D 537 (Example 4.16).

EXAMPLE 4.14. Schubert, Sonata in A minor, D 784, movt. 1 (mm. 38–61)

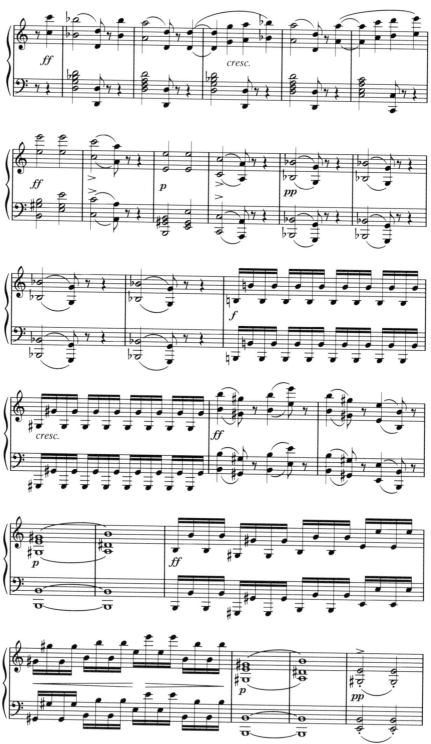

EXAMPLE 4.15. Schubert, Sonata in A minor, D 784, Andante (mm. 1–10)

EXAMPLE 4.16. Schubert, Sonata in A minor, D 784, movt. 3 (mm. 51–59)

SONATA NO. 14 IN C MAJOR D 840 (*RELIQUIE* SONATA, HENLE EDITION III/10)

This sonata, composed in April 1825, was first published by F. Whistling (Leipzig) in 1861 with the mistaken title "Schubert's Last Sonata." The publisher apparently wanted to explain why only its first two large-scaled movements are complete. Schubert, however, had nearly finished the third movement, a Menuetto with the tempo indication Allegretto. Only the final movement in sonata form, in which each theme appears as if part of a miniature rondo, breaks off in the middle of the development, thus being left incomplete, indeed. Evidently Schubert found the thematic material (related somewhat to the finale of Beethoven's C-major Sonata op. 2 no. 3) too trivial compared to that of the opening movements.

Of the several attempts to complete the work, those by Ernst Krenek (1921) and Paul Badura-Skoda (1976) deserve attention. Krenek uses the material in a free, romantic way, whereas Badura-Skoda remains far closer to Schubert's own musical style and pianistic idiom. For the completion of the Menuetto, which breaks off at the key of the lowered supertonic, he uses a procedure found in Schubert's sixth *Moment Musical* in the same key.

As in D 784, the first movement of this sonata sounds like a piano reduction of a symphony. Again, this composition somehow foreshadows Mussorgsky's *Pictures at an Exhibition*, yet, strangely enough, as in the case of Mussorgsky, such a technique loses its impact if orchestrated (even if a master like Maurice Ravel is the orchestrator). Why is this so? Perhaps the piano evokes or suggests a "heavenly orchestra" that can exist only in the listener's imagination. Less orchestral and more pianistic is the utterly beautiful second movement of this sonata, which starts like a paraphrase of Pamina's aria in G minor, "Ach, ich fühls, es ist verschwunden," from Mozart's *Magic Flute*.

SONATA NO. 15 IN A MINOR D 845 (HENLE EDITION I/6)

During April and May of 1825, Schubert wrote another A-minor sonata, which was soon published in Vienna (March 1826) as his *Première grande sonate* with a dedication to the Archduke Rudolph. This was Schubert's first piano sonata to be published, and it met with immediate success: "In the matter of expression and technique, although it preserves a praiseworthy unity, it moves so freely and originally within its confines, and sometimes so boldly and curiously, that it might not unjustly have been called a Fantasy. In that respect it can probably be compared only with the greatest and freest of Beethoven's sonatas." So one reviewer reported in the Leipzig *Allgemeine musikalische Zeitung* on 1 March 1826.

This work is noted for its concentrated form and unity of thematic material. The first movement is based on only two rhythmic ideas; the subsidiary and closing subjects are derived from the opening theme. This return to a nearly monothematic sonata form (of course, the marchlike modulating section *is* in fact based on a different theme) can be seen also in Haydn's last sonatas and symphonies. Schubert thus returns here to a pre-Beethoven concept of unity to achieve a strong control of form. In the development, Schubert proved that he could write—when he wished to—a development *à la* Beethoven: We find a typical Beethovenian elaboration of the main theme with its fragmentation into small particles. And yet the work is as truly in Schubert's own language as is any of his other works. No one but Schubert could write the exciting coda, which, through a series of fantastic harmonic progressions, rises from the darkest register to a most powerful climax. The welding together of the development and the recapitulation is another striking feature of this Allegro moderato. The *Allabreve* sign at its beginning should encourage performers not to play it too slowly.

The second movement, an *Andante con mosso* in the relative key of C major, is a variation movement that suggests a mood of comfort and relaxation. With its repeated G at the beginning, it bears a certain resemblance to the *Arietta* of Beethoven's Piano Sonata Op. 111, which has the same meter and key. But whereas Beethoven seeks redemption from suffering through an exaltation of the spirit, turning his mind to the higher spheres, Schubert seems to find relaxation in the realm of nature, which is also eternal and divine. The last variation of the Andante bears witness to this.

The autograph of the sonata is lost. Paul Badura-Skoda was the first to discover that in this movement, apparently due to an engraver's oversight, four bars are missing in the first variation.[12] No Viennese composer of the classical period would purposely shorten the first variation. Such engraving mistakes happened not infrequently and must be remedied, of course (Schumann once found a similar mistake in the first edition of Mozart's G-minor Symphony K. 550). Paul Badura-Skoda's reconstruction of these bars is printed in the Henle edition. A slightly different solution for their reconstruction is suggested by Howard Ferguson in his Associated Board edition of Schubert's sonatas.

The energetic Scherzo is contrasted with a sublime unearthly Trio, which seems to symbolize the journey of the soul to faraway lands where neither joy nor sorrow can penetrate (Example 4.17).

The last movement, in rondo form, is one of Schubert's most elaborate movements. All its themes are based on a single melodic device, a diatonic four-note motive, either in descending or ascending order. The ascending version gains predominance in the central A-major section, which also provides a light contrast to the prevailing dark mood. After the return to the original key of A-minor, the two forms of the main motive, descending and ascending, are directly opposed to each other in strident contrapuntal clashes. From this point until the very end, these two themes are constantly interwoven; finally they are torn into small segments in a whirlwind, a kind of *danse macabre*, that brings the work to a shattering close.

EXAMPLE 4.17. Schubert, Sonata in A minor, D 845, Trio (mm. 127–50)

SONATA NO. 16 IN D MAJOR D 850 (*GASTEIN* SONATA, HENLE EDITION I/7)

This sonata was composed during a holiday in August 1825 in Gastein, Austria (hence its name). It was published as Schubert's *Seconde grande sonate* in Vienna in April 1826 with the opus number 53 and was dedicated to Carl Maria von Bocklet, a professional pianist who became Schubert's friend (Bocklet later participated in the first performance of the E-flat major Piano Trio in the only public concert Schubert arranged himself).

The *Gastein* Sonata is perhaps Schubert's happiest piano work. If the exuberant first movement seems to depict a sunlit mountain landscape, the second movement, an Andante, evokes a feeling of pious meditation in the woods, a scene for which Thomas Merton might be the predestined author to find the proper description. Throughout this sonata an element of the "Austrian symphonic style" is prevalent: the mere joy of harmony. One is reminded of a Bruckner anecdote. As a friend recalled, Bruckner once played repeatedly a chord in D-flat major exclaiming: "Isn't it beautiful?" This parallel is significant: In works of this kind the mere beauty of harmonies and harmonic progressions assumes an importance similar to the thematic process in works by Beethoven. Often Schubert enriches the harmony through an unexpected, colorful modulation *(Ausweichung)* into a mediant tonality, or through just a touch of such a key in a subject (as for instance in measure 7 of the theme of the second movement).[14]

The third movement, an extended Scherzo, is in fact, a Czech *furiant,* and its Trio is like a litany sung in church. As mentioned before, its melodic germ is derived from material of Schubert's first piano sonata, D 157.

The last movement, a Rondo, starts like a hiking song, depicting the serene wayfarer enjoying the marvels of wandering with new outlooks on a beautiful landscape at every turn of the road (Example 4.18; see also

EXAMPLE 4.18. Schubert, Sonata in D major, D 850, Rondo

Illustration 4.1a and 4.1b). The second episode might evoke the feeling of a boat ride on a lake, and the end seems to suggest joyful dancing. In this movement Schubert proves himself more typically Austrian than anywhere else in his sonatas. To a lover of that kind of music, Joseph Haydn's last symphony in D major, Hob. I/104, might come to mind.

ILLUSTRATION 4.1. Schubert, Sonata in D major D 850. a. Rondo b. Enlargement of mm. 3–5. Reproduced courtesy of the Österreichische Nationalbibliothek, Vienna.

SONATA NO. 17 IN G MAJOR D 894 (HENLE EDITION II/8)

In the autograph Schubert entitled this sonata *IV. Sonate für das Pianoforte allein* and added the date "October 1826." Because of the Viennese publisher's reluctance to accept Schubert's idea of a sonata, it was published in Vienna in April 1827 as *Fantasie, Andante, Menuetto und Allegretto* op. 78 with a dedication to Joseph Edlen von Spaun. As for the number

"IV," we do not know which sonata Schubert intended to publish as no. III. Perhaps he had already given a manuscript of one of the earlier sonatas to a Viennese publisher who rejected it. But which one? Most likely, at this point in his career Schubert considered the unpublished Sonata in A minor D 784 as the contender for no. III, and, perhaps, he even intended to disown all his other sonatas.

There is an undeniable resemblance between the first movement, in sonata form (no fantasy at all!), and the opening movement of Beethoven's Fourth Piano Concerto. Both start with the same G-major triad, and both let the piano sing like "a lark in the sky." Yet the mere *sound* of Schubert's chord is even more beautiful than Beethoven's; Schubert does not double the third in the lower octave (Examples 4.19a–b). The contemplative mood of this opening gradually gives way to the dancelike subsidiary theme. Several gigantic outbursts of energy occur in the development before the movement ends in total calm.

After the extended first movement follows a rather fluid light Andante in $\frac{3}{8}$, which more than once foreshadows Gustav Mahler in his idyllic mood. The conventional roles of the first and second movement are

EXAMPLE 4.19a. Schubert, Sonata in G major, D 894, movt. 1 (mm. 1–5)

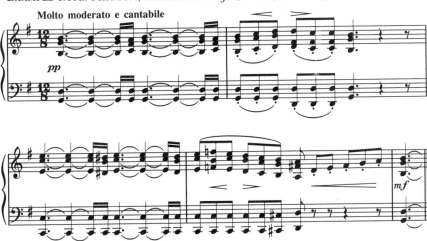

EXAMPLE 4.19b. Beethoven, Piano Concerto No. 4 Op. 58, movt. 1 (mm. 1–5)

nearly reversed: the Andante sustains a more active motion throughout than the restrained first movement with its heading *Molto moderato e cantabile,* and the tranquility that marks its beginning and ending. (Interestingly enough, in the first edition of this Andante Schubert eliminated all the turns he had written in the autograph [e.g., measure 3]. In my opinion it is indeed a mistake to reinstate these turns in modern editions.)

The Menuetto became celebrated and something of a popular hit in the nineteenth century. Brahms paid a tribute to the Trio by imitating its harmonic progressions in his first Rhapsody op. 79 no. 1 in the same key of B major. The last movement is a "nature song" containing elements of the hurdy-gurdy and popular march music, the song "Frühlingssehnsucht" (D 957 No. 3), tears, and smiles. No one but Schubert could unite such a diversity of thoughts and moods!

Sonatas of the Late Period

The last three sonatas are well-known works. In spite of their "heavenly length" (Schumann) and their technical difficulty, by now they belong to the standard repertoire of pianists. Schubert habitually drafted compositions of this scope and importance but apparently did not always keep these drafts. Fortunately, in this case sketches of all three sonatas are extant, and recently they were published in a facsimile edition. A comparison between draft and fair copy gives interesting insights into Schubert's method of composition. As in the drafts of the E-flat major Trio D 929, Schubert invented more thematic material than necessary; thus, some musical ideas in the drafts were ultimately abandoned, while others appeared in slightly varied ways.

There is a striking resemblance between the circumstances surrounding the creation of Mozart's last three symphonies and Schubert's last three piano sonatas. Both cycles were created in an incredibly short period of time and represent the undisputed peak in the composers' symphonic and pianistic outputs. The creation of works of such magnitude in only a few weeks is miraculous.[13] Each group consists of one tragic work in a minor key and two more serene major-key works. But there are some differences: Mozart still had three years to live after having finished his cycle, whereas Schubert died only six weeks after completing these three sonatas. This accounts, perhaps, for the character of vigorous self-assertion in Mozart's *Jupiter* Symphony versus the serene resignation in Schubert's last sonata—the wayfarer bids farewell at the end of his life's journey.

By Schubert's lifetime the dualistic thematicism of the early classical sonata had systematically been enlarged to accommodate the principle of ternary structure in sonata form. This process was developed mainly by Beethoven; it culminated in Bruckner's and Mahler's symphonies. In the last group of sonatas Schubert wrote three distinct themes or groups of themes in his sonata-form movements. Moreover, most of the subjects appear not only twice but three times. For a detailed analysis the interested reader is referred to Arthur Godel's book *Schuberts letzte drei Klaviersonaten.*

Sonata No. 18 in C minor D 958 (Henle Edition II/9)

The C-minor Sonata D 958 is one of Schubert's darkest works and is even more somber in content than the *Death and the Maiden* String Quartet. Despite an energetic powerful opening, its first movement ends as hopelessly as any music can. The main theme has been compared by some commentators with Beethoven's Thirty-two Variations in the same key. Though the rhythm of both works suggests that of a sarabande, other resemblances are rather superficial. While Beethoven's theme ascends only to the sixth above, Schubert's subject rises like a rocket over more than two octaves (Example 4.20). In one of his last songs ("Der Atlas" D 957/8), Schubert used a similar rhythm most effectively. The key to understanding the song as well as the sonata theme is the phrase "Die ganze Welt der Schmerzen muß ich tragen" ("I must carry the entire world of pain"; Example 4.21). The second subject enters after a general pause (measure 39). In total contrast to the energetic, detached first theme, it has a "feminine" character, tranquil and legato, based on a most beautiful melody in E-flat major. Everything seems to be peaceful until the uncanny shift from E flat to D flat creates the impression of unworldliness; time is interrupted, life faces death. If these two measures were left out, nothing harmonic would be missing; yet the essential message would be lost.

The Adagio, one of the few genuine Adagio movements Schubert wrote, is like a prayer over "De profundis." It is followed by a sad, melancholy minuet and a gigantic, powerful finale based on a tireless, sustained tarantella rhythm (incidentally, this is the only external resemblance to the finale of Beethoven's op. 31 no. 3, with which the finale is often mistakenly compared). This movement suggests riding through a dark and never-ending night. Only at the center of the movement is the tarantella rhythm briefly interrupted by a magical B-major section that is like a dream of a distant past happiness, a dream gradually dispelled in one of the longest sustained crescendos in piano literature. The end of this movement, and thus of the sonata, recalls the haunted spirit of a *danse macabre.*

Sonata No. 19 in A major D 959 (Henle Edition II/10)

Though the second sonata of the final group has always been overshadowed in popularity by her more gentle sister, no. 20 in B-flat major, it is in no way inferior. It is a lofty work that attains the highest peaks of expression. "Lofty" is indeed the term that comes to mind when we consider the powerful, awe-inspiring opening theme of the first movement. No other word can aptly describe the crystalline beauty and purity of the

EXAMPLE 4.20. Schubert, Sonata in C minor, D 958, movt. 1 (mm. 1–21)

EXAMPLE 4.21. Schubert, "Der Atlas," D 957/8 (mm. 1–4, 49–56)

second subject or the "wanderings into distant countries" of the development. One more blissful moment of this movement needs to be mentioned: At the very end, the "lofty" theme is stated again, this time in a mysterious *pianissimo*. It is like a serene farewell.

If ever sadness was expressed in music, it was expressed in the Andantino movement where a sorrowful melody is "sung" in F-sharp minor and A major alternately. The new harmonization in A major, however, gives the melody such a different meaning that one barely recognizes it—a striking example of the expressive power of harmony in classical music. The middle section of the Andantino, a "chromatic fantasy," is one of Schubert's boldest pages, perhaps a stark vision of all the horrors of war and destruction, of the day of judgment, the *dies irae*. After this eruption, an equally dramatic recitative leads back to the immensely sad theme in the recapitulation. The contrast is comparable to the Andante movement of Beethoven's Piano Concerto No. 4 in G major with its pleading "soloist" and the orchestra's firm answers: "No."

After this visionary movement the Scherzo brings us "back to earth." But in such a context it would be too simple merely to write a charming Viennese dance movement. Behind Schubert's apparent ease there is a note of nostalgia, and a sudden descending scale in *fortissimo* reminds us of past horrors—it is, *nota bene,* the same C-sharp minor scale that had marked the climax of the second movement.

The Rondo finale contains one of Schubert's most beautiful liedlike themes, evoking the joys of spring and peace. It is nearly identical to the *Allegretto quasi Andantino* from the Sonata op. 164 D 537 of March 1817. But a lifetime of creative work lies between the movements. Promise becomes fulfillment, so that the later movement is in every respect fuller and richer. How exquisite is the counterpoint Schubert devises when the theme is quoted in the baritone register! Again, Schubert invites us to follow the wanderings of his soul. For a last time, in the development, the dark brooding region of C-sharp minor is reached again—and surpassed. For a last time, the mystery of another world touches the music and brings it to a standstill, as in the coda of the first movement. In a sense, the last pages summarize the whole musical and spiritual experience of this magnificent work. Thus it is only fitting that the very last chords recall the lofty theme with which the sonata began—from Eternity to Eternity.

Sonata No. 20 in B-flat major D 960 (Henle Edition II/11)

The opening of Schubert's last sonata has the majesty and calm with which man should face his final moments. It closely resembles the opening stanza of Schubert's lied "Am Meer" (D 957/12) from the same year, 1828: "Das Meer erglänzte weit hinab im letzten Abendscheine" ("The sea was shining in the last glow of the sunset"). The last glow evokes an infinite sense of beauty, of nostalgia, of memories and regret; and precisely these emotions seem to be represented in the first movement, where the calm of the opening gives way to a process of intensification. In the development the Mozartian third subject is gradually transformed until it becomes nearly identical to the opening lines of the lied "Der Wanderer," expressing the grief of the homeless wayfarer. Schubert's quotation of his celebrated early song (D 489) leads to a powerful climax that symbolizes anguish and despair. Only gradually does the storm subside and the calm of the opening return.

The second movement, *Andante sostenuto,* is considered by many musicians to be the crown of Schubert's piano music. (See Illustration 4.2.) It is a lament in the distant key of C-sharp minor with a comforting middle section in A major related to the music of "Der Lindenbaum" from *Die Winterreise,* where nature (the tree) consoles the unhappy pilgrim: ". . . und seine Zweige rauschten, als riefen sie mir zu, 'Komm her zu mir, Geselle, hier findst Du deine Ruh' " (". . . and its branches rustled, as if they called to me, 'Come here to me, lad, here you'll find peace' "). The lament returns, but gradually the minor key gives way to the major (C and C-sharp major), and the movement ends blissfully.

The sonata could very well end here, thus resembling somewhat Beethoven's last piano sonata, op. 111. However, Schubert intended to bring the listener back to earth, ever so gently and gradually. The unearthly Scherzo (*con delicatezza*) with its more somber, pensive, subdued Trio prepares the way for the Rondo.

This Rondo finale opens with a question mark in C minor, rather like a "false" entrance—which is, however, affirmatively answered by the cadence in B-flat major. The opening remarkably resembles that of Beethoven's last finished composition, the finale he wrote for the String Quartet in B-flat major op. 130 to replace the *Grosse Fuge.* The transcendent quality of Schubert's finale is indescribable. Again the eternal wayfarer is invoked, but here without any sense of resignation or bitterness. There are turbulent passages, too, and the interruptions at the end taste a little like death. But the sonata concludes positively, in a mood of happiness, with an exuberant presto outburst.

The Fantasies

Three complete fantasies for piano solo by Schubert have survived: an early one in C minor D 2E (formerly D 993), a newly discovered one in C major D 605A (*Grazer* Fantasy), and the famous one in C major D 760, published in 1823 as op. 15, the so-called *Wanderer* Fantasy. There existed perhaps another Fantasy in E-flat major (D Anhang I,10; described in 1923 by W. Pauker). Supposedly it was composed in 1825 in Gmunden; today it is lost.

The C-minor Fantasy D 2E is one of Schubert's earliest known compositions. It clearly shows the influence of Mozart studies yet looks ahead to Schubert's own pianistic style. Its first printed version appeared in an article by Jörg Demus (1978/79).

Illustration 4.2. Schubert, Sonata in B-flat major D 960, middle section of the second movement; autograph. In m. 86 (penultimate system, 1st bar) Schubert clearly wrote the notes d[1] on the third beat; nearly all editions have here incorrectly C-sharp. The placement of the thirty-second notes leaves no doubt that Schubert wanted them to be played as sixteenth triplets throughout. Reproduced by permission of the Österreichische Nationalbibliothek, Vienna.

*Fantasy in C major D 605A (*Grazer *Fantasy)*

This beautiful work was probably composed in 1818. It was discovered only in 1969 in the estate of Rudolf von Weis-Ostborn (from Graz, Austria, hence the title) in a copy, the title page of which was written by Schubert's friend Josef Hüttenbrenner. The title reads: *Fantasie für das Pianoforte Componirt von Franz Schubert;* a note underneath, also written by Hüttenbrenner, informs us that he once lent the original manuscript to Professor Pirkert.

Undoubtedly a genuine work of Schubert, the fantasy greatly resembles other piano works of the year 1818. Typical features include chromatic runs and a use of the polonaise rhythm (see the Rondo for Piano *à 4* in D major D 608 and the Sonata in C major D 613/612). This fantasy is composed in a cyclic form: the opening elegiac *bel canto* theme reappears toward the end, where it fades away in a nostalgic mood. Actually the form is fairly complex: what we have is a free rondo form in which parts of the main theme reappear "in disguise" in different keys and rhythmic variations, separated by "free" episodes, such as the refreshing *alla polacca* in the distant key of F-sharp major (measure 55), and the virtuoso episode in G major reminiscent of Carl Maria von Weber toward the end. The theme itself is a kind of Rossini-like march, though it also resembles a characteristic motive in Beethoven's Triple Concerto, op. 56. The "hidden" reprises of the theme occur in the A-flat major section (measure 129) and the E-major section (measure 213); fragments of the main theme, however, appear throughout the work, a technique that foreshadows the later *Wanderer* Fantasy.

Fantasy in C major D 760 (Wanderer *Fantasy)*

In November 1822, Schubert rapidly composed his *Wanderer* Fantasy, his most monumental and most technically demanding piano composition. It occupies a special position, not only among Schubert's works but doubtless as one of the most important piano compositions of all times. Its creation can be viewed as a turning point in Schubert's career. Written during the period of crisis in 1822 and 1823, it belongs to a series of works distinguished by enormous emotional tension, dramatic power, and concise, audacious construction. Composed during the same year as Beethoven's last piano sonata, the fantasy points to the future in a decisive manner scarcely equaled by any other work of the time. The seeds of the symphonic development of the nineteenth century are present, from the new formal design of the fantasy to the rhythmic motive present in all four sections (or quasi movements) of the work. In Elaine Brody's view,

> From its innovative design spring such musical landmarks as Liszt's B-Minor Sonata, his E-flat Concerto, and the vast literature of symphonic poems including those by Liszt and Richard

Strauss. With only a slight stretch of the imagination, Wagner's "Leitmotive[-technique]" and Franck's cyclical works, beginning with his F-Minor Trio of 1841, can be seen as an extension of Schubert's inventive technique. With unexpected boldness Schubert seized the chisel from Beethoven and sculpted a work whose significance cannot be overemphasized. Through his use of thematic transformation, the composer achieved thematic unity and formal cohesion in the several movements of a large work by interrelating these sections through expansion, contraction and fragmentation of one and the same melody. (Brody, 24).

The rhythmic motive with which the fantasy starts dominates especially the first section. Only in the Adagio is this motive easily recognized as a quotation from the well-known song "Der Wanderer" (hence the name; see Example 4.22). The main focus of interest concerns the words "die Sonne dünkt mich hier so kalt" ("the sun here seems to me so cold"). Here, in the Adagio, the quotation appears in the same tempo and mood as in the lied. Thus, it is recognized far more easily than in the first movement, and the subject corresponds especially well to the mood of the poem.

In its grandiose "orchestral" use of the piano, Schubert's *Wanderer* Fantasy stands as a guidepost to the future. Recognized as a masterpiece immediately after its appearance in February 1823, it was greeted enthusiastically in the *Wiener Zeitung*, and, on 30 April 1823, in the Leipzig *Allgemeine musikalische Zeitung*. Such critical acclaim is remarkable, for the fantasy must have sounded surprisingly modern to the ears of contemporary listeners.

The *Wanderer* Fantasy influenced Liszt in several ways, not only in the form of his symphonic poems. The use of mediant relationships may be traced back to Schubert's work. Liszt also arranged Schubert's fantasy as a piano concerto—an enterprise, however, that was not too successful, insofar as Schubert's work was altered so much that it became more an idiomatic piece of Liszt than of Schubert.

Other Piano Pieces

For approximately a century after Schubert's death, his miscellaneous piano pieces were nearly his only piano works that were occasionally heard in public. The *Impromptus* and *Moments Musicaux* have remained "evergreens" in the repertoire of pianists and amateurs and have retained an appeal comparable to that of Schubert's most popular songs. Indeed, in some of these pieces the songlike element is so overtly felt that they might easily be termed "songs without words."

That other equally fine solo pieces failed to gain as much popularity as the *Impromptus* and *Moments Musicaux* was due to the fact that for a long period they remained unknown. Thus, the masterly *Drei Klavierstücke* op.

EXAMPLE 4.22. Schubert, "Der Wanderer," D 489 (mm. 23–31)

posth. D 946 were published only in 1868 (Brahms was their first editor), and the two incomplete *Impromptus* in C major D 916B and C minor D 916C (1827) appeared only in 1978! When Jörg Demus completed them in 1986, he titled them Schubert's *Sonate oubliée* and proposed as a middle movement the *Allegretto* in C minor D 900. Let us take a closer look at the most important collections of these shorter pieces for piano.

Six Moments Musicaux D 789 (op. 94)

We know little about the history of the *Moments Musicaux*. Even such questions as whether they were conceived as a cycle or conceived in their present order remain unanswered. After nos. 3 and 6 appeared separately in 1823 and 1824 (their titles were not Schubert's but an invention of the publishers), and when all six were published as a set in 1828, they immediately became favorites of the musical public in Vienna and elsewhere. Some reveal one special feature characteristic of Schubert, his fondness of nature, a trait that often comes to the fore in his lieder but also in his instrumental chamber music. Like Beethoven, Schubert was a genuine wanderer who turned to nature as a constant source of inspiration and consolation. Not surprisingly, reflections of the endearing Austrian landscape may be seen in some of his *Moments Musicaux*.

The very opening of *Moment Musical* No. 1 in C major offers a typical *Jodler* motive, of a kind one can still hear sung in the Austrian Alps. Later on, the cuckoo, another symbol of the open air, appears before a restatement of the *Jodler* motive, this time answered by an echo. The trio of this piece might be entitled "At the Brook," for it expresses a mood similar to that of the second movement of Beethoven's *Pastoral* Symphony.

Moment Musical No. 2 (A-flat major) is a poignant, somber song. After a passionate outcry of anguish toward the end, it closes in peaceful resignation. *Moment Musical* No. 3 in F minor, perhaps Schubert's best-known composition, is typically Viennese in its relaxed pace. The mood of the music, unassuming as it may be, defies verbal description; a paradoxical expression such as "smiling through tears" might come closest to describing it. A sweet melancholy also pervades *Moment Musical* No. 4 in C-sharp minor. Its regular gray patterns in the middle register of the piano suggest perhaps a landscape under a gentle continuous rain, now and then falling more heavily after an occasional gust of wind. Brahms used a similar motion in his *Regenlied*. In the Trio the sun seems to break timidly through the clouds with a faint beam of light, but soon the returning rain disperses light and, with it, hope.

After so much delicacy, a more energetic moment is overdue. In *Moment Musical* No. 5 (F minor) the tepid air is cleared suddenly by a violent storm with fierceness, protest, and fury. Then, as abruptly as it started, the storm ends with a rather unexpected turn to F major. After the last thunderbolt there is suddenly bright sunshine.

The last *Moment Musical*, No. 6 in A-flat major, is the most songlike of all—only the words are missing. According to an old Viennese tradition, the work should not be played too slowly. Himself a singer by training, Schubert carefully avoided very slow tempo indications in most of his works, vocal or instrumental, to take into account the limitations imposed by breathing. This *Moment* shares its key and general mood with no. 2 but adds an element of finality. Schubert, the tone poet, seems to have gone here beyond all sorrow and suffering, even if he still recalls them. In this last *Moment* he enters a new world, a realm of inner peace where suffering is transformed into bliss.

Four Impromptus D 899 (op. 90)

The Impromptus show Schubert at the very peak of his mastery. The planned sequence of flat keys was altered only by the publisher Haslinger who, twenty-nine years after Schubert's death, took it upon himself to transpose the third Impromptu from G-flat to G major, surely to improve sales. (Haslinger also added a tasteless change in the harmony—inconceivable but true, there are still pianists who play that version today!).

The subtlety of the original key relationships deserves attention. No. 1, a C-minor Impromptu with a C-major ending, gives way to no. 2, in the mediant above, E-flat major, which then ends in the minor, the reverse of the minor-major transformation. That a cheerful, flowing piece in E-flat major should end "tragically" in E-flat minor is utterly new. (It has a later counterpart in Brahms's E-flat major Rhapsody op. 119 no. 4, among others). From the point of view of cyclic form, the minor key conclusion of no. 2 affords a strong connection to the following no. 3 Impromptu in G-flat major (relative major of E-flat minor). The broad melodic spans over a constant triplet accompaniment in that Impromptu suggest the poetic content of the *Gesang der Geister über den Wassern* (D 484).

The fourth Impromptu needs a full page to break free of the G-flat major tonality; it begins in A-flat minor, the second degree of G-flat major. Its principal key, however, is A-flat major, a key closely related to C minor, and a connecting link to the first Impromptu, whose exposition (after the dirgelike introduction) is likewise in A-flat major. The formal design of the first Impromptu, despite its incipient suggestions of sonata form (which Schumann noticed), cannot be categorized and remains a miracle of its own. The principal idea is worked out rather like a *Leitmotif*, a "leading" motive that appears in a succession of variants, interrupted only twice by a subsidiary theme that goes against all rules by appearing in A-flat major and in G major at the recapitulation, and that is derived from the closing motive of the principal theme (measure 73). Equally admirable is the interruption of the predominant triplet motion in the G-minor episode at measures 125 ff. and the return to the simple march rhythm in the closing measures.

Four Impromptus D 935 (op. 142)

The four Impromptus D 935 may be less original with regard to form than the Impromptus D 899, but the first of the set is one of the most beautiful pieces in the whole of piano literature. The second and third are the only ones to strike an elegiac Viennese tone. The variation theme of the B-flat major Impromptu is especially closely related to the *Rosamunde* theme, which Schubert also quoted in the A-minor String Quartet, a sign that Schubert himself was fond of this beautiful melody (Example 4.23).

EXAMPLE 4.23. Schubert, Impromptu in B♭ major, D 935/3 (mm. 1–8)

The final Impromptu of this set, a truly brilliant piece of piano music, must not be played with too much haste, despite the virtuoso passages. The cross-rhythms at measures 7, 63, and elsewhere have the character of a Czech *furiant,* showing that Bohemian music was present in Vienna and not without effect on Schubert.

Three Klavierstücke *(Impromptus) D 946 op. posth.*

Music "more eloquent than words" (Mendelssohn)—these words may characterize the last three piano pieces. Indeed, they often express states of mind for which verbal equivalents can hardly be found. The first piece displays a strong contrast between the passionate, tormented mood of the main part and the contemplative, almost religious atmosphere of the central section. (An originally conceived episode in A-flat was carefully canceled by Schubert himself.) The second piece is based on a touchingly simple tune in E-flat major that contrasts with two episodes, one in a dark, despairing C minor, the other in a luminous A-flat minor. This second episode seems to evoke the chant of otherworldly spirits. Here Schubert created piano sonorities of sublime beauty rarely encountered elsewhere in piano music.

The opening of the third piece brings us "back to life." Its principal section, marked by syncopations and frequent groups of five-bar phrases, betrays Slavic influence. Thus, it may come as no little surprise that the main motive is similar to the opening of Tchaikovsky's First Piano Concerto (written much later!). A bold modulation from C to D flat indicates a radical change of mood. The dreamy second part, also displaying free metrical groups, shows an inner relation to the lied "Die Sterne" (D 939) composed in January 1828, in which the stars are a guide for the lonely pilgrim. They float in the spheres as "messengers of love."

Performing Schubert's Piano Works

Schubert, the only Viennese classical composer who was actually born in Vienna, was thoroughly Viennese by nature. Thus, not only his personal character but also the culture of Vienna, especially during the *Wiener Kongress* (1814–15), shaped the style of his music.

The first task of a musician approaching Schubert's piano music is to find the proper tempo, the *tempo giusto*. It is not always easy to interpret Schubert's tempo indications. For most of his opening movements, Schubert preferred moderately fast tempo designations such as Allegro moderato or only moderato. These must be weighed against a fashionable tendency to play very fast, often with a somewhat "shallow" display of virtuosity. To perform the opening movement of Schubert's last sonata in B-flat major as an Adagio instead of an (Allegro) Molto moderato tempo is, therefore, a grave mistake. On the other hand, today it happens even more frequently that Schubert's central Andante movements are played much too slowly and thus create the impression of a "not so heavenly" length (Schumann coined the term *heavenly length* in an enthusiastic review of the "Great" C-major Symphony). Schubert preferred such designations as Andante, *Andante con moto,* and *Allegretto quasi Andantino* for so-called "slow" movements. Even his rare movements entitled Adagio need not be played in a dragging tempo. An indirect proof may be found in Schubert's metronome indications for several of his songs, particularly for those in slow motion. Thus, "Wanderer's Nachtlied" D 224 ("Der Du von dem Himmel bist") has the indication *Langsam, mit Ausdruck* (i.e., *Adagio espressivo*). It also has the indication MM ♩ = 50, a tempo faster than this song is ever performed today. Similarly, one should remember that Schubert's Menuettos, Scherzos, and final movements always call for a fresh, lively interpretation.

A brief note, finally, about the performance of the Impromptu D 935 (op. 142 no. 4): Schubert's typical notation of the accompaniment, with the bass note on beats 1 and 3 marked *pizzicato,* makes considerable demands on the pianist. The melody must be "sung" (simply and not sentimentally) with the fingers close to the keys. The player must also avoid obliterating the bass staccato by clumsy pedaling.

Regrettably, the scope of this essay does not allow a discussion of Schubert's chamber works with piano; indeed, Schubert wrote some of his most beautiful compositions in this genre. His *Trout* Quintet, his Piano Trios in B-flat major and E-flat major, his many Duos for piano four hands, and his violin sonatas have always been favorites of Schubert lov-

ILLUSTRATION 4.3. Death mask of Franz Schubert. Courtesy of The Curtis Institute of Music, Philadelphia.

ers, long before the piano solo works (with the exception of the *Impromptus, Moments Musicaux,* the *Wanderer* Fantasy, and some dances) became popular. The wealth of Schubert's legacy to the musical world is overwhelming and, when we consider the brevity of his life, truly a miracle. In many ways for Schubert the piano was the medium through which that miracle worked its wonder.

Notes

1. Donald Tovey, "Tonality," *Music and Letters* 9 (1928): 41f.

2. Maurice Brown in "The Schubert Piano Sonatas," notes for *The Complete Piano Sonatas* [of Franz Schubert], RCA Victor Records, New York, 1971.

3. Twice, however, it seems that he considered a selection—see the discussion of the sonatas below, page 126.

4. See Eva Badura-Skoda, "On Schubert's Choral Works," *American Choral Review* 24 (1982): 83–90.

5. Howard Ferguson counts twenty-two sonatas in his edition (Associated Board of the Royal Schools of Music); the Henle edition contains twenty-one sonatas. See also M. J. E. Brown's article on Schubert in *The New Grove Dictionary of Music and Musicians* and its list of works as well as Brown's article "Towards an Edition of the Pianoforte Sonatas" in his *Essays on Schubert.*

6. "The Schubert Piano Sonatas," notes by Maurice Brown for *The Complete Piano Sonatas* [of Franz Schubert].

7. Program notes for Badura-Skoda's recording of *The Complete Piano Sonatas.*

8. O. E. Deutsch in *Schubert: Thematic Catalogue of All His Works* rightly listed all five movements as the Sonata in E, convinced that these movements belonged together, but thought that Schubert may have considered omitting one of the Scherzos. In the second (German) edition of the *Thematic Catalogue (Thematisches Verzeichnis,* Kassel, 1978), the new editors unfortunately separated the movements, listing only two as authentic parts of the Sonata and the other three under the number D 459A as separate *Klavierstücke*—certainly a misunderstanding of Schubert's intention. Like all other early publishers, in 1843 Klemm preferred to publish "Piano Pieces" rather than "Sonatas" because they sold better. Tellingly, Klemm later issued an arrangement for four hands as *Große Sonate in fünf Sätzen!*

9. British and Continental Music Agencies, London, 1948.

10. See this fine edition published by the Associated Board of the Royal Schools of Music.

11. Maurice Brown, "The Schubert Piano Sonatas."

12. Paul Badura-Skoda, "Missing Bars and Corrupted Passages in Classical Masterpieces," *The Music Review* 22 (1961): 98–100.

13. As stated above (p. 101) some drafts for these sonatas were written on paper acquired several months earlier and may have been composed during the spring of 1828. See Robert Winter, "Paper Studies and the Future of Schubert Research," in *Schubert Studies,* eds. Eva Badura-Skoda and Peter Branscombe, Cambridge, 1982, p. 252; and Ernst Hilmar's preface to the facsimile edition of the drafts of the sonatas D 958, 959, and 960, published by Akademische Druck und Verlagsanstalt Graz, 1988.

14. University Library, Lund, Sweden, Taussig Estate.

Selected Bibliography

Badura-Skoda, Eva, and Branscombe, Peter, eds. *Schubert Studies: Problems of Style and Chronology.* Cambridge, 1982.

Badura-Skoda, Paul. Program notes to *The Complete Piano Sonatas* [of Franz Schubert]. LP sound recordings in four albums, twenty-four sides. Paul Badura-Skoda, piano. RCA Victrola VICS 6128–6131. New York, 1971.

Brody, Elaine. "Mirror of His Soul: Schubert's Fantasy in C major (D760)," *The Piano Quarterly* 104 (1978/79): 23–33.

Brown, Maurice J. E. *Schubert: A Critical Biography.* London, 1958.

———. *Essays on Schubert.* London, 1966.

———. "The Schubert Piano Sonatas," essay accompanying the RCA recording of *The Complete Piano Sonatas* [of Franz Schubert]. Paul Badura-Skoda, piano. New York, 1971.

———, with Eric Sams, "Franz Schubert," in *The New Grove Dictionary of Music and Musicians.* London, 1980.

Brusatti, Otto. "Zwei unbekannte Klavierwerke Schuberts," *Schubert-Studien,* Veröffentlichungen der Österreichischen Akademie der Wissenschaften, vol. 341. Vienna, 1978. Pp. 33–42.

Demus, Jörg. "Two Fantasies: Mozart's Fantasy in C minor K 475 and Schubert's Fantasy in C minor D 993," *The Piano Quarterly* 104 (1978/79): 9–13.

Deutsch, Otto Erich, *Schubert: Thematic Catalogue of All His Works in Chronological Order.* London, 1951.

———. *Franz Schubert: Briefe und Schriften.* Vienna, 1954.

———. *Schubert: Die Dokumente seines Lebens.* Leipzig, 1964.

———. *Franz Schubert: Thematisches Verzeichnis seiner Werke in chronologischer Folge.* Kassel, 1978.

Gál, Hans. *Franz Schubert, oder die Melodie.* Frankfurt am Main, 1970.

Godel, Arthur. *Schuberts letzte drei Klaviersonaten (D 958–960).* Baden-Baden, 1985.

Griffel, Michael L. "A Reappraisal of Schubert's Methods of Composition," *Musical Quarterly* 63 (1977): 186–210.

Hilmar, Ernst, ed. *Franz Schubert: Drei große Sonaten für das Pianoforte, D 958, D 959, und D 960 (frühe Fassungen), Faksimile nach den Autographen.* Tutzing, 1987.

Schubert, Franz. *Fantasie C-Dur "Wanderer Fantasie" (D 760).* Edited by Paul Badura-Skoda. Vienna, 1965.

———. *Impromptus, Moments musicaux, Drei Klavierstücke.* Edited by Paul Badura-Skoda. Mainz/Wien, 1968.

———. *Klaviersonaten,* vols. I und II. Edited by Paul Mies. Munich, 1971.

———. *Klaviersonaten,* vol. III. Edited by Paul Badura-Skoda. Munich, 1976.

———. *Complete Pianoforte Sonatas.* Edited by Howard Ferguson. London, 1978.

Schwarz, Vera, ed. "Die ersten Interpreten Schubertscher Klaviermusik," in *Zur Aufführungspraxis der Werke Franz Schuberts.* Beiträge zur Aufführungspraxis 4. Munich, 1981. Pp. 105–110.

Vetter, Walther. *Der Klassiker Schubert,* 2 vols. Leipzig, 1953.

Whaples, Miriam. "Schubert's Piano Sonatas of 1817–1818," *Piano Quarterly* 104 (1978/79): 34–37.

CHAPTER FIVE

In Defense of Weber

Michael C. Tusa

It is not uncommon in the history of music for the judgments of one era to be overruled by those of another. A case in point is the piano music of Carl Maria von Weber (1786–1826). Though fashionable in the nineteenth century, Weber's piano music has largely disappeared from the consciousness of modern musicians and audiences. To a certain extent this reversal was mirrored in the critical reception of Weber's piano music. In 1824, two years before the composer's death, the German music critic A. B. Marx assessed Weber's piano works as "next to Beethoven's indisputably the most important and valuable of the current day, indeed often surpassing [Beethoven's] in grandeur and elaboration" (*Berliner allgemeine musikalische Zeitung* [hereafter *BamZ*] 1: 217). By the second half of the nineteenth century, however, critics were less inclined to praise Weber's piano music; indeed, W. H. Riehl attributed the enduring popularity of Weber's piano pieces solely to the fact that they happened to have been composed by the author of the famous opera *Der Freischütz* (Riehl, 2: 300).

Several factors explain the discrepancy between contemporary acclaim and posterity's neglect. For one, the tremendous success of *Der Freischütz* has led history to view Weber primarily as an opera composer and to regard the rest of his output as an ancillary effort; Weber's contemporaries, however, saw him as a multitalented composer, conductor, concert pianist, and music critic who cut a conspicuous figure on the German musical scene well before the triumphant premiere of *Der Freischütz* in 1821. That much of the virtuosity in Weber's piano music—an element essential to its conception—was superseded by the technical demands of Chopin, Liszt, and their successors doubtless affects the way modern performers and listeners respond to the works; for Weber's contemporaries, of course, many of the effects presented stunning innovations and unprecedented difficulties.

Perhaps more telling, the recognition of the great Viennese composers as *the* points of reference for form and compositional technique in instrumental music surely worked against Weber, whose output seemed to represent an abrupt, radical, and altogether unpredictable departure from the high classical style. Traditional analytical techniques rooted in the study of the Viennese classics fail to yield meaningful insights about Weber's works, especially those in the large forms. Such criteria as level of contrapuntal ingenuity, degree of motivic development, or manifestations of the "organic" metaphor play little role in Weber's music, and any attempt to measure Weber's music by these yardsticks inevitably leads to negative results. In part, Weber's distance from the classical style must be seen as a consequence of the peripatetic lifestyle of his first thirty years, which afforded him little prolonged contact with the Viennese school, or, for that matter, with any school of composition.

If, then, we may explain why Weber's piano music has disappeared from the acknowledged nineteenth-century canon, there are nevertheless compelling reasons why these works should now be known. They formed an important part of the environment that nurtured the later giants of the piano, and their admirers included all the major figures of the next generation, Schumann, Chopin, Mendelssohn, and Liszt, the last of whom especially championed Weber's solo piano music through frequent public performances.[1] They reflect as well as any other body of piano music several issues critical to early nineteenth-century music: (1) accelerating development in piano technique and sonority; (2) the widening gulf between amateurs and professionals, and a concomitant redefinition of musical genres; (3) the reliance on poetic conceptions to shape all or part of a composition; (4) the exploitation of the exotic; and (5) the vogue of dance music. Moreover, they challenge the modern analyst to devise critical approaches appropriate to their aesthetic. By avoiding as much as possible evaluative comparisons with the classical style, we shall attempt to approach these works sympathetically, to view them from the perspective of Weber's day, and to appreciate what they can still offer to our own time.

Variations

Despite his great pianistic gifts, Weber never emphasized music for the piano over his other compositional interests, and his output for piano is thus quite small.[2] In addition to three concerted works written for his own public performances and a few easy pieces for amateurs, there exist only eight sets of variations, four solo sonatas, and five single-movement pieces.[3] Weber's earliest piano music is dominated by variations; in a genre that traditionally emphasized brilliance, his outstanding pianistic abilities found a ready outlet. His unsystematic training in composition, perhaps an impediment to success in larger forms, had no negative effect on the variations, where structure and invention are guided by a predetermined theme (Puchelt, 55–56).

Although he made no attempt to redefine the traditional premises of the genre, Weber's distaste for formula and imitation, evidenced by his biting satire on the variations of the Abbé Josef Gelinek,[4] nevertheless led him to seek out in his own sets a personal tone marked by a number of stylistic features. One concerns the frequent allusions in the variations to non-German nationalities, either in the manner in which a theme is varied or in the very choice of subject. The former category includes the *Mazurka* eighth variation of op. 5 (J. 40), the *Polacca* seventh variation of op. 7 (J. 53), and the Spanish Boleros in opp. 9 (J. 55) and 40 (J. 179). The last category is represented by Weber's last two sets, on Russian and Gypsy themes respectively (J. 179 and J. 219). Such exoticisms, which recur throughout Weber's output, are part of his inheritance from his most important teacher, the composer-theorist-organist Abbé G. J. Vogler (1749–1814), a talented but eccentric figure whose numerous pursuits included the collecting and arranging of melodies from different nations.

A second category of stylistic features that distinguish Weber's variations includes his particular contributions to piano technique, evident already in his very first piano work, the op. 2 variations, composed when the young virtuoso was only thirteen years old. Weber used the genre to display the full range of his own pianism, as attested by his own performances of op. 9 and op. 28 in semi-public concerts. Thus the variation sets make few concessions to the amateur performer, except for the eighth and last set, op. 55, which was expressly commissioned by an amateur. In addition to emphasizing velocity of scalar and arpeggiated passagework (the technical legacy of the eighteenth century), Weber's variations frequently call for advanced wrist and forearm techniques in both hands: fast octaves (already in op. 2); legato octaves (op. 28, var. 3); rapid staccato chords (op. 28, var. 7); and large, rapid leaps in the left hand (op. 7, var. 5 and var. 7). Significant too as a characterization of Weber's style is the fact that certain traditional virtuosic techniques are *not* especially stressed in his works, such as trills, hand crossing, rapid-tone repetition, and the elaborate passagework of Johann Nepomuk Hummel and other members of the Viennese school.

Weber's criticisms of Hummel, prompted by two concerts the great pianist gave in Prague in April 1816, point up a third feature of Weber's piano style that first emerged in his variations. Admiring the unprecedented precision of Hummel's playing and his great gifts in improvisation, Weber nevertheless felt compelled to criticize the Viennese pianist for his failure to take full advantage of the instrument: "the true, deeper study of the nature of the instrument," he wrote to Friedrich Rochlitz, "has remained wholly foreign to him."[5] Two traits in particular seem to grow from Weber's own desire to expand the sonorous potential of the piano. First, thickly scored left-hand chords frequently encompass the span of a tenth (Example 5.1). Their intended rich resonance was doubtless facilitated by the peculiarities of Weber's own hand structure; yet, their impracticability for hands of average size was frequently criticized during Weber's own life, to which the composer responded that he only called for such reaches where they seemed "inescapably necessary for the musical thought" (C. Weber, 1908, 185). Second, many of the new sounds that Weber sought to coax out of the piano arose from his apparent view of the instrument as a surrogate for some other medium: the tremolo inspired by orchestral music (op. 2, var. 3; op. 40, var. 8); the placement of the melody in the top of the left hand to emulate the warm sound of the cello (op. 28, var. 7); the four-voice legato writing related to the vocal model of chorale harmonizations (op. 7, var. 6); and the stylized recitative in the sixth variation of op. 9. These approximations of orchestral or vocal sonorities, also found in the sonatas, remind us that Weber was one of the first composers to approach the piano arrangements of his operas with the goal of suggesting as much orchestral detail as possible (Riehl, 276–77).

EXAMPLE 5.1. Weber, Variations, Op. 9. Variation 4 (*Spagnuolo moderato*, mm. 118–121)

In their form, Weber's variations witness the development of an increasingly personalized approach and a willingness to experiment cautiously within the relatively narrow confines of the genre. Composed at the outset of his career, the *Six Variations on an Original Theme* op. 2 (J. 7, 1800)[6] reveal a composer not strongly influenced by the sophisticated architecture of Mozart's sets. The variations proceed without any changes in tempo, meter, or internal structure from one to the next; Weber's concern for overall structure is rudimentarily manifested in his use of the minor mode to mark the midpoint in the set (Variation 3) and in reserving the most brilliant writing for the concluding Variation 6. The *Variations on a Theme from Vogler's "Castor und Pollux"* op. 5 (J. 40, 1804), the first product of Weber's studies with Volger in Vienna during 1803 and 1804 (after Weber abstained from composition during nearly a year of study), are also conservative in form. By the young composer's own admission written according to a "system" devised by Volger,[7] all of the variations adhere scrupulously to the melodic contour and phrase structure of the theme.

In contrast, the *Variations on a Theme from Vogler's "Samori"* op. 6 (J. 43, 1804), a more brilliant set originally composed for piano and *ad libitum* accompaniment of violin and cello, suggest that during his stay in Vienna the young composer may have absorbed more than just Vogler's instruction. Perhaps the clearest indication is the pairing of the slow, penultimate Variation 6 with the finale (labeled *coda*) in a different meter, in emulation of Mozart's approach. That Weber was also exposed to Beethoven's most recent piano works is hinted by the minor-mode "Marche funèbre" of Variation 6 that, like its counterpart in Beethoven's op. 34, is connected to the finale via a transition in the major mode.[8] Another possible influence of op. 34 is the way in which Weber sets apart adjacent variations by pronounced changes of mood and character, with variations of relatively greater brilliance (nos. 1, 3, 5) followed by nonvirtuosic variations in slower tempi (nos. 2, 4, 6).

Composed in 1807, the Variations on the Italian song "Vien quà Dorina bella" op. 7 (J. 53),[9] one of Weber's best works for solo piano, is the first to reveal an individual voice, especially in the characteristic dotted rhythms of Variations 2 and 7. As in op. 5, Weber here indulges his tendency to alternate between graceful (nos. 1, 2, 4, 6) and more brilliant variations (3, 5, 7). What is more, the variations now have recognizable characters: thus, no. 4 is a *Siciliano,* no. 6 is described as a *Chorale,* and the finale begins as a *Polacca.* For the first time, too, Weber allows himself to depart from rigid adherence to the harmonic structure of the theme, particularly in Variations 2, 4, and 6; and a fermata on the dominant in measure 22 of the theme is composed out as additional measures of dominant harmony in all variations except no. 6. The finale carries Weber one step closer to Mozart's finales, for it begins as a complete *Polacca* variation of the theme but then detours in the extended coda from its home key, C major, to A-flat major, in which the theme reappears over a rippling arpeggiated sextuplet accompaniment. Further modulation leads to a final, partial *Da Capo* of the theme over a second-inversion tonic triad in the warm tenor register (executed by the left-hand thumb), following which the melody dissolves in the lowest reaches of the piano for a quiet ending. Weber's satisfaction with this set led him to keep it in his repertoire, for he played it at court in Copenhagen as late as 1820 (M. Weber, 2: 262). Jähns (68) considered the work the oldest cornerstone of Weber's reputation, an assertion that is perhaps indirectly corroborated by the finale of Hummel's well-known *Armide* Variations op. 57 of about 1811 to 1815, which emulate Weber's two-key treatment of the *Da Capo* almost step-for-step.

The Variations op. 28 (J. 141) on the romance "A peine au sortir de l'enfance" from Méhul's *Joseph* represent Weber's masterpiece in the genre. Although written in September 1812, this set may have originated in a concert in Munich on 11 November 1811, when Weber was asked to improvise on this theme by the Queen of Bavaria.[10] Perhaps because it grew so directly out of performance, it is his most virtuosic work for solo piano. Except for the funeral march of its penultimate variation, it downplays the pointedly "characteristic" variations of the earlier sets and instead demonstrates an array of technical difficulties, not only in the overtly brilliant variations but also in those that adopt a more graceful or songlike approach. Thus the work is an important antecedent to Schumann's *Symphonic Études* and Brahms's *Paganini* Variations, and it still offers a valuable collection of études that explore such techniques as rapid broken chords (Variation 2), legato left-hand octaves (Variation 3), quick grace notes and two-note slurs (Variation 4), wrist rotation and finger crossing (Variation 5), and fast, staccato chordal and octave technique (Variation 7).

As many writers have noted, Weber's last two variation sets fail to reach the same level as the *Joseph* Variations, perhaps because by this time the composer had begun to outgrow the genre. The *Variations on a Gypsy Melody* op. 55 (J. 219, 1817), commissioned by an amateur musician who presumably supplied the theme, are unassuming and technically undemanding.[11] The Variations op. 40 (J. 179)[12] on the Russian song known in Germany as *Schöne Minka* (composed 1814–15) introduce technical difficulties that match those of the *Joseph* set, especially the double-note writing in Variations 3 and 9, but as even Weber's fervid apologist Jähns pointed out, the work becomes a little monotonous by its frequent treatment of the theme as an unvaried *cantus firmus* in Variations 2, 4, 6, and 7 (Jähns 192). The most striking feature of this work lies in its slow *Introduzione*, the only one among Weber's variation works, which not only adumbrates the theme but also hints at figurations subsequently used in Variations 1 (mm. 14–15), 3 (m. 16), 5 (m. 17), 2 (m. 18), 6 (m. 19), 8 (m. 20), 7 (m. 21), and 9 (mm. 22–25). Weber's intent clearly is to suggest an improvisation that spawns the entire work. One may also hear references to the preceding variations in the long coda of the "Espagnuola" finale, a synopsis of previous materials perhaps inspired by two of Dussek's variation sets.[13] Admittedly, the allusions in the finale are somewhat disguised by their combinations with and absorption into the bolero rhythm of Variation 9, but the uses of texture, rhythm, and gesture are striking enough to suggest several references: to the steady sixteenths of Variation 1 (mm. 205–208); the triplet left-hand figuration of Variation 2 (mm. 209ff); the fast turns and octaves of Variation 5 (mm. 235–38); the four-voice style of Variation 4 (mm. 239–47); the double thirds of Variation 3 (mm. 258–66); and the combination of melody and triplet accompaniment in one hand of Variation 6 (mm. 268–75).

Sonatas

Composed between 1812 and 1822, Weber's four piano sonatas are, on the whole, prototypes for the "grand sonata" of the nineteenth century. Normally cast in four movements (only no. 3 has three), the sonatas offer an ample measure of pianistic brilliance and full sonorities. Although Weber conceived them for private use and performed them only in intimate circles, the sonatas make technical demands, especially for the left hand, that raise them above the capabilities of most amateurs, a fact that Weber wryly noted when he attempted to teach the first sonata to the Grand Duchess of Weimar.[14] With the rise of the solo recital as a legitimate public concert institution, these sonatas quickly moved onto the concert stage, especially under the hands of Liszt.[15] Nevertheless, to claim that the pieces are not "genuine" sonatas because they are concert- rather than chamber-sonatas (Riehl, 269–74) is to overlook the tradition for extroverted virtuosity that runs through many sonatas by Clementi, Dussek, and even Beethoven. And even F.-J. Fétis, who tended to judge Weber harshly, conceded that his piano sonatas were "of the highest order and of an incontestable originality" (Fétis, 8: 434).

The sonatas exhibit a number of features that stamp them as the product of a single mind. Their finales are invariably cast in rondo form and normally entail a kind of perpetual motion; Dussek and Beethoven could easily have provided models for this approach. Although all four finales incorporate certain aspects of sonata form, only the second really approximates the Viennese sonata-rondo form. The "minuets" are actually fast, aggressive dances close to the mold of Beethoven's one-beat-per-bar *scherzi*,[16] and at times they also resemble *Walzer* in quick tempo. Whereas cross-rhythms, hemiola, and other kinds of syncopation are featured in the minuets, the trios achieve a sense of calm and relaxation through greater metric regularity. The first movements also betray certain family characteristics, such as their adherence to the traditional tonal scheme of sonata form, their predilection for songlike main themes that do not lend themselves well to thematic development (no. 3 is again exceptional), and their overreliance on the diminished-seventh chord as a means to pivot quickly from one key to another. The slow movements demonstrate the greatest formal variety: the second and fourth are cast as rondos, the former in an unusual ternary form, and the third is a theme-and-variations movement that also partakes of rondo form. They exhibit a simple melodic style, indebted to vocal models like folk song, choral song, and the operatic cavatina; only rarely do they indulge in the elaborate *fioritura* of the Viennese school.

Despite these conventional traits, each sonata impresses as a distinct individual and exhibits a sense of unity, to be sure not based on the elegant unifying techniques in Beethoven's mature works, which Weber clearly did not understand, but rooted instead in feeling, gesture, and sonority.[17] Significant in this regard is the fact that Weber typically began composing a sonata with a movement other than the opening Allegro. Although this habit is often adduced as evidence of his difficulty with sonata form, more telling is its relation to the way in which he composed his operas, which he normally began by setting the pieces that established the main colors of the drama. Seen in this light, the movement first composed in an instrumental cycle perhaps gives us a clue to the basic tone of the work as a whole.

The C-major Sonata op. 24 (J. 138), composed in Berlin between April and August 1812, lets us test this hypothesis. Its starting point was the Rondo, a Presto perpetual motion study that Weber himself called *"L'Infatigable."*[18] Clearly the finale set the tone for what became Weber's most cheerful and playful sonata and perhaps also inspired certain details that come to the fore in earlier movements. Thus the cascading diminished-sevenths near the end of the Rondo may have suggested similarly prominent figures throughout the first movement, and the strong pull towards E minor in the finale's first episode perhaps determined the choice of that key for the Menuetto. The accented nonchordal melody tones frequently encountered in the finale also resonate through the sonata, especially in the first and second movements.

With respect to form each movement reveals some idiosyncrasy that sets it apart from textbook models. Like Hummel's Sonata in E-flat op. 13, the first movement begins with a cadential gesture that introduces the main theme, and, as in Hummel's piece, this gesture is treated extensively during the development. But unlike the classically oriented Hummel, whose introduction firmly establishes the tonic, Weber obscures the key until measure 4. His introductory gesture represents a diminished-seventh of D minor, and one of the principal goals of this movement is to convert that gesture into a tonic-defining *dominant*-seventh of C major, an event that finally occurs at the end of the movement. More critical for the piece than the four-square main theme (mm. 5–19), which evokes the choral singing so popular in Weber's day, is the sixteenth-note appoggiatura figure that begins at measure 20, the first significant climax in the movement (Example 5.2). Exemplifying Weber's love of thick sonorities and his facility with rapid lateral motion of the arm, this figure also forms the basis for the second theme and is treated in the latter part of the development. The recapitulation is far from orthodox: Weber separates its tonal and thematic components so that the lyrical part of the main theme returns in E-flat major as a "false recapitulation" (m. 98)[19]; then, after further modulation, the tonic returns with a forceful restatement of the second paragraph (m. 114). The "false recapitulation" thus turns out to be the only recapitulation of the first theme, an effect perhaps inspired by the first movement of Beethoven's op. 10 no. 2.

The second movement also defies an easy formal classification. It consists of four sections that can be diagrammed *ABCA'*. The three basic sections are highly contrasted. The simple F major melody of *A* is followed by a florid *bel canto* section in C major for *B*. The new melody of *C*, again featuring accented nonchord tones, begins quietly in C minor but quickly becomes more animated and modulates to D-flat major for the climax of the movement (m. 48). The reprise of the first section is greatly

EXAMPLE 5.2. Weber, Piano Sonata in C, Op. 24, movt. 1, (mm. 20–24)

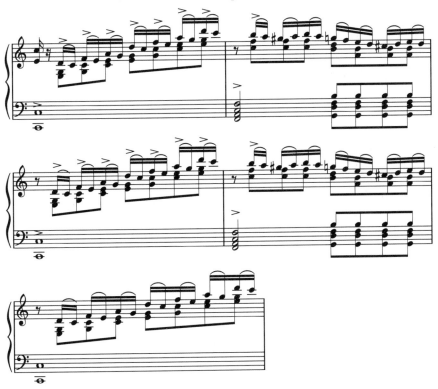

altered (m. 65): here the melody is reduced to its first phrase, which We-ber subsequently varies by changing its register and accompaniment; the movement closes with the motive of the C given as a quiet ostinato. The movement may be seen as an example of Weber's tendency to a mosaiclike construction, an approach that works well if the abrupt changes between the disparate sections are explained by poetic or dramatic clues but that remains puzzling in a purely instrumental piece.[20] Weber's friend the theorist-composer Gottfried Weber found the form of the movement problematic and suggested in a review that the movement would have been easier to grasp had the composer restated at least part of the main theme between the second and third sections of the movement (*Allgemeine musikalische Zeitung* [hereafter *AmZ*] 15 [1813]: 597). Ever open to con-structive criticism, Weber followed this advice in his next sonata.

The third movement, in E minor, is a study in cross-rhythms and double thirds. The Menuetto proper is a full-blown sonata form that modulates not to the conventional relative major but to the submediant, C major, the tonic for the entire cycle. In general, once Weber moves away from the first movement, he seems more willing to explore nontraditional key relationships (as in the finales of op. 49 and op. 70, discussed below). With the fourth movement Weber once again demonstrates his distance from the classical style with a rondo formally closer to Dussek's than Mozart's or Beethoven's examples. Essentially a five-part scheme (*ABA'CA"*) that eschews the sonata principle, the movement does modulate to the dominant in *B* and also incorporates some development of the main theme between *C*, which begins as a traditional *minore*, and *A"*, procedures that can be observed in Dussek's Sonata in B-flat major op. 24 (1793). Like the Rondo Finale in Dussek's *Farewell* Sonata op. 44 (1800), the last statement of the refrain is modified to effect closure by prolonging the progression from V ($^{6}_{4}$–$^{5}_{3}$) to I through 15 measures. Frequently published as a separate piece, the so-called *Perpetuum mobile*, the Finale is also an excellent étude for velocity and finger independence of the right hand, a fact recognized by Weber, who practiced the piece in C-sharp major to limber up stiff fingers (Jähns, 161), and by Brahms, who inverted melody and accompaniment to arrange the piece as a left-hand study.[21]

The Sonata in A-flat major op. 39 (J. 199, 1814–16) presents an entirely different world. In certain respects the work relies more closely on the classical style. Thus, the Rondo recalls the graceful style of the finales of Mozart's Sonatas K. 333 and K. 533/494 and especially Beethoven's Sonata op. 22. Significantly, among Weber's sonatas, the Rondo is the only finale to approximate classical sonata-rondo form, with the first episode treated as a second theme in the dominant, the third as a development of the two main themes, and the fourth as a transposition of the second theme to the tonic. Classical key structures support the first and second movements, the latter another rondo that draws on the sonata principle. Yet, anyone familiar with this sonata recognizes that in gesture and sound it is arguably Weber's most romantic sonata, an impression confirmed by certain subtleties of form.

Once again the Rondo was the first of the four movements Weber composed, and perhaps suggested to him some material for treatment in the preceding movements. For example, the tonic pedal points in its refrain and coda are related to the *tremolando* pedal point in the main theme and coda of the first movement. The graceful mood of the Rondo and its relatively uninterrupted unfolding are matched by the intimacy and seamlessness of the first movement,[22] in which the second theme emerges gradually and with no clear break from the preceding transitional material; thus, at the end of the bridge (m. 42) a new melody is introduced in C minor that blossoms into E-flat major (m. 46, Example 5.3a). Equally telling for the cyclic conception are the resemblances between the second themes in the first, second, and fourth movements, all of which are built around the contrary motion of stepwise descent in the right hand and arpeggiated ascent in the left (Example 5.3a–c). In the outer movements the reprises of the second themes are treated similarly. The last statement of the second theme in the finale furnishes the movement's climax through its dynamic, register, and brief combination with the refrain; in the first movement, the reprise of the second theme also assumes a climactic function by eliminating its previous tonal and modal ambiguity and by greatly expanding its original sonority and dynamic with a much fuller and more energetic accompaniment (Example 5.3d). This "apotheosis" of the second theme explains the most unorthodox formal feature in the first movement, its rearrangement of the recapitulation so that the intensified second theme is heard *after* the original closing group and immediately before the brief coda, thereby placing the climax as near to the end of the movement as possible. Such thinking, of course, is directly related to the heroic reinterpretations of second themes in Weber's mature opera overtures, and perhaps later inspired the grandiose transformations of lyrical melodies in so many of Liszt's works.

For this writer, the second sonata is Weber's greatest contribution to the genre, though, to be sure, it is far from a perfect work. The bridge and

EXAMPLE 5.3a. Weber, Piano Sonata in A-flat, Op. 39. movt. 1, 2d theme (mm. 44–47)

EXAMPLE 5.3b. Weber, Piano Sonata in A-flat, Op. 39. movt. 2, 2d theme (mm. 45–48)

EXAMPLE 5.3c. Weber, Piano Sonata in A-flat, Op. 39. movt. 4, 2d theme (mm. 45–48)

EXAMPLE 5.3d. Weber, Piano Sonata in A-flat, Op. 39. movt. 1, 2d theme (recapitulation, mm. 169–170)

development in the first movement exemplify Weber's overreliance on the diminished-seventh, almost as a crutch, to effect modulation, and on the whole the succession of keys in modulatory sections seems capricious and haphazard.[23] From a classical perspective, the strong pull to the subdominant of the dominant (that is, the original tonic) in the closing theme of the first movement (mm. 56–60) vitiates the tonal principles on which first-movement form traditionally rests. In addition, many passages are cast in an unrelievedly homophonic texture in which the left hand routinely repeats some of Weber's most widely spaced chords.

Nevertheless, because of its numerous intrinsic beauties, the work seems to have left its mark more strongly on posterity than any of Weber's other sonatas. Thus the cascading broken chords in the first-movement coda of Chopin's B-minor Sonata are indebted to the corresponding passage in Weber's sonata, and the pianistic layout and metric complication in the Menuetto are undeniably similar to passages in the same key in the "Préambule" and "Marche" of Schumann's *Carnaval* (Dale, 49). Liszt's *Dante* Sonata nearly quotes the Rondo's second theme, and the second movement also seems to anticipate Liszt in the way that its main theme is scored to suggest instruments other than the piano. The first two phrases impress as a sustained soprano melody with pizzicato accompaniment, and the third phrase places the theme in a tenor or cello range at the top of the left hand with plucked sounds on either side; both effects occur, slightly modified and in reverse order, in Liszt's great *Funérailles*. The rhetorical gestures and overall shape of the slow movement also suggest a connection to *Funérailles*: Weber's slow movement is a funeral march that builds to a heroic vision, with the chordal closing theme over a triplet ostinato octave bass, before sinking into a quiet ending (Example 5.4). The Andante may have reached Schubert shortly after its publication in December 1816; the last statement of the main theme (mm. 98–106), which veers from its expected harmonic course as it is combined with the constant triplet motion of the middle section, anticipates a similar effect in the slow movement of the younger composer's B-major Sonata (D. 575), composed in August 1817.

The compositional history of the D-minor Sonata op. 49 (J. 206) differs from that of the other sonatas in two important points: (1) Weber composed it in a concentrated period of three weeks in November 1816, immediately after completing op. 39; and (2) he began work on the sonata with the first movement. The sonata presents numerous expressive and stylistic contrasts to op. 39, as if the composer sought to explore a complete antithesis to the prior work. Unlike the intimate, lyrical, seamless style of op. 39, the third sonata offers elements of tension, contrast, drama, and even disjunction, within and between movements.

These features are especially prominent in the first movement, characterized by irregular phrase lengths, unexpected harmonic twists, and a proliferation of sharply differentiated materials. At the broadest structural level this tendency toward contrast entails (for once) the use of dissimilar themes to articulate the main tonal plateaus of the movement: an aggressive, motivic main theme, marked *feroce*, and a lyrical second theme whose shape and demeanor bring us close to Agathe's aria in *Der Freischütz*. Friedrich Rochlitz, who discussed op. 39 and op. 49 in a major review, criticized disruptive rhythmic and harmonic elements in the first

EXAMPLE 5.4. Weber, Piano Sonata in A-flat, Op. 39. movt. 2 (mm. 85–94)

movement for their lack of "natural flow" and "symmetry" (*AmZ* 20: 686). Yet Weber, who thanked the influential writer for his comments, claimed to "have his reasons" for what he did;[24] although he never explained the underlying idea of the movement in writing, it seems to play out a Beethovenian metaphor of struggle culminating in triumph. Thus the struggle to hold together the centrifugal, disruptive forces of the exposition is joined in the development, which, for once, does work over the first theme extensively and culminates in a symbolic victory with a "heroic" recapitulation that reinterprets the main theme in three significant ways: (1) through the change to the major mode; (2) through placing the theme in a more brilliant register; and (3) through contrapuntal combination of the first theme (x) with a prominent secondary motive (y) and a rhythmic figure from the closing group (z; Example 5.5).

EXAMPLE 5.5. Weber, Piano Sonata in D minor, Op. 49. movt. 1, recapitulation (mm. 183–192)

The second and third movements on the whole avoid such dramatic rhetoric. The slow movement presents a novel approach to form, in which a theme and set of variations is twice interrupted, perhaps to parallel the disruptive tendencies of the first movement. Between the second and third variations lies a thirty-one measure section that, in its free treatment of the theme, recitative style, and modulation to the remote key of A-flat major, may best be considered a fantasialike development. The third and fourth variations are separated by an impassioned episode of new material in the subdominant. The four-measure introduction bears little relationship to the simple theme or its elaborations but serves to recall the harmonic progression (I-IV-I) that begins the first movement.

In the absence of a Menuetto, the triple-meter finale assumes some of the rhythmic character of Weber's typical *scherzi*. Without doubt Weber's most high-spirited finale, and arguably his most successful, the third movement is an odd sonata-rondo that turns on three distinct themes: (1) a refrain with perpetual-motion tendencies; (2) a *Walzer*-like episode in the subdominant; and (3) a *scherzando*-like episode, first presented in the dominant. A recapitulation satisfies the sonata principle by partially transposing both of the episodes to the tonic, and to cap off the movement with a tour de force Weber combines the last statement of the refrain with the *scherzando* theme, a gesture that recalls the contrapuntal high point of the first movement. The combination also reveals the *scherzando* melody to be a free inversion of the refrain.

Dedicated to Rochlitz, the Sonata in E minor op. 70 (J. 287) perhaps suggests those paths Weber might have explored within the genre had he lived longer (Warrack, 277). Pianistically much leaner than any of his preceding works—a response to Rochlitz's criticisms of opp. 39 and 49?—the work also demonstrates a new interest in imitative counterpoint.[25] In addition, the work manifests an especially heightened concern for unity within the separate movements and the cycle as a whole. If these new features reflect the continued maturation and refinement of Weber's instrumental style, we may also relate many of the work's novelties to underlying poetic impulses first disclosed many years later by Julius Benedict, who studied with Weber from 1821 to 1824:

> The first movement, according to Weber's own ideas, portrays in mournful strains the state of a sufferer from fixed melancholy and despondency, with occasional glimpses of hope, which are, however, always darkened and crushed. The second movement describes an outburst of rage and insanity; the Andante in C is of a consolatory nature, and fitly expresses the partly successful entreaties of friendship and affection endeavoring to calm the patient, though there is an undercurrent of agitation—of evil augury. The last movement, a wild fantastic Tarantella with only a few snatches of melody, finishes in exhaustion and death. None but Weber himself could give the true picture of this fierce struggle of reason against the demon of insanity which this fine composition so graphically describes (Benedict, 155).

To be sure, Benedict is not always the most reliable witness,[26] but in this instance his recollection of Weber's intention seems quite plausible. First of all, by his own admission, Weber believed that concertos in the minor mode required definite imagery to guide the aesthetic response of the listener. Thus in 1815 he conceived a piano concerto in F minor with the explicit dramatic-psychological progression, Separation-Lament-Pain-Consolation-Reunion-Joy; this conception eventually became the famous *Konzertstück* op. 79.[27] Second, the expression marks throughout the sonata lend credence to a programmatic conception, from the melancholy *con duolo* at the beginning of the first movement to the *consolante* of the third. In Weber's autograph the finale is explicitly designated a Tarantella, a *topos* traditionally associated with delirium (Illustration 5.1).[28] Typically enough, Weber declined to communicate this program, and his two other decidedly programmatic piano works, the *Konzertstück* and *Aufforderung zum Tanze* (see below), were also published without an official acknowledgment of their narrative backgrounds, suggesting that the composer wished his works to be judged primarily on musical grounds.[29]

ILLUSTRATION 5.1. Weber, Sonata in E minor, Op. 70 movt. 4. Autograph score. Bibliothèque nationale, Paris.

On the local level, the first movement lends itself particularly well to a psychological interpretation. Thus the economical movement essentially turns on the juxtaposition and interplay of two basic melodic ideas that embody opposing moods. The austere main theme, a musical symbol for melancholy or depression (*con duolo*), employs almost exclusively descending contours in predominantly eighth-note motion (Example 5.6a); opposed to this is the melody of the bridge section (*con agitazione*), which surges upward in constant sixteenth-note motion spread between the two hands, as if to throw off the shackles of melancholy through action (Example 5.6b). The second theme begins in the key of G major with a melody (m. 39) closely related to the opening theme and then continues with a near note-by-note transposition of the first theme into the relative major. Accompanied now by a widely spaced left-hand pattern and placed in a higher register, the melancholy theme thus assumes some prospect of comfort or hope. The exposition closes with a quiet reiteration of the rising figures from the bridge. Weber's treatment of the recapitulation suggests a psychological resolution of the opposition. Following immediately upon the truncated first theme, the second theme now begins in E minor but is temporarily able to recapture the warmth of the major mode at measure 134 (*con anima*). The expanded closing group, which compensates for the omission of the bridge in the recapitulation, replays in miniature the struggle of the development section but is unable to recapture a mood of optimism. Thus the coda (m. 166) witnesses the "triumph" of depression, for the main theme is heard one last time over a quiet, seemingly exhausted version of the rising motive (*murmurando*).[30]

As has been noted in the Weber literature, the efforts to unify the entire sonata are more conspicuous in this work than in any of Weber's

EXAMPLE 5.6a. Weber, Piano Sonata in E minor, Op. 70. movt. 1, main theme (mm. 1–12)

EXAMPLE 5.6b. Weber, Piano Sonata in E minor, Op. 70. movt. 1, bridge (mm. 21–25)

other sonatas (Newman, 252; Warrack, 276; Marinaro, 30–31). Especially striking are the relationships between the first and second movements, evidently composed at the same time; according to Weber's diary, the Menuetto was composed on 28 August 1819, and the first movement was completed only three days later.[31] The Menuetto replays the idea of opposition in various ways. Whereas the Menuetto proper is informed by the stepwise descent of the main theme from the first movement, the rising contours of the Trio recall the bridge and closing group of the first movement (Examples 5.7a–b). Moreover, the rhythmic contrast between the two sections also finds its parallel in the first movement, for the Menuetto moves in fast quarter notes, while the Trio moves in constant eighth notes to suggest a dizzying *Walzer*. Significantly different in the second movement, however, is the reversal of dynamics, so that the descending figure is no longer melancholy but aggressively manic (*Presto vivace ed energico*), while the rising pattern is but a quiet shadow of its former self, referring explicitly to the defeated *murmurando* quality that obtained at the end of the first movement.

EXAMPLE 5.7a. Weber, Piano Sonata in E minor, Op. 70. Menuetto (mm. 1–7)

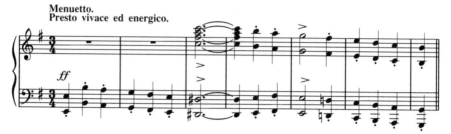

EXAMPLE 5.7b. Weber, Piano Sonata in E minor, Op. 70. Trio (mm. 1–8)

The last two movements, composed between 1820 and July 1822, do not exploit the same dichotomy, perhaps because by this point in the sonata the "healthy," rising impulses have been thoroughly suppressed. That the C-major refrain of the slow movement avoids referring to the stepwise descent of the first two movements lends credibility to Benedict's program, according to which the point of view has temporarily shifted from the suffering protagonist to his friends; furthermore, the music seems to evoke the sound of choral song through its chordal setting, a musical metaphor for companionship (Example 5.8). Episodes that tend toward the minor mode and exhibit more angular melodic contours offer further instances of a psychologically motivated "mosaic," in this case anguished outbursts that nearly manage to overpower the consoling refrain; thus the last statement of the refrain begins forcibly in E minor, the cyclic tonic, before restoring a sense of calm.

The finale evidently makes the first use in European art music of the tarantella, a South Italian folk dance, here employed not for its value as "local color" (as was so often later the case), but instead for symbolism that

EXAMPLE 5.8. Weber, Piano Sonata in E minor, Op. 70. movt. 3 (mm. 1–8)

Andante consolante, quasi Allegretto

was apparent to all educated persons: the dance's alleged power to cure the mental derangement of tarantism. Thus, even without Benedict's explanation, the last movement provides the sensitive listener with a clue to the symbolism of the entire sonata. The ending of Benedict's program perhaps ought to be refined, however, for the exhaustion at the end of the tarantella traditionally does not connote death, but rather the abatement of hysteria.[32] As a portrait of the protagonist, the refrain of the finale returns to the descending contour of the first two movements, although its initial chromatic ornament may also be subtly related to the theme of the Andante (Example 5.9). The frenzied, obsessive rhythms of this tarantella, nearly all derived from the opening four measures, are a psychologically apt manifestation of perpetual motion that Weber favored in his finales. In its form, the movement is cast as a rondo with some references to sonata form, although the antipode to E minor here is C major, a feature that can be related to the use of that key in the slow movement and perhaps ultimately to the deceptive cadence on a submediant C-major triad in the main theme of the first movement (m. 8). Thus the first episode of the finale initially presents C major as a submediant harmony (m. 44) that progresses to the dominant through an augmented-sixth chord, and the second episode is predominantly in C major (m. 105); both C-major passages are partially recapitulated in E major near the end of the movement to satisfy the requirements of the sonata principle, even if in somewhat unorthodox fashion. Perhaps for symbolic reasons (the long-sought cure?) the finale ultimately breaks through to E major at the *fortissimo* fourth statement of the refrain (m. 271). The exhaustion associated with the dance as a sign of restored sanity is then graphically portrayed at

EXAMPLE 5.9. Weber, Piano Sonata in E minor, Op. 70. Finale (mm. 1–12)

the very end of the movement, for the last measures of the sonata restore the minor mode and quietly bring the refrain down from e³ to the bottom of the keyboard. There it gradually dissolves in a process of rhythmic augmentation before the abrupt conclusion of the last five measures.

Other Works

Weber's few remaining works for solo piano divide into two general categories. In the first belong works for amateurs; these consist of three sets of authenticated functional dances[33] and three sets of four-hand pieces. With the exception of the four-hand *Huit pièces* op. 60 (1818–19), all of Weber's extant amateur pieces were composed before 1812, at a time when the young composer was eager to make a name for himself with works that could easily be published. Having attained public recognition, however, Weber sought to distance himself from appearing to pander to the masses; thus he published his last set of waltzes (J. 143–48) anonymously.[34] These unassuming pieces should not go unnoticed. Weber's functional dances are excellent examples of the type of music that composers of all ranks turned out at the beginning of the nineteenth century to meet the tremendous vogue for social dancing. Within his own oeuvre they laid the groundwork for the *Freischütz* waltz and the *Invitation to the Dance*. Conceding the limited capabilities of the swelling amateur market, the various four-hand pieces of op. 3, op. 10, and op. 60 are well removed from the technical demands of the two-hand works; nevertheless, their charm as amateur music may have led Hindemith, the twentieth century's great exponent of *Gebrauchsmusik,* to base his colorful *Symphonic Metamorphoses on Themes of Weber* on themes from op. 10 and op. 60.

The second category comprises five well-known compositions of moderate length, all cast in some version of rondo form and concentrated in the years 1808 and 1819.[35] The *Momento capriccioso* op. 12 (J. 56, composed 1808, published 1811) is closely related in its cross-rhythms to the minuets of Weber's sonatas and in its perpetual-motion tendencies to their finales. Dedicated to his youthful friend Meyerbeer, a fellow student of Abbé Vogler and by all accounts a tremendously gifted pianist,[36] the *Capriccio* (as it was also called) is an understated étude in fast, pianissimo, staccato chordal and octave technique that looks ahead to the elfin style of many of Mendelssohn's works. The *Grande Polonaise* in E-flat major op. 21 (J. 59), also composed in 1808, is the first of Weber's concert dances, works that transform the popular dances of the day into independent piano pieces for the salon or concert hall. Avoiding the bolero rhythm familiar from Chopin's Polonaises ($\sqcap$ $\sqcap\sqcap$), it relies extensively on grace notes and Weber's idiosyncratic dotted rhythms to effect, like the *Polaccas* within the variation sets, elegance and *courtoisie* rather than heroism.[37]

The three works from the fruitful summer of 1819 differ from those of 1808 in their greater emphasis on brilliant passagework. The graceful *Rondo brillante* in E-flat major op. 62 (J. 252) is, pianistically and structurally, Weber's closest approximation to the elegant rondos of Hummel and the Viennese school; much of its classical sonata-rondo form is filled with scales and broken chords in thirty-second notes (Illustration 5.2). The *Polacca brillante* in E major op. 72 (J. 268) is distinguished from the earlier Polonaise by a more playful mood, a point emphasized in Weber's instruction that the piece be performed *mit Keckheit* ("with impudence") and by the quirky rhythms of the refrain; Ignaz Moscheles named it *L'Hilarité* to suggest its inherent humor.

By far the most famous of Weber's compositions for solo piano is the *Aufforderung zum Tanze (Invitation to the Dance)* Op. 65 (J. 260; Illustration 5.3). Like the other pieces of 1819, *Invitation* also exploits the glittery brilliance of right-hand passagework, facilitated in this piece by its key, D-flat major, which is especially suited to scales and broken chords. The historical significance of this familiar piece should not be underestimated. It represents the first significant attempt to transform the dominant social dance of the day, the waltz, into a concert piece for piano; thus, it is the progenitor for the concert waltzes of Chopin and later pianist-

ILLUSTRATION 5.2. Weber, *Rondo brillante*, Op. 62. Autograph score. Bibliothèque nationale, Paris.

ILLUSTRATION 5.3. Weber, *Aufforderung zum Tanze*, Op. 65. Autograph score. Pierpont Morgan Library, New York.

composers.[38] Its quick tempo (*Allegro vivace*) marked a break from the more moderate tempi of the *Walzer, Ländler,* and *Deutscher* practiced at the beginning of the nineteenth century.

In addition, the *Invitation* profoundly influenced the later form of the waltz, as composers like Johann Strauss, Jr., adopted its slow introduction and imitated some aspects of its internal structure. In Weber's day functional waltzes, normally consisting of two strains of eight measures each, were treated either as loose suites of dances, the approach exemplified in Schubert's waltz sets, or as a pair of dances organized like the classical minuet into a large ternary form (Waltz-Trio-Waltz D.C.); Weber followed the latter approach in his own functional waltzes. The *Aufforderung* actually appropriates elements of both approaches to suggest the *impression* of a ball but at the same time creates a larger coherent form than previously attempted for the waltz. Specifically, the *Aufforderung* combines four different waltzes of two strains each into a large structure that partakes of rondo form (the first strain of Waltz 1 recurs as a refrain after Waltz 2)[39] and ternary form (the first two waltzes are recapitulated in the last major section of the piece); a modulatory transition replete with a "false recapitulation" of the second strain of Waltz 1 leads from Waltz 4 to the reprise (see Table 5.1).[40] Of course, such recall techniques later became the norm in works by masters of the genre.

Aufforderung zum Tanze is of great interest too for its poetic program. The work presents a miniature courtship ritual explained to Jähns by Weber's wife Caroline, the work's dedicacée, who received the "program" from the composer as he first played it for her (Jähns, 284). The Introduction represents a male dancer's attempt to convince a female to dance with him. Rejected at first, he repeats his request more forcefully; the lady accedes, and they converse awhile before the dance begins. To convey these images, communicated to the world at large only through the title of the work, Weber symbolically alternates between two distinctive registers, a baritone-tenor range in the left hand for the male's questions and comments and a right-hand soprano range for those of the female. An opposition of rising and falling contours also reflects the question-answer dichotomy of the first sixteen measures (Example 5.10). As the dance approaches, the two "characters" metaphorically "take their place" by moving together in parallel tenths.[41]

The body of the piece has no specific program, for it obviously represents the dance proper; yet, commentators have drawn attention to certain expressive features that may be based in a poetic conception. First, the two basic moods in the waltz reflect the distinction between the brilliant and the intimate that Schubert designated, respectively, as "Noble" and "Sentimental" (Guignard, 28); to the former belong Waltzes 1, 2 (*brillante ma grazioso*), and 4 (*feroce*), to the latter the quiet third waltz (*wiegend*). Second, the waltz seems to refer to the Introduction, albeit in oblique ways. Thus the contours of the first strain of Waltz 1 can be heard as a

TABLE 5–1.
Aufforderung zum Tanze

Introduction (Moderato) D♭ 1		
Waltz 1 (*Allegro vivace*) ‖: a :‖: b :‖ D♭ 36	Waltz 2 (*brillante, ma grazioso*) ‖: c :‖: dc′ :‖ D♭ 60	Waltz 1 ‖: a :‖ D♭ 88
Waltz 3 (*wiegend*) ‖: e :‖: fe′ :‖ D♭ 96	Waltz 4 (*feroce*) ‖: g :‖: h :‖ g f C f 200	Transition ext. on g- "false recap." of b- ext. ----------------C----------------V/D♭ 223
Waltz 1 ‖: a :‖ b D♭ 301	Waltz 2 c c′ ext. D♭ 325	Waltz 1 a′ ext. D♭ 381
Coda (Moderato) D♭ 408		

"brilliant" metamorphosis of the question-answer complex at the beginning of the Introduction (Stenger, 35), and the second strain of Waltz 3 temporarily resumes the registral dialogue of the Introduction, as if the dancers take advantage of the more intimate section to exchange pleasantries. Finally, Weber's extremely fast tempo has been interpreted to symbolize the rather passionate relationship between the two dancers.[42] The brief coda resumes the registral metaphors of the Introduction to bring the scene to its fitting conclusion: the male thanks his partner, she replies, and they retire quietly. In performance, this poetic ending presents something of a problem, however, for after the dizzying conclusion of the waltz, the coda can appear as an anticlimax to the listener who is not aware of the work's imagery.

It would be inappropriate to make undue claims for Weber's piano music. The early nineteenth century produced a number of talented pianist-composers who languish in the shadows cast by Beethoven,

EXAMPLE 5.10. Weber, *Aufforderung zum Tanze.* Introduction (mm. 1–15)

Chopin, Schumann, and Liszt, and by no means should Weber be considered the one outstanding figure among these lesser lights; Dussek was arguably a more fertile composer, and Hummel certainly a more polished one and probably a greater influence on piano technique. Nor are Weber's works entirely representative of the *Virtuosentum* that dominated piano music in the "Age of Beethoven." But precisely because his music stood somewhat apart from much of the piano music of his day, it did speak to his contemporaries and immediate successors with an original voice. By placing pianistic brilliance and sonority in the service of poetic content he opened up worlds that would be further explored throughout the nineteenth century.

Notes

1. For Chopin's knowledge and uses of Weber's piano music see Eigeldinger, 78, 96, 191 (n. 141), and 315; for Mendelssohn's assimilation of Weber's piano style, see below, p. 184. Liszt's first exposure to Weber's piano music is described in Lenz, 12–20. Liszt's repertoire, cited in Walker, 446–47, included the four sonatas, the *Polacca brillante,* the *Momento capriccioso,* the *Aufforderung zum Tanze,* and the *Konzertstück* in F minor.

2. Weber's piano music is available in various editions, although a critical edition is still needed. Here works are identified by their opus numbers and the "J." numbers assigned by Jähns. For specific studies see Riehl, Georgii, and Marinaro, as well as significant discussions in Egert, 92–101; Dale, 43–53; and Newman, 246–60.

3. Weber's *Six Fughettas* op. 1 (1798), although frequently included with the keyboard works, were actually published in open score and represent an abstract kind of composition. The young Weber is known to have written three sonatas and an unspecified number of variation sets, which he offered to the publishers André and Simrock in November 1801, but they have not survived. See Rosenthal, 437–46. According to Weber's "Autobiographical Sketch" of 1818, these lost works were destroyed in a fire; see C. Weber, 1981: 251. In addition, Weber's diary, cited in Jähns, 438, records work on a set of piano études in 1820 and 1821; unfortunately, no trace of these studies survives.

4. C. Weber, 1981: 18.

5. Letter of 22 April 1816, in M. Weber, 1: 517. See also the letter to Gottfried Weber of 24 April 1816 in Bollert and Lemke, 75; a tamer version of this criticism was included in his published review, trans. in C. Weber, 1981: 181–82. In fairness to Hummel, Weber's remarks predate Hummel's later piano works, especially the magnificent Sonata in F-sharp minor op. 81, which do explore a broad palette of sonorities.

6. Weber's early variation sets up through op. 9 were originally published without opus numbers; the composer retrospectively supplied them in his own catalogs of his works. The first edition of op. 2 was lithographed by the teen-aged Weber himself. Facsimiles from this early example of musical lithography are published in Hauswald, 100–102.

7. See Weber's letter of 2 April 1804 to Thaddäus [Ignaz] Susann, cited in Jähns, 56.

8. The variation also recalls strikingly the Funeral March in Beethoven's op. 26.

9. The song is variously attributed to Antonio Bianchi (1758–1817) and Francesco Bianchi (1752–1810). See Hansell, 673.

10. Jähns, 163. See also Münster, 377–78.

11. Weber seems to have been somewhat unclear about the provenance of the theme. In a letter to his wife of 30 August 1817, quoted in M. Weber 2: 112, he described it as a "Polish" theme, and a *Stichvorlage* of the work with corrections by Weber in the Bibliothèque nationale in Paris labels the theme a "Thema russo."

12. Also published as op. 37.

13. Op. 71 no. 2 and the Variations on *Partant pour Syrie.*

14. See his letter to Hinrich Lichtenstein of 1 November 1812, cited in Jähns, 161.

15. Riehl, 263. On Liszt's Weber repertoire see n. 1.

16. An entry in Weber's diary for 28 August 1819 actually calls the Menuetto of Sonata no. 4 a Scherzo (Jähns, 346).

17. Weber criticized the "confusion" of Beethoven's music in a letter to Hans Georg Nägeli of 21 May 1810 (Nohl, 178–79). On the question of unity in Weber's instrumental music see Hatch, which appeared after the present essay had gone to press.

18. See Weber's diary entry of 12 April 1812 (Jähns, 161).

19. As in many false recapitulations in the classical style, there is a subtle change in accompaniment, so that the auditor without absolute pitch recognizes something is amiss in the return.

20. Marinaro, 12–17, stresses the potentially poetic nature of this movement by reference to gestures and accompaniments in several slow arias from Weber's operas.

21. The movement seems also to have left its mark on various perpetual motion pieces by Mendelssohn, including op. 7 no. 4, the posthumously published *Perpetuum mobile* op. 119 (see p. 184), and more generally, the finales to the posthumous B-flat major Sonata op. 106 and the F-sharp minor Fantasia op. 28.

22. Georgii, 21, aptly speaks of the "unendliche Melodie" of the first movement.

23. In his review of op. 39 (*AmZ* 20: 685), Rochlitz complained that the "main threads" of the movement at times threatened to "slip away" from the auditor.

24. Letter to Rochlitz of 16 October 1818, quoted at length in Jähns, 214.

25. Noteworthy are the canon in the development of the first movement, the loose imitation in the Menuetto, and the canonic writing in the third movement.

26. See Tusa, 122. The first edition of Benedict's Weber biography was published in 1881.

27. See the letter to Rochlitz of 14 March 1815, cited in Jähns, 338. Weber finished the work in 1821.

28. Paris, Bibliothèque nationale, Mus. ms. 400. This title is omitted in many published editions.

29. As Weber noted in the letter to Rochlitz cited in n. 27 "Since I profoundly hate all musical works with titles, it will be devilishly unpleasant for me to accustom myself to this idea [the programmatic conception of the planned F-minor concerto], which nevertheless presses upon me inexorably and wishes to convince me of its effectiveness. In any event I should not wish to perform the piece in a place where I am not already known, for fear of being misunderstood and grouped with the musical charlatans." On the program of the *Konzertstück* see Kirsch.

30. In printed editions the expression mark *murmurando con duolo* is applied to both voices; in Weber's autograph, however, *murmurando* is clearly applied to the left hand and *con duolo* to the main theme in the right hand.

31. Jähns, 346. My chronology differs from the interpretation offered by Warrack (275–76) that the Tarantella was composed immediately after the Menuetto. The diary entry for 31 August 1819 is *Allegro der Sonate E moll vollendet*. To be sure, the first movement is marked Moderato, but Weber almost always referred to the first movement in a sonata form as an Allegro; moreover, the tempo for the Tarantella is *Presto vivace ed energico*.

32. See Weber's own characterization of the dance in his unfinished novel *Tonkünstlers Leben* (C. Weber, 1981: 338): "for just as the bite of the tarantula

makes people dance, it is not long before they sink exhausted to the ground—cured."

33. In addition, Weber possibly had two prior sets of *Favorit-Walzer* published anonymously. See Jähns, 167 and 440–41.

34. See Weber's letter of 30 November 1812 to F. F. Flemming (Jähns, 167).

35. One short work attributed to Weber that has recently surfaced, a brief *Adagio patetico* in C-sharp minor, was presumably composed for an album during the composer's fateful trip to London in 1826. A facsimile of the Cramer edition is in Temperley, 15: 257.

36. In a notice about Meyerbeer's *Alimelek* published in 1815 Weber called him "one of the finest, if not actually the finest, pianist of today" (C. Weber, 1981: 139).

37. Liszt later appropriated the slow introduction of this Polonaise to serve as the introduction for his piano-orchestra arrangement of Weber's op. 72.

38. Hummel's *Apollo-Saal* Waltzes op. 31, occasionally cited as the starting point for the concert waltz for piano (e.g., Carner, 28), were originally written for orchestra and thus were truly intended for dancing. On the relationship of the *Aufforderung* to Chopin's waltzes see Stenger, 80–84.

39. Weber's autograph describes the work as a Rondo, and in the first edition the work is titled *Rondo brillant*.

40. Slightly different interpretations of the form are advanced by Guignard, 27–30, and Viertel, 436–45.

41. A sensitive discussion of the poetic impulses and their realization is offered by Viertel, 445–54.

42. According to Riehl, 296, the basic *Affekt* of the *Aufforderung* was "Pathos der Liebe," to the exclusion of other traditional connotations of the waltz.

Selected Bibliography

Benedict, Julius. *Weber*. New edition. London, n.d.

Bollert, Werner, and Lemke, Arno, ed. "Carl Maria von Webers Briefe an Gottfried Weber." *Jahrbuch des Staatlichen Instituts für Musikforschung Preußischer Kulturbesitz 1972*. Berlin, 1973. Pp. 7–103.

Carner, Mosco. *The Waltz*. New York, 1948.

Dale, Kathleen. *Nineteenth-Century Piano Music*. London, 1954.

Egert, Paul. *Die Klaviersonate im Zeitalter der Romantik*. Vol. 1, *Die Klaviersonate der Frühromantiker* (no further volumes appeared). Berlin, 1934.

Eigeldinger, Jean-Jacques. *Chopin vu par ses élèves*. Rev. ed. Neuchâtel, 1979.

Fétis, F.-J. "Weber." *Biographie universelle des musiciens*. 2d ed. Paris, 1875. Vol. 8, 428–34.

Georgii, Walter. *Weber als Klavierkomponist*. Halle, 1911.

Guignard, Silvain. *Frédéric Chopins Walzer*. Collection d'études musicologiques, 70. Baden-Baden, 1986.

Hansell, Sven. "Antonio Bianchi." *New Grove Dictionary of Music and Musicians*. London, 1980.

Hatch, Christopher. "Weber's Themes as Agents of 'a Perfect Unity.' " *The Music Review* 48 (1988): 31–42.

Hauswald, Günter, ed. *Carl Maria von Weber: Eine Gedenkschrift*. Dresden, 1951.

Jähns, Friedrich Wilhelm. *Carl Maria von Weber in seinen Werken: chronologisch-thematisches Verzeichniss seiner sämmtlichen Compositionen.* Berlin, 1871.

Kirsch, Winfried. "Carl Maria von Webers *Konzerstück* f-moll opus 79." *Studien zur Instrumentalmusik. Lothar Hoffmann-Erbrecht zum 60. Geburtstag.* Edited by Anke Bingmann, Klaus Hortschansky, and Winfried Kirsch. Frankfurter Beiträge zur Musikwissenschaft, 20. Tutzing, 1988. Pp. 363–94.

Lenz, Wilhelm von. *The Great Piano Virtuosos of Our Time.* Translated by Madeleine R. Baker. New York, 1899.

Marinaro, Stephen John. "The Four Piano Sonatas of Carl Maria von Weber." D.M.A. treatise, University of Texas at Austin, 1980.

Münster, Robert. "Zu Carl Maria von Webers Münchener Aufenthalt 1811." *Musik, Edition, Interpretation. Gedenkschrift Günter Henle.* Edited by Martin Bente. Munich, 1980. Pp. 369–83.

Newman, William S. *The Sonata since Beethoven.* 3d ed. New York, 1983.

Nohl, Ludwig. *Musikerbriefe.* Leipzig, 1867.

Puchelt, Gerhard. *Variationen für Klavier im 19. Jahrhundert.* Hildesheim, 1973.

Riehl, W. H. "K. M. von Weber als Klaviercomponist," *Musikalische Charakterköpfe.* 2d ed. Stuttgart, 1862. Vol. 2, 260–301.

Rosenthal, Albi. "Franz Anton und Carl Maria von Weber in der Frühgeschichte der Lithographie." In *Festschrift Rudolf Elvers zum 60. Geburtstag,* edited by Ernst Herttrich and Hans Schneider. Tutzing, 1985. Pp. 437–46.

Stenger, Alfred. *Studien zur Geschichte des Klavierwalzers.* Europäische Hochschulschriften, Series 36, 1. Frankfurt am Main, 1978.

Temperley, Nicholas, ed. *The London Pianoforte School 1766–1860.* Vol. 15. New York and London, 1985.

Tusa, Michael C. "Weber's *Große Oper*: A Note on the Origins of *Euryanthe*." *19th-Century Music* 8 (1984–85): 119–124.

Viertel, Matthias S. *Die Instrumentalmusik Carl Maria von Webers.* Europäische Hochschulschriften. Series 36, 20. Frankfurt am Main, 1986.

Walker, Alan. *Franz Liszt.* Vol. 1, *The Virtuoso Years.* New York, 1983.

Warrack, John. *Carl Maria von Weber.* 2d ed. Cambridge, 1976.

Weber, Carl Maria von. *Sämtliche Schriften.* Edited by Georg Kaiser. Berlin and Leipzig, 1908.

———. *Writings on Music.* Translated by Martin Cooper. Edited by John Warrack. Cambridge, 1981.

Weber, Max Maria von. *Carl Maria von Weber: ein Lebensbild.* 3 vols. Leipzig, 1864–66.

CHAPTER SIX

Piano Music Reformed: The Case of Felix Mendelssohn Bartholdy

R. Larry Todd

Mendelssohn is today generally not highly esteemed as a composer of piano music, yet the piano played a central role in his career. Some twenty-five years separate his earliest preserved efforts for the instrument (circa 1820) from what were perhaps his final piano works, the *Lieder ohne Worte* op. 102 nos. 3 and 5, composed in December 1845, less than two years before his death.[1] All told, the piano repertory comprises some 150 compositions. Of these, Mendelssohn released about seventy in seventeen *opera*; roughly twenty-five other works appeared posthumously during the nineteenth century in eleven additional *opera*.[2]

Whether composing for the piano or for other media, Mendelssohn habitually used in his sketches a two-stave, treble-bass format, suggesting that if he did not work at the piano, the sound of the instrument was never far removed from the wellspring of his inspiration. Mendelssohn's powers as a keyboard performer and improviser—at the piano and organ alike—were widely celebrated and documented by such witnesses as Ferdinand Hiller, Ignaz Moscheles, Robert Schumann, Hector Berlioz, Joseph Joachim, and Goethe, among others.[3] His fastidious, elegant style of performance was especially highly prized. In an age of virtuosity, declared his early biographer, W. A. Lampadius,

> Mendelssohn's skill as a virtuoso was no mere legerdemain, no enormous finger facility, that only aims to dazzle by trills, chromatic runs, and octave passages; it was that true, manly *virtus* from which the word virtuoso is derived; that steadfast energy which overcomes all mechanical hinderances, not to produce musical noise, but music, and not satisfied with any thing short of exhibiting the very spirit of productions written in every age of musical art. The characteristic features of his playing were a very elastic touch, a wonderful trill, elegance, roundness, firmness, perfect articulation, strength, and tenderness, each in its

needed place. His chief excellence lay, as Goethe said, in his giving every piece, from the Bach epoch down, its own distinctive character.[4]

These *encomia* aside, Mendelssohn's own piano music has not withstood the test of time unscathed. For the most part, it impresses as comfortable (*gemütlich*), secure music for the salon. Its reliance on older models, for example, the music of J. S. Bach, and its generous applications of rigorous counterpoint were noticed by Robert Schumann for whom, to adopt Leon Plantinga's interpretation, Mendelssohn's piano music was somehow not "fully congruent with the expectations of present-day musical culture."[5] Mendelssohn's keyboard style also exudes a certain sentimental, even saccharine quality—regrettably reinforced after his death by numerous editions of the *Lieder ohne Worte* adorned with fanciful, unauthorized titles—that reflects the conservative temper of the *Restaurationszeit* in Germany and the Victorian period in England.

Occasionally Mendelssohn himself expressed dissatisfaction with his piano music. After finishing the *Rondo brillant* op. 29 for piano and orchestra in 1834, he confessed to Ignaz Moscheles: "My own poverty in shaping new forms for the pianoforte once more struck me most forcibly whilst writing the Rondo. It is there I get into difficulties and have to toil and labor, and I am afraid you will notice that such was the case" (Moscheles, 1888: 85). Later that year, in another letter to Moscheles: "You once said it was time I should write a quiet, sober piece for the pianoforte, after all those restless ones; and that advice is always running in my head and stops me at the outset, for as soon as I think of a pianoforte piece, away I career, and scarcely am I off when I remember, 'Moscheles said, etc.' and there's an end to the piece" (Moscheles, 1888: 121–22). In 1835, Mendelssohn wrote to Ferdinand Hiller: "I have some new pianoforte things, and shall shortly publish some of them. I always think of you and your warning whenever an old-fashioned passage comes into my head, and hope to get rid of such ideas." And again in 1838, to Hiller: "Pianoforte pieces are not exactly the things which I write with the greatest pleasure, or even with real success; but I sometimes want a new thing to play, and then if something exactly suitable for the piano happens to come into my head, even if there are no regular passages in it, why should I be afraid of writing it down?" (Hiller, 43–44, 131).

But if Mendelssohn judged his own piano music severely, he maintained a no less critical gaze toward the piano music of his own time. The music of Beethoven remained beyond reproach for him, and he also highly esteemed the piano works of his close friend (and senior by fifteen years) Moscheles and selected works by Weber (the sonatas, *Aufforderung zum Tanze*, and *Konzertstück*). Little else, however, elicited his critical approbation. Of Schubert's piano music, Mendelssohn knew relatively little,[6] and his opinions about Schumann's piano music have apparently not survived. As for Chopin and Liszt, he clearly admired their pianistic prowess and position as virtuosi of the highest order. On hearing in 1838 of the lionization of the pianist Theodor Döhler, Mendelssohn typically reacted, "What very different stuff Liszt and Chopin are made of! [Chopin] has more soul in his little finger than all Döhler has from top to toe" (Moscheles, 1888: 170). Nevertheless, Chopin's—and especially Liszt's—music gave Mendelssohn pause. Thus to Moscheles he confided in 1835, "A book of Mazurkas by Chopin and a few new pieces of his are so mannered that they are hard to stand"; and, in 1837, "Chopin's new things, too, I don't quite like, and that is provoking"[7] (Moscheles, 1888: 129, 156). In 1840, after Liszt's visit to Leipzig, Mendelssohn expressed himself at length about that phenomenon and the music of Liszt's *Glanzzeit*:

> His playing, which is quite masterly, and his subtle musical feeling, that finds its way to the very tips of his fingers, truly delighted me. His rapidity and suppleness, above all, his playing at sight, his memory, and his thorough musical insight, are qualities quite unique in their way, and that I have never seen surpassed.[8] . . . The only thing that he seems to me to want is true talent for composition, I mean really original ideas. The things he played to me struck me as very incomplete, even when judged from his own point of view, which, to my mind, is not the right one. . . . Liszt's whole performance is as unpremeditated, as wild and impetuous, as you would expect of a genius; but then I miss those genuinely original ideas which I naturally expect from a genius. (Moscheles, 1888: 203–04)

But Mendelssohn reserved his most scathing criticism for the dozens of second-rate virtuoso pianists who crisscrossed Europe pandering their glittery pianistic wares to the public. For Mendelssohn and for Schumann, they represented philistinism at its most pronounced in modern European culture. Thus Friedrich Kalkbrenner, who had dared to claim Chopin as his pupil, Mendelssohn compared to a "little fish patty" or "indigestible sausage"; he saw little if any merit in Sigismond Thalberg's ostentatious fantasias; and, for Henri Herz, he reserved this withering rebuke:

> Well, if he will only abstain from writing Variations for four hands, or . . . winding up with those Rondos that are so frightfully vulgar, . . . then . . . let him be made King of the Belgians,[9] or rather Semiquaver King. . . . He certainly is a characteristic figure of these times, of the year 1834; and as Art should be a mirror reflecting the character of the times,—as Hegel or some one else probably says somewhere,—he certainly does reflect

most truly all salons and vanities, and a little yearning, and a deal of yawning, and kid gloves, and musk, a scent I abhor. If in his latter days he should take to the Romantic and write melancholy music, or to the Classical and give us fugues, . . . Berlioz can compose a new symphony on him, "De la Vie d'un Artiste," which I am sure will be better than the first. (Moscheles, 1888: 112–13)

By 1837 Mendelssohn could only offer this pessimistic assessment: "For really the piano music of the present day is such that I cannot make up my mind to play it through more than once; it is so desperately empty and poor that I usually get tired of it on the first page" (Moscheles, 1888: 156). Nevertheless, Mendelssohn continued to compose for the piano and to emulate, as in all his music, rigorously high, if traditional, artistic standards. We shall consider his piano oeuvre in four categories: (1) early student works from the 1820s; (2) the *Songs without Words* (*Lieder ohne Worte*), which occupied Mendelssohn's attention intermittently between the late 1820s and 1840s; (3) mature works of the 1830s and 1840s in large forms; and (4) mature works of the 1830s and 1840s in short forms.

Early Works: The Student Period

Mendelssohn's earliest surviving piano works date from the early 1820s when he was studying piano with Ludwig Berger and theory and composition with Carl Friedrich Zelter in Berlin and beginning to appear in the concert life of the city.[10] They include a *Recitativo* (which also survives in a version with strings), several sonatas, variations, fugues, fantasias, études, and various other pieces. For the most part these youthful efforts[11] reveal Mendelssohn's distinctly conservative bent and the marked influence of Zelter's traditional instruction, which led the impressionable student through figured bass, chorale, canon, and fugue. There are few signs here of the music of Beethoven, Weber, or other contemporaries; rather, Mendelssohn initially seemed intent on modeling his compositions on the eighteenth-century works of Haydn and Mozart and especially of J. S. Bach. Thus a D-major set of variations set down probably in 1820 is based on a square-cut, eight-bar symmetrical theme that could almost pass for Haydn, followed by a contrasting theme in the minor that is suspiciously close to a theme from a Haydn sonata (Example 6.1a–b). The remainder of the composition oscillates between major and minor variations, a technique reminiscent of Haydn's variations in alternating modalities. Into each D-minor variation, however, Mendelssohn incorporates a canon, first at the octave, then at the third and fifth. This contrapuntal display can point only to his intense study of Bach's music.[12]

EXAMPLE 6.1a. Mendelssohn, Theme and Variations in D major (ca. 1820), mm.
1–8, 17–21

EXAMPLE 6.1b. Haydn, Sonata in D major (Hob. XVI:19), movt. 3 (mm. 17–24)

Considerably more ambitious in scope is the Piano Sonata in G minor, completed on 18 August 1821. Mendelssohn performed it before

Hummel and likely before Goethe during the youth's first visit to Weimar in November of that year, but the sonata was published only posthumously in 1868 as op. 105. It comprises two fast sonata-form movements that enclose a contrasting, cantabile Adagio. Especially noteworthy in the outer movements is their monothematic design; both movements are built up from short, concise motives, a procedure often encountered in the sonatas of Haydn and Clementi. Thus, Mendelssohn extracts the thematic material for the first movement from an initial half-step, G-F♯, which is immediately set against its mirror, D-E♭.[13] Subsequently the half step reappears in a bass line that unfolds a chromatic descending fourth; this traditional figure, in addition to the liberal amount of counterpoint, imbues the movement with a distinctly eighteenth-century hue (Example 6.2). In much the same way, Mendelssohn's one-movement Sonata in B-flat minor of 1823 employs an essentially monothematic approach to sonata form; in addition, it begins with a slow introduction, which returns later in the movement, again bringing to mind similar experiments by Clementi and by Clementi's pupil and Mendelssohn's piano teacher Ludwig Berger.[14]

EXAMPLE 6.2. Mendelssohn, Piano Sonata in G minor, Op. 105, movt. 1 (mm. 1–3, 5–9)

In February 1824 Zelter set his imprimatur on Mendelssohn's progress by declaring him a mature musician in the brotherhood of Sebastian Bach, Mozart, and Haydn.[15] Significantly, Zelter excluded Beethoven and other contemporary composers from his musical pantheon, though by this time his prize pupil was broadening the scope of his piano music beyond the eighteenth-century models he had already essayed. For example, in June 1821, shortly after the premiere of *Der Freischütz* in Berlin, Mendelssohn heard Carl Maria von Weber introduce his *Konzertstück.* The performance deeply impressed the young composer, who adopted the telescoped form and other features of the *Konzertstück* in a number of works.[16] An especially striking example of the debt to Weber is the *Perpetuum mobile* in C major, which Mendelssohn recorded in Moscheles's album during his first English sojourn of 1829 (Moscheles, 1873: 150) but left unpublished; it appeared posthumously in 1873 as op. 119. In many ways Mendelssohn's piece is modeled on Weber's famous *perpetuum mobile* finale from the Piano Sonata in C major op. 24, the same movement Brahms later arranged as a study for the left hand. Example 6.3a–b offers two comparisons: the opening measures, which share rapid descending figuration in the treble supported by similar staccato harmonies in the bass, and fortissimo closing passages with bass octaves.

The keyboard idioms of other virtuosi, such as Johann Nepomuk Hummel and Ignaz Moscheles (who, when he gave Mendelssohn some finishing lessons in 1824, noted in his diary, "I am quite aware that I am sitting next to a master, not a pupil"; Moscheles 1888: 1), also are evident in Mendelssohn's piano works of this time. Thus, a Capriccio in E-flat mi-

EXAMPLE 6.3a. Mendelssohn, *Perpetuum mobile* in C major, Op. 119 (mm. 1–4, 180–81)

EXAMPLE 6.3b. Carl Maria von Weber, Piano Sonata in C major, Op. 24, Finale (mm. 1–4, 326–328)

nor (ca. 1823) exhibits virtuoso figuration with wide leaps, and a Prestissimo in F minor (1824) and Vivace in C minor (1825) were conceived as études, Mendelssohn's response to "advances" in piano technique. On the other hand, Mendelssohn continued to explore the world of Bachian counterpoint. In 1824 he penned a double fugue in G minor, and in 1826 a lyrical Andante in D major that includes as a contrasting middle section a strict canon at the octave. Also in 1826, not long after finishing the *Midsummer Night's Dream* Overture, Mendelssohn conceived a deeply felt fugue in E-flat major; its subject quotes a passage from the *St. Matthew* Passion, which Mendelssohn first came to know in 1823 and then revived in performance in Berlin on 11 March 1829 (Examples 6.4a–b).[17]

But undoubtedly the major new influence, from around 1823, was the music of Beethoven. Numerous specific allusions to Beethoven's piano sonatas occur in Mendelssohn's piano music of the 1820s;[18] in addition, the debt extends to elements of tonal and structural planning. One example is the Piano Sonata in B-flat major, finished on 31 May 1827 but

EXAMPLE 6.4a. Mendelssohn, Fugue in E-flat major (1826), mm. 1–8

EXAMPLE 6.4b. J. S. Bach, *St. Matthew Passion*, Recitative (No. 15), mm. 14–15

published posthumously in 1868 as op. 106. The similarities of this work to Beethoven's magisterial op. 106, the *Hammerklavier* Sonata, have been noted in the literature (see Newman); indeed, Mendelssohn performed the *Hammerklavier* only a few months before finishing his op. 106 sonata.[19] Both are in B-flat major, both begin with a rising figure that highlights the third scale degree, D, and both employ in their first movements a submediant relationship. Furthermore, as in the *Hammerklavier*, Mendelssohn's second movement is a minor-keyed Scherzo, albeit a Scherzo in $\frac{2}{4}$ time, as if to recall the $\frac{2}{4}$ Presto middle portion of Beethoven's Scherzo (mm. 81ff.). For the third movement Mendelssohn attempted a contemplative Andante in the distant key of E major, perhaps his response to Beethoven's extraordinary F-sharp minor Adagio in the *Hammerklavier*. The light-hearted finale, strongly reminiscent of Weber, is linked to the slow movement by an extended transition that not only effects the necessary modulation (from E major to F major as dominant preparation) but also quotes the opening motive of the first movement. In addition, midway through the finale Mendelssohn recycles the material of the Scherzo, a technique clearly derived from Beethoven's Fifth Symphony. These thematic recalls from the first and second movements evidence Mendelssohn's growing interest at this time in the use of cyclic techniques to strengthen the underlying sense of organic thematic unity.[20]

Mendelssohn's piano music of the student period culminated in three compositions: the Capriccio in F-sharp minor op. 5, Sonata in E major op. 6, and *Sieben Charakterstücke* (*Seven Characteristic Pieces*) op. 7, which appeared in Berlin between 1825 and 1827, the first piano works he released for publication. Robert Schumann regarded the Capriccio as a "classic" masterpiece; upon hearing it Rossini was reminded of the sonatas of Domenico Scarlatti.[21] Its untoward technical difficulties were duly noted in the *Allgemeine musikalische Zeitung*.[22] Fittingly enough, in 1835 Mendelssohn designated the work as a birthday present for the sixteen-year-old prodigy Clara Wieck.[23] Formally, the work consists of two alternating sections, ABAB. The capricious character of the A section derives from a series of treacherously expanding leaps and an early jolting turn to unstable diminished-seventh harmonies. The B section, in contrast, is deliberately studied in character: Here Mendelssohn sets a sturdy fuguelike subject against a rushing countersubject in sixteenth notes. With characteristic zeal he indulges his contrapuntal whim by systematically exploiting the subject, first in mirror inversion and then in combination with the prime form.

Like the Piano Sonata op. 106, Mendelssohn's Piano Sonata in E major op. 6 may be viewed as a response to Beethoven's late piano sonatas, though the influence of Weber is again clearly felt in a scintillating finale. In this work, according to Schumann, Mendelssohn touched "Beethoven with his right hand, while looking up to him as to a saint, and being guided at the other by Carl Maria von Weber (with whom it would be more possible to be on a human footing"; Wolff, 210). Among the Beethovenian influences we may mention: (1) the singing, cantabile style of the first movement and its softly dampened sonorities (see the opening of Beethoven's Sonatas opp. 101 and 109, and the second movement of op. 90); (2) tonal relationships by step, as in the second movement, a Minuet in F-sharp minor (see Beethoven's op. 101); (3) experimentation with special pedal effects; (4) the use of widely spaced chords and broad registers; (5) the recall in the finale of material from the first movement (see Beethoven's op. 101) and the device of linking movements; and (6) the use of a free recitative and fugato in the third movement.

The last cited owes its inspiration to the Adagio of Beethoven's op. 101. Like Beethoven, Mendelssohn begins his slow movement with a first-inversion E-major harmony and then introduces a thematic idea sprung from a neighbor-note ornament encircling the pitch E (Example 6.5a–b). While Beethoven subsequently subjects the motive to imitative counterpoint, Mendelssohn goes further and presents the motive in a full-fledged fugato with four descending entries. Notwithstanding this strict, contrapuntal elaboration, Mendelssohn's opening unfolds as a fantasylike recitative without regular bar lines (*Adagio e senza tempo*). Eventually this gives way to an ariosolike Andante in F-sharp major ruled in triple time. A transition returns us to the recitative, which recommences on the dominant; the Andante then reenters a step lower, in B-flat major. Finally, in an extended transition, the dominant B-natural is clarified, and the music progresses through a gradual intensification of texture directly into the finale. The adventuresome tonal plan based on steps (E-F♯; B-B♭-B) may be attributed to Beethoven[24]; even so, the result is a highly effective and forward-looking approach to the problem of unifying the disparate movements of the sonata. Schumann prized Mendelssohn's op. 6 as among the best piano sonatas of the time.

EXAMPLE 6.5a. Mendelssohn, Piano Sonata in E major, Op. 6, movts. 2–3

EXAMPLE 6.5b. Beethoven, Piano Sonata in A major, Op. 101, Adagio (mm. 1–4, 9–12)

Mendelssohn broached a new direction in the *Sieben Charakterstücke*, a group of seven diverse pieces of varying lengths. Tonally the group is unified through the use of sharp keys centered on E (Example 6.6a); in addition, the group obtains a certain programmatic shape by the inclusion of short, subjective titles that Mendelssohn added to suggest individual moods or characters. Some pieces reveal decidedly historicizing tendencies, as critics have noticed (Wolff, 120–21; *BamZ* 4 [1827]: 289; *Amz*

30 [1828]: 63). Thus no. 1 offers thickly imitative, Bachian textures; no. 3 is a buoyant fugue in a Handelian vein; and no. 6 (titled *Sehnsüchtig*), in binary form, evokes the baroque sarabande. No. 5 is a contrapuntal tour de force; it is a fugue filled with special devices, as "though the composer officially wished to demonstrate how diligently he had studied and mastered his subject through counterpoint" (*AmZ* 30 [1828]: 63). Here, however, the model is neither Bach nor Handel but Beethoven; marked *Ernst, und mit steigender Lebhaftigkeit* ("Seriously, and with rising energy"), no. 5 presents an acceleration fugue that takes as a point of departure the fugal finale of Beethoven's Piano Sonata in A-flat major op. 110. Not only does Mendelssohn's subject bear a certain resemblance to Beethoven's sequential subject, but, like Beethoven, Mendelssohn applies erudite—for 1827, *recherché*—devices, as when he combines the mirror form of the subject in stretto against the prime form in augmentation (Example 6.6b).

The three remaining pieces of op. 7 form a decided contrast. Nos. 2 and 4 are études (Mendelssohn treats the running sixteenth-note figuration of the latter in an opening fugal exposition); most progressive of all is the final piece, a light-hearted Scherzo punctuated by mischievous staccato work. Its title, *Leicht und luftig* ("Light and airy"), raises intriguing questions about Mendelssohn's programmatic purpose. Hermann Franck, a friend who reviewed op. 7 in 1827 (*BamZ* 4 [1827]: 288), attempted to describe its peculiar (*fremdartige*) character: "All flies past hastily, without rest, gathering together in colorful throngs, and then scattering in a puff. So this splendid piece impresses as a fleet-footed daughter of the air. Individual chords seem to sting before they resolve; again and again one is teased, as if in a foggy dream. All seems to resolve in a mild, limpid twilight, an indescribably lovely effect." Franck's interpretation brings to mind Mendelssohn's masterpiece of 1826, the *Midsummer Night's*

EXAMPLE 6.6a. Mendelssohn, *Sieben Charakterstücke*, Op. 7, Key Plan

EXAMPLE 6.6b. Mendelssohn, *Charakterstück* (Fugue), Op. 7 no. 5 (mm. 95–101)

Dream Overture, with which, in fact, op. 7 no. 7 shares several stylistic features. Both are in E major, and both make use of descending tetrachords spanning the fourth E-B (Example 6.6c–d). What is more, the *Charakterstück* ends with an unexpected though revealing turn: broken arpeggiations in E minor well up from the depths of the piano. Significantly, the play on modality (major vs. minor) is the crucial device in the overture by which Mendelssohn transports us from the ceremonial world of Theseus's court in Athens to the elfin world of Oberon and his train in the forest. Not surprisingly, for Schumann, the *Charakterstück* represented a "forecast" of the overture.

EXAMPLE 6.6c. Mendelssohn, *Charakterstück* ("Leicht und luftig"), Op. 7 no. 7 (mm. 1–6)

EXAMPLE 6.6d. Mendelssohn, Overture to *A Midsummer Night's Dream*, Op. 21 (mm. 8–11)

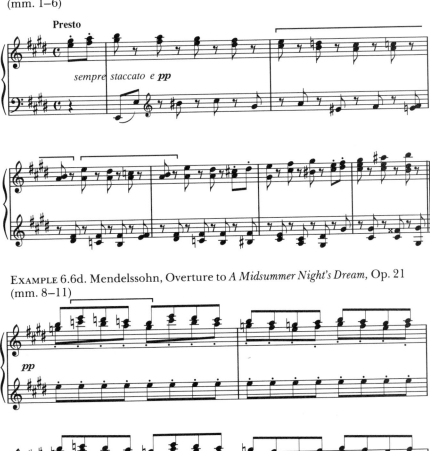

Songs without Words (*Lieder ohne Worte*)

With the *Songs without Words,* most of which appeared during the 1830s and 1840s, Mendelssohn developed the musical genre to which his reputation as a composer of piano music became inseparably attached. Designed primarily for amateur domestic music making, these highly popular piano pieces struck resonant chords in respectable middle-class households throughout Europe, where the piano enjoyed increasing status as the preferred instrument. Attempts have been made to trace the origins of the *Songs without Words* to various character pieces of Schubert, Dussek, Tomášek, and Mendelssohn's teacher Ludwig Berger—thereby diminishing the scope of Mendelssohn's contribution—but with limited success.[25] The documentary evidence, though scanty, firmly indicates that the term and concept of *Lied ohne Worte* originated with Mendelssohn or his circle sometime during the late 1820s; indeed, from his talented sister Fanny Hensel, whose own piano Lieder began to appear in print toward the end of her life (in 1846 and 1847), we learn that the genre may have been inspired by a kind of musical game the siblings played as children.

In a little known letter written to her brother in 1838, Fanny compared Mendelssohn's textless "piano songs" to the then fashionable technique, popularized by Liszt and other virtuosi, of transcribing texted songs for keyboard performance: "Dear Felix, when text is removed from sung lieder so that they can be used as concert pieces, it is contrary to the experiment of adding a text to your instrumental lieder—the other half of the topsy-turvy world. I'm old enough to find many things utterly tasteless in the world at present: that may well fall into that category. But shouldn't a person think a lot of himself . . . when he sees how the jokes that we, as mere children, contrived to pass the time have now been adopted by the great talents and used as fodder for the public?"[26]

This child's play aside, the new piano genre touched on a fundamental problem that confronted nineteenth-century aestheticians of music: in Friedhelm Krummacher's formulation, how to make instrumental music, now enjoying more and more autonomy from vocal music, comprehensible to the public.[27] Understandably, the inherent contradiction in the title *Lieder ohne Worte* initially created confusion. Thus, the theorist Moritz Hauptmann, before he had an opportunity to examine the first book of Mendelssohn's new pieces, mistook them for a kind of vocal exercise: "What is it all about? Is he really in earnest? To be sure, in strictness, pure Lyric has no words, but that means no intelligence—no form, therefore no Art. . . . Still, Songs without Words must be uncanny, I think; I am not very fond of Crescentini's Solfeggios, because they seem to me to tax unduly the singer's power of expressing what he feels."[28]

Robert Schumann, who reviewed three volumes of Mendelssohn's *Songs without Words,* offered this conjecture about the origins of the pieces: "Who of us in the twilight hour has not sat at his upright piano (a grand piano would serve a statelier occasion), and in the midst of improvising has not unconsciously begun to sing a quiet melody? Should one happen to be able to *play* the cantilena along with the accompaniment, above all, should one happen to be a Mendelssohn, the loveliest 'song without words' would result. Or, still easier: to choose a text and then, eliminating the words, give in this form one's compositions to the world" (Wolff, 210). Inevitably the interpretation of these compositions as songs with suppressed texts provoked further questions, and in 1842 Marc-André Souchay asked Mendelssohn about the specific meanings of some *Songs without Words*. Here are parts of Mendelssohn's celebrated reply:

> People often complain that music is too ambiguous; that what they should think when they hear it is so unclear, whereas everyone understands words. With me it is exactly the reverse, and not only with regard to an entire speech, but also with individual words. These, too, seem to me so ambiguous, so vague, so easily misunderstood in comparison to genuine music, which fills the soul with a thousand things better than words. The thoughts which are expressed to me by music that I love are not too indefinite to be put into words, but on the contrary, too definite. . . . If you ask me what I was thinking of when I wrote it [the *Song without Words*], I would say: Just the song as it stands. And if I happen to have had certain words in mind for one or another of these songs, I would never want to tell them to anyone because the same words never mean the same things to different people. Only the song can say the same thing, can arouse the same feelings in one person as in another, a feeling which is not expressed, however, by the same words.[29]

Thus for Mendelssohn, music represented a higher form of language, one that communicated its meaning with a precision unmatched by the ambiguities of mere words.

With due deliberation, then, Mendelssohn left most of his *Songs without Words* untitled. Though they typically have clear songlike qualities (e. g., lyrical treble melodies supported by an arpeggiated form of accompaniment) and are frequently cast in a ternary song form, suggesting again the trappings of the texted art song, for the large majority their poetic meaning or the types of poetic texts they represent remain unknown. Of the thirty-six Lieder Mendelssohn published, only five have titles he authorized. The three minor-keyed *Venetianische Gondellieder* (*Venetian Gondola Songs*), op. 19 no. 6, op. 30 no. 6, and op. 62 no. 5, project the distinctive features of the barcarolle: in $\frac{6}{8}$ time, they display melancholic treble melodies against a cross-current of undulating, arpeggiated accompaniments. Op. 38 no. 6, titled *Duetto,* was written in 1836 at the time of Mendelssohn's engagement to Cécile Jeanrenaud. Throughout much of the Lied, the melodic material alternates between soprano and tenor registers; in the closing section the melody appears doubled at the octave in both voices. Op. 53 no. 5 is appropriately titled *Volkslied* (*Folksong*); with its open-spaced chords and strident introductory fifths (Example 6.7a), it captures something of the rough-hewn quality of the first movement of Mendelssohn's *Scottish* Symphony op. 56 and looks ahead to the A-minor episode of the finale to Brahms's Piano Sonata op. 1.

EXAMPLE 6.7a. Mendelssohn, *Lied ohne Worte* (*Volkslied*), Op. 53 no. 5 (mm. 1–2)

A few other titles were evidently suppressed by Mendelssohn. For example, the autograph of op. 53 no. 3 is titled *Gondellied,* and an autograph copy of op. 53 no. 4 bears the heading *Abendlied* (*Evening Song*).[30] One piano Lied which Mendelssohn composed in 1844 but left unpublished is titled *Reiterlied* (*Rider's Song*); driven by an infectious staccato rhythm, this delightful piece contains an extended canonic passage, doubled at the octave, to convey the idea of a pursuit.[31] Finally, four other songs have titles either attributed to Mendelssohn or to his circle. Thus op. 19 no. 3, which resounds with horn calls, is patently a *Jägerlied* (*Hunters' Song*) or *Jagdlied* (*Hunting Song*), a favorite *topos* of romantic music and poetry alike. Op. 62 no. 3 (*Andante maestoso*, $\frac{2}{4}$ time) is a *Trauermarsch* (*Funeral March*); op. 62 no. 6, with its delicate, harplike accompaniment, is the celebrated *Frühlingslied* (*Spring Song*); and op. 67 no. 4, introduced by a swirling turnlike figure, is a *Spinnerlied* (*Spinning Song*).[32] But here the list ends, notwithstanding the superabundance of unauthorized, overtly sentimental titles ("Sweet Remembrance," "Consolation," and the like) which publishers saw fit to append after Mendelssohn's death.

The great majority of the *Songs without Words* fall into three categories; a few songs defy ready classification. The most frequent type, the solo Lied, is featured at the beginning of each set; other examples that display soprano melodies include op. 38 nos. 2 and 3; op. 53 nos. 2, 4, and 6; op. 62 no. 6; op. 67 no. 6; op. 85 nos. 3, 4, and 6; and op. 102 no. 4. Into a second category fall the duets, which have two treble melodic lines, typically doubled in thirds or sixths, as in the *Venetian Gondola Songs* op. 19 no. 6 and op. 62 no. 5; the *Duetto* op. 38 no. 6 contraposes soprano and tenor melodic lines. A few Lieder suggest a hybrid between the solo and duet types. Thus, op. 19 no. 2, op. 30 no. 6 (the second *Venetian Gondola Song*) and op. 67 no. 2 begin as solo Lieder but continue with passages displaying duetlike textures (Example 6.7b). In an extension of the duet, at least two Lieder, op. 53 no. 3 and op. 62 no. 2, suggest trio or quartet textures,

EXAMPLE 6.7b. Mendelssohn, *Lied ohne Worte*, Op. 67 no. 2 (mm. 5–6, 29–30)

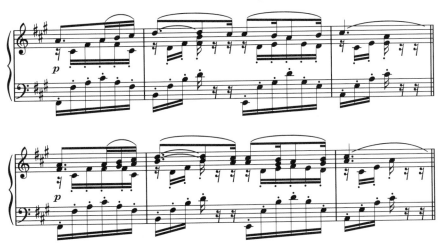

EXAMPLE 6.7c. Mendelssohn, *Lied ohne Worte*, Op. 53 no. 3 (mm. 9–12)

with three or four treble melodic lines (Example 6.7c). The third category, the partsongs, are distinguished by homophonic textures; among these are op. 19 nos. 3 and 4, op. 30 no. 3, op. 38 no. 4, op. 53 no. 5 (*Volkslied*), op. 62 no. 4, op. 67, no. 5, op. 85 no. 5, and op. 102 no. 6. The third and fourth Lieder of op. 19 stand in a special relationship: not only are they in A major, but they both make use of the same horn-call figure associated with the hunt. Indeed, Mendelssohn may have intended both as *Jägerlieder* or *Jagdlieder* (Example 6.7d).

This tripartite division of the *Lieder ohne Worte* into solo songs, duets, and partsongs mirrors a similar division in Mendelssohn's texted songs

EXAMPLE 6.7d. Mendelssohn, *Lied ohne Worte* (*Jägerlied*), Op. 19 no. 3 (mm. 6–9) and *Lied ohne Worte*, Op. 19 no. 4 (mm. 6–9)

into solo Lieder, duets, and choral partsongs. What is more, among the texted Lieder we may find precisely those titles—*Frühlingslied* (op. 34 no. 3, op. 71 no. 2), *Volkslied* (op. 63 no. 5), *Gondellied* (op. 57 no. 5), and *Jagdlied* (op. 59 no. 6, op. 120 no. 1)—applied by Mendelssohn or his circle to some of the *Songs without Words*. In all likelihood, the inspiration for the *Songs without Words* lay in the wealth of German romantic lyric poetry, and the step from texted to textless song, from poem (whether an actual poem or abstract poetic type) to pure instrumental music, was facilitated by the composer's ever fertile imagination.

Mendelssohn evidently began to compose *Lieder ohne Worte* during the later 1820s for the albums of friends and family; a letter from his sister Fanny dated 8 December 1828 refers to a "*Lied ohne Worte*, of which he has composed several recently."[33] Not until 1832, however, did he contemplate the possibility of publishing a collection of these pieces. In July his first volume appeared as op. 19 in London, Bonn, and Paris, followed in 1833 by a volume of songs *with* words, published as op. 19b (Illustration 6.1).[34] In preparing op. 19 Mendelssohn drew upon some older piano pieces and created a few new ones to insure a suitable balance between Lieder in major keys (nos. 1, 3, and 4) and minor keys (nos. 2, 5, and 6), between relatively short (no. 4) and longer Lieder (nos. 3 and 5), and among various types, including the solo Lied (no. 1), duet (no. 6), and partsong (nos. 3 and 4). Five additional volumes of *Lieder ohne Worte* appeared during Mendelssohn's lifetime: opp. 30 (1835), 38 (1837), 53 (1841), 62 (1844), and 67 (1845), all with dedications to women, including, in the case of op. 62, Clara Schumann. Then, after Mendelssohn's death, two additional volumes appeared, opp. 85 (1850) and 102 (1868). These were assembled from miscellaneous pieces in the composer's *Nachlass*, and among them figured some that he had rejected for inclusion in op. 67,

ILLUSTRATION 6.1. Mendelssohn, *Melodies for the Pianoforte* (*Lieder ohne Worte*), op. 19, autograph title page and number 3. Reproduced by permission of the Huntington Library, San Marino, California.

the sixth and last set published under his supervision. Though opp. 85 and 102 may in no way be regarded as authentic *opera*, a manuscript source does survive that provides some clues about Mendelssohn's plans for a seventh volume of *Lieder ohne Worte*. Bearing an autograph title page dated 4 April 1846 (Illustration 6.2), the manuscript includes copies of op. 85 nos. 1, 2, 3, and 5, the *Reiterlied*, and op. 102 no. 2. Represented are the solo Lied (op. 85 no. 1), the duet (op. 102 no. 2), the partsong (op. 85 no. 5), and the programmatic piece with title (*Reiterlied*), in accordance with the composer's usual procedure.

Mendelssohn's catalog of works includes several other pieces that, though not specifically titled, are essentially *Lieder ohne Worte*. Among these are the *Gondellied* in A major, a Duet without Words that appeared separately in 1838; and the six *Kinderstücke* (*Children's Pieces*) op. 72, composed in London in 1842.[35] Nor was the *Lied-ohne-Worte* style limited to Mendelssohn's piano music. Mendelssohn titled at least one posthumous chamber work, for cello and piano, a *Romance sans paroles* (op. 109), and the slow movements of the Piano Trios opp. 49 and 66, String Quartets op. 44, the Piano Concerto in D minor op. 40, and the Violin Concerto in E minor op. 64 are essentially further examples of the genre. What is more, many other composers emulated the *Lied-ohne-Worte* style. Several of Robert Schumann's *Phantasiestücke* op. 12 may be regarded as *Lieder ohne Worte*, as may the slow movements of Brahms's piano sonatas opp. 1, 2, and 4;[36] related to them are the versions of Liszt's three *Petrarch Sonnets* for solo piano.[37] Spohr, Stephen Heller, Henry Litolff, Tchaikovsky, and Fauré composed songs without words. The young Richard Strauss produced one example for full orchestra in 1883 and later transformed Mendelssohn's *Gondellied* op. 19 no. 6 into a *Wiegenlied* in the *Symphonia domestica* of 1903.[38] Finally, some measure of their enduring significance as a kind of *topos* in European culture is found in literature. The venerable Sherlock Holmes plays Mendelssohn's Lieder on request in the second chapter of *A Study in Scarlet* (1888) as a "testimony to his power on the violin." In Samuel Butler's scathing indictment of Victorian society, *The Way of All Flesh* (posthumously published in 1903), the protagonist Ernest Pontifex engages in a conversation about "modern music" with Miss Skinner, and comes to the conclusion that he "never did like modern music"; "with his mind's ear" he seems to "hear Miss Skinner saying, as though it were an epitaph: STAY / I MAY PRESENTLY TAKE / A SIMPLE CHORD OF BEETHOVEN / OR A SMALL SEMIQUAVER / FROM ONE OF MENDELSSOHN'S SONGS WITHOUT WORDS." "Songs without Words" figure in the music-laden imagery of the Sirens episode in James Joyce's *Ulysses* (1922); and Aldous Huxley, in the fourth chapter of *After Many a Summer Dies the Swan* (1939), describes a "ridiculous Englishman with a face like a rabbit's and a voice like Songs without Words on the saxophone."

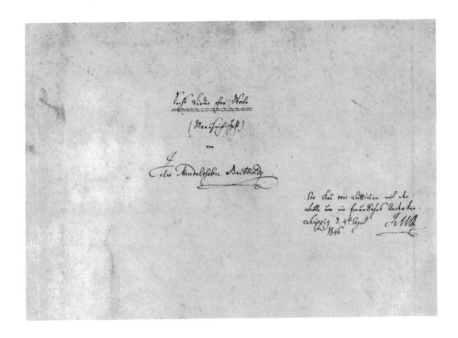

ILLUSTRATION 6.2. Mendelssohn, *Sechs Lieder ohne Worte* (*Manuscript-Heft*), auto-graph title page and copy of no. 5, *Reiterlied* (Stanford Memorial Music Library). Courtesy of the Department of Special Collections, Stanford University Libraries.

Mature Works: The Large Forms

Mendelssohn produced only five mature piano works of ambitious scope. Three of these, the Fantasia in F-sharp minor (*Scottish Sonata*) op. 28, *Six Preludes and Fugues* op. 35, and *Variations sérieuses* op. 54, appeared in print during his lifetime; two additional variation sets were published posthumously as opp. 82 and 83. The three-movement Fantasia, like the Schumann Fantasy op. 17, was conceived as a three-movement piano sonata; the Preludes and Fugues reflected Mendelssohn's desire to preserve the heritage of Bach's *Well-Tempered Clavier* and to renew the art of fugal writing; and the *Variations sérieuses* was Mendelssohn's contribution to a musical album in honor of Beethoven.

The origins of the Fantasia remain obscure. Its final version dates from 1833, though the original version, titled *Scottish* Sonata (*Sonate écossaise*), was probably composed as early as 1828.[39] The work thus belongs to a group of compositions inspired by Scottish subjects,[40] including the *Hebrides* Overture and the *Scottish* Symphony, though significantly, the Fantasia was drafted *before* and thus uninfluenced by Mendelssohn's celebrated Scottish sojourn in 1829. Whether or not a particular Scottish program for the *Fantasia* existed is not known; characteristically, Mendelssohn left no clues about its meaning when he suppressed the original title upon publishing the work in 1834. Still, certain features, notably in the first movement, betray the likelihood of some programmatic inspiration: the use of widely spaced harmonies and chords with open fifths, blurred, open pedal techniques, and dramatically spaced dissonant crescendos, all of which look ahead to similar special effects in Mendelssohn's later Scottish works.

The Fantasia comprises three movements, played without separation, in progressively faster tempos: Andante, Allegro, and Presto, the last a dramatic, full-length sonata movement that carries the structural weight of the composition. The probable source for this plan was Beethoven's *Sonata quasi Fantasia* (*Moonlight* Sonata, op. 27 no. 2), which suggests, like Mendelssohn's Fantasia (*Sonate écossaise*), a mixture of genres. But the resemblance is primarily external, for Mendelssohn fills his *Fantasia* with distinctively original material. In the first movement, the brooding, melancholy Andante is prefaced by a series of rapid, hushed arpeggiations that rise from the depths of the piano. Out of this shadowy opening emerges a loose sonata form based on two melodious sections in the tonic minor and relative major; the arpeggiations of the opening return to provide a kind of connective tissue between the contrasting groups. In the center of the movement Mendelssohn works up the arpeggiations into a dramatic crescendo with rising chromatic scales in the bass. A recapitulation of the two principal themes follows; then, in the coda we are left with an open-pedal passage in which the first theme momentarily reappears, echolike, an effect not unlike the close of the *Hebrides* Overture (Example 6.8).

EXAMPLE 6.8. Mendelssohn, Fantasia in F-sharp minor (*Sonate écossaise*), Op. 28, movt. 1 (closing measures)

Mendelssohn's most substantial piano work, the *Six Preludes and Fugues,* appeared in 1837 as op. 35. Combining freshly composed preludes with several earlier, independent fugues, he arranged the entire collection in a tonal plan based on alternating minor and major keys, with three sharp keys and three flat keys (E minor, D major, B minor, A-flat major, F minor, B-flat major). Several of the preludes have distinctly étudelike characters; in fact, Mendelssohn evidently viewed the work as a juxtaposition of technical and contrapuntal studies, for he first intended to title it *Six Études and Fugues.*[41] The first prelude explores a technical device developed by Sigismond Thalberg during the 1830s and then exploited by Liszt and other pianists, the so-called three-hand technique. In this device melodic material is entrusted primarily to the two thumbs in the middle register of the piano, and rapid figuration, often in some arpeggiated form, is executed above and below (Example 6.9). Mendelssohn used the technique in a variety of other piano works as well, including the Prelude in E minor (1842, without opus number), the Étude in B-flat minor op. 104b no. 1, and the Piano Concerto No. 2 in D minor. This last work's first movement displays arpeggio passages, through which, in Moscheles's words, "the melody seems to push its way" (Moscheles, 1888: 168).

Other preludes feature a three-part texture with a treble melodic line supported by a running, sixteenth-note inner voice and walking bass (no. 2); a scherzolike arpeggiation study in staccato articulation (no. 3); a duetlike texture with two melodic lines in imitative counterpoint (no. 4); and *cantabile* soprano melodic lines supported by chordal accompaniments—pulsating, tremololike chords in no. 5 and arpeggiated

EXAMPLE 6.9. Mendelssohn, Prelude in E minor, Op. 35 no. 1 (mm. 1–3)

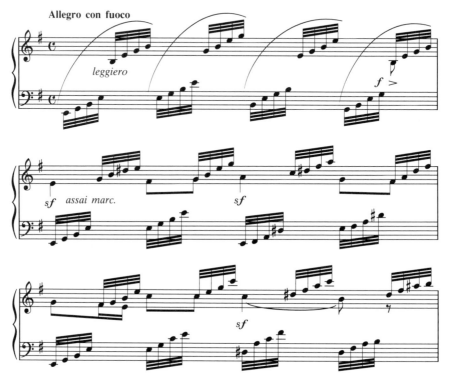

block chords in no. 6. The conclusion of the fifth prelude is especially striking. The descending melody momentarily appears in an inner voice before reappearing in the soprano to pause on a diminished-seventh harmony. This dissonance resolves to a pulsating measure of the tonic F, but unexpectedly in the major mode, a striking historicism that alludes to the *tierce de Picardie* and the music of J. S. Bach (Example 6.10).

But it is the six fugues, of course, that reinvigorate the spirit of the *Well-Tempered Clavier.* Here is how Robert Schumann considered the question of Mendelssohn's debt to Bach:

> In a word, these fugues have much of Sebastian and might de-
> ceive the sharp-sighted reviewer, were it not for the melody,
> the finer bloom, which we recognize as modern; and here and
> there those little touches peculiar to Mendelssohn, which iden-
> tify him among a hundred other composers. Whether review-
> ers agree or not, it remains certain that the artist did not write
> them for pastime, but rather to call the attention of pianoforte
> players once more to this masterly old form and to accustom
> them to it again. That he has chosen the right means for suc-
> ceeding in this—avoiding all useless imitations and small arti-

EXAMPLE 6.10. Mendelssohn, Prelude in F minor, Op. 35 no. 5 (mm. 68–73)

ficialities, allowing the melody of the cantilena to predominate while holding fast to the Bach form—is very much like him. (Wolff, 214–15)

In Schumann's view, then, Mendelssohn was attempting not necessarily to invoke the music of J. S. Bach directly but to explore in a modern keyboard idiom the style of fugal writing—more and more becoming, in 1837, an antiquated art.

Still, the fugues "have much of Sebastian." Thus the subject of the second fugue (D major) offers what is clearly a rhythmically simplified version of the subject from Bach's D-major Fugue in the *Well-Tempered Clavier*, Book I (Example 6.11a–b. Schumann was impressed enough by

EXAMPLE 6.11a. Mendelssohn, Fugue in D major, Op. 35 no. 2 (mm. 1–8)

EXAMPLE 6.11b. J. S. Bach, Fugue in D major, *Well-Tempered Clavier*, Book I (mm. 1–3)

the lyricism of Mendelssohn's subject, however, to suggest that the fugue might be mistaken for a *Song without Words.*) To be sure, Mendelssohn's fugues do not lack those specialized "paper intricacies" for which Bach was celebrated. Thus, in the third fugue (B minor), Mendelssohn applies mirror inversion to his subject and later combines the two forms, first in stretto at the fourth and, at the conclusion of the fugue, in simultaneous contraposition. Similarly, in the first fugue (E minor), the winding, chromatic subject reappears in mirror inversion, though here, perhaps, this erudite procedure is overshadowed by those "touches peculiar to Mendelssohn." For one, the fugue culminates in a freely composed chorale in E major, with accompaniment in octaves, and concludes with a short Andante postlude in the major; for another, it is designed as an acceleration fugue, perhaps in homage not to Bach but to the fugal finale of Beethoven's Piano Sonata op. 110. In a similar way, the fourth fugue (a double fugue in A-flat major) draws its subject not from Bach but from Beethoven's op. 110, also in A-flat major; here Beethoven's sequence of rising fourths is filled in with stepwise motion (Example 6.12a–b).

Opus 35 was one of three cycles in which Mendelssohn explored contrapuntal styles of writing. In 1837, he also released his *Three Preludes and Fugues for Organ* op. 37, and in 1844 and 1845, a period when he was editing selected organ works of Bach,[42] Mendelssohn composed the *Six Organ Sonatas* op. 65. Other composers around this time sought to renew their art through counterpoint: thus, Chopin studied the music of Bach during the 1840s, as did Clara and Robert Schumann, whose work culminated in Clara Schumann's *Three Preludes and Fugues* op. 16 and Robert Schumann's *Six Fugues on BACH for Organ* op. 60. But for Chopin and the Schumanns this study of counterpoint represented a relatively concentrated undertaking; for Mendelssohn, opp. 35, 37, and 65 represented an ongoing commitment to the rejuvenation of modern music through traditional counterpoint.

Mendelssohn's three sets of piano variations, opp. 54, 82, and 83, all date from the summer of 1841 (a piano duet arrangement of op. 83 followed in 1844). Of these the *Variations sérieuses* op. 54 is often acknowledged as his masterpiece for the instrument, though the details of its creation are still not well known. In March 1841 the Viennese publisher Pietro

EXAMPLE 6.12a. Mendelssohn, Fugue in A-flat major, Op. 35 no. 4 (mm. 1–9)

EXAMPLE 6.12b. Beethoven, Piano Sonata in A-flat major, Op. 110, Finale (mm. 27–30)

Mechetti invited Mendelssohn to contribute a piano work to a Beethoven album, to be published in a limited edition whose sales would benefit efforts underway to erect a Beethoven monument in Bonn. The album appeared in December 1841 with Mendelssohn's variations and works by Chopin, Czerny, Liszt, Moscheles, and other pianists.

Mendelssohn's choice of "serious" variations was his response to the Beethoven tribute.[43] In fact, the op. 54 alludes to at least two Beethoven works, the *Thirty-Two Variations* in C minor for piano and, appropriately enough, the String Quartet op. 95, which Beethoven labeled *Serioso*. As is well known, Beethoven's variations are constructed upon the traditional descending chromatic fourth, the chaconne bass pattern associated since the seventeenth century with the lament and other serious topics. Now, though this chromatic figure is not directly stated in Mendelssohn's theme, careful analytical prodding reveals that the two are not unrelated. First of all, embedded in Mendelssohn's theme and accompaniment are several descending scalelike lines (Example 6.13a). Thus, in the theme the initial A descends to a G-sharp; this pitch, though it literally skips by tritone to a D above, may also be heard to descend to the G-natural in the contiguous tenor voice, and from there to continue downward through F and E. A complete octave descent, in fact, may be traced, beginning in the tenor (D-C-B♮), then shifting to the alto (B♭-A-G) and concluding in the soprano (F-E-D). To be sure, these descents are not strictly chromatic and by themselves do not constitute invocations of the chaconne pattern. But convincing evidence is at hand: Mendelssohn's composing score of the *Variations sérieuses,* dated 4 June 1841,[44] contains several rejected variations, one of which clearly states the descending chromatic bass, reinforced at the octave with rapid figuration in the treble (Example 6.13b). Evidently, Mendelssohn did associate the chromatic bass with his theme.

EXAMPLE 6.13a. Mendelssohn, *Variations sérieuses* in D minor, Op. 54, Theme (mm. 1–4)

EXAMPLE 6.13b. Mendelssohn, *Variations sérieuses* in D minor, Op. 54, Rejected Variation (Kraków, Biblioteca Jagiellońska, *Mendelssohn Nachlass* 35)

Mendelssohn's composing score of op. 54 provides one other clue that links the work to Beethoven. The original version of the tenth variation, a fugato, resembled the fugal subject from the slow movement of the *Serioso* Quartet, a subject that unfolds another version of the descending chromatic figure (Examples 6.14a–b; see also Illustration 6.3). The final version of Mendelssohn's tenth variation deviates clearly enough from the Beethoven, yet some tell-tale signs of the source remain, including rhythmic similarities and the use of the chromatic pitches B-flat and G-sharp as auxiliary tones to the fifth scale degree A (Example 6.14a, m. 2; 6.14b, m. 42).

EXAMPLE 6.14a. Mendelssohn, *Variations sérieuses* in D minor, Op. 54, Fugato (Variation 10), mm. 1–5, and Rejected Version (see Illustration 6.3)

EXAMPLE 6.14b. Beethoven, String Quartet (*Serioso*), Op. 95, *Allegretto ma non troppo* (mm. 39–42)

If the *Variations sérieuses* stand as a kind of homage to Beethoven, they also represent a major contribution to the nineteenth-century theme and variation. Mendelssohn devised the work as a theme with eighteen variations, in which the final variation functioned as an expanded coda. The first nine variations describe a course that gradually builds in intensity, through the use of increasingly faster rhythmic values and, in the fourth variation, the application of canon. Following the comparatively restrained tenth and eleventh variations, marked Moderato, the process of intensification resumes: in the twelfth and thirteenth, the theme is transferred from the soprano to the inner register; the thirteenth variation offers yet another example of the three-hand technique. The next two variations mark a second structural pause. The fourteenth is a lovely major-key variation in which the theme, still situated in an inner voice, is concealed by a lyrical soprano line (Example 6.15). In the harshly dissonant fifteenth, marked *Poco a poco più agitato*, the theme is finally disembodied and broken up among various registers (Example 6.16). In the sixteenth and seventeenth variations, Mendelssohn introduces brilliant virtuoso figuration that builds to a climax: the theme is reintroduced intact over a dramatic dominant pedal point and finally, in the culminating coda, presented in unrelenting syncopation. Near the end we hear an arpeggiated flourish on a diminished-seventh harmony; then, a few quiet chords outline the descending tonic minor triad.[45]

In his two other sets of variations, Mendelssohn chose themes of contrasting characters: "sentimental" for op. 82 and "gracious" for op.

ILLUSTRATION 6.3. Mendelssohn, *Variations sérieuses,* Op. 54 (Kraków, Biblioteca Jagiellońska, *Mendelssohn Nachlass* 35, f. 31). Autograph.

83.[46] Though meticulously crafted, these works do not measure up to the stature of op. 54. In choosing a serious tone for op. 54, Mendelssohn was indeed looking back at Beethoven's achievements, and that glance sufficed for him to create a worthy successor to Beethoven's C-minor Variations. In turn, op. 54 influenced later works in that genre. Notable examples in the serious style include two by Brahms, the Variations in D ma-

EXAMPLE 6.15. Mendelssohn, *Variations sérieuses* in D minor, Op. 54, Variation 14 (mm. 1–4)

EXAMPLE 6.16. Mendelssohn, *Variations sérieuses* in D minor, Op. 54, Variation 15 (mm. 1–4)

jor op. 21 no. 1 and, of course, the finale of the Fourth Symphony, based on a *rising* passacaglia figure. Example 6.17 gives one example of how Brahms alluded, consciously or unconsciously, to Mendelssohn's op. 54. The tenth variation of op. 21 no. 1—a variation in D minor—revives for a moment the eleventh variation of Mendelssohn's set. Mendelssohn's disjunct melodic configuration—A-G-D-C♯—may be traced in the same register in the Brahms. What is more, Mendelssohn's eighth-note turn figure (measure 3) resurfaces, and both examples are supported by a tonic pedal point. As had Mendelssohn, so did Brahms find inspiration in musical tradition.

EXAMPLE 6.17a. Mendelssohn, *Variations sérieuses* in D minor, Op. 54, Variation 11 (mm. 1–4)

EXAMPLE 6.17b. Brahms, *Variations on a Theme by the Composer,* Op. 21 no. 1, Variation 10 (mm. 1–4)

Mature Works: The Short Forms

The rest of Mendelssohn's piano music includes several short and intermediate-length compositions that fall conveniently into three groups: four works to which he assigned opus numbers (opp.14, 15, 16, and 33), six pieces he published separately in various albums and periodicals, and five works that appeared posthumously (opp. 104a and b, 117, 118, and an Andante and Presto). Miscellaneous other pieces and fragments survive in manuscript and await further study.[47] A cluster of three works appeared in 1830 and 1831 as opp. 14, 15, and 16, the *Rondo capriccioso, Fantasy on an Irish Song,* and *Three Fantasies or Caprices.* Precious little is known about the origins of op. 15, a keyboard fantasy on the Irish song "The Last Rose," which was popularized during the nineteenth century in settings by such composers as Beethoven, Moscheles, and Flotow. Considerably more is known about opp. 14 and 16, which had their origins in 1828 and 1829.

The *Rondo capriccioso* was conceived in 1828 as an Étude in E minor; an incomplete autograph of this version, which consisted of only the Presto, survives (Illustration 6.4). Some two years later Mendelssohn reworked the piece, apparently as a present for the talented Munich pianist Delphine von Schauroth; on 13 June 1830 he dated his second autograph, which now included the lyrical Andante introduction and transition to the original Presto.[48] Mendelssohn himself frequently performed the work, and it quickly entered the repertoire as a favorite virtuoso showpiece. Analysis reveals how, when he added the Andante, he took pains to link it thematically to the Presto: the two principal ideas describe descending forms of the tonic major and minor triads, with several structural pitches embellished by auxiliary tones (Example 6.18a–c). The device of joining slow and fast movements was likely influenced by Carl Maria von Weber's *Konzertstück*; indeed, the *Rondo capriccioso* is not unlike the condensed second and third movements of a concerto and presages similar procedures Mendelssohn followed in his two three-movement piano concertos, opp. 25 and 40, and in two shorter works for piano and orchestra, the *Capriccio brillant* op. 22 and *Serenade und Allegro giojoso* op. 43, which, like op. 14, have slow movements linked to fast finales.

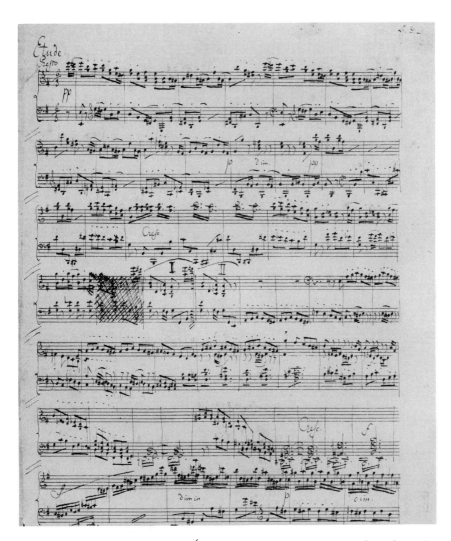

ILLUSTRATION 6.4. Mendelssohn, Étude (early autograph version of *Rondo capriccioso*, op. 14), Pierpont Morgan Library, New York.

The three Fantasies op. 16 (also designated Caprices) were written during Mendelssohn's visit to Wales in September 1829 as presents for the three daughters of John Taylor, an Englishman who operated several lead mines. As a houseguest at Taylor's summer residence at Coed Du, Mendelssohn sketched the scenery of the Welsh countryside during the day and improvised at the piano during the evening. The first piece, the opening of which brings to mind the opening of the *Scottish* Symphony (jotted down two months earlier), was inspired by the sight of carnations and roses. The rising diminished-seventh arpeggiations in the Andante

EXAMPLE 6.18. Mendelssohn, *Rondo capriccioso,* Op.14 (a–b, mm. 4–8, 27–30) and Analytical Reduction (c)

sections were evidently meant to suggest "the sweet scent of the flower rising up."[49] The second, a spirited Scherzo in E minor, was inspired by a creeping plant with trumpet-shaped flowers. Mendelssohn's Presto sought to capture the music that "the fairies might play on those trumpets."[50] With its gossamer textures, mock trumpet fanfares, and light staccato work in the high register, it effectively transports us to the world of the *Midsummer Night's Dream* Overture. As in the overture, Mendelssohn introduces a descending tetrachord figure in the minor (Example 6.19), and plays on the major versus minor modal duality by directing the Scherzo to conclude in a delicately scored passage in E major. The third fantasy, a gently undulating Andante, was Mendelssohn's representation of a rivulet; its original title, *Am Bach* (*By the Brook*), and thick, dark textures (e. g., mm. 50ff.) encourage comparisons with the celebrated slow movement of the same title in Beethoven's *Pastoral* Symphony. But despite all these extramusical elements, Mendelssohn suppressed the urge to provide special titles when he published op. 16, allowing instead the (for him) superior language of absolute music and the listener's imagination to remain unencumbered.

EXAMPLE 6.19. Mendelssohn, Scherzo in E minor, Op. 16 no. 2 (mm. 1–8)

The Three Caprices op. 33, in A minor, E major, and B minor, were composed between 1833 and 1835 and published in 1836. Each begins with an introductory section that proceeds to a full-fledged movement in sonata form. The introductions range from a few measures of chords that hint at a thematic outline (no. 2), to more fully developed Adagios that pause on the dominant (nos. 1 and 3). The opening Adagio of no. 1 presents a series of rising arpeggiations above a descending chromatic bass. Improvisatory in character, it recalls the tradition of the keyboard fantasia; indeed, the tempo marking *Adagio quasi fantasia* demonstrates, as does the title of op. 16, that for Mendelssohn the distinction between the caprice and fantasy was not clearly drawn. As Carl Czerny attempted to explain, the essential character of the caprice resided more in its "singular or even eccentric ideas, than in the form."[51] The main bodies of the Caprices represent more or less straightforward sonata movements but suffer perhaps from their undue length and overworking of the thematic material. Still, Robert Schumann was favorably impressed by the second, which he compared, somewhat cryptically, to Walt's "cross-country summer flights" in Jean Paul's *Die Flegeljahre* (Wolff, 213). At least one passage, marked by a gently syncopated figure in the treble, brings to mind a similar texture in Schumann's *Des Abends* from the first *Phantasiestück* of op. 12, composed the following year in 1837 (Examples 6.20a–b).

EXAMPLE 6.20a. Mendelssohn, Caprice in E major, Op. 33 no. 2 (mm. 37–39)

EXAMPLE 6.20b. Robert Schumann, *Phantasiestück* ("Des Abends"), Op. 12 no. 1 (mm. 1–4)

Mendelssohn's six occasional piano pieces require only a brief comment here. Two appeared in contemporary music journals. The B-minor Scherzo, composed in London in June 1829, appeared that year in the *Berliner allgemeine musikalische Zeitung*, a Berlin music journal edited by the music theorist Adolf Bernhard Marx. The *Gondellied*, to which we have already referred, was published in Dresden in 1838 and then reprinted by Schumann in a supplement to the fourteenth volume of the *Neue Zeitschrift für Musik* in 1841. Four other pieces were solicited by publishers for special albums. The *Scherzo a capriccio* appeared in the *Album des pianistes* published by Schlesinger in Paris in 1836; the *Andante cantabile e presto* appeared in the *Musikalisches Album* from Breitkopf & Haertel in 1839; the Étude in F minor was written as an "étude de perfectionnement" for the *Méthode des méthodes de piano* edited by Fétis and Moscheles for Schlesinger in 1840; and the Prelude and Fugue in E minor appeared in the album *Notre temps* from Schott in 1842 (for the occasion Mendelssohn joined a newly composed prelude, a kind of study in the three-hand technique, to a youthful fugue from 1827). Though rarely heard today, these pieces present the full range of Mendelssohn's favored pianistic styles: the capricious, lightly scored scherzo; the *Lied ohne Worte*; the two-movement concert piece with a lyrical slow movement linked to a fast finale; the piano study; and, finally, the fugue, the traditions of which influenced so much of his music.

A final group of five works appeared posthumously between 1860 and 1872. The *Andante* in B-flat and *Presto agitato* in g, joined together as *Zwei Clavierstücke*, were probably composed separately. The Andante suggests a *Lied ohne Worte*; the Presto is a short movement in sonata form. Two compositions in E minor were issued in 1872 as opp. 117 and 118. The Allegro op. 117, a ternary-form movement with a contrasting middle section in the major, may have been written in 1836 for F. W. Benecke, the uncle of Mendelssohn's wife, Cécile.[52] The Capriccio in E minor op. 118, composed in 1837, begins with a lilting *Lied-ohne-Worte* Andante in E major linked to a fast Allegro in E minor; the combination of slow and fast movements recalls the op. 33 Caprices.

Of greater interest musically are the two sets of Preludes and Études, which appeared in 1868 as opp. 104a and 104b. At least four of these pieces, opp. 104a nos. 1–3 and 104b no. 1, were composed in 1836 and may have been intended for Mendelssohn's planned cycle of études and fugues, which ultimately appeared in 1837 as the *Six Preludes and Fugues* op. 35. The first étude of op. 104b, in B-flat minor, offers a fine specimen of a study in the three-hand technique. What is more, the three "preludes" op. 104a actually have the character of études. No. 1 is an octave study, while nos. 2 and 3 are built on running scalelike figures (designed for the left hand in no. 2 and broken between the left and right hands in no. 3). Also, the tonalities of op. 104a—B-flat major, B minor, and D major—suggest that they may have been originally linked to three of the fugues from op. 35 in the same key, nos. 6, 3, and 2.

Mendelssohn's piano music marks few if any new stylistic departures in the distinguished nineteenth-century piano repertoire. Though impeccably crafted, his finely chiseled piano compositions are usually thought not to convey the depth and dramatic power of Beethoven's piano music, the lyrical warmth of Schubert's, the rich harmonic and tonal palette of Chopin's, or the bold, literary imagination of Schumann's, nor to rival in any way the formidable technical demands of Liszt's piano music or its challenging programmatic designs. Instead, Mendelssohn was content to preserve strong artistic ties to the past and to build cautiously on the foundations of earlier models. Almost certainly, his piano music was intended in large part as an antidote to what he regarded as the excesses and mediocrity of much contemporary piano music. His reform-minded efforts avoided the shifting sands of public taste in order to reembrace and reaffirm traditional compositional procedures. And if he relied heavily on exemplary historical models, that reliance was applauded in many quarters as a necessary corrective. Though twentieth-century criticism has not always received this repertoire kindly, the broader historical view may yet recognize Mendelssohn's substantial efforts on behalf of the piano.

Notes

1. The six *Kinderstücke* (*Children's Pieces*) op. 72, which appeared in London in 1847 shortly after Mendelssohn's death, were composed in 1842. See also n. 35.

2. A comprehensive catalog of Mendelssohn's music is still lacking. For the most current list of the piano music see *The New Grove Early Romantic Masters 2* (London, 1985), pp. 273–75.

3. See Hiller, 5; Moscheles, 1873: *passim*; C. Mendelssohn-Bartholdy, *Goethe and Felix Mendelssohn Bartholdy* (London, 1874), 11ff.; W. S. Rockstro, *Mendelssohn* (London, 1884), 96, 112; H. F. Chorley, *Modern German Music*, 2 vols. (London, 1854, rep. 1973) 1: 49ff.; *Neue Zeitschrift für Musik* 13 (1840): 56; and Sir George Grove's "Mendelssohn" article for *Grove's Dictionary of Music and Musicians*, rep. in 2d ed., J. A. Fuller Maitland, ed. (London, 1904–10) 3:161–63.

4. W. A. Lampadius, *Life of Felix Mendelssohn Bartholdy*, trans. W. L. Gage (1865: reprinted, Boston, 1978), pp. 175–76.

5. Leon Plantinga, "Schumann's Critical Reaction to Mendelssohn," in *Mendelssohn and Schumann: Essays on Their Music and Its Context*, ed. J. W. Finson and R. Larry Todd (Durham, 1984), 12.

6. In 1839 Diabelli brought out the first edition of Schubert's Piano Sonata in A minor D. 784, with an honorary dedication to Mendelssohn. Schumann may have introduced Mendelssohn to some of Schubert's other piano sonatas and pieces. Schumann's favorable perusal of the manuscript of the "Great" Symphony in Vienna led Mendelssohn to perform a truncated version of that work in Leipzig in 1839.

7. For a more balanced account of Mendelssohn's view of Chopin, see Hiller. The mazurkas that provoked Mendelssohn were probably the Four Mazurkas op.

17, which appeared from Breitkopf & Haertel in 1835; the fourth mazurka, in A minor, an especially chromatic work, concludes with a celebrated "open-ended" cadence. See also p. 233.

8. Ferdinand Hiller related Mendelssohn's observing Liszt, in 1832, flawlessly sightread his Piano Concerto in G minor op. 25 (Hiller, 26–27).

9. A reference to the Belgian Revolution, reportedly sparked by a performance of D.-F.-E Auber's *La muette de Portici* in Brussels in 1830.

10. Mendelssohn's first public performance as a pianist occurred on 28 October 1818 with the horn player Joseph Gugel; other early public performances took place on 31 March 1822 at the Schauspielhaus, where Mendelssohn participated in a performance of a double concerto by Dussek, and on 5 December 1822 at a concert of the soprano Anna Milder-Hauptmann. See Rudolf Elvers, "Ein Jugendbrief von Felix Mendelssohn," *Festschrift für Friedrich Smend* (Berlin, 1963), 95; and the *Allgemeine musikalische Zeitung* (hereafter *AmZ*) 24 (1822): 273, and 25 (1823): 55.

11. Several pieces are scattered in a workbook of composition exercises Mendelssohn undertook under Zelter's supervision; see Todd, 1983. Many others survive in manuscript in the Mendelssohn Nachlass of the Deutsche Staatsbibliothek, Berlin.

12. See further, Todd, 1983: 72–73.

13. Rearranged, the two half steps form the common baroque fugal subject of a perfect fifth bordered by a diminished seventh: D-G-E♭-F♯.

14. An edition of the sonata is available (New York, 1981). See the first movements of Clementi's op. 13 no. 6 and op. 34 no. 2, and of Berger's Sonata in C minor. The latter is reprinted in *The London Pianoforte School*, ed. N. Temperley, 20 vols. (New York, 1984), 15:9–25.

15. The occasion was a rehearsal of Mendelssohn's Singspiel *Die beiden Neffen* on his fifteenth birthday (3 February 1824).

16. For example, the Piano Concertos opp. 25 and 40, the *Capriccio brillant* op. 22, and, as we shall see below, the *Rondo capriccioso* op. 14.

17. For an edition of these compositions see Mendelssohn, *Early Works for Piano*, ed. R. Larry Todd (Cambridge, 1985). See also, Todd, 1990: "A Mendelssohn Miscellany," and 1990: "From the Composer's Workshop."

18. See Todd, 1990: "A Mendelssohn Miscellany," and Godwin.

19. In February 1827 in Stettin. See *Berliner allgemeine musikalische Zeitung* (hereafter *BamZ*) 4 (1827): 83.

20. As in the finales of the Sextet op. 110 and the Octet op. 20.

21. See the foreword to Schumann's *Studies on Caprices of Paganini* op. 3 and Wolff, 120; the Rossini anecdote is recorded in Hiller, 58.

22. *AmZ* 29 (1827): 688.

23. B. Litzmann, *Clara Schumann: Ein Künstlerleben* 3 vols. (Leipzig, 1925) 1:89.

24. Cf. the Arioso (*Klagender Gesang*) and concluding fugue of op. 110, which modulate from A♭ minor/A♭ major to G minor/G major for the return of the arioso and the mirror inversion of the fugue.

25. See Kahl and Siebenkäs; for a comparison of Mendelssohn's *Lieder ohne Worte* with Wilhelm Taubert's *Minnelieder,* see Glusman. It should be stressed that the exact nature of Fanny Mendelssohn's role in the creation of the genre remains unclear.

26. Letter of 7 September 1838. *The Letters of Fanny Hensel to Felix Mendelssohn,* ed. and trans. M. J. Citron (New York, 1987), 261.

27. Krummacher, "Mendelssohn's Late Chamber Music: Some Autograph Sources Recovered," in *Mendelssohn and Schumann,* 73.

28. A Schöne and F. Hiller, eds., *The Letters of a Leipzig Cantor,* trans. A. D. Coleridge, 2 vols. (London, 1892) 1:96–97.

29. Letter of 15 October 1842. G. Selden-Goth, ed., *Mendelssohn Letters* (New York, 1947), 313–314.

30. Sächische Landesbibliothek, Dresden; regarding op. 53 no. 3, see Jost, 159ff.

31. The *Reiterlied* is available in Rudolf Elvers's critical edition of the *Lieder ohne Worte* (Munich, 1981).

32. A special case is the *Herbstlied,* a duet with words (op. 63 no. 4) that Mendelssohn also notated as a *Lied ohne Worte.* The two versions were completed on 16 October 1836. See further Jost, 127ff.

33. S. Hensel, *Die Familie Mendelssohn 1729 bis 1847,* 2 vols., 15th ed. (Berlin, 1911) 1: 222.

34. A facsimile of Mendelssohn's assignment of the copyright of op. 19 to Novello is in Moscheles, 1888: 67. The original English title for op. 19 was *Melodies for the Pianoforte (alone)* (see Illustration 6.1).

35. The last opus Mendelssohn prepared for the press, op. 72, appeared with six of seven pieces written in June 1842 for the children of F. W. Benecke, whom Mendelssohn visited in England. The first English edition erroneously referred to these pieces as Christmas presents. See the *Musical Times* (hereafter *MT*) 32 (1891): 592. A modern, complete edition prepared by H. O. Hiekel is available (Munich, 1969).

36. See the study by George Bozarth, "Brahms's *Lieder ohne Worte:* The 'Poetic' Andantes of the Piano Sonatas," in *Brahms Studies: Papers Delivered at the International Brahms Conference, The Library of Congress, Washington, D.C., 5–8 May 1983,* ed. G Bozarth (Oxford, 1990), 345–78.

37. Among Liszt's transcriptions of Mendelssohn's texted Lieder for piano solo is a collection of seven arrangements from opp. 19b, 34, and 47, which appeared in 1841 with a dedication to Mendelssohn's wife, Cécile (Searle 547).

38. Further examples are cited in Jost, 20ff.

39. See Fanny's letters to Felix of 23 [May] and 4 June 1829 in *The Letters of Fanny Hensel to Felix Mendelssohn,* 41, 50.

40. See R. Larry Todd, "Mendelssohn's Ossianic Manner, with a New Source—*On Lena's Gloomy Heath,*" in *Mendelssohn and Schumann,* 139–40.

41. See his correspondence with Breitkopf and Haertel in 1835, in Felix Mendelssohn Bartholdy, *Briefe an deutsche Verleger,* ed. Rudolf Elvers (Berlin, 1968), 42, 45. Coincidentally, Carl Czerny's collection of preludes and fugues, *The School of Playing Fugues and of Performing Polyphonic Compositions and Their Particular Difficulties on the Piano in 24 Large Studies,* began to appear in 1837 as op. 400, with a dedication to Mendelssohn.

42. See Rudolf Elvers, "Verzeichnis der von Felix Mendelssohn Bartholdy herausgegebenen Werke Johann Sebastian Bachs," in *Gestalt und Glaube: Festschrift für Oskar Söhngen* (Berlin, 1960), 145–49.

43. The appeal for funds was announced in *AmZ* in 1835, and the monument was unveiled in 1845 with a gala concert directed by Liszt.

44. Mendelssohn Nachlass, vol. 35, Biblioteca Jagiellońska, Kraków.

45. Jack Werner attempted to link this cadence to one employed in traditional Jewish services for Passover. See "The Mendelssohnian Cadence," *MT* 97 (1956): 17–19.

46. Letter of 30 July 1841 to his sister Rebecka. (New York Public Library, Mendelssohn Family Correspondence).

47. See the listing in *The New Grove Early Romantic Masters 2*, 274–75. An edition of Mendelssohn's *Albumblatt* in A major for Ottilie von Goethe (1830) is now available (Wiesbaden, 1984).

48. Conservatoire Ms. 198, Bibliothèque nationale, Paris.

49. Letter of Anne Taylor in *Grove's Dictionary of Music and Musicians*, 2d ed., 3:161–63.

50. *Ibid.*

51. Carl Czerny, *School of Practical Composition*, op. 600, trans. J. Bishop, 3 vols. (ca. 1848, reprinted, N.Y., 1979) 1:89.

52. See Margaret Crum, *Catalogue of the Mendelssohn Papers in the Bodleian Library, Oxford* (Tutzing, 1983), 2:6.

Selected Bibliography

Eppstein, Hans. "Zur Enstehungsgeschichte von Mendelssohns Lied ohne Worte op. 62, 3." *Die Musikforschung* (hereafter *Mf*) 26 (1973): 486–90.

Glusman, Elfriede. "Taubert and Mendelssohn: Opposing Attitudes toward Poetry and Music." *The Musical Quarterly* (hereafter *MQ*) 57 (1971): 628–35.

Godwin, Jocelyn. "Early Mendelssohn and Late Beethoven." *Music and Letters* 55 (1974): 272–85.

Hiller, Ferdinand. *Felix Mendelssohn Bartholdy: Letters and Recollections*. Translated by M. E. von Glehn. 1874. Reprint. New York, 1972.

Hochdorf, Louise. "Mendelssohns *Lieder ohne Worte* und der Lieder-ohne-Worte-Stil in seinen übrigen Instrumentalwerken." Ph.D. dissertation, University of Vienna, 1938.

Jost, Christa. *Mendelssohns Lieder ohne Worte*. Tutzing, 1988.

Kahl, Willi. "Zu Mendelssohns Liedern ohne Worte." *Zeitschrift für Musikwissenschaft* 3 (1920–21): 459–69.

Kahn, Johannes. "Ein unbekanntes 'Lied ohne Worte' von Felix Mendelssohn." *Die Musik* 16 (1923–24): 824–26.

Moscheles, Ignaz. *Recent Music and Musicians*. Translated by A. D. Coleridge, New York, 1873.

———. *Letters of Felix Mendelssohn to Ignaz and Charlotte Moscheles*. Edited by F. Moscheles. Boston, 1888.

Newman, William S. "Some 19th-Century Consequences of Beethoven's 'Hammerklavier' Sonata, Op. 106." *Piano Quarterly* (hereafter *PQ*) 17 (1969): 12–18.

Parkins, Robert C. "Mendelssohn and the Erard Piano." *PQ* 32 (1984): 53–58.

Reininghaus, Frieder. "Studie zur bürgerlichen Musiksprache: Mendelssohns 'Lieder ohne Worte' als historisches, ästhetisches und politisches Problem." *Mf* 28 (1975): 34–51.

Siebenkäs, Dieter. "Zur Vorgeschichte der Lieder ohne Worte von Mendelssohn." *Mf* 15 (1962): 171–73.

Sirota, Victoria. "The Life and Works of Fanny Mendelssohn Hensel." D.M.A. dissertation, Boston University, 1981.

Temperley, Nicholas. "Mendelssohn's Influence on English Music." *ML* 43 (1962): 224–33.

Tischler, Hans, and Louise H. "Mendelssohn's Songs without Words." *MQ* 33 (1947): 1–16.

———. "Mendelssohn's Style: The *Songs without Words*." *Music Review* 8 (1947): 256–73.

Todd, R. Larry. "The Instrumental Music of Felix Mendelssohn Bartholdy: Selected Studies Based on Primary Sources." Ph.D. dissertation, Yale University, 1979.

———. "A Sonata by Mendelssohn." *PQ* 29 (1981): 30–41.

———. *Mendelssohn's Musical Education: A Study and Edition of his Exercises in Composition.* Cambridge, 1983.

———. "A Mendelssohn Miscellany." *Music and Letters* 71 (1990): 52–64.

———. "From the Composer's Workshop: Two Little-Known Fugues by Mendelssohn." *Musical Times* 131 (1990): 183–87.

Wolff, Konrad, ed. *Robert Schumann: On Music and Musicians.* Translated by P. Rosenfeld, New York, 1946.

CHAPTER SEVEN

Hearing Poland: Chopin and Nationalism

Jeffrey Kallberg

We know Chopin in many ways. Biographers derive countless stories from his brief life; some weave stark chronicles of the events of his daily existence, others emplot his days as a kind of gothic romance. Theorists of every faith find fodder for their methods in his music; we can study his formal, harmonic, rhythmic, melodic, and contrapuntal processes from perspectives as diverse as those of Riemann, Schenker, Forte, and Narmour. Critics and historians offer glimpses of the composer in relationship to contemporaries like Berlioz and Liszt, or as foreshadowing figures like Wagner and Debussy. Others discover in his music the embodiment of the Polish national spirit, or even, in one case, a prefiguration of mainland Chinese resistance to foreign aggression—a curious feat of critical legerdemain.[1] And, obviously, pianists reveal strikingly different visions of Chopin through their performances, as a sampling of the recordings from the likes of Koczalski, Hofmann, Lipatti, Rubinstein, and Pollini quickly confirms. In this sheer variety we can see something of the high value Chopin enjoys in our culture: he admits—or, depending upon one's point of view, withstands—investigations of all kinds.

Any of these approaches could profitably be explored, for a corollary of my opening sentence is that many different factors affect our knowledge of Chopin. Biography informs criticism, which informs theory, and so on: any permutation can and probably should be defended and embraced. In this essay, however, I opt for a predominantly historical course. I will examine some of the consequences of understanding Chopin as part of the culture of his time and demonstrate how knowledge of a small slice of what Chopin and his music meant to his contemporaries can affect how our own cultures engage with him. Market forces in part suggest such a plan; historical orientations are still lacking among general treatments of the composer, although useful, often excellent, modern biographical, theoretical, and analytical approaches are readily available (Abraham; Samson, 1985; Temperley). More important, a historical orientation can both reveal a number of categories of thought about Chopin that have faded from consciousness since his death and correct certain anachronistic ways of perceiving his music. This disjunction between past and present musical cultures is my main concern.

Historically, the nature of "nationalist" expression in Chopin's musical works has been a provocative point of fissure. From the start, the Polish element in Chopin's music has provoked perceptions of foreignness, of strangeness. To judge from the trepidation and curiosity with which many modern pianists approach these compositions (especially the mazurkas), they still have the ability profoundly to unsettle us. But the reasons that Chopin's contemporaries perceived his music to be strange may not be the same as our reasons. The possibility of such a rupture in experience opens the way for our historical investigation.

Hearing Poland

If asked to identify the most famous Pole in history, most people in the West would probably name Chopin. Chopin seems inextricably linked with his native origins; his Polishness constitutes one of the primary images through which modern listeners filter his music. Textbook accounts of Chopin's music, for example, routinely center their discussions on statements such as, "Although Chopin lived in Paris from 1831, he never ceased to love his native Poland or to be afflicted by her misfortunes."[2] This primary image would seem to imply in turn a close and pervasive relationship between Chopin's entire oeuvre and nineteenth-century Polish history and culture. And that this epoch evokes highly charged memories—throughout the nineteenth century, the state of Poland existed only in the minds of a disenfranchised citizenry—further solidifies this relationship. To hear Chopin, it appears, is in some sense to "hear Poland."

Does this modern image accurately reflect that of Chopin's own time? In effect, this question asks us to reconstruct the nature of national expression in the 1830s and 1840s. How should an inquiry proceed that attempts such a reconstruction? To speak of the links between sound and culture, or of music as an expression of national ideals, is necessarily to view musical meaning as a social phenomenon shared by all participants in the sonic experience, that is, by composers, performers, and listeners alike. Conversely, it is to reject the often-made claim that an examination of nationalism in music should focus on inherent characteristics of the music alone, on shared devices found in a number of different compositions. To the degree that such devices exist, they provide only factual information about nationalism in music; they do not explain its meanings. Rather than dwell exclusively on the constituent features of Chopin's nationalist compositions (though a discussion of some of these features certainly will aid our grasp of the meanings of nationalism), we need also to recover nineteenth-century contexts and traditions, and to lay bare the perceptions of both Chopin and his audiences.

We need, then, to expose some of the historically specific strands of meaning that clung to Chopin's "nationalist" compositions. Genre—the type or kind of a composition (that is, mazurka, polonaise, nocturne, and so forth)—stands at the center of this quest, for it was one of the primary means by which "nationalist" ideas could be represented through instrumental music in the 1830s and 1840s. As with meaning generally, genre too should be understood as a communicative concept, which in turn makes us aware of ways in which music interacts with society. In particular, an examination of genre often reveals otherwise hidden ideological agendas and associations in music without texts.

Two genres in particular served Chopin's nationalist purposes: mazurkas and polonaises. (Now and then, especially in his early years, he essayed other works with national resonances, like the *Fantasy on Polish Airs* op. 13 or the *Krakowiak* op. 14.) Both genres traced their dance and vocal origins back to Poland (the mazurka was cultivated primarily in folk spheres, the polonaise in more aristocratic circles). Hence one reason Chopin turned so often to these distinctly Polish kinds was that their familiar rhythmic and formal gestures enabled him directly to evoke memories of different aspects and strata of Polish culture.

On the whole, mazurkas called forth sharper reactions than polonaises, partly because mazurkas as cultivated instrumental music were relatively novel; indeed, Chopin was chiefly responsible for their rise in popularity. The polonaise, on the other hand, had been well known as an instrumental genre since the eighteenth century. In addition, the mazurka carried an aura of strangeness, a quality missing in the familiar polonaise. What accounted for this feeling of foreignness? Some measure of it must have been provoked by certain constructive elements of the mazurkas that are idiosyncratic, arcane, and unsettling—these adjectives represent reactions both of Chopin's contemporaries and of modern listeners.

The Mazurkas

The mazurkas provide a marvelous index of Chopin's career. He wrote more of them than any other genre (we know of at least fifty-eight separate works entitled "Mazurka," and mazurkas also appear embedded within pieces like the F-minor Concerto op. 21, the *Andante spianato* from op. 22, and the F♯-minor Polonaise op. 44). What is more, they span his entire career, from 1826 to 1849. Of these, plainly the most important and influential were the forty-one mazurkas he released in eleven published sets throughout the 1830s and 1840s. The Mazurkas opp. 6 and 7 counted in the first group of publications Chopin sold to a Parisian publisher shortly after his arrival in the city; the Mazurkas op. 63 were among the last works he put before the public prior to his death in 1849.

That Chopin issued his mazurkas in sets of three or four works partly reflects a convention of the publishing industry: shorter compositions sold better when grouped together with other like kinds. But the sets also gave Chopin the opportunity to experiment with principles of musical structure of a higher order. In particular, he often attempted to articulate musical connections between the numbers of the set. In his more arcane moments, he explored different sorts of tonal relationships. The four numbers of the Mazurkas op. 41, for example, exhibit a kind of "logical" succession of tonic keys: E minor, B major, A-flat major, C-sharp minor.[3] In the Mazurkas op. 59 he tried the idea of tonal recall, where an unusual key featured in one work is brought back in another. Here, the most striking moment of the A-minor Mazurka (op. 59 no. 1), the shift to G-sharp minor at the moment of reprise (Example 7.1, Illustration 7.1), is recalled in the parallel major by the tonic key of the A-flat major Mazurka (op. 59 no. 2).

EXAMPLE 7.1. Chopin, Mazurka in A minor, Op. 59 no. 1 (mm. 79–82)

More perceptually apparent, however, are Chopin's concerns with closure at the level of the set. To speak of closure at this level is mostly to speak of codas, which loom important throughout Chopin's mazurkas. For the moment, I will defer discussion of the role of these codas with respect to overall form in the genre. Here instead I need simply note some of the characteristics of these codas: their considerable length; their tendency to incorporate the most dramatic musical gesture of the piece (whether a chromatic peroration, as in the Mazurka in F-sharp minor op. 59 no. 3, or an extended sequential passage, as in the C-sharp minor Mazurka op. 50 no. 3); the derivation of a portion of it from the body of the work (as in the opening of the coda to the C-sharp minor op. 41 no. 4); and the occasional presence of a new theme, always at the conclusion of the coda (see Example 7.2, from op. 59 no. 3). These new themes are unlike any others in Chopin: their range is extremely restricted, they employ mainly congruent motion, their harmonies are diatonic and highly cadential. In their striking restriction of means and their use of highly stable and unambiguous musical material, they take on an epigrammatic character.[4]

ILLUSTRATION 7.1. Opening page of the German first edition (published by Stern in Berlin) of Chopin's Mazurka in A minor op. 59 no. 1. Notice the missing sharps in the last measure of the fourth system (m. 20), an oversight corrected in pencil by an earlier owner.

How then do these codas effect closure at the level of the set? Chopin quite carefully deployed his codas, reserving the most complex of them

EXAMPLE 7.2. Chopin, Mazurka in F♯ minor, Op. 59 no. 3 (mm. 147–154)

for the concluding numbers of opuses. These concluding numbers them-selves were usually the longest of the set, a feature reviewers occasionally noticed:

> The fourth [mazurka of op. 30] is very dreamy and fantasti-cally dallying [*tändelnd*], restless and gloomily profound. For that reason it is also the longest; the picture otherwise could not take shape.[5]

> The third of these national romances [the Mazurkas, op. 50], in C♯ minor, enters into substance by a canon at the octave, a very nice effect; it is more extended than the other two, but the six pages of which it is composed do not have tedious passages.[6]

The redoubled effect of length upon length, of an intricate coda adjoined to an extended primary structure, lends much to the sensation of closure at the level of the set.

Even more significantly, Chopin saved his idiosyncratic epigrammatic themes, those very special and maximally closed melodies, for the ends of codas attached to the last number of a set (other examples include the B♭-minor op. 24 no. 4 and the C♯-minor op. 41 no. 4). The positioning of these epigrammatic themes contributes to their effect; by virtue of the complex and structurally unstable material that precedes them, the themes take on even more closural weight. In any case, the position of such themes at the termini of sets strongly suggests that Chopin intended to secure closure at the level of the opus in the mazurkas.

Chopin's concern for such higher level closure does not necessarily mean that he wished his sets to be played only integrally. We have no clear evidence that Chopin ever performed in public any of his sets from beginning to end. At best he seems to have admitted pairing pieces from his sets; most often he appears to have selected individual works from them. While Chopin's own practices as a pianist might in this case seem at odds with his procedures as a composer, a more critical interpretation would view both practices as reflecting Chopin's pluralistic notions about the purposes of his published sets. Clearly he desired performances of individual numbers; but for those pianists who wished to play the entire set, he also tried to ensure what might be termed the "compatibility" of the numbers when played in sequence.[7] Modern pianists would do well to follow this flexible model in their performances.

A discussion of codas inevitably raises the issue of form in the individual mazurkas. Indeed, Chopin's innovative treatment of form stands as one of the most intriguing and enjoyable aspects of this genre for modern listeners. Interestingly enough, however, form seems not to have been a pressing concern of Chopin's contemporaries. Reviewers occasionally used a formal term such as "Trio" to refer to a portion of a composition or gave a kind of narrative description through which readers might discern the shape of a piece. More often, however, they commented on expressive qualities. Chopin's mazurkas were not understood as autonomous formal designs; rather their forms were subsumed under other categories, including genre and expression.

Nonetheless, form plainly matters to *us*, and other composers just as plainly learned from Chopin, so some commentary on the nature of form in the mazurkas remains necessary. Or better, some commentary on the nature of formal principles: Chopin showed such ingenious variety with respect to form that it makes little sense to construct a typology in this area. (Moreover, avoiding discussion of such familiar—and rather baggy—formal concepts as "ternary" brings us somewhat closer to the attitude of Chopin's contemporaries.) Instead, I will point to some of the significant formal strategies Chopin used in the genre, strategies that serve the idiosyncratic expressive goals of the genre. In particular, I will focus on those aspects of formal structure that derail expectations of stability and normalcy (variously construed). Having begun my discussion with codas, I will continue my progress backward with reprises.

Chopin's reprises often do not reaffirm the theme or thematic complex that opened a work. Instead, they undercut it. Radical foreshortening was one means by which he achieved this effect. He made particularly striking use of this strategy in his later mazurkas (good examples include op. 59 no. 2 in A-flat major and op. 59 no. 3 in F-sharp minor), but he adumbrated it also in some earlier ones (see op. 17 no. 4 in A minor and op. 24 no. 4 in B-flat minor). The reprise in the A♭-major Mazurka op. 59 no. 2 is paradigmatic (Example 7.3). Two techniques combine to tinge the returning principal section with unfamiliarity: the curtailment of the original length (from 44 to 12 measures) and the revoicing of the tune (we expect it in the soprano, not tenor, register). This brief reprise then resolves directly into an extended coda, a familiar consequence of its instability. Gerald Abraham observed more than half a century ago that Chopin's codas often seem to offer a sort of structural compensation for abbreviated reprises (Abraham, 46–47).

Chopin sometimes undermined reprises through different techniques. I have already mentioned the striking turn of harmonic events at the moment of reprise in the A-minor Mazurka op. 59 no. 1 (see Example

EXAMPLE 7.3. Chopin, Mazurka in A♭ major, Op. 59 no. 2 (mm. 69–80)

7.1); the outlandishness of the G♯-minor episode not only weakens the stability of the reprise, it also enables a retrospective tonal connection with the second number of the set. In op. 41 no. 4, the Mazurka in C-sharp minor (Example 7.4a), the reprise opens first on A major (briefly flirting with a pseudo-canon) and then, upon returning to the tonic, settles onto a dominant pedal, serving to shift structural weight onto an extended coda (in which, again as if to compensate for the equivocal reprise, we hear the theme thundered out unambiguously in octaves). A similar combination of canon (now realized) and dominant pedal besets the opening of the reprise of the F♯-minor Mazurka op. 59 no. 3 (Example 7.4b), and once more results in a prolonged coda.[8]

Of course, not all reprises in mazurkas sap the structural stability; many present a more or less full and unadulterated accounting of the principal theme or thematic complex. Especially in his earlier mazurkas, Chopin favored complete returns of the opening section of the piece; indeed, at times he simply notated a *da capo* repeat at the end of the contrasting section (op. 7 no. 2 in A minor; op. 17 no. 1 in B-flat major). But while these unvaried reprises avoid ambiguity in the area of formal return (and consequently tend not to be followed by codas of any length), they often

EXAMPLE 7.4a. Chopin, Mazurka in C♯ minor, Op. 41, no. 4 (mm. 65–76)

EXAMPLE 7.4b. Chopin, Mazurka in F♯ minor, Op. 59 no. 3 (mm. 97–103)

stand as part of an insistently reiterative design that itself provokes amphibolous responses to formal closure.

In many of the early mazurkas (as well as in some of the later ones), the opening theme returns literally several times. To some degree, this repetitiveness of structure magnifies the construction of the individual themes themselves, where pervasively reiterated short melodic and/or rhythmic motives abound (Example 7.5).[9] But the whirling, breathless quality of these individual themes, when repeated literally several times, has a striking effect on the nature of closure at the level of the piece. Each successive statement of the theme recalls earlier ones and prefigures later ones that presumably will occur in the future. The illusion of an unending chain of repeating themes is broken only by the understanding of conventional duration for the piece at hand.[10] Consequently, when a piece ends after one of these literal returns, the termination sounds artificial: it simply stops rather than closes (see op. 7 no. 1 in B-flat major).

Already in the early mazurkas, Chopin occasionally tempered the sense of abruptness by subtly altering the final statement of the principal theme (see the ends of op. 6 no. 3 in E major and op. 7 no. 3 in F minor). This slight bit of functional differentiation hints to the listener that closure is imminent. As he continued to write mazurkas, he sought to lessen the sense of openness of structure in the genre in other ways, some of which have already been mentioned: expansive codas and modified returns of principal themes (i. e., foreshortened reprises, altered tonality and/or texture). But these strategies themselves depended upon an awareness of the lack of differentiation that results from literal repetition and return, and hence they did not represent a radical shift in Chopin's understanding of the genre.

EXAMPLE 7.5. Chopin, Mazurka in A♭ major, Op. 17 no. 3 (mm. 1–16)

Determining how far to extend the reiterative thematic chain concerned Chopin throughout his career. Indeed, corrections pertaining to repetition and return appear with enough frequency in the manuscript and printed sources for his mazurkas to suggest a unique relationship of these concepts to this genre. In several instances, he remained fundamentally ambivalent about how many times to repeat a principal theme. For example, variants in the sources for the B♭-major op. 7 no. 1, which include an autograph manuscript, a scribal copy, and the printed editions, transmit a number of possible schemes of formal repetition. Both the autograph manuscript and the scribal copy date from before the publication of the work in 1832–33. The scribal copy also gives vague directions for repetition and return. The following table summarizes the variants in formal repetition schemes in op. 7 no. 1:

Autograph		‖:A:‖ B‖:A:‖	C‖:A:‖		
Scribal Copy	1)	‖:A:‖ BA	CA	(BA?)	*or*
		‖:A:‖ B‖:A:‖	C‖:A:‖	(B‖:A:‖?)	
	2)	‖:A:‖: BA :‖	CA	(‖:BA:‖?)	*or*
		‖:A:‖: BAA‖	C‖:A:‖	(‖:BAA:‖?)	
Printed versions		AA ‖:BA :‖:	CA :‖		

Possibly the scribal manuscript does not reflect in any way Chopin's own conception of the form of the piece. Yet, because the manuscript was copied before the work was published, we cannot summarily dismiss it. Its vague directions could reflect the equivocal state of a Chopin autograph now lost, a possibility supported by the ambiguity in demonstrably authentic sources for other mazurkas from op. 7.[11]

The most striking feature of all these versions is that none sounds superior to any other; further, no one ending sounds superior to another. Because of the illusion of an unending chain of repetitions of the principal theme, no statement of this theme is prospectively identifiable as the final one. The endings sound equally abrupt whether the concluding formal segment stands as CA, C‖:A:‖, or ‖:CA:‖. It follows then that any selection from among these formal options seems arbitrary. What is important to remember, however, is that this arbitrariness, or ambiguity, reflects something essential about the nature of the genre itself. Indeed, Chopin wittily drew attention to this facet of the genre in the brief op. 7 no. 5 in C major, whose final bar points the pianist back to measure 5 with the direction *Dal segno senza Fine. Senza Fine*: the pianist can draw the piece to a close where she or he wants. Op. 7 no. 5 states overtly what others of its kind imply quietly: mazurkas embrace an aesthetic of formal ambiguity.

That a single work might allow a variety of formal plans can be a troubling notion to those accustomed to finding *the* "authentic" text, *the* "definitive" version for a given composition. But a little probing into the musical culture of the nineteenth century reveals that this problem hinges entirely on an anachronistic notion of what the "musical work" represents. Composers and audiences of the day did not necessarily view scores as unique, invariable forms of their music. Consider, for example, the multiple texts of Beethoven's *Leonore/Fidelio*, the three versions of *Tancredi* that Rossini produced in 1813, the various interpretations of what came to be called *Mazeppa* that Liszt published between 1826 and 1852, and the various forms of Schumann's *Symphonic Études*, first before publication, then in the first edition, and finally in the second edition of 1852.

Above all, consider the status of Chopin's own texts: the multiple manuscript and printed sources for his compositions never preserve identical versions. Many of these variants are minor, but many are not. Their sheer abundance often overwhelms editors (and a glance at the critical notes for some of their editions—good choices are the Paderewski, Henle, and Universal editions—confirms this), who then conceive of the conflicting readings as "problems" to be "solved." But here again, anachronistic viewpoints fog the way, for surely the variants reflect something essential both to Chopin's art in particular, and the constitution of a work of art generally in the first half of the nineteenth century. For Chopin and his listeners, a musical work was a fluid, not fixed, concept.

Hence the aesthetic of formal ambiguity that affects some of the mazurkas should be understood in terms of the relatively fluid conception of the "musical work" fostered by Chopin and his contemporaries. And once we allow the seemingly peripheral category of ambiguity to occupy a central role in our perception of the genre, a number of other related structural features of the mazurkas emerge, features that similarly bring to the foreground what might appear to be marginalized and unstable types of musical experience.

Ends of mazurkas again provide some of the best examples of destabilization in Chopin's music. The abruptness with which many mazurkas conclude often serves to frustrate a sense of secure closure. Chopin sometimes upset closure by tonal means as well. Perhaps the most famous instance occurs in the A-minor Mazurka op. 17 no. 4. Here the final four measures recapitulate almost identically the opening four measures of the piece. What seemed initially a gesture of thematic anticipation—the rising third in the inner voice of the chordal progression matches the rising third that opens the principal theme (Example 7.6a)—now distantly recalls, at the end of the coda, the events of the body of the Mazurka (Example 7.6b). As it does so, it simultaneously diffuses tension (Chopin tried to

EXAMPLE 7.6a. Chopin, Mazurka in A minor, Op. 17 no. 4 (mm. 1–5)

EXAMPLE 7.6b. Chopin, Mazurka in A minor, Op. 17 no. 4, Coda (mm. 129–132)

convey this to performers through his direction *perdendosi,* "dying away") and leaves this tension harmonically unresolved (the piece ends on a VI[6] chord). But while this extraordinary conclusion is well known (op. 17 no. 4 is one of the few mazurkas continuously favored by pianists since Chopin's time),[12] in fact it is atypical of the genre. Indeed, by both diffusing tension and avoiding strong closure it more closely resembles the sort of coda found in nocturnes.

More characteristic of the genre are the final measures of op. 30 no. 2 in B minor (Example 7.7a). While the piece seems to end with the firmest, most closed of gestures (in both versions of the ending), in fact the final cadence falls on F-sharp minor, not on B minor where the piece began ("though we scarcely observe it," Schumann wrote).[13] Now B minor last seems secure as the tonic of the piece in measure 16; all articulations of B minor after that point lack the stability normally associated with the tonic (e. g., mm. 33 and 37). In some ways then, we might profitably construe the Mazurka as beginning in the subdominant (B minor) and ending on the tonic (F-sharp minor). Still, normally we expect that the first key established in the piece will both function as the tonic and return in conjunction with the opening theme. Neither expectation is realized. Instead we witness an interesting variation on the reiterative formal strategy discussed above. Each section unfolds through the pervasive repetition of the two-measure motive that begins it (Example 7.7b); one of the sections returns near-literally as well, but the surprise is that it is the second section, not the first. Hence the conclusion of the piece, despite the apparent solidity of its closure, brings together a number of strategies designed to unsettle listeners: it stops after a chainlike series of near-literal motivic and sectional repetitions; it lacks a return of the opening section, substituting in its place a return of the second section; and it does not end in the key in which it began.

EXAMPLE 7.7a. Chopin, Mazurka in B minor, Op. 30 no. 2 (mm. 61–64)

(German Edition)

EXAMPLE 7.7b. Two-measure motives (mm. 1–2, 17–18, 33–34)

Of course, the majority of mazurkas do not scotch orderly tonal closure. Indeed, most mazurkas securely reaffirm the tonic when they end,
and many do so in the context of a relatively stable return of the principal
theme. (I have already mentioned as a special instance of this typical phenomenon the epigrammatic themes that fall at the end of some codas to
mazurkas.) Rather, the two contrary examples just discussed remind us
that, in a genre where musical experience is pervasively destabilized, even
the most conventional of expectations might be overturned.

Since form was little remarked upon in discussions of the genre in
the 1830s and 1840s, we can only assume that some of these unusual strategies contributed to its perceived ethos of strangeness. What was noted,
however, and what stood in the minds of Chopin's contemporaries as
among the most striking and often most unorthodox features of his mazurkas, was their pervasive chromaticism. Even fellow composers were
perplexed by this feature. Mendelssohn's conservative feathers were apparently ruffled by Chopin's op. 17: "A book of Mazurkas by Chopin and
a few new pieces of his are so mannered that they are hard to stand."[14]
Ludwig Rellstab, an even more hidebound critic and poet, heaped scorn

on Chopin's first two books of mazurkas, opp. 6 and 7: "In search of ear-splitting dissonances, tortured transitions, piercing modulations, disgusting dislocations of the melody and rhythm, he is unremitting and—we would say—inexhaustible."[15] Other reactions were less blustery, even positive:

> The mazurkas [op. 30] are national and so individual that the author is not at all to be mistaken. For all that, they are not as dissonant as the earlier ones. (Fink, *AmZ* 40 [1838]: 668).

> Thus the second of these mazurkas [of op. 63] is peculiarly charming owing to the uncertain mixture, often encountered in Chopin, of major and minor scales directly in the melody. He reaches so far at the end [see Example 7.8]

[EXAMPLE 7.8. Chopin, Mazurka in F minor, Op. 63 no. 2 (mm. 55–56)]

> that the minor third arrives just after its true mark. From such indecision, as when the tonic comes forth, also originates that hazy effect that results in a yearning expression, and that remains unattainable to Chopin's imitators; indeed for he himself it has already become a mannerism. (*AmZ* 50 [1848]: 214).

While remarks of this sort were sometimes levied against Chopin's style in general (Rellstab, for example, fired similar salvos at the composer's early nocturnes), they nonetheless reveal the extent to which dissonance was associated specifically with the mazurkas. In this genre, dissonance had become a "mannerism" that identified Chopin "unmistakably."

The opening eight-measure phrase of Chopin's first published mazurka, op. 6 no. 1 in F♯-minor, establishes the centrality of dissonant chromaticism to the genre (Example 7.9a). Sequences govern the phrase, diatonic ones in the first half, chromatic ones in the second. (That chromaticism in the mazurkas often emerges out of a diatonic context only augments its restive effect.) The second phrase slithers semitonally downward from C♯″ to F♯′; in using the seventh chord as its principal sonority, it momentarily suspends awareness of a local harmonic basis. As Jim Samson has observed, it is only the regularity of the phrase structure that mollifies the uneasy progression of chromaticism, and that heralds the return to diatonicism (Samson, 1985: 112). The tensive relationship between diatonicism and chromaticism established in op. 6 no. 1 recurs often in the mazurkas; one similar instance, made all the more remarkable by its parallel fifths, occurs in the coda of op. 30 no. 4, in C-sharp minor (Example 7.9b). And by Chopin's later mazurkas, chromatic sequences grow more extended and sometimes articulate the most provocatively unstable

EXAMPLE 7.9a. Chopin, Mazurka in F♯ minor, Op. 6 no. 1 (mm. 1–8)

EXAMPLE 7.9b. Chopin, Mazurka in C♯ minor, Op. 30 no. 4 (mm. 128–133)

gesture of the piece. In the coda to op. 50 no. 3, in C-sharp minor, a densely chromatic "meta-sequence" gathers strength over sixteen measures, finally to deliver a mighty climax on a six-four chord (Example 7.9c).

EXAMPLE 7.9c. Chopin, Mazurka in C♯ minor, Op. 50 no. 3 (mm. 157–173)

Such chromatic forays clearly represented a "foreign" element of the genre; chromaticism as the embodiment of the "exotic" then easily encouraged among western European listeners a perceptible link to the national origins of the mazurka. Chromaticism in effect stood synecdochically for the mazurkas as a whole: the strangely dissonant byways represented cogently the sheer otherness of this relatively unknown and foreign genre (Illustration 7.2).

Other unusual chromatic features served further to convey exoticism in the genre. Chief among these is the quirky modality that suffuses many of the mazurkas. We have encountered this already in the frame to the A-minor Mazurka op. 17 no. 4 (Example 7.6); when the phrase opens the piece—that is, before any hint of an A-minor tonic has been heard—the harmony seems to suggest either Aeolian on A or Dorian on D. A similar ambiguity affects op. 41 no. 1 (Example 7.10): the first two measures of the piece point toward a tonic of A minor, or perhaps Dorian on A, but as the phrase progresses, the sense of the tonic is deflected first toward a diatonic E minor, and finally to Phrygian on E. (Chopin himself showed some perplexity about the tonality of this piece: in his sketch, he first labeled the tonic "A minor" and then changed this to "E minor.")

More common still (particularly in Chopin's earlier mazurkas) are modally inflected melodies. In the trio of op. 7 no. 1 in B-flat major, an open fifth drone (seemingly in the wrong key) intensifies the exotic, folkloristic effect of the sharpened fourth melodic degree (Example 7.11a).[16] Even more eerie is the octave passage that commences the central section of op. 24 no. 4 in B-flat minor (Example 7.11b). Here the vocabulary of church modes fails to convey the phrase's full sense of strangeness, a good portion of which derives from its sharp juxtaposition with a most stable, diatonic, and homophonic cadence in F major.[17]

EXAMPLE 7.10. Chopin, Mazurka in E minor, Op. 41 no. 1 (mm. 1–8)

ILLUSTRATION 7.2. An example of a vocal *kujawiak*—one of the folk types generally thought to form the background of the art mazurka—taken from a collection of folk poetry and music contemporary with Chopin (Kazimierz Władysław Wójcicki, *Pieśni ludu Biało-Chrobatów, Mazurów i Rusi znad Bugu* [Warsaw, 1836], 2 vols., 1: after p. 184). The raised fourth degree in the melody and the open fifths in the bass seem particularly suggestive *vis-à-vis* Chopin.

EXAMPLE 7.11a. Chopin, Mazurka in B♭ major, Op. 7 no. 1 (mm. 45–51)

EXAMPLE 7.11b. Chopin, Mazurka in B♭ minor, Op. 24 no. 4 (mm. 53–60)

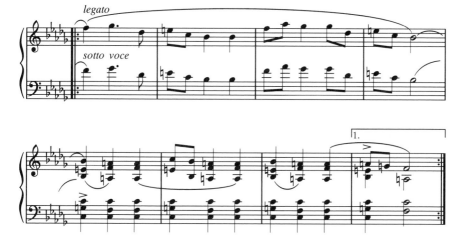

The acerb Rellstab alerts us that dissonant chromaticism alone did not discomfort listeners: "disgusting dislocations" of rhythm also contributed to the ambience of otherness in the genre. Rellstab reacted to the rhythmic patterns notated on the printed page, but other listeners were astonished by Chopin's rhythmically inflected manner of performance. I shall explore briefly both aspects of rhythm in the genre.

Syncopated rhythms represent the stylized feature that Chopin most persistently applied from the peasant models for the mazurka. In danced mazurkas, the second or third beat accents would have been accompanied by foot stomping; the memory of this earthy practice surely encouraged the perception of a strong element of exoticism in the ordinarily rarified atmosphere of his salon pieces (Example 7.12a). Strong indeed: it is difficult to find mazurkas in which the accentual stress is *not* constantly shifted away from the first beat in the measure and onto the second or third beat. The dogged whirl of syncopation often results in a restless dynamism that contributes to the instability perceived in many of Chopin's reiterative themes. Other times, the unsettling effects are more local, as in the first measures of the E-major Mazurka op. 6 no. 3, where the accents temporarily efface the basic triple meter of the genre (Example 7.12b).

EXAMPLE 7.12a. Chopin, Mazurka in D major, Op. 33 no. 2 (mm. 1–8)

EXAMPLE 7.12b. Chopin, Mazurka in E major, Op. 6 no. 3 (mm. 1–6)

Chopin's most storied form of rhythmic perturbation was, of course, rubato. Listeners marveled again and again over his rhythmically free manner of performance; it became a critical commonplace that one could not play Chopin properly until one heard the master himself at the keyboard. The very concept of rubato, though in fact known for centuries, became associated specifically with Chopin.[18] Because Chopin himself notated the term most frequently in the mazurkas (some three-fourths of its appearances take place in this genre), and because rubato played an important role in the folkloristic antecedents to Chopin's mazurkas (constantly shifting accents were a feature of the *mazur*; Eigeldinger, 120, 147), a special affinity grew between the concept and this kind.

Evidence from his pupils and familiars suggests Chopin employed two basic types of rubato.[19] The first is described by his pupil Wilhelm von Lenz, who cited one of Chopin's favorite aphorisms:

> What characterized Chopin's playing was his rubato, in which the totality of the rhythm was constantly respected. "The left hand," I often heard him say, "is the choir master [*Kapellmeister*]: it mustn't relent or bend. It's a clock. Do with the right hand what you want and can." He would say, "A piece lasts for, say, five minutes, only in that it occupies this time for its overall performance; internal details are another matter. And there you have rubato." (Eigeldinger, 50)

In other words, in this type of rubato the accompaniment remains rhythmically constant; all rhythmic variation occurs in the melodic lines.

The second, more common type of rubato consists of agogic modifications of pace relative to the basic tempo. These may last for a portion of a phrase or for an entire period. However long they last, though, the rhythmic variations take place simultaneously in the melody and accompaniment.

Perhaps the most remarkable of all of the dislocating effects of Chopin's playing of rubato was his ability to make musically sophisticated listeners call into question the notated meter of mazurka. A number of observers, among them Charles Hallé, wondered whether mazurkas were really written in duple, not triple meter:

> It must have been in 1845 or 1846 that I once ventured to observe to him that most of his Mazurkas (those dainty jewels), when played by himself, appeared to be written, not in $\frac{3}{4}$, but in $\frac{4}{4}$ time, the result of his dwelling so much longer on the first note in the bar. . . . The more remarkable fact was that you received the impression of $\frac{3}{4}$ rhythm whilst listening to common time. (Eigeldinger, 72)

Chopin reacted to Hallé with amusement, but a similar encounter with Meyerbeer led to an explosion. Meyerbeer overheard a student of Chopin's performing the C-major Mazurka op. 33 no. 3 (Example 7.13) and insisted that the piece was in $\frac{2}{4}$, even while Chopin beat time on the piano with his pencil. Three performances by himself, stomping out the time with his feet, failed to convince Meyerbeer, and the two parted angrily (Eigeldinger, 73). For Meyerbeer and for Hallé, their encounters with the mazurka were, in this way at least, confrontations with the foreign and strange.

EXAMPLE 7.13. Chopin, Mazurka in C major, Op. 33 no. 3 (mm. 1–4)

Mazurkas that are embedded within other genres deserve brief mention, for the ethos of the genre on a few occasions works its destabilizing effects outside its normal context. That is, when transplanted into another genre, the mazurka continues to act as an agent of dislocation. For example, much of the peculiarity of the Nocturne in G minor op. 15 no. 3 derives from its heavy overlay of mazurkalike gestures (I will return to this piece below). Similarly, the idiosyncratic character of the Polonaise in F-sharp minor op. 44—at one time Chopin thought the work resembled a fantasy as much as a polonaise[20]—results in large part from the *Tempo di Mazurka* passage in its central section (Example 7.14). This passage doubly unsettles. First, it derails the Trio that began some forty measures earlier, hence skewing the usual formal plan for the middle section of a polonaise. Second, the passage imports into the piece some of the connotations of strangeness that customarily adhere to the genre (its insistently reiterative phrases particularly contribute to the *topos*). Composers had long turned to generic mixture as a way to expand the expressive range of a host kind. And Chopin did indeed broaden the staid and aristocratic polonaise with the help of the uncanny mazurka: the tensive, unstable worlds of Chopin's Polonaise in A-flat major op. 53 and Polonaise-Fantasy op. 61 owe much to the generic implant in op. 44.[21]

Nationalist Responses

How did listeners in Chopin's day construe the nationalist element in his mazurkas? Did they "hear Poland" in the same way we do? A cursory look at reactions to the mazurkas from the 1830s and 1840s quickly uncovers a paradox: The view today that Chopin was the embodiment of nineteenth-century Polish culture has worked to obscure the full range of

EXAMPLE 7.14. Chopin, Polonaise in F♯ minor, Op. 44 (mm. 127–143)

nationalist expression originally conceived and perceived in his music. Andrzej Walicki reminds us that Polish nationalism had many meanings in the 1830s and 1840s (Walicki, 1982). From these, we can identify two principal varieties: cultural and political. "Cultural" nationalism evoked images of Polish customs, beliefs, social forms, ethnic groups, and language but omitted any overt sense of the political status of the country. In "political" nationalism, the issue of the sovereignty of Poland lay at the expressive core of the composition; if more general cultural resonances were felt, they were at the periphery. The two types of musical nationalism were plainly related; indeed, as time passed, they merged into the more general concept commonly mentioned in our modern histories. But in Chopin's day, the differences between the two types stood more to the fore and particularly help us understand the gradual shift in attitude that characterized responses over the span of his career.

Composers constitute a special class of listener: their own conceptions plainly can affect the responses of audiences, yet just as plainly, they cannot govern them completely. Chopin did not leave many verbal clues that testify to his understanding of the nationalist element in his mazurkas. Those that he did jot down are rather general, as in this comment from 1831: "You know how I have wanted to feel and in part have approached the feeling of our national music."[22] Yet the very generality of such statements is suggestive. In light of Chopin's abiding avoidance of political activism, they imply that he gravitated most comfortably to expressions of cultural nationalism. While he might have hoped that listeners to mazurkas would reflect on the Polish political situation (following the Russian defeat of the Poles' 1830 "November Uprising," the plight of Poland was much discussed throughout Europe during the 1830s and 1840s), Chopin probably did not compose mazurkas in order to stimulate political thought.

Apparently his early mazurkas were successful. Granted, the circumstances of certain listeners, in particular Chopin's Polish critics, influenced their responses: yoked by Russian censorship, they could only latently encode what they might perceive to be political sentiments in Chopin. But it is difficult to detect anything but purely cultural resonances in most early Polish criticism. For example, Chopin's premiere performances in March 1830 of his F-minor Piano Concerto op. 21, which includes a mazurka finale, elicited responses of the following sort:

> It is also pleasing to the Polish people when reflecting on such a magnificent talent, nay even genius, to remember that in the greater part of his compositions as well as in his performance the spirit of the nation was evident. . . .

> The land which has given him life by its songs has influenced the character of his music. This is evident in the works of this artist where the sound of many of his melodies seems to be a joyful echo of our native harmony. The simple mazurka becomes transformed at his touch while it still preserves its own peculiar flavor and accent. To capture the charming simplicity of such native refrains as Chopin does with his exquisite playing and brilliant composition, one has to have a certain sensitivity to the music of our fields and woodlands and the songs of the Polish peasant. . . .

> Our native songs which appear in his works, far from making them tiresome, serve as an ingenious background of ideas. . . . They have this common trait, that they all strive to bring forth their own stamp of individuality as well as that of the nation which influenced their character.[23]

Such reactions reveal the characteristic cultural awareness in Polish national responses. For Polish listeners, the genre was entirely familiar. Hence not only were certain traits of the mazurka understood as representations of folk customs and sounds, but they were also heard to reflect Poland as a nation, with its distinctly individual spirit (Illustration 7.3). Indeed, to judge from much Polish criticism, Chopin's mazurkas served as something of a rallying point for national pride.

MAZUR

z okolic Warszawy.

ILLUSTRATION 7.3. A *Mazur* from the Warsaw region, in his characteristic dress. (Wójcicki, *Pieśni ludu,* 2: before p. 25).

"Awareness," of either the cultural or political variety, could hardly be said to characterize the initial responses of western European listeners. Indeed, what stands out most in this criticism is a pervasive rhetoric of novelty and peculiarity. How different the following excerpts from western European reactions to Chopin's early published mazurkas sound from those coming from Polish pens. Hector Berlioz authored the first, in 1833; the second comes from an 1833 German periodical; the third, from an 1834 French newspaper:

> His melodies, all impregnated with Polish elements, have something naively untamed about them that charms and captivates by its very strangeness.[24]

> He who is more intimately acquainted with the charming, and, in this genre, particularly inimitable dance of Poland, he who is aware of how the dancing pair knows gracefully and securely how to adapt to each altered accent, will know how to appreciate the piquancy of the peculiar rhythm in the mazurkas. . . . It extends a special spirit of sadness through the often singularly accentuated desire to dance, like a deep and secretly sighing power that governs only more uncannily through the great contrast. (*AmZ* 35 [1833]: 200)

> M. Chopin has acquired a quite special reputation for the spiritual and profoundly artistic manner in which he handles the national music of Poland, a genre of music that still remains very little known to us. . . . The true Polish mazurka, such as M. Chopin reproduces for us here, carries so particular a character, and at the same time adapts with such advantage to the expression of a sombre melancholy as well as to that of an eccentric joy—it is suitable as much to love songs as to war songs— that it seems to us preferable to many other musical forms.[25]

From these western European critics emerges a more general expression of the sense of dislocation, the confrontation with the unknown that we explored above in our musical discussion. The critics seem compelled to talk in terms of strangeness, peculiarity, singularity, uncanniness, and eccentricity. This special vocabulary indicates that the early mazurkas of Chopin had a rather different resonance for audiences in western Europe than for those in Poland. For both groups, the early mazurkas elicited reflections on cultural traits, but only the French and German critics remarked on the added notion of strangeness. Western European listeners heard in the early mazurkas a celebration—or, for the likes of Rellstab, a lamentation—of the exotic, untamed Polish culture.

Around the time of Chopin's full maturity, that is, in the mid-1830s, we detect a shift in perceptions in both western and eastern European critics. Now expressions of political nationalism crop up more frequently.

Some critics even began "hearing Poland" not just in mazurkas and polonaises but throughout Chopin's music.

The prescient Schumann was one of the first overtly to comment on the political overtones of Chopin's mazurkas, an expressive element that he felt sometimes worked to their detriment:

> Combined with all this and the favorable influence of the moment, Fate also distinguished Chopin among all others by endowing him with an intensely original nationality, specifically Polish. And because this nationality now goes forth in black raiments, it attracts us all the more firmly to this thoughtful artist. . . . If the mighty autocratic monarch of the north knew what a dangerous enemy threatened him in Chopin's works, in the simple tunes of his mazurkas, he would forbid this music. Chopin's works are cannons buried in flowers.
>
> In his origins, in the fate of his country, rests the explanation of his merits and also of his defects. When speaking of enthusiasm, grace, of presence of mind, passion and nobility, who does not think of him? But who also does not when it is a question of strangeness, morbid eccentricity, even hate and wildness!
>
> All of Chopin's earlier poems bear this impress of the most acute nationality.[26]

Schumann went on to suggest that the national element in Chopin's music had recently begun to wane in favor of more universal modes of expression that would only increase his significance in the world of music. But more important for us is the direct manner with which Schumann drew the issue of the sovereignty of Poland, a nation he garbed in black mourning raiments, into the perceptual world of the mazurkas. To do so was to propose a relatively new mode of experience for the genre. Relatively new: even when the nationalist element is understood as political, we find once more a western critic conjoining the notions of nationalism and strangeness.

It did not take much prompting for Poles to hear nationalism as pervading Chopin's music. Since the defeat of the Poles' "November Uprising" led to severe political repression, expressions of cultural nationalism were all that could be printed. Yet it is not difficult to perceive political undertones in some Polish commentary. We sense it in the opening salvo of an 1836 overview of Chopin's career; its nationalist sentiments echo more directly later in the text:

> Poland has lately given the musical world a genius the equal of whom does not and certainly will not exist for a long time: it is Chopin . . . this creator of the romantic school of music, or the Shakespeare, Byron, Mickiewicz of pianists. . . .

> We may safely maintain that not any nation may boast of
> such a great, truly national composer. In Chopin's works,
> every note is national, every note beautiful—truly beautiful—
> divine—each thought sublime, heavenly![27]

Like the earlier Polish criticism, this review offers up Chopin as a figure
for national admiration and pride. But its language is surreptitiously suggestive. Polish readers might well have interpreted the linking of Chopin
with such revolutionary romantic figures as Byron and Adam Mickiewicz
(the great Polish poet who had been imprisoned by the Russians in the
1820s) as covert testimony to the political power of his music. And this
political force was made all the more potent since "every note" of his music
was "national" and "divine."

French critics too framed perceptions of the mazurka directly in
terms of the political oppression of Poland. Consider the opening words
from a review of Chopin's Mazurkas op. 50 published in 1843 in Paris:

> The mazurka, as M. Chopin creates it, is a musical elegy, a waltz
> more noble in its shape . . . but stamped with sadness and
> naivety. It is said that there is always a memory of the absent
> and oppressed country in the melodies of this pianist-
> composer. Fortunate are countries that have poets like
> Thomas Moore and Chopin; through their songs, they keep
> alive the traditions and the love of the country where they were
> born, and nurse it with a sweet and noble hope of liberation.[28]

What brought about this shift in attitude that we have detected in Schumann, the Polish, and the French critics? I think we may trace it to two
works that Chopin either conceived or was understood to have conceived
(more on this distinction below) as explicit expressions of political nationalism: the Nocturne in G minor op. 15 no. 3, which dates from 1833, and
the Ballade in F major op. 38, which Chopin began in 1836 and completed
in 1839. Before we examine these works, we may note that, as genres, neither the nocturne nor the ballade originally called forth nationalist associations. In other words, Chopin articulated his most explicitly political
statements through "neutral" genres in which the political message could
stand forth all the more clearly. Hence, in Chopin's practice we find justification for my distinction between "cultural" and "political" nationalisms.

The G-minor Nocturne is one of Chopin's most idiosyncratic works.
Unorthodox gestures stand out on every page. Many of the stylistic devices ordinarily found in nocturnes do not appear in this piece. The melodies are barren and static (not florid, as in earlier nocturnes); the rhythmic
stress falls repeatedly on the second and third beats (Example 7.15a); and,
most striking, there is no return at the end to the opening theme. The
piece seems to present a strange conjury of genres: at various times, it
sounds more like a mazurka, at times more like a *religioso* chorale (Exam-

ple 7.15b). Critical reactions to the piece invariably commented in some way on its fundamental generic ambiguity.[29]

EXAMPLE 7.15a. Chopin, Nocturne in G minor, Op. 15 no. 3 (mm. 1–13)

EXAMPLE 7.15b. Chopin, Nocturne in G minor, Op. 15 no. 3 (mm. 89–96)

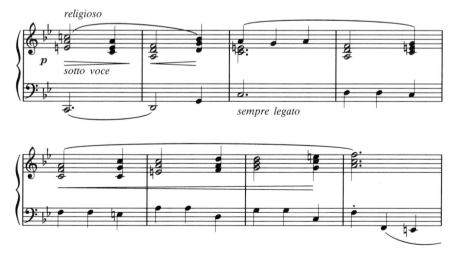

Chopin's fusion of the nocturne, mazurka, and *religioso* music into one heterodox work went beyond a simple experiment in combining seemingly uncombinable types. Indeed, the striking mixture of the nocturne, the "national" mazurka, and the "religious" chorale must have resonated provocatively among the Polish emigré community in Paris, for it expressed some of the key tenets of Polish romantic nationalism.[30] In particular, it drew on the distinctive ethos of a particular branch of the Polish nationalist project—messianism. The Polish romantic messianists, among whom numbered the poet Mickiewicz, believed that the coming war to liberate Poland would lead to the religious redemption of all mankind. Their writings generally promoted an idiosyncratic blend of nationalism, universalism, and religion.[31]

The central components of the messianic brand of Polish romantic nationalism practically read like a description of Chopin's Nocturne in G minor, particularly in its blend of the "nationalistic" mazurka and the "religious" chorale. The Nocturne's lack of a clearly defined national identity might have been perceived as "universal" or "international." And while it may seem unusual that the generally apolitical Chopin composed such a political work, his letters suggest that during his first two years in Paris (1831–33) he was more aware than usual of nationalist concerns. Some of this awareness developed in response to urgings from various quarters that he compose an opera on a Polish national subject. In any case, the striking parallel between the generic content of Chopin's opus and the idiosyncratic beliefs of the Polish romantic messianists bears witness that Chopin was receptive to at least some of their aims, both cultural and political.

The political import of the G-minor Nocturne may have struck one non-Pole: Robert Schumann. In a letter to Stephen Heller, Schumann remarked that op. 15 no. 3 was "one of my favorite pieces."[32] In fact, he went so far as to try to compose a set of variations on it. Is it outlandish to suppose he liked this piece for the implied political meaning of its mixture of genres? If so, the political message in the Nocturne might have led in 1836 to his hearing similar content in the mazurkas. It would not be surprising if he were among the first in the West to do so; after all, Schumann was also one of the first to doff his cap to the genius of Chopin.

Only Chopin's fellow emigrés and perhaps a few kindred spirits like Schumann were aware of the political message of the Nocturne. The political nationalism associated with Chopin's F-major Ballade attracted much greater attention. Two contemporary writers implied that Chopin's Ballade represented the plight of the Polish pilgrim, separated from his or her homeland after the "November Uprising." A third figure, the ubiquitous Schumann, stated that Chopin based the piece on certain unnamed poems by Mickiewicz.[33] All this would have been interesting enough news about a composer who was extraordinarily reserved about revealing programmatic intentions in his music. But the titillating circumstances that attended one of the publications intensified the public's curiosity. At roughly the same time that Félicien Mallefille's laudatory, quasi-dramatic interpretation of Chopin's Ballade appeared in print, Chopin supplanted Mallefille as the object of George Sand's affections. Mallefille was so distraught over this development that he apparently attempted to assault Sand. The desire to escape the resultant air of scandal contributed to the new couple's fateful decision to flee to Mallorca.

Whether Chopin actually did intend the Ballade to be heard politically is another question. Given that the three writers functioned independently of one another (though both Probst and Schumann could have known the Mallefille article), and given that at one time or another they all had dealt directly with the composer, we might accept at least the gist of their accounts as true. Certainly the genre itself encourages expectations of programmatic meaning, hidden or otherwise: ballades are supposed to tell tales. And certain aspects of the structure of the piece favor the perception of extramusical meaning. In particular, the breaks in continuity caused by juxtaposition of sections having sharply different characters or tempi mirror features found in demonstrably "narrative" instrumental works such as the popular battle pieces of the early nineteenth century.[34]

But for our purposes, the actual "truth" is not as important as the resultant diffusion of a politically inspired story in the Ballade, a story that people took to be true. For it was this greater exposure of what readers understood to be Chopin's personal credo that decisively altered the reactions of his listeners. After 1838, audiences commonly imputed motives of political nationalism to Chopin. And often these perceptions extended into realms where Chopin may only have conceived cultural resonances. The comments of Chopin's pupil Wilhelm von Lenz are typical of this trend:

> Chopin's Mazurkas are the diary of his soul's journey through the socio-political territories of his Sarmatian dream-world! There his playing was truly at home; *in them resided* Chopin's originality as a pianist. He represented Poland, *the land of his dreams,* in the Parisian salons under Louis-Philippe—salons which *his* viewpoint allowed him to use as a political platform. Chopin was the *only political* pianist. He *incarnated* Poland, he *set* Poland *to music!*[35]

Nourished by remarks like Lenz's, the tendrils of political nationalism spread after Chopin's death, and led to the generalized concept of "nationalism" often encountered today.

"Hearing Poland" in Chopin's day, then, meant both something less and something more than it does today. As something less, the scope of nationalist perception was more limited in terms of the genres where it might occur. As something more, listeners engaged a greater variety of cultural and political nationalist messages. This greater variety should not surprise us: sound and national culture, complex phenomena on their own, become no less complex when joined in the service of nationalism.

In this essay, I have touched on only a few of the abundant means of expression that were bound up with Chopin's forays into nationalist composition. Yet we nonetheless can detect the richness—and often the uncanniness—of meanings that nationalism conveyed in Chopin's time. And for the mazurkas, this awareness encourages a tempting thought, not at all paradoxical: with some probing into history, we might mitigate our own perceptions of strangeness through our understanding of the strangeness of the past.

Notes

1. Ting Shan-Teh, "What Makes the Chinese People Accept and Appreciate Chopin's Music," in Lissa, 399–403.

2. Donald J. Grout and Claude Palisca, *A History of Western Music,* 4th ed. (New York, 1988), 687.

3. "Logical" here refers to the tonic-dominant pairs of E-B and A♭-C♯. Some editions distort the numbering of this set, placing the C-sharp minor Mazurka first. This confusion resulted from shuffling the order of individual numbers in the manuscript Chopin sent to his German publisher. But overwhelming documentary evidence (including manuscript numerations and a publisher's contract in Chopin's hand) confirms the opening position of the E-minor Mazurka.

4. In other genres, Chopin occasionally essayed similar epigrammatic themes at the ends of codas, though usually not as fully formed as those in the mazurkas; two examples are the Nocturne in E major op. 62 no. 2 and the Prelude in D-flat major op. 28 no. 15. Chopin may have learned the technique from Beethoven; an epigrammatic theme caps the opening variation movement of the Sonata in A-flat major op. 26 (one of Chopin's favorite teaching pieces).

5. G. W. Fink, "Die neu-romantische Schule," *Allgemeine musikalische Zeitung* (hereafter *AmZ*) 40 (1838): 668.

6. *Revue et Gazette musicale de Paris* 10 (1843): 179.

7. On this subject, see my "Compatibility in Chopin's Multipartite Publications."

8. The appearance of formal counterpoint in these two later mazurkas highlights the importance of counterpoint generally in Chopin's late period. In the mazurkas, we can see other passages of canonic imitation in op. 50 no. 3 in C-sharp minor; op. 56 no. 2 in C major; and op. 63 no. 3 in C-sharp minor. Imitative passages also occur in the Ballade in F minor op. 52, the Nocturne in E major op. 62 no. 2, and the last movement of the Violoncello Sonata op. 65. Chopin's interest in counterpoint went beyond imitation, as testifies the careful part writing in a work like the Nocturne in B major op. 62 no. 1.

9. Motivic repetitiveness also characterizes the melodies of Polish folk mazurkas.

10. Again, the folk mazurka may have provided models of this formal effect to Chopin. Sectional repeats were often taken *ad libitum* in the folk *mazur, oberek,* and *kujawiak* (individual but related genres that were subsumed in art music under the single label *mazurka*); the chains of repetitions could extend for some time.

11. I discuss these sources more fully in "The Problem of Repetition and Return in Chopin's Mazurkas."

12. Though in many cases—to judge by the performances—for the wrong reason: rarely does one hear this piece played at the proper tempo. Chopin's metronome indication of ♩ = 152 should be taken at face value. The languorous pace adopted by most pianists distorts the expressive values of the piece. Mazurkas are dances, not dirges.

13. *Neue Zeitschrift für Musik* (hereafter *NZM*) 19 (1838): 179–80.

14. Ignaz Moscheles, *Letters of Felix Mendelssohn to Ignaz and Charlotte Moscheles*, ed. F. Moscheles (Boston, 1888), 129.

15. *Iris im Gebiete der Tonkunst* 4 (1833): 111.

16. Eugene Narmour convincingly argues that such dissonances are not mere "escape notes," but rather structurally transformed dissonances that represent one of Chopin's most important contributions to the development of harmonic language. See Narmour, 77–114.

17. Chopin tried something similar in the middle section of the F-minor Mazurka, published incompletely and posthumously as op. 68 no. 4. (I wish to thank the students in Leo Treitler's seminar on the Chopin mazurkas, held in Spring 1989 at the Graduate Center of the City University of New York, for drawing this similarity to my attention.) But in this piece (probably sketched around 1846, and left unfinished by the composer), the alteration of dissonant chromaticism and pure diatonicism is prolonged to the point of banality; indeed, this may have been one reason why he abandoned the piece. A complete edition of this middle section appears in Fryderyk Chopin, *The Final Composition: Mazurka in F Minor Op. Posthumous (Fontana Op. 68 no. 4), A Completely New Realization*, ed. Ronald Smith (New York, 1975). For a discussion of problems of this mazurka with respect to Chopin's final years, see my "Chopin's Last Style."

18. A glossary of Italian musical terms published in *Le pianiste* 1 (1834): 103, identifies Chopin as the composer who employed the term *rubato* most often.

19. The best presentation and discussion of this evidence is in Eigeldinger, 49–52, 70–73, 118–123, 145–48.

20. Letters of 23 and 24 August 1841 in Chopin, 2:341 and 2:32.

21. For a further discussion of the role of instability in opp. 53 and 61, see my "Chopin's Last Style."

22. Letter of 25 December 1831 in Chopin, 1:210.

23. The three excerpts come from reviews in the *Powszechny Dziennik Krajowy*, 19 March 1830, and *Kurjer Polski*, 20 and 26 March 1830, cited and translated in Attwood, 209, 211–12, 215.

24. *Le rénovateur*, 15 December 1833, cited and translated in Eigeldinger, 71.

25. *Gazette musicale de Paris* 1 (1834): 210.

26. *NZM* 4 (1836): 137–39. I have modified somewhat Paul Rosenfeld's standard translation published in Robert Schumann, *On Music and Musicians*, ed. Konrad Wolff (1946; reprint ed., New York, 1969), 132.

27. Antoni Woykowski, "Chopin," *Przyjaciel Ludu*, 9, 16, and 23 January 1836, 223–24, 230–31, and 237–39.

28. *Revue et Gazette musicale de Paris* 10 (1843): 179.

29. For a full discussion of the generic anomalies in this piece, see my "The Rhetoric of Genre: Chopin's Nocturne in G Minor."

30. We have some proof that it did in a piece by a fellow Polish emigré, Edward

Wolff, that is plainly modeled on the Chopin nocturne. Wolff entitled his piece *Nocturne en forme de Mazurke*, making his homage clear. But its significance for the present argument is that it was authored by a Pole, that is, by a person particularly apt to sense the political meaning of the generic mixture in the Chopin Nocturne.

31. For an exemplary analysis of Polish romantic messianism, see Walicki.

32. Stephen Heller, *Lettres d'un musicien romantique à Paris*, ed. Jean-Jacques Eigeldinger (Paris, 1981), 93.

33. The first writer, Félicien Mallefille, expressed himself at length in "A M. F. Chopin, sur sa Ballade polonaise," *Revue et Gazette musicale de Paris* 5 (1838): 362–64. The second writer was Heinrich Albert Probst, the Parisian agent for Breitkopf & Härtel, one of Chopin's German publishers. In a letter to his employers dated 10 March 1839, he referred to the eventual op. 38 as "a Pilgrim's Ballade." The full letter appears in Wilhelm Hitzig, " 'Pariser Briefe': Ein Beitrag zur Arbeit des deutschen Musikverlags aus den Jahren 1833–40," *Der Bär: Jahrbuch von Breitkopf & Härtel 1929/30* (Leipzig, 1930), 65. Schumann's remarks came in a review of the Ballade in *NZM* 15 (1841): 141–42.

34. Perhaps the clearest example of this phenomenon in the ballades occurs in op. 38, in the form of the contrast between the lilting *Andantino* in F major that opens the piece and the agitated *Presto con fuoco* in A minor that follows.

35. "Die Grossen Pianoforte-Virtuosen unserer Zeit aus persönlicher Bekanntschaft: Liszt–Chopin–Tausig," *Neue Berliner Musikzeitung* 22 (1868), cited and translated in Eigeldinger, 71.

Selected Bibliography

Abraham, Gerald. *Chopin's Musical Style*. London, 1939.

Attwood, William G. *Fryderyk Chopin: Pianist from Warsaw*. New York, 1987.

Belotti, Gastone. *F. Chopin l'uomo*. 3 vols. Milan-Rome, 1974.

———. *Saggi sull'arte e sull'opera di F. Chopin*. Bologna, 1977.

Chomiński, Józef M. *Fryderyk Chopin*. Translated by Bolko Schweinitz. Leipzig, 1980.

Chopin, Fryderyk. *Korespondencja Fryderyka Chopina*. Edited by Bronisław Edward Sydow. 2 vols. Warsaw, 1955.

Eigeldinger, Jean-Jacques. *Chopin: Pianist and Teacher as Seen by His Pupils*. Translated by Naomi Shohet, Krysia Osostowicz, Roy Howat. Edited by Roy Howat. Cambridge, 1986.

Hedley, Arthur. *Chopin*. London, 1974.

Higgins, Thomas, "Tempo and Character in Chopin." *Musical Quarterly* 59 (1973): 106–20.

Kallberg, Jeffrey. "Chopin in the Marketplace: Aspects of the International Music Publishing Industry." *Notes* 39 (1983): 535–69, 795–824.

———. "Compatibility in Chopin's Multipartite Publications." *Journal of Musicology* 2 (1983): 391–417.

———. "Chopin's Last Style." *Journal of the American Musicological Society* 38 (1985): 264–315.

———. "The Problem of Repetition and Return in Chopin's Mazurkas." In *Chopin Studies*, edited by Jim Samson. Cambridge, 1988. Pp. 1–23.

————. "The Rhetoric of Genre: Chopin's Nocturne in G Minor."*19th Century Music* 11 (1988): 238–61.

Kobylańska, Krystyna. *Rękopisy utworów Chopina. Katalog.* 2 vols. Cracow, 1977.

————. *Frédéric Chopin. Thematisch-bibliographisches Werkverzeichnis.* Translated by Helmut Stolze. Munich, 1979.

Lissa, Zofia, ed. *The Book of the First International Musicological Congress Devoted to the Works of Frederick Chopin.* Warsaw, 1963.

Narmour, Eugene. "Melodic Structuring of Harmonic Dissonance: A Method for Analysing Chopin's Contribution to the Development of Harmony." In *Chopin Studies,* edited by Jim Samson. Cambridge, 1988. Pp. 77–114.

Samson, Jim. *The Music of Chopin.* London, 1985.

————, ed. *Chopin Studies.* Cambridge, 1988.

Temperley, Nicholas. "Fryderyk Chopin." *The New Grove Early Romantic Masters 1.* New York, 1985. Pp. 1–96.

Walicki, Andrzej. *Philosophy and Romantic Nationalism: The Case of Poland.* Oxford, 1982.

CHAPTER EIGHT

Schumann and the Marketplace: From Butterflies to Hausmusik

Anthony Newcomb

A number of issues confront the person who wants to place Schumann's solo piano music in its full context. Some of these issues are chronological or historiographical ones, which the performer may think he or she can safely ignore. Others, however, directly affect the text to be played.

First and most fundamental: Schumann's piano music can scarcely be regarded as a single oeuvre, for it contains at least three different stages. Although these succeed each other in time, they are not three phases in an evolving style, such as one posits for Beethoven—phases differing from one another in important ways, but involving generically comparable pieces developing out of one another in a kind of unfolding narrative. In Schumann's case, these phases are rather three separate, distinct compositional enterprises, separated by fundamental compositional and aesthetic changes of course rather than by gradual stylistic development.

The first phase is the one most pianists and listeners know as Schumann's piano music. This phase includes opp. 1–23, which are all solo piano music; it comes to a close with opp. 26, 28, and 32, none of which was composed later than 1839. (A rough chronological chart of composition and publication of the solo piano music is given in Table 8.1, which makes clear that opus number is not a reliable index of the chronology of either composition or publication.)

The second phase is the series of polyphonic studies of 1845 (opp. 56, 58, 60, and 72), whose roots seem to lie partly in Schumann's response to the historicist movement and the Bach revival of the midcentury and partly in his personal search for psychological order, objectivity (a much-used word in Schumann criticism of his day), and distance. These polyphonic pieces I have called studies in compositional (as opposed to pianis-

258

tic) technique in Table 8.2, which attempts to plot chronologically Schumann's activity as a composer of piano music by rough generic families.

Most of the third phase falls into the category that I have called in Table 8.2 *Hausmusik*. In some sense, the compositional studies of 1845 may be seen as a harbinger of this third phase, since one subgroup of *Hausmusik* has a didactic or pedagogical purpose. As the name *Hausmusik* implies (I shall return to discuss it at length later), none of the music from this third and last phase seems to have been designed primarily as public concert music.

A second and related issue is that one can scarcely speak of a single Schumann.[1] His aesthetic attitudes, or at least his perception of his own relation to the musical culture around him, changed widely—one might even say wildly—during his career. As with the changes of compositional style, one needs to ask in what sense and why this was true. This is not just an academic question, of interest for the music historian alone. The answers affect the attitude the performer will take toward the various versions of various pieces produced by Schumann at various times in his career, and the attitude he or she will take toward aesthetic questions such as the presence and function of captions, titles, and the like.

A third issue, again related to the previous one, involves the sources for the study of Schumann's music. Many of Schumann's piano works come down to us in a number of musical sources, both manuscript and printed. These sources do not offer a single version, either among themselves or individually within themselves. In fact, they often seem not even to progress toward a single final version but rather to swing between various distinct alternative versions. As a group, they force us to question what notation is supposed to establish inflexibly, what an "Urtext edition" might mean, and to what extent the composer's intention included the concept of a single definitive text.

The issue of sources for the study of Schumann's music is raised not only by the various musical sources surrounding a given piece but also by the various kinds of verbal documents surrounding a given period in Schumann's life. Our access to both verbal and musical sources has increased at a dizzying rate, especially in the past dozen years.[2] Much of this material either has quite recently become available (the later diaries) or is still incompletely available (the compendium of information surrounding the early piano music (*Quellenkat*), the letters between Clara and Robert (*Brfw*), or the complete correspondence announced by Boetticher, for example[3]). Thus Schumann scholarship has still to digest—even to ingest—this rich banquet, and any summary at this stage will show a situation in rapid flux.

Furthermore, in regard to nonmusical sources, one should keep in mind that the overwhelming majority of verbal material quoted as evidence of Schumann's views on any given matter is quoted from the published essays brought together by Schumann in the *Gesammelte Schriften*,

TABLE 8.1. Schumann's Solo Piano Music: A Rough Overview of Periods of Compositional Activity and Dates of Publication

Opus	1	2	3	4	5	6	7	8	9	10	11	12	13	14	15	16	17	18	19	20	21	22	23	26
1828																								
1829																								
1830																								
1831																								
1832																								
1833																								
1834																								
1835																								
1836																								
1837																								
1838																								
1839																								
1840																								
1841																								
1842																								
1843																								
1844																								
1845																								
1846																								
1847																								
1848																								
1849																								
1850				+												+								
1851																								
1852													+											
1853													+											
1854																								
1855																								

+ = Re-editions supervised by Schumann (for opp. 5, 6, 13, 14, 16)

Within the vertical columns for each opus, solid vertical lines indicate periods for which compositional activity on the opus is documented; the horizontal line at the bottom of each column indicates the date of publication.

Dotted lines for opp. 99 and 124 indicate the protracted periods from which the various pieces in these opp. come.

Bracketed opus numbers designate works for four hands or two pianos.

260

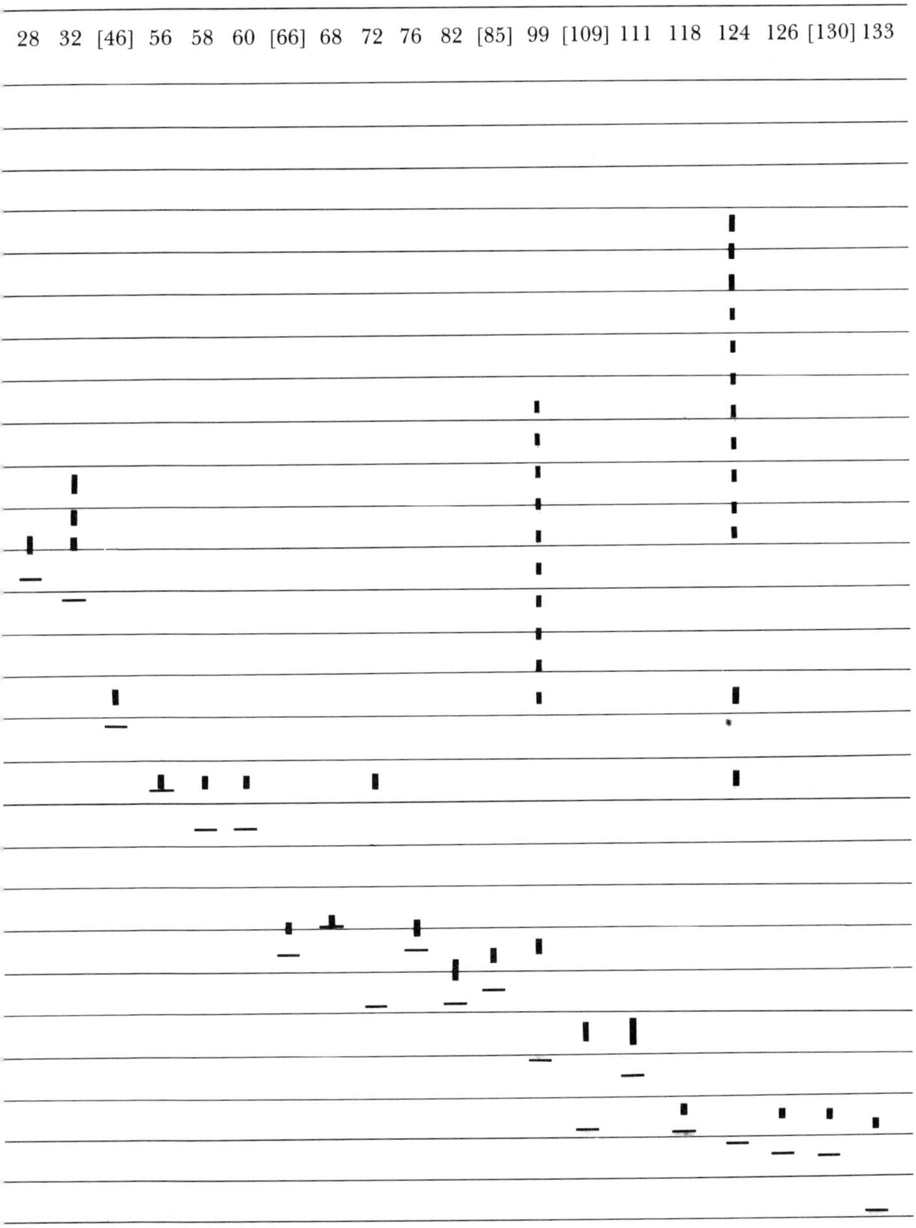
28 32 [46] 56 58 60 [66] 68 72 76 82 [85] 99 [109] 111 118 124 126 [130] 133

TABLE 8.2. An Overview of Schumann's Piano Music by Broad, Generic Category

Year	Easy Pieces, *Hausmusik, Instruktives*; Didactic, Diversional	Smaller Forms		Variations (all characteristic)	Etudes		Compositional (*Strenger Satz*)	Larger Forms (Sonata-related cycles or movements)
		Exoteric, modest	Esoteric, ambitious		Characteristic	Virtuoso		
1828	Polonaises			[Louis-Ferdinand]				
1829								[C-Minor Piano Quartet]
1830			Op. 2	Op. 1 [Paganini B Min. (Dale 1952: 17)]		Op. 7		
1831			Op. 4	[Orig. Theme G Maj. (Dale 1952: 17)]				[G-Minor Symph.] Op. 8
1832						Op. 3		
1833				Op. 5; [Schubert, *Sehnsuchtswalzer*, Beethoven, Op. 92/2 Chopin, Op. 15/3]		Op. 10		
1834			Op. 9	[Op. 9]				Op. 11
1835					Op. 13			
1836			Op. 6					Op. 14
1837		Op. 12	Op. 16					Op. 17
1838		Op. 15						[F-minor Sonata]
1839		Opp. 18, 19, 23, 28, 32	Opp. 20, 21					Op. 22
1840			Op. 26					[Op. 26]

TABLE 8.2. An Overview of Schumann's Piano Music by Broad, Generic Category (continued)

	Easy Pieces, Hausmusik, Instruktives; Didactic, Diversional	Smaller Forms Exoteric, modest	Esoteric, ambitious	Variations (all characteristic)	Etudes Characteristic	Virtuoso	Compositional (Strenger Satz)	Larger Forms (Sonata-related cycles or movements)
1841								
1842								
1843								
1844								
1845							Opp. 56, 58, 60, 72	
1846								
1847								
1848	Opp. 66, 68		Op. 76					
1849		Op. 82						
1850		Op. 85						
1851	Op. 109 [Op. 99]	Op. 111						
1852								
1853	Opp. 130, 118, 126 [Op. 124]		Op. 133				[Op. 126]	[Op. 118]

Dates are roughly those of composition, save for opp. 99 and 124, whose brackets signify that they are special cases. Brackets may also signify secondary generic categories (for opp. 9, 26, 118, 126) and unpublished works (variation sets and sonata types of 1828–33).

especially as presented in the well organized, indexed, and annotated fifth edition edited by Martin Kreisig (1914, hereafter *Ges Schr*). These essays are most often quoted or cited without date, as if Schumann's opinions were consistent across time. One tends to forget that most of the essays in the *Gesammelte Schriften* come from the period 1834 to 1839, so that they represent only the first of the three Schumanns proposed above. The letters and diaries that represent the later two Schumanns are scattered in various publications, are not so well indexed, annotated, and organized, and are often published only in excerpted form, or (in the case of the later diaries) have only very recently become available.[4] Thus the verbal Schumann that we know tends also to be the Schumann of the first phase.

The two great surveys, describing and discussing all of the piano music, are those by Wolfgang Gertler (1931) and Kathleen Dale (1952). Edler (1982) offers a shorter, recent survey.[5] All the documentary material, both verbal and musical, pertaining to opp. 1–13 is now available in the *Quellenkataloge* by Wolfgang Boetticher. There is no need to recapitulate all this material here, even if space allowed. Instead, I shall first survey the field quickly and completely, according to the rough generic families that I have suggested in Table 8.2, in order to suggest a reason behind the abrupt change of compositional and aesthetic course noted above. I shall then turn to some questions raised by recent scholarship in connection with the second and third issues raised above.

In surveying Schumann's output from the 1830s, one should first note what is *not* to be found there. There are no fantasies, variations, capriccios, rondos, and so forth based on favorite operatic tunes, such as loomed large on recital programs of the virtuosi and in publishers' offerings.[6] Instead, Schumann's earliest published works, those of 1831 and 1832, occupy different generic realms and establish at least the basis for his production across the rest of the decade. Op. 1 is a set of variations, but of a riddling kind—not a set of figurational variations on a fixed and well-known tune, but a set of highly characteristic (in the sense, "full of character") variations on an unfamiliar theme. In op. 1, as often in later pieces of the same type, the theme was self-invented and, especially in the harmonically wide-ranging finale, is less a theme than a motivic cell or a shifting network of motives. This tendency toward loosening of the variation form is carried much further in the op. 5 Impromptus—in truth a free set of variations partly on a structured tune, partly on a motivic bass-voice idea, whose kinship to the finale of the *Eroica* Symphony was noticed in a review of 1837 by Liszt.[7] Op. 2 is Schumann's best known and most original generic innovation—the interconnected cycle of small-form character pieces, usually offered with some sort of programmatic title(s) or caption(s).[8] Op. 3, generically the most traditional of the first three publications, is a series of figurational études transcribed from Paganini's *Capricci* op. 1 and explicitly addressing certain details of piano technique.[9] Such virtuoso études were a prominent feature in publishers' catalogs of the 1830s and in the review column of Schumann's *Neue Zeitschrift für Musik.*

It was this last, most typical genre that would quickly disappear from Schumann's production as the decade progressed. As Boetticher has shown,[10] the Toccata op. 7 started as an étude in 1830 but was transformed in 1832 into something closer to a sonata-form movement. In 1833, Schumann produced the second set of arrangements for the piano of Paganini *Capricci*—a complement to op. 3 that had been part of Schumann's original conception.[11] The last appearance of anything like the étude genre in Schumann's output is op. 13, a complicated generic hybrid on which Schumann worked from late 1834 into 1836. The generic étude that enters into the hybrid is now more the *étude charactéristique* than the virtuoso étude of dazzling figurational display. As the title *Symphonic Études* announces, op. 13 also incorporates an element of the large-scale symphonic (or sonata) cycle, a genre that came increasingly to occupy Schumann's published output in the second half of the decade (see Table 8.2). In op. 13, the symphonic element was apparently the larger scale, transformational development of thematic-motivic material across a sizable span of time. The main formal background against which this transformational development occurs, however, is Schumann's distinctive understanding of the variation set, as suggested in op. 1 and carried in increasingly personal and unconventional directions in opp. 5 and 9, before being grafted onto the étude and the symphonic cycle in op. 13.[12]

At the same time as he was working on op. 13, Schumann began working on what were to become his first published essays in the sonata cycle, opp. 11, 14, and 17.[13] All of these, especially opp. 11 and 17, were exceptionally bold and unconventional formal hybrids. Thus, by 1834 Schumann was concentrating on his own personal conception of the variation set, on the cycle of usually interdependent, highly characteristic pieces, and on the large and formally unconventional sonata cycle. That is to say, Schumann was—from the beginning really, but by 1834 certainly— a generic renegade as far as the market for piano music in the 1830s was concerned. (Compare the solo piano output of Henselt, Moscheles, Ries, and even Clara Wieck in the 1820s and 1830s.) He showed no signs of moving toward a commercially more acceptable, generically more conventional published output as the decade progressed. Indeed, he became generically less conventional and more ambitious up to 1838, when some signs of retrenchment begin to appear.

This is not to say that Schumann during the 1830s set out consciously on a commercially impractical course—indeed, he was always extremely attentive and sensitive to published reactions to his work.[14] He may simply not have known what could and what could not succeed in the marketplace. As a young composer, he was part of a close and insulated circle of friends. Moreover, Leipzig was not London, or Paris, or Berlin, nor even the musical center of northern Germany that it was soon to become. Finally, the professional and commercial context for the composer of piano music in the 1830s was in a state of extraordinary flux. New generic types, new performance venues and techniques, new publishers, and new markets were appearing right and left, north and south.[15] The resulting scene must have been as unstable and unpredictable as the rock music scene of the 1960s, even to the most commercially sensitive and savvy—and there is no evidence that Schumann was either.[16]

Yet he did eventually need to figure out how to make his living from this professional and social context. As is well known, by the early 1830s he was forced to abandon his dreams of becoming a virtuoso pianist because of problems with one of his fingers. He did not have the social gifts that would enable him to survive as a performer in house-concerts and as teacher of the well-to-do. Unless he were to try to survive on musical journalism alone, he needed to figure out how to wring some reasonable income out of his activity as a publishing composer. The difficulty of satisfying this need, as it dawned on him during the last years of the decade, may well account for the hints of retrenchment noted above. The protracted struggle with Clara's father, begun in 1838 and lasting into 1840, concerning Clara's proposed marriage with Robert—a struggle that came to focus more and more on demands from Wieck's side for evidence of financial security for Clara—could only have made this need clearer and more pressing.[17]

The influence of Clara herself should also not be neglected. In a letter from March 1838 Robert complains loudly: "But Clara, what has happened to you? You write that I should write quartets—but '*please good and clear*'—that sounds indeed like something from the mouth of a Dresden *Fräulein*."[18] In a letter of 4 April 1839 from Paris, Clara complains in her turn:

> Listen Robert, won't you for once compose something brilliant, easily understandable, and something without titles, something that is a complete, coherent piece, not too long and not too short? I would so love to have something of yours to play in concerts, something written for an audience. Admittedly, that is degrading for a genius, but politics demands it now; once one has given the public something that it understands, then one can also put something a bit more difficult before it—but the audience must first be won over. . . . See if you can—maybe variations? You wrote such things once—can't you do so again? Or a Rondo?[19]

A similar passage of September 1839 from her diary laments, "I would play [Robert's compositions] gladly, but the public doesn't understand them."[20] She goes on to hope that she can convince him to write for orchestra.

Suggestive, then, are the signs that Robert's move toward more conventional styles and genres comes at the same time as the struggle to prove himself professionally and financially worthy of marrying Clara. The earliest instance, *Kinderszenen* (op. 15), may be something of a serendipitous accident. Robert's first mention of these pieces comes in a passage directly preceding that quoted above from his letter to Clara of March 1838:

> As if in response to your words, where you once wrote "ich käme Dir auch manchmal wie ein Kind vor," I obediently got into my piano garb, and I wrote away at the 30 quaint little things, of which I chose twelve [sic] and called them "Kinderscenen." You will have fun with them, but frankly you will have to forget yourself as a virtuoso.[21]

The *Kinderszenen* may also have been influenced by the ideals of *Hausmusik,* a kind of German answer to the technically undemanding branch of French salon music, for the term was first brought to prominence in Schumann's own *Neue Zeitschrift* in a series of articles of 1837 (Becker). Whatever the impulse behind it, op. 15 quickly became Schumann's first commercially successful publication, to judge both by reviews of his career published in the mid-1840s (see below) and by Robert's delighted letter from April 1839 about sales figures, also quoted below.

At the same time or shortly thereafter, Schumann revised the G-minor Sonata (op. 22) to render it simpler and clearer, partially at least because of Clara's pressure to do so.[22] In early 1839 come the *Arabeske* and the *Blumenstück* (opp. 18 and 19)—texturally, technically, and formally a much simpler kind of music, which seems to move generically toward a higher level of salon music.[23] Opuses 23, 28, and 32, all from later in 1839, follow the same path toward a musically and technically less demanding style, more acceptable to the dilettante.

This proposed stylistic change of direction in 1838 and 1839 was far from single-minded, however. During these same years Schumann worked on the revision of op. 17 and the composition of opp. 20 and 21, among his most ambitious and formally most unconventional works.[24] He also composed *Kreisleriana* (op. 16), a cycle without the captions and titles of opp. 9 and 6, but with the same technical difficulties and the same intense quirkiness and quick shifts of mood. And the composition of the *Faschingsschwank aus Wien* (op. 26), begun early in 1839 and likewise large and formally ambitious, seems to have stretched even into early 1840.[25]

But with op. 26 came the end of the early piano music, and of Schumann's piano music as most people know it. In explaining this abrupt change of direction, we might reasonably reject the conclusion that Robert's spring of youthful romantic inspiration ran dry around 1840—the songs of 1840 would certainly contradict this; also the conclusion that his mind was showing early signs of the disintegration that was to lead him to the mental institution some fourteen years later—the magisterial and immediately appreciated Piano Quartet, Piano Quintet, and Second Symphony would certainly contradict this. He had simply decided, on some level at least, to stop beating his head against the wall. He had recognized that the style of music that he found most natural and by which he placed most store had not found public acceptance and would seemingly never gain him the kind of public recognition that he needed to survive professionally. He had to try something else.[26]

In order to understand better the social and professional pressures that Schumann was attempting to interpret and respond to, we might well survey the most important reactions that Schumann's piano music elicited from his contemporaries, both because the earliest of these reactions were ones he would have read and reacted to, and because they tell us the values of the musical culture in and for which Schumann worked. These reactions are remarkably uniform in their judgments.[27] Carl Kossmaly, in the first large-scale retrospective review of Schumann's output (1844), notes that the early piano music strove too much for strange, puzzling effects and "Bizarreries."[28] He also complains that the music is often so difficult to play that only the Liszts and Thalbergs of the world can produce even an acceptable performance.

Franz Brendel's detailed and searching article of 1845, the most important early survey of Schumann's output, echoes and expands these remarks. Brendel notes that Schumann's pieces (he discusses only the small-form piano music, opp. 2, 6, 9, 12, and 16, in any detail, without commenting on his choice) have by then achieved some diffusion, but by no means that which they deserve. He cites five reasons for this failure to find a broad audience (Brendel, 91, col. 2). First, little has been written about the pieces in musical journals.[29] Second, the pieces are exceptionally difficult technically and yet not grateful to play. The way things are now—although they will soon change, he says—they cannot be played by virtuosi in concert, one of the main avenues for their becoming known.[30] Third, only a longer acquaintanceship will reveal their *tiefere Geist*. At the outset, before one conquers the technical difficulties, everything is completely bewildering. This is an important matter, says Brendel, for he knows from experience that many pianists give up on the pieces after the first reading. Fourth, the modern, youthful tone (*Stimmung*) of the pieces puts off many older players (as it does, he says, potential readers of Heine's poems). Lastly the harmonic harshness discourages some people, though one can find the same harshness in Beethoven, even in Mozart.

In this extraordinarily specific summary, Brendel covered all the points that later critical retrospectives would repeat, in versions more or less complete.[31] A later, substantial overview of Schumann's compositions published in 1850 noted that the early works "disappeared without leaving a trace" ("gingen spürlos vorüber") and attributed this to a lack of attention to "reality" ("den Wirklichen")—a reproach roughly equivalent to the oft-repeated one that Schumann's early work was too "subjective," or lacked "objectivity."[32] Ambros in 1860 remarked succinctly that Schumann's early piano pieces were "too difficult to play and to understand for the common dilettante; for the professional musician they were too eccentric and too far outside the habitual and the traditional rules of art."[33]

These observations all reveal the problematic area into which Schumann had strayed as far as audiences for his piano music were concerned. As private music, for meditation and enjoyment at home, it was technically too difficult to play, even if bourgeois audiences had wanted to reflect on and come to terms with its challenges to musical understanding.[34] On the other hand, the challenges to musical understanding posed by its formal games, by its complex textures and persistent syncopations, and by its extremely quick rate of emotional change made it inappropriate for the diversion-oriented public concert of the 1830s. Even the well-disposed Liszt and Clara Wieck had to admit that they found little or no success playing Schumann's music in public concerts in the period from 1835 to 1855 (cf. Liszt's letter of 1857 to Wasielewski, printed in Was, Appendix G).[35]

The one arena in which especially Clara reported real success with Robert's early piano music was in the private concert for connoisseurs, where the difficulties, unconventionalities, and rapid changes of mood in Robert's music might better be understood and enjoyed.[36] Schumann's music of the 1830s was, as Dahlhaus has commented, music for private rooms and the specially initiated.[37] (Kossmaly notes that Schumann's piano music was known "as yet only in a small, if select and musically knowledgeable circle.") Unfortunately, this was scarcely the kind of market that could support a composer through the sale of published music on the open market.[38] It was not even enough to make his name known on any broad front. Thus, quite understandable was Robert's conclusion that, in the face both of father Wieck's financial demands and (Robert hoped) of impending marriage, he had to change directions.

After the flood of songs of 1840 (technically accessible to amateurs), he turned first toward more conventional forms and traditional genres, as suggested by the formally straightforward new finale of op. 22, as well as by Clara's repeated urgings. The new, more public pieces included the String Quartets op. 41, the Piano Quartet and Quintet, the B-flat Symphony and the first version of the D-minor Symphony, the piano fantasy that became the first movement of the Piano Concerto, and the oratorio *Das Paradies und die Peri*. The strategy was successful. These were in fact the works that soon gave Schumann the public recognition that he sought, and that lastingly imprinted his name on the musical culture of his time.

In summer of 1844 through winter of 1845 came a nervous crisis and collapse, followed by a new immersion in the works of J. S. Bach, for which purpose Schumann acquired a pedal attachment to his piano. The result of the Bach study and the pedal piano were the Fugues, *Skizzen,* and *Studien* of opp. 56, 58, 60, and 72 (the latter published only in 1850). The study and veneration of Bach had been a constant in Schumann's life since his earliest days as a musician, but it had never before in his published music taken the form of direct imitation of baroque formal, rhythmic, and textural types such as one sees and hears especially in opp. 60 and 72.[39] This Bach study may have resulted from Schumann's impression that Bach's fugal polyphony offered the rigor, firmness, stability, and "objectivity" that his battered psyche needed. One should also remember, however, that, on the one hand, the midcentury Bach movement leading to the founding of the Bach Gesellschaft in 1850 was centered around Schumann's friends and colleagues in Leipzig and Dresden, and, on the other, almost all important German composers participated in some way in the midcentury Bach revival.[40] In any case, these four publications form a compact, isolated, and atypical group in Schumann's output.[41]

When Schumann returned to piano music in 1848, after these anomalies of 1845 and the string of generically traditional chamber music pieces with piano in 1846 and 1847, it was to explore in opp. 66 and 68 the vein uncovered in op. 15, a vein that had proved to be both successful and culturally significant.

The latter is particularly important. Schumann's change of direction in the 1840s was not just a cynically calculated, commercially motivated change. The changed aesthetic goals represented in the late pieces both for piano and for small ensemble were part of an important cultural movement in Germany's musical world of the 1840s—a movement embraced with deep conviction by at least part of Schumann's always divided personality. This movement and Schumann's response to it are primary factors in the second issue proposed at the beginning of this essay—the changes in Schumann's aesthetic attitudes.

As a background to these changes, let me recall one aspect in particular of the aesthetic that preceded them. In his discussion of op. 6, Brendel identified a characteristic of Schumann's early piano music that we may (with Brendel) recognize as an essential part of the aesthetic of this early style, while at the same time recognizing in it part of the difficulty presented by the early piano music for its potential public, either as virtuoso concert music or as middle-class domestic music for the relaxation of amateurs. Brendel remarks that "these juxtapositions [he is referring to Florestan and Eusebius], this splintering of the composition into opposites, these vacillations and struggles are highly significant; they reveal to us that *Humor* is the principle of Schumann's early compositions." Schumann explained the concept *Humor* in a letter of 1839 to a French-speaking admirer, and the entire passage is worth quoting at length: "It is unfortunate that there exist no good and precise words in the French language for precisely those peculiarities and concepts most deeply rooted in the German nationality, such as *Gemüthliche (Schwärmerische)* and *Humor*, which is the happy blending together of *Gemüthlich* and *Witzig*. But this is an integral part of the whole character of both nations. Are you not acquainted with Jean Paul, our great writer? From this man I have learned more counterpoint than from my music teacher."[42] This splintered, quicksilver quality of rapidly changing moods made the music too unsettling for either the concert hall or the parlor of the average bourgeois. Schumann himself acknowledged what he often referred to as his "rapid changes [of mood]" ("rascher Wechsel," which he also connected with Jean Paul) as a reason why his music was inappropriate for domestic concerts or the concert hall.[43]

Ambros (56) stressed even more strongly the importance of the young Schumann's oft-declared admiration for the novelist Jean Paul, Schumann's explicit model for *Witz* and *Humor*.[44] Ambros went on to remark that Schumann's adherence to the aesthetic of Jean Paul was fine when and where Jean Paul was admired (Jean Paul's most influential novels were written between 1793 and 1805, the novels and tales of his spiritual successor E. T. A. Hoffmann between 1814 and 1822). Now that "his form is considered barbaric and tasteless, one holds the rich treasures of mind that it contains worthless."

In fact, the aesthetic of Jean Paul was already largely alien to the culture of the German *Vormärz* (1830–48), and Schumann seems to have recognized this on some level.[45] During the 1840s both the above-noted quick changes of mood and the sometimes violent surface discontinuities disappear from Schumann's music; at the same time the ecstatic mentions of Jean Paul's novels disappear from Schumann's diaries. We may deduce from this that Schumann came consciously or unconsciously to back away from the wild swings of mood and jolting reversals of direction characteristic of Jean Paul's narrative technique.

Nonetheless, one should keep in mind that the early piano music comes from the years of infatuation with the novels of Jean Paul, and that its aesthetic goals should be understood with that background in mind, however distant that background may be from us now. The aesthetic of the early Romantic novel prized incompleteness, interruption, digression, juxtaposition of opposites, even the avoidance of unequivocal closure (Blackall, *passim*, esp. 263–65). These same aesthetic goals are intrinsic to Schumann's early style. We should realize this not just as a piece of intellectual history; the way we perform and hear this music is affected by these goals as well. Surface discontinuity and riddling juxtapositions are an aesthetic ideal to be projected as strongly as possible, not an aesthetic defect to be covered up insofar as possible. Early Schumann should not be played like Brahms, or like middle-period Beethoven, or like late Schumann.[46]

A crucial factor in Schumann's change of aesthetic stance in the 1840s and in what I propose as his turning away from Jean Paul may have been his reaction to what Carl Dahlhaus (1982: 65) calls the furor of German cultural politics in the turbulent 1840s. Many cultural critics of the time saw the survival in music of early romantic ideas such as Jean Paul's not as the preservation of a precious poetic ideal, but as a flight inward, a turning away from life, from society and the people, from the demands of a new day. From around 1840 onward, through the revolutions of 1848 and beyond, questions about the social significance of music became increasingly pressing in the German press (Lichtenhahn, 12). These questions rapidly came into focus around the institutions of lay musical culture: *Musikvereine, Singakademien, Liedertafeln,* musical education, and finally the home.[47] Around these last two institutions the concept of *Hausmusik* took shape in the 1840s; this concept, in turn, was the focus of a large musical-cultural movement that had profound effects on Schumann's later piano music.[48]

As the word implies, *Hausmusik* was defined primarily by place of performance, and only secondarily by style or genre. It was music for performance at home—as opposed to concert music, which is public, and salon music, which is semiprivate. In fact, in the area of piano music, *Hausmusik* formed the German answer or counterpart to the salon music of the French. It was also thus defined by nationality as well as by local venue. Its characteristics were understood to place the German national traits of seriousness, simplicity, and *Volksthümlichkeit* in opposition to the frivolous, artificial French national characteristics.[49] Finally, *Hausmusik* had a social dimension. It was music of the broad middle class, as opposed to salon music, which was music of exclusive society (Lichtenhahn, 10). It was thus part of the goals of *Hausmusik* to improve the level of musical education of this lay middle class.

The term *Hausmusik* first came up in a series of articles published in Schumann's *NZfM* (1837–1839) and written by the Leipzig organist, musicologist, and early music enthusiast (as we would now say), C. F. Becker.[50] The subject of these articles was the traditional place of modest music-making in German culture of past centuries. Part of *Hausmusik* was thus a cultural-didactic crusade for the revival of the "pure and true" music of the German musical past, a crusade into which fit easily the keyboard music of J. S. Bach—the *Well-Tempered Clavier* and the *Clavierübung,* Parts I and II, the music by which he was principally known to the German musical world of the mid-nineteenth century.[51] (So, too, did Schumann's fugues and fughettas of opp. 72 and 126, partly as didactic examples, partly as echoes of a great German musical past.)

All of these aspects had flowed together to form a broad musical-cultural movement by the late 1840s in Germany. It was the headwaters of this future river of music that Schumann stumbled upon, perhaps inadvertently, with op. 15. When he returned to piano music with opp. 66 and 68 of 1848, he returned to the socially important and musically well-formed category of *Hausmusik.*[52] Alfred Dörffel's review of op. 68 is one of the clearest statements of the ideals of *Hausmusik* (*NZfM* 30 [1849]: 89–91). After dividing Schumann's career into three periods (as was becoming common) and putting op. 68 near the beginning of the third, citing especially the "objectivity of the expression,"[53] Dörffel continues:

> The Master appears *volksthümlich* in the noblest fashion; the small pieces make their effect immediately and surely through their simplicity, and also through the natural strength that surges through them. . . . How very well suited they are to instruction—that is, not just to the technical education of the hand, but also to musical education in the general sense—must make the entire work extremely welcome to piano teachers.

The most famous visual icon of the movement, Ludwig Richter's woodcut *Hausmusik* (Illustration 8.1) done as the frontispiece of Wilhelm Heinrich Riehl's widely popular song album of the same name (1856), was reportedly inspired by "Winterzeit/II" from op. 68. Richter reported a performance in his presence of op. 68 by Clara, during which "the composer sat by her side with closed eyes and whispered before the beginning of each new piece the title and a few explanatory comments." Richter reported Schumann's comments on "Winterzeit" as follows: "The surrounding forests and fields are covered in snow; thick snow blankets the streets of the city. It is dusk. A light snow begins to fall. Inside in the cozy room the old people sit by the fire and watch the joyful frolicking of the children with their dolls."[54]

ILLUSTRATION 8.1. Frontispiece to Wilhelm Heinrich Riehl, *Hausmusik* (1856)

To this culture and this set of aesthetic goals the remainder of Schumann's piano music (and the music for small ensemble, such as opp. 73, 94, 102, 113, 132) is directed. We must keep in mind the aesthetic stance and social purpose behind his music, just as we must remember the model of Jean Paul behind the early piano music. The usually faultless Kathleen Dale (90–91) seemingly misjudges op. 82 because she thinks of it as concert music for public performance. Even if it is now presented as such, one should remember that Schumann apparently conceived it otherwise.

By the late 1840s, music for solo piano seems to have come to mean *Hausmusik* for Schumann. This change in attitude may help explain why pieces drafted but rejected for publication in the 1830s and early 1840s were acceptable around 1850 (opp. 99, 124). Did the change of audience and function now make these simpler pieces seem appropriate? Another stylistic aspect of these early pieces eventually published in opp. 99 and 124 raises questions. The pieces, most supposedly from the 1830s and very early 1840s, lack the formal whimsy and the textural, harmonic, and rhythmic complexity of the early piano music. Some of op. 124 seem simple-minded, almost inept. Did the later Schumann in fact "straighten them out" for the later publication?[55] Or had he simply not put them through a late stage of technical refinement and development such as he would have for publication in the earlier period (see n. 41)?

This change in attitude should also be borne in mind in evaluating Schumann's sometimes disparaging later pronouncements about the value of his early piano music. In answer to an exploratory letter from a new admirer in Vienna, Schumann wrote on 10 May 1852: "It seems to me that you are too laudatory, and this about youthful works, such as the sonatas, whose partial failures are only too clear to me. Such a well-meaning recognition might be more justified at least in part by my later, larger works, such as the symphonies and the compositions for chorus."[56] Wasielewski (Was, 121) relates an anecdote from "the Düsseldorf years" (i. e., 1851ff.). He expressed to Schumann the wish to hear some of the early piano pieces played by Clara, to which Schumann replied "confused stuff" ("wüßtes Zeug"). The comment was, says Wasielewski, half ironic, half serious.

The change in attitude becomes most serious for the musician of to-day when considering Schumann's later re-editions of his own early piano music. First of all, Schumann reveals his own typically divided attitude by caring enough about the pieces, in spite of his occasional dismissive comments, to return to at least some of them and re-edit them. Second and more seriously, the musician who revised them was much different from the one who had created them. The question must arise as to which version should be considered the more authentic.

Schumann was already thinking of the necessity of a re-edition of opp. 5 and 6 in November 1842, because he felt the original publications were not getting enough distribution.[57] But he seems to have lost interest at this point, and the first of the projects for re-edition of the piano music to come to fruition was that for op. 16 (together with a revised edition of the *Liederkreis*, op. 39) in early 1850. His letter of 20 November 1850 to his publisher Whistling does not indicate that faithfulness to the original conception was a primary concern in his enterprise. "The *Kreisleriana* are much revised. Unfortunately, I spoiled my things so often in earlier times, and wantonly so. All that has now been expurgated."[58] Schumann seems to have maintained a typical ambivalence of opinion on this matter. In the early "Denk-und-Dichtbüchlein," he had expressed a clear preference for first versions:

> The first conception is always the most natural and the best. Reason errs, intuition not.
>
> *On Alteration in Composition*: Often two readings can be equally valid (Eusebius). The original is usually the better (Raro).

And Schumann republished these aphorisms in the *Gesammelte Schriften* in 1854.[59] In spite of all this, Schumann did revise his earlier pieces for the new editions of opp. 5, 6, 13, 14, and 16 between 1850 and 1853. (The alterations to op. 16 were mostly in the nature of adding repeat signs, probably to reduce the impression of *rascher Wechsel* mentioned above, and firming up the closure of individual pieces to increase their autonomy. The original version can be heard played by Charles Rosen on Nonesuch 79062 and Etcetera ETC 3001.)

As I have already emphasized, it was a substantially different Schumann who revised these pieces, and this divergency has posed a problem for thoughtful editors of modern editions almost since the appearance of the revisions.[60] For the Gesamtausgabe, Clara Schumann printed both versions (with the exception of op. 16). Later "practical" editions usually use the revised editions as models, though some note "substantial" variants from the earlier versions. Wolfgang Boetticher, in his summary of text-critical matters preparatory to his new "Urtext" edition of Schumann's piano music for Henle, comes out strongly in favor of the authority and reliability of the first editions (1968a: 48–59), only to revert without explanation to the second edition as the primary source for his text.[61] In the same article, Boetticher chronicles many instances where details of the first editions were silently emended (often regularized, or straightened out) for the Gesamtausgabe.[62] Given the difficulty of the matter of performance indications (see below) and the careful attention that Schumann gave to the visual appearance of publications of his music (see Hoffmann, xxviii–xxxvi), photographic reproductions of an authoritative exemplar of the first editions of each of Schumann's early piano works would seem to be an item of first priority, for the sake of pianists and scholars alike. Might not a publisher successfully undertake such a venture?

It might be appropriate at this point to remark that the range of editions available to the present-day student of Schumann's piano works is unusually wide. Two fundamental editions, the Gesamtausgabe edited by Clara Schumann and Johannes Brahms and the "instruktive Ausgabe" issued contemporaneously under the editorship of Clara Schumann, were first published roughly a century ago and remain available even today. The Gesamtausgabe is currently available in photographic reprint (New York: Dover—though with the omission of some material published in the Gesamtausgabe, such as alternative early versions, or the completed variations not included in the published edition of op. 13). This Gesamtausgabe tried to come as close as possible to what we now call an Urtext—reprinting the original printed edition with no personal additions or recommendations from the editor.[63] Then, as now, it was marked by a complete absence of critical commentary.

Clara's "Instruktive Ausgabe" adds many recommendations for performance—tempo indications, dynamics, fingerings, and expressive markings—not found in the original editions. This particular kind of edition, from the hand(s) of a famous virtuoso and incorporating his or her approach to the pieces, became a commonplace in the late nineteenth and early twentieth centuries.[64] Of the many published, several are still available today. Clara's version of this kind of edition, of course, could and did claim a particular authority not accessible to everyone—she appealed on the title page to her use of "manuscripts and personal communication" as a basis for her edition. Her edition, or a descendant of it, is still available (Wiesbaden: Breitkopf and Härtel, ed. Wilhelm Kempff).

Finally, a number of current scholarly editions incorporate the most recent background information on the pieces and the various sources for them, sometimes giving more than one version for those movements where the divergencies between sources are great enough to warrant this, and in other cases incorporating more or less detailed notes on the variants between the sources. Of these current editions, the one that has come the closest to completion is that edited by Wolfgang Boetticher (Munich: Henle); only the last of five volumes has yet to appear.[65] For the most complete assembly of contextual material surrounding each individual work (relevant correspondence and diary entries, description of sources both manuscript and printed, contemporary reviews, and so on), the user must go to the volumes of the *Quellenkatalog* (*Quellenkat*), also edited by Boetticher, as complements to the Henle edition.[66] The combination of the *Quellenkatalog* and the Henle edition provide as complete a body of information surrounding each work as can be obtained anywhere. The *Quellenkatalog*, however, can be found only in major research libraries. Failing this, the edition by H. J. Köhler (Leipzig: Peters) provides a compact and admirable compendium of background material, plus a modern scholarly edition with differing versions or notes on variants. A similar balance is offered by the few editions of Schumann's piano music in the Wiener Urtext Edition (Vienna: Universal and Schott).

The kind of unresolvable quandary that led Clara Schumann (and Brahms) to publish two versions of op. 13 plus five unpublished variations in the Gesamtausgabe can serve to introduce the third issue to which I referred at the beginning of this essay: What is notation supposed to establish inflexibly, what might an "Urtext edition" mean, and to what extent did the composer's intention include the concept of a single definitive text? Much of the most interesting work in recent Schumann scholarship has centered on the ramifications of this issue, as they appear in connection with individual works. Exploring these ramifications will lead us into often unresolved questions of detail in connection with particular works or movements.

The *Impromptus* op. 5 are the first cycle to bring up the question of whether the first edition (1833) or the revised edition (1850) should be used as the basis of a modern edition (and performance). A comparison of the second with the first version (both are printed in the Gesamtausgabe) shows Schumann's tendency to remove the most unconventional and musically challenging parts of the piece (see especially the excised fantasia-like penultimate variation) and to clarify closure at the end of the piece, alterations that conform to Schumann's aesthetic of 1850 more than to that of the early 1830s, when the piece was created. Whether the final version from the hand of the author would be judged the more authoritative one becomes, in cases like this, less than self-evident.[67]

The issues become yet more complicated when one introduces the evidence offered by the autograph manuscripts and the fair copies reviewed and annotated by Schumann. Again and again, the sources for the cycles of character pieces show a constant reordering of pieces, and hence of moods and keys within the cycle, as well as a lingering indecision about what should be included and what excluded. Linda Correll Roesner's article on the *Davidsbündlertänze* gives a fine account of one instance of the indecision concerning ordering. The number of cases in which Boetticher finds evidence in the manuscripts for this kind of indecision suggests that it was endemic to Schumann's approach to the genre.[68]

The indecision revealed by a comparison of these manuscript sources with the first editions goes beyond number and order of sections. Roesner also carefully analyzes the variations in dynamic markings, accents, slurs, pedaling, captions, and such in order to conclude that Schumann "often postponed a final decision about the placement of expression marks until very late in the process of finalizing a work." She goes on to suggest that "the many changes of expression that one encounters between the various stages of composition in the works of the 1830s and early 1840s may be attributable to the possibility that Schumann continually 'heard' the details differently" (1984: 62), adducing a comparison of two pieces from op. 6 copied by Schumann into souvenir albums with the published version of those same pieces. Here again, detailed performance instructions differ significantly among the various versions.

One might combine this evidence with that noted by Jeffrey

Kallberg in his review of Jean-Jacques Eigeldinger's *Chopin: Pianist and Teacher as Seen by his Pupils*: "Excerpts throughout the book, for example, reinforce the sense that both Chopin and his audiences adopted a more flexible attitude toward his musical texts than we do today." Kallberg goes on to cite evidence, principally drawn from editions annotated by Chopin during lessons, involving changes in pedaling, phrasing, accentuations, and indications of tempo and character, as well as outright reversals of notated dynamics. In addition, the annotations "sometimes delete large chunks of music; other times they add to the score by means of ornamental variants. The annotations occur across the totality of Chopin's output, from early works through late ones."[69]

Schumann, writing about his own *Concert Études* op. 10 as part of a review of a number of such publications (1836, *Ges Schr* 1:213), suggests that in public performance his pieces might be provided with "a free, short, appropriate introduction." He also remarks, "In No. 5 I omitted all performance indications on purpose, so that the student can plumb the heights and depths himself. I hope that this procedure may seem most fitting for testing the interpretive strength of the pupil." If one recalls the early diary entry reprinted in the *Denk- und Dichtbüchlein* (1832, *Ges Schr* 1:28) and quoted above ("*On Alteration in Composition*: Often two readings can be equally valid"), or the above quoted observations of the eminent Schumann scholar Akio Mayeda concerning Schumann's tendency to hold simultaneously a number of contrasting viewpoints about the same subject matter, one may begin to believe that the possibility Roesner suggested cautiously—that Schumann "continually 'heard' the details differently . . . in effect reinterpreted the music" (1984: 64)—indeed merits our serious attention. Evidence from a number of sides indicates that Schumann liked to hold in unresolved tension a number of possibilities and to resist an exclusive, definitive decision. Thus, his love of masks and multiple personalities, and of varied performance indications. In this light, one might also view differently the controversy over Clara's alterations of some of Robert's metronome marks when she edited the *Gesamtausgabe*. First, as Kämper has shown, alterations large enough to be significant were rare, and concentrated in the *Kinderszenen*.[70] Second, there is evidence that neither Robert nor Clara took metronome markings to be as precisely binding as we tend to do. When Clara (on tour in Paris) had received the printed edition of op. 15, Robert wrote:

> Have you received the *Kinderscenen?* How do you like it? Do charming pictures rise before you? Please play the "bittendes Kind," the "Kind im Einschlummern" and "der Dichter spricht" only half as fast [*nur ja noch einmal so langsam*] as you have in the past. That is quite arrogant of me, isn't it? But I know you, Klärchen, and your fire!

This, when she had the edition with its metronome markings in front of her.[71] A similar detail involves the editions of the Second Symphony. In the published orchestral score of 1847, the last movement is marked $\d = 170$, or so says Krüger in his review of the score (*AmZ* 50/22–23 [1848]), remarking that this tempo is impossibly fast. In the four-hand piano version of 1848, made by Robert, the last movement is marked $\d = 150$, a significant change. The general impression is that neither tempo was chosen with tremendous care or precision.

As with tempi and expressive markings, so with the closely related titles and captions for pieces or collections of pieces. Schumann seems to have considered his choices not as definitive and exclusive—not as unique verbal explanations of the content of the music, but as appropriate examples of the kind of meaning or images that might be aroused by the music. He maintained consistently that these titles and captions were conceived after the composition of the pieces, as "subtle indications for performance and understanding," and that the individual piece was not the response to the stimulus offered by the verbal image, but rather the verbal image was *one* of the appropriate responses to the stimulus offered by the piece.[72] The information assembled by Edward Lippman concerning the various explanations offered for the imagery behind op. 2 (314–20, 337–38), and the various titles conceived at various times for the movements of op. 17 and op. 23 reinforce the impression of Schumann's ambivalence and resistance to finality in these matters.

In the case of both op. 17 and op. 23, Schumann finally dropped the titles entirely after considering at least two alternatives for each set of movements. In the case of op. 23 he dropped the titles on the specific advice of Clara, who saw them as a source of misunderstanding for the public.[73] In 1845 Franz Brendel also remarked that Schumann's titles had aroused "vigorous opposition" in a public that saw them as "pre-existent schema, according to which the composer worked."[74] He also remarked how poetic and appropriate to the music were Schumann's titles, as opposed to the modish and irrelevant ones tacked on most salon music of the time. Thus the titles pleased some and displeased others. Nonetheless they represented a way of interpreting and reflecting about music that was deeply ingrained in even the most cultivated professional musicians of the time. As examples of the extravagant extent to which these verbal interpretations of music could go, one has only to consult Robert's letter to Clara of 21 April 1838, in which he gives an elaborate scenario for *In der Nacht* of op. 12, based on the story of Hero and Leander (*Brfw*, 1:154), or Franz Brendel's rather circumstantial narrative account of op. 2 (83). The problem with putting such interpretations, or even less elaborate ones, before a public for whom verbal meaning was primary was that this public might easily assume that the verbal meaning was ontologically primary in the case of the artwork, and that the musical meaning was a secondary translation of that primary meaning. In fact, quite the reverse was true, but many listeners missed this point, then as now. An analogy might be made with the titles in the works of Paul Klee. Neither the visual nor the verbal element is a one-to-one translation of the other; the meaning of the artwork is in the interaction of the two.

Thus the evidence of the letters, the various seemingly finished autograph sources, and printed editions. The hypothesis is worth entertaining that Schumann saw himself as providing materials out of which he or another gifted performer could make a performance, but that he was reluctant to fix definitively many details of that performance.[75] (The evidence Kallberg offered concerning Chopin suggests that this attitude toward the notated text may not have been restricted to Schumann.) In pursuing this hypothesis, we may profitably review the various relatively finished forms (as opposed to fragmentary sketched details) in which Schumann wrote down this material. From these we may be able to get some idea of the various ways Schumann may have considered hearing his own piece.

Here the various manuscript versions are crucial and revealing. They offer not only varying performance indications; they can also offer entire movements or variants omitted from editions published during Schumann's lifetime, and they can tell us where these might have gone. A famous example is given by the variations omitted from both editions of op. 13 published during Schumann's lifetime but issued later on the basis of autograph manuscripts as an appendix to the Gesamtausgabe. Unfortunately, the Gesamtausgabe said nothing about where the variations might have gone in the piece, and consequently pianists often inserted them as a block at some point in Schumann's revised second edition of the work. The autographs can tell us of the different orderings Schumann imagined for the pieces of opp. 12 and 13, and they can offer one additional piece for op. 12, finally rejected from Schumann's published edition and not issued in the *Gesamtausgabe*.[76]

The complexity of the questions raised here is well illustrated in the case of the *Quasi variazioni* movement of the Sonata in F minor, op. 14, which Roesner has carefully analyzed (1975). Roesner finds evidence of three, perhaps four, different orderings in the autograph manuscript, which also served as a printer's source for the first edition. (See Table 8.3 for my understanding of the various versions, plus a simple formal and harmonic analysis of each section.) One may count four versions by including the one produced by the red roman numerals in Schumann's hand (Roesner, 1975: 117, n. 27). (It is not clear to me why the version produced by these roman numerals could not have been one considered by Schumann before the first edition, when the original variation V had not yet been excised.)

All of these versions are in some sense reasonable. Typically, the process of revision was one of simplification, and the version in the published editions is the simplest (see Table 8.3). Variation I, which remains faithful to the head phrase of the *Andantino* in melody and texture but

TABLE 8.3. Op. 14, *Quasi variazioni*

Schumann's MS*: In the Variation numbering,
Roman numerals = Original Ordering in MS
(Arabic Numerals) = Ordering in Published Editions

Version Ordered by Red Roman Numerals
(cf. Roesner 1975: n. 27)

Editions of 1836 and 1853

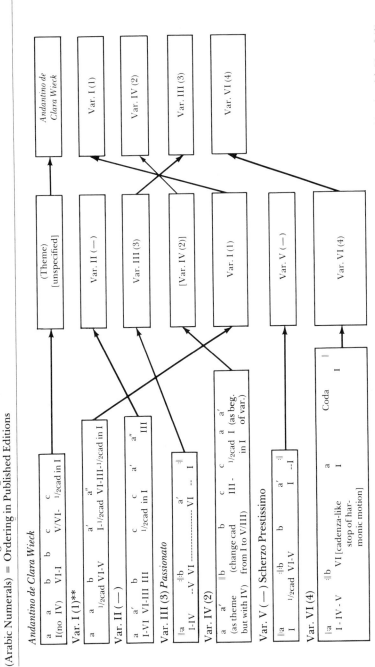

Andantino de Clara Wieck

Var. I (1)**

Var. II (—)

Var. III (3) *Passionato*

Var. IV (2)

Var. V (—) Scherzo Prestissimo

Var. VI (4)

*Also the order of the "projected second edition" (cf. Roesner 1975: 114), which may omit the *Andantino*, and begin with Var. I (1).
**"Melodie de C. W." in "projected second edition."

omits its third phrase and only hints at its second, retains its leading position in all but one version. Indeed, if we are to believe the version of the "projected second edition shortly after the first" proposed by Roesner (p. 114), the *Andantino* was at one time dropped, and the movement began with Variation I. In the version represented by the red roman numerals, Variation I(1) (the numbering system is explained in Table 8.3) is moved to the antepenultimate position, where it can serve as a rounding return to the theme, and where its quiet homophonic ending can serve as a good foil to the scherzo-like Variation V(–), whose lightness in turn serves as a fine contrast to the turbulent *espressivo* of the final variation. The final variation, because of its cadenzalike slowing of harmonic motion and extension of the dominant preparation for the final return (mm. 118ff.), and because of its homophonic coda, must always be last and was always so placed. For the published edition, Variation V(–) was dropped, allowing Variation I(1) to return to its original position. Surprising in this published version is the omission of Variation II(–), with its reference to the repeated third phrase of the theme, which had disappeared in Variation I(1), and its welcome tonal contrast through a final cadence in the key of III. Once Variation II(–) was excised, Variation IV(2) was brought forward, providing the reference to the third phrase of the theme that Variation II(–) had formerly provided and, because of a rounding return to the first phrase after the third phrase, ending with a full instead of a half cadence for the first time in the movement. In this published version, the two variations that are most distant from the structure of the *Andantino* (no variation ever reproduced its anomalous *aabbcc* structure) are now placed at the end, whereas in the first three versions Variation III(3), the most distant from the *Andantino,* had been placed as a central departure, followed by a return to something close to the *Andantino* in the form of Variation IV(2) before the scherzo-like Variation V(–) as preparation for the finale. If we accept these interpretations, then we have here materials for three or four different—though feasible—variation sets. It seems justifiable at least to try each out in performance. At the very least, if one does play one or both of the excised variations, now printed in the Henle edition, one should probably put them in one of the configurations Schumann imagined for them.

The cyclical references to other movements of the sonata in the last two variations of the published version have not, to my knowledge, been noticed (the headmotif of the *Andantino* itself, of course, echoes the beginning of movement 1). In Variation III(3), the chromatic gesture descending in the right hand through e-natural and e-flat, and the immediate repetition of this gesture transposed by sequence up a fourth echoes the opening gesture of the principal theme of the first movement (mm. 2–5; Example 8.1a–b). The opening gesture of Variation VI(4) clearly echoes that of the Scherzo of the second published edition of 1853 (Example 8.1c–d).

EXAMPLE 8.1a. Schumann, Piano Sonata in F minor, Op. 14. *Quasi variazioni*, variation 3 (mm. 1–4)

EXAMPLE 8.1b. First movement (mm. 1–5)

The cyclical interconnections of all four movements of the 1853 edition, including this Scherzo (which was not present in the *Concert sans orchestre* version of 1836) raises the question of the relation of these four movements to the other F-minor Scherzo found preceding this D-flat-major Scherzo in the autograph of 1836. The hypothesis is initially attractive that Schumann abandoned this first F-minor Scherzo as soon as it was

EXAMPLE 8.1c. *Quasi variazioni,* variation 4 (mm. 1–2)

EXAMPLE 8.1d. Scherzo (mm. 1–2)

drafted, and replaced it in his developing cyclical conception of the whole sonata with the D-flat-major Scherzo that follows it in the manuscript and that was published in the full version of the piece (the 1853 edition). We are tempted to think, in other words, that Schumann never thought of both scherzos as part of the same sonata. A sonata cycle with two scherzos would not have been extremely unusual, but one with two scherzos in a row would have been. Nonetheless, a look at the autograph makes this hypothesis untenable. The F-minor scherzo is headed "Scherzo 1° Vivacissimo" in the ink of the original drafting, and the D-flat-major scherzo is headed "Scherzo 2do. Promenade" in the same original penpoint and ink. With a later pen and ink used for revisions to the autograph some time after the engraving of the first edition Schumann then crossed out the original "Scherzo 2do. Promenade." and wrote "Scherzo. Promenade. Intermezzo." (cf. Illustration 8.2). Finally, he deleted "Promenade" and "Intermezzo" with the later pen and ink, leaving only "Scherzo." Thus Schumann's idea about the particular character of the D-flat-major Scherzo (Promenade/Intermezzo) seems to have survived for a good while, but his idea about the two scherzos does not seem to have survived beyond the first drafting of the movement. What remains puzzling is that the thematic material of the F-minor Scherzo has no cyclical interconnections with the other four movements, such as those one can hear between all the other movements. This, and the unrelieved F-minor tonality, suggests that Schumann had soon abandoned the idea of the F-minor Scherzo as part of this piece—perhaps even by the time he was struggling with the *Quasi variazioni.* It thus appears likely that the inclusion of the F-minor

ILLUSTRATION 8.2. Schumann, Op. 14, autograph (London, British Library, Ms. addl. 37056), beginning of D-flat-major Scherzo

Scherzo with the other four movements does not provide a succession of movements ever conceived of by Schumann.

One last aspect of what Schumann's manuscript versions can tell us has been suggested in another stimulating and valuable article by Roesner (1977). Here she uses the various autograph versions of the first movement of the Sonata in G minor, op. 22, to arrive at some hypotheses about Schumann's compositional methods in large-scale sonata movements. In brief, she proposes that he made cut-and-paste alterations, removing entire sections of a movement and replacing them with other independently conceived sections, and that he made large-scale alterations in the structural ordering of a movement at a relatively late stage.

In assessing this argument, I would first make a clear distinction between the putting together of sonata-form movements and the ordering of the various movements in a cycle of small pieces. The evidence of Schumann's cutting, inserting, and reordering, incontrovertible in the latter case, is not nearly so clear in the first. Roesner (101–2) compares the continuation of the first theme and the transition of the first movement of op. 22 (as given in the Berlin autograph of the movement, prepared some time after October 1835) with the version of that same section that appears in the printed edition of 1839 (the manuscript source for which is not known to exist). I do not interpret the changes that she identifies in the same way as she does. (Her first example [pp. 100–101] gives the section as found in the Berlin autograph, which stood in place of the material beginning at m. 24 of modern editions; her second example [p. 103] gives the immediately following section in the autograph. Example 8.2 here puts the two together.) The material at the beginning of the example does not suggest to me "a second theme in the tonic area of the exposition" (102), but a development of the head motif of theme 1 (the scalar descending fourth). It is followed by a figurationally simplified version of the present transitional material (Example 8.2, mm. 20–25 = published edition, mm. 24–29; Example 8.2, mm. 32–52 = published edition, mm. 36–56). The modulation has been slightly shortened (by excising mm. 26–31 of the example), and the arrival at the second theme (which begins in m. 68 of ex. 8.2 and m. 59 of the modern edition) has been simplified in the published version by excising from the manuscript version an extraordinary dominant prolongation of great harmonic and figurational complexity (mm. 53–67 of ex. 8.2—see especially mm. 53–60). This is not cut-and-paste replacement of an entire section; it is the judicious revision of a section. And no structural alteration is involved, in the sense that the succession of functional elements, even the material in them, remains the same. The later version simply cuts out the most complex developments of this material, in favor of a simpler, more straightforward approach.[77] Whether this produces an improved movement is another question. It is true that the second version is more "succinct" (Roesner, 102), but this is not everyone's goal—not Jean Paul's, for instance, or that of Schumann of the earlier 1830s.

The second theme (Example 8.2, mm. 68ff., replaces mm. 59–70 of the modern edition) does indeed use different material from that in the published version. The second theme of the manuscript version is, if anything, closer to the first theme of the movement and hence should be praised for its organic unity (again, not everyone's goal).[78] But here

EXAMPLE 8.2. Schumann, Piano Sonata in G minor Op. 22, mvt. 1, Continuation of First Theme, Transition, and Second Theme in Exposition (Berlin, Deutsche Staatsbibliothek, Mus. ms. autogr. Schumann 38; after Roesner, 1977). © 1977 by the Regents of the University of California. Reprinted from *Nineteenth Century Music*, Vol. I, No. 2, November, 1977, pp. 97–109, by permission.

Example 8.2. *continued*

Example 8.2. *continued*

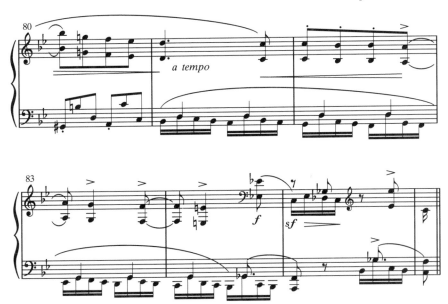

Roesner criticizes the manuscript theme for having a markedly contrast-ing midsection and a return, and hence being "almost a perfectly rounded miniature, a *papillon* that just happens to be employed as the secondary theme in a sonata movement." This is, she says, inappropriate to the so-nata idea (1977: 102). Even if rounded, self-contained second themes were in fact inappropriate to the sonata idea, this particular one scarcely gives the impression of self-containment or even rounding, principally because of the shifting nonclosure of the initial idea in both occurrences. What is noteworthy in the manuscript version of the second theme is the harmonic complexity of its midsection. Again this harmonic complexity and distant tonal excursion are excised in the final version, where the en-tire second theme is replaced by a well-closed, tonally straightforward theme, which is repeated in slightly varied fashion to open out into the closing material (the same in both versions). Again, we see Schumann's tendency to revise slightly in order to simplify, to make the path to his goals more direct and linear. But no structural revisions have been made. The functional succession of events, the keys, even the rough proportions have remained the same.

Finally, I cannot agree with Roesner's interpretation of Schumann's marginal notation on the manuscript of the exposition concerning the transition of both exposition and recapitulation (1977: 106–8). Schu-mann's "NB. Dieses B gilt erst Seite 5" (see 1977: 107, Plate I) means not that the engraver should remove the section between Schumann's B and C from the exposition and replace it on p. 5, but that he should replace the section between B and C on p. 5 with the section between B and C from the exposition, while leaving the section in the exposition as well. The meaning of the indication, in other words, is: "this B becomes significant only on p. 5, with reference to the B and C also to be found on p. 5. Here (on p. 1) this B has no meaning. Ignore it." Schumann was thus proposing to replace the transition in the recapitulation (Example 8.3, after Roesner, 1977: 108), with the version of the transition in the exposition (see Example 8.2), thus shortening and harmonically simplifying the transition in the recapitulation and, more importantly, saving the modal contrast in the recapitulation for the beginning of the second theme itself, instead of anticipating it in the transition, as he had initially thought of doing. A new joint to the second theme in the recapitulation was then fashioned on an attachment D, whose place is indicated in the recapitulation, but which no longer survives. This perfectly reasonable interpretation of Schumann's marginal notation arguably gives a better transition in the recapitulation. It also has the advantage of not leaving the utterly nonsensical transition in the exposition that would result from the excision of the passage B through C in Roesner's Example 1.

The point of all this detail is that the evidence concerning op. 22, movement 1, does not indicate a "piecemeal approach to composition," achieved by "the piecing together of many such [idea] sketches." What we

EXAMPLE 8.3. Schumann, Piano Sonata in G minor, Op. 22, mvt. 1, Deleted Transition in Recapitulation (Berlin, Deutsche Staatsbibliothek, Mus. ms. autogr. Schumann 38; after Roesner, 1977) © 1977 by the Regents of the University of California. Reprinted from *Nineteenth Century Music*, Vol. I, No. 2, November, 1977, pp. 97–109, by permission.

*ms:c

EXAMPLE 8.3. *continued*

see by comparing the draft and the published version of the movement is a revision for greater concision and simplicity and for better effect at the return of the second theme in the recapitulation.

A recently located fair copy of the early version of the *Fantasie* op. 17 raises yet another question concerning material existing in a completed, and in some sense authorized, manuscript version but excised from the final published version—a question akin to those surrounding opp. 12, 13, and 14. This fair copy, which includes corrections and comments in Schumann's hand, seems to have been prepared as the printer's source for the published version issued by Breitkopf in 1839. Among other revisions made after this copy was prepared, Schumann crossed out a return of the end of the first movement at the end of the last.[79] We know that op. 17 had been brought to virtual completion in the summer of 1836,[80] and that Robert considered it finished enough to offer to a publisher in December of that year.[81] To judge by the fair copy—whether this be the 1836 version or a subsequent revision it was, in any case, a version thought in a finished enough state to have it copied for the engraver—a complete early version of the piece had the cyclical return at the end, and Schumann thought enough of this version to call its first movement "probably my most refined to date." Should we consider this version to be a possible performance alternative? Again, Charles Rosen thinks so and has recorded it on the three-record set of early versions cited above.

These closing measures of the first movement of op. 17 (mm. 296–end) raise yet another question, pertaining especially to our understanding of op. 17 in this century. It has long been a commonplace to say that this coda quotes the last song of Beethoven's song cycle *An die ferne Geliebte* (a piece not in the C major of op. 17, but in E-flat). Other commentators, myself among them, have then seen the quotation as being carried forward by Schumann to a second level through another reference in the last movement of the C-major Symphony.[82] In my work on the reception of that symphony, I was surprised to find that no one had mentioned the putative reference to Beethoven in the last movement until a tentative and somewhat difficult note in the third, much revised, edition of Wasielewski's biography in 1880. Subsequently I have been surprised to note that no one mentioned the putative quotation in the first movement of op. 17 until the second edition of Hermann Abert's *Robert Schumann* in 1910 (p. 64—the passage is absent from the first edition; see p. 58 of that edition). Again, I was forced to wonder whether the Beethoven reference was made by Schumann or created by a more recent critical tradition. The possible Beethoven quotation at the end of the first movement of op. 17 is not extraneous to the rest of the music—is not embedded in musical quotation marks, so to speak, as is the quotation from *Papillons* in "Florestan" of *Carnaval* or the "Stimme aus der Ferne" in the last *Novellette*. This passage in the coda is clearly and progressively derived from previous material in the movement (see Example 8.4). Appropriately enough, the coda returns to the closing theme of the exposition and recapitulation in slightly varied form, adding to it a consequent-like cadential phrase. The occurrence makes perfect musical sense without positing any reference outside the movement. Given that no one seems to have noticed, or at least mentioned, the quotation of Beethoven for almost seventy years, might it be that for Schumann and for the musical culture of the nineteenth century, the quotation was not there—or at least that it was not for them part of the content and meaning of the piece, as we now consider it?

The initial version of the *Fantasie* offered to Kistner in December 1836 indeed contained a Beethoven quotation—from the slow movement of the Seventh Symphony. "In den 'Palmen' [the original title of the last movement] kommt das Adagio [sic] aus der A dur-Symphonie vor," wrote Robert in a letter to Kistner of 19 December 1836 (*BNF*2, 421: "In the

EXAMPLE 8.4. Schumann, *Fantasie*, Op. 17, First Movement

Palmen appears the Adagio from the A-major Symphony."). Erler (1887, 1:102–3), after printing this letter, added, "Dieser beabsichtigte Anklang an die 'siebente' Beethoven's ist nachträglich ganz entfernt worden." ("This intended reminiscence of Beethoven's Seventh was subsequently removed completely.") He would certainly seem to have been right, to judge by the published edition of the *Fantasie*. A quotation from one of Beethoven's most beloved pieces would, of course, have been in place in a piece offered by "Florestan and Eusebius" as a contribution to the Beethoven Monument of 1837 (see the same letter). The function of this quotation would have been less clear in a Fantasy of 1839 dedicated to Liszt, to say nothing of the function of a quotation from a much less known song cycle. But the function of the song quotation is not the issue; it is rather that no one seems to have recognized any such quotation as part of the piece, not even Clara in her ecstatic and detailed letter of appreciation upon receiving the piece.[83]

Just as the first movement of op. 17, final revisions for which were made in Winter 1838–39, may be Schumann's "most refined" version of a sonata-form first movement, so various of the contemporaneous *Novellettes* are his most refined version of the alternation/rondo-form movement, and the entire cycle of op. 21 (which Schumann repeatedly insisted upon as a cycle)[84] was his most formally ambitious and harmonically adventurous version of the cycle of character pieces. Since no complete recording of the cycle is currently in the catalog, and since several of the inner pieces especially seem to have fallen into relative neglect, we might well examine the fifth *Novellette* as an example of the degree to which Schumann's harmonic, metric, and formal imagination had grown powerful and audacious by the end of this period of his early piano music.

In comparing any of the *Novellettes* with the individual movements of the cycles opp. 6, 12, and 16, one is first struck by their much greater size, formal complexity, and motivic development. No. 5, by no means the longest, has 254 moderately fast $\frac{3}{4}$ measures. Diagrammatically it is in a roughly rondolike form: A B A' C A" D A" B' C-Coda. The initial thematic unit (mm. 1–12) exemplifies on the level of the individual phrase the irregularities of construction that characterize the piece as a whole (Example 8.5). This goes beyond the detail of syncopation within a regular measure, for which Schumann is well known, to a bewildering variety of metrical displacements and motivic extensions producing four-beat motivic units in $\frac{3}{4}$, five-measure phrases, and implied shifting of downbeats, such as to frustrate any sense of regularity at either the measure or the phrase level. Such a section should lay to rest the accusation that Schumann suffered from four-square phraseology and from a lack of vital interplay between meter and motivic rhythm.

The B section of the piece (mm. 33ff.) shows a similar metrical complexity (Example 8.6a). The right hand is a big hemiola, but cutting across the accents of the written $\frac{3}{4}$ measure. Meanwhile the left hand marches in three-beat units syncopated against both the implied $\frac{3}{2}$ hemiola of the right hand and the written $\frac{3}{4}$ of the piece. Harmonically as well, the material is richly complex, especially in its always-varied repetitions. In one instance of local harmonic variation, the a' return of this material in the a b a' form of the B section (mm. 53–56) is considerably increased in harmonic complexity. The later, large-scale return of the entire B section is varied still further, both motivically and harmonically, to incorporate a transformation of the head motive of the C section (mm. 88–95; Example 8.6b) in a harmonically complex phrase that slides from D major to F-sharp major to G major and back to D major in just eight measures (mm. 197–205; Example 8.6c). The ensuing transition to the closing section of the piece (mm. 219–30; Example 8.6d), fashioned from the head motive of the C section as transformed in the preceding B' section, has a local harmonic complexity equal to Chopin's mazurkas of the late 1840s.

Formally, too, the piece shows an almost riddling play with the function of the various sections. For example, instead of a rounding return to the initial section as at the end of the conventional rondo form, we have a transformational series in which the stable, relatively tuneful C episode invades the B material as shown above, then supplants the A material (incorporating into itself an accompanimental reference to the head motive

EXAMPLE 8.5. Schumann, *Novellette*, Op. 21 no. 5, Head Motive of A Section (mm. 1–12)

of A) to achieve formal closure and end the piece. The swirling and unstable A material itself has meanwhile come to be used functionally as transitional material between the more stable episodes (see mm. 112–43 and 170–96). (The play with the function of refrain and episode here is similar to the one in the rondo-form last movement of op. 41 no. 3, which I analyze in greater detail in Newcomb, 1987.)

The mercurial sixth *Novellette* is even more complex in its formal functions. Its initial theme, frivolous and full of redundancy, soon disappears entirely. It turns out to have been a kind of introduction, although it

EXAMPLE 8.6a. Schumann, *Novellette,* Op. 21 no. 5, Head Motive of B Section (mm. 33–36; 53–56)

does not sound so at first (since it is clearly formed and stable to the point of banality). The B material that succeeds it (mm. 17ff.), a contrasting transformation of a motif from the A section, turns out to be the main theme of the movement, and it returns in varied form after a vast midsection to close the piece. This vast midsection itself, defined by repetition as

EXAMPLE 8.6b. Schumann, *Novellette,* Op. 21 no. 5, Head Motive of C Section (mm. 88–95)

EXAMPLE 8.6c. Schumann, *Novellette,* Op. 21 no. 5, Return of B Section (mm. 197–205)

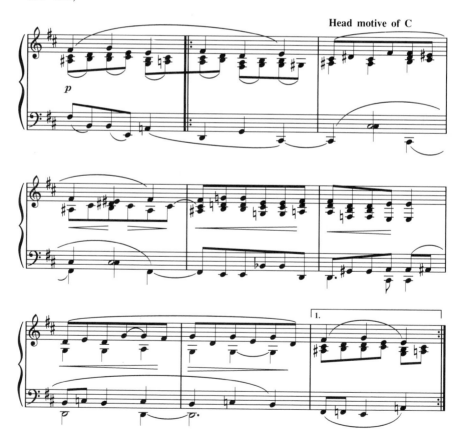

EXAMPLE 8.6d. Schumann, *Novellette,* Op. 21 no. 5 (mm. 219–30)

a block transposed down a half step, is developed out of a noncontrasting variant of the B material, such that one does not sense the beginning of the midsection, but comes to understand it as a contrasting section only after one is well into it. Shifting sectional functions, blurred sectional boundaries, and sectional interrelations through motivic transformation give the whole sizable piece a formally puzzling, almost enigmatic quality that then serves as a foil to the straightforward stability and bluff bravura of the seventh piece as the cycle continues.[85]

Never again after 1840 would Schumann return to such ambitious complexities in his solo piano music. If our interpretation is correct, Schumann decided shortly after these splendid pieces were published to abandon the whimsical and complex style they embodied in favor, first, of other genres (and their associated styles), and then, when he returned to solo piano music, in favor of a style more attuned to the institutional and cultural ideals of the midcentury. The irony of the situation sketched here is that the early style was abandoned at least partially because it found no place in the musical culture of its time; it was replaced by other styles that more easily belonged to that culture. Yet only twenty years later, it was the early style that took hold in the serious recitals of the later nineteenth century, and it is this style that has since preserved Schumann's name in the annals of piano music, while the style designed for public acceptance has virtually disappeared from the canon.

Notes

1. See Mayeda, 116: "In the case of Schumann it seems to me especially appropriate to distinguish between various simultaneous personalities. Schumann did not develop in a linear fashion. It is far more characteristic for Schumann to see himself in a lifelong alternation between contrary poles. These poles constitute his personality considered as a whole."

2. See *Tgb, Brfw, Album, Quellankat,* and the new autograph source for op. 17 reported in Walker.

3. Boetticher, 1981: 103, announced a complete correspondence to be published by Schott in 1982. No volume has yet appeared.

4. See Boetticher, 1981, for a summary of the various sources for Schumann's correspondence. In Boetticher, 1984: 8, the reappearance of the *Correspondenz* in the Biblioteca Jagiellońska in Kraków is reported.

5. See Dale (85 pages) and Gertler (172 pages). See also Edler, 119–49, 188–94.

6. Chopin's Variations on "Là ci darem la mano," subject of a famous early (1831) review by Schumann, was of this genre. Like the Chopin, Schumann's op. 1 was originally conceived with orchestral accompaniment. In his introduction to the *Gesammelte Schriften* (written in 1854), Schumann observed that the publications of Herz and Hünten, both composers of this broad genre, dominated the offerings of keyboard music in the 1830s. This generic category was what the review columns of *NZfM* called *Mode- und Fabrikartikeln.* The category is summarized in an entertaining fashion in the chapter "Piano Fodder" in Loesser.

7. The original review is in the *Revue et Gazette musicale de Paris* of 12 November 1837, reprinted in Was, Appendix F (pp. 274ff.).

8. See Lippmann.

9. Schumann's detailed preface in French and German to these *Studien,* published in the Gesamtausgabe (Series 7, no. 1, 22–29), has unfortunately not been retained in the widely available Dover reprint.

10. Boetticher, 1980; see also *Quellenkat* 2:10–24.

11. As Schumann himself pointed out in a review of 1836 (*Ges Schr* 1:212), he exercised much more freedom in arranging the Paganini originals in the second set. Schumann's creative role in selecting, transcribing for the piano, and ordering these entrancing pieces would repay further study. Is the lack of attention paid to them by performers and musicologists alike due to our prejudice against the use of other composers' material?

12. Kathleen Dale sees the manifold possible realizations of the variation idea as the thread that ties together Schumann's early piano music (p. 13). All three generic types represented by opp. 1–3 can be seen as having some element of variation in them: op. 1 explicitly, op. 3 in the varied transformation of Paganini's originals, and op. 2 in the varied reuse of material from the four-hand polonaises of 1828, never published in Schumann's lifetime but now available in modern edition. Moreover, during the early years of his career (1828–34), Schumann worked on at least six other variation sets that were never completed or published during his lifetime (entered in brackets on Table 8.2—see Dale, 15–17). These unpublished works are: Variations for four hands on a theme by Prince Louis Ferdinand (1828); Variations on the *Rondeau à la clochette* from Paganini's B-minor Concerto (1830); Variations on an original theme in G (1831); Variations on Schubert's *Sehnsuchtswalzer* (op. 9 no. 2, D. 365/2, 1833); Variations on the second movement of Beethoven's Seventh Symphony (1833–34, now available in modern edition, ed. Robert Münster [Munich: Henle, 1976], and in recording, Teldec 6.42787, Cyprien Katsaris, piano); and Variations on Chopin's Nocturne in G minor, op. 15 no. 3.

13. The concern with sonata form and the sonata cycle was not new with the second half of the decade: an unpublished piano quartet from 1829 and a first movement of a symphony in G minor completed and performed in 1832 are now published in modern edition. The most recent chronicle of Schumann's concern with the sonata form and the sonata cycle is in Kapp, 42ff.

14. See the early reviews copied into his diaries (*Tgb* 1:424–33) under the heading *Zur Besserung* (read in Boetticher, 1941, as *Zur Besinnung*) and his later compilation of reviews under the heading *Zeitungsstimmung* (Boetticher, 1941: 626).

15. Loesser gives a vivid sense of this ferment.

16. He showed intense commercial concern and at least some skill in the case of the *NZfM*. I am speaking here of his sense for the commercial market for piano music, or even the commercial aspect of professional music making in general.

17. See especially Borchard, 174–80 and 244–55.

18. "Aber Clara, was ist denn mit Dir geworden? Du schreibst, ich solle Quartetten machen—aber '*bitte recht klar*'—das klingt ja wie von einem Dresdner Fräulein." (*Brfw* 1:121).

19. "Höre Robert, willst Du nicht auch einmal etwas Brillantes, leichtverständliches componiren, und Etwas das keine Ueberschriften hat, sondern ein ganzes zusammenhängendes Stück ist, nicht zu lang und nicht zu kurz? ich möchte so gerne Etwas von Dir haben öffentlich zu spielen, was für das Publikum ist. Für ein Genie ist das freilich erniedrigend, doch die Politik verlangt es nun einmal; hat man dem Publikum Etwas geliefert dass sie verstehen, kann man ihm auch dann Etwas Schwereres vorführen,—doch das Publikum muss erst einmal gewonnen sein. . . . Sieh, dass Du es kannst, vielleicht Variationen? Du schreibst ja schon einmal Welche—kannst Du es nicht noch einmal? oder ein Rondo?" (*Brfw* 2:469–70).

20. Quoted partially in Litzmann 1:372–73. A more complete version is given in translation in Reich, 272.

21. "War es wie ein Nachklang von Deinen Worten einmal wo Du mir schriebst 'ich käme Dir auch manchmal wie ein Kind vor'—kurz, es war mir ordentlich wie im Flügelkleid und hab' da an die 30 kleine putzige Dinger geschrieben, von

denen ich ihrer zwölf ausgelesen und 'Kinderszenen' genannt habe. Du wirst Dich daran erfreuen, musst Dich aber freilich als Virtuosin vergessen" (*Brfw* 1:121). Schumann later claimed to have conceived these pieces as part of the *Novellettes*, on which he was working at the same time. Cf. *BNF2*, 423.

22. See *Brfw* 1:108 (letter of Clara to Robert of 3 March 1838). "One thing: do you plan to leave the last movement just the way it was before? It would be preferable to change it a bit and make it easier, for it is altogether too difficult. I understand it by now and even play it if I have to, but the public, the audience even of connoisseurs, for whom one really writes, does not understand it." ("Doch eins: willst Du den letzten Satz ganz so lassen wie er ehemals war? Ändere ihn doch lieber etwas und erleichtere ihn, denn er ist doch gar zu schwer. Ich versteh' ihn schon und spiele ihn auch zur Noth, doch die Leute, das Publikum selbst die Kenner, für die man doch eigentlich schreibt verstehen das nicht.") See also Robert's letter to Clara of 1 December 1839. After debating which of the *Novellettes* would be appropriate to play in concert in Berlin (he advised the E major, then the D major no. 2), he continues, "But if you don't want to play either, then it would be best to stick with the G-minor Sonata (but *without* the Scherzo), because that piece develops one characteristic mood [*Character*] in an understandable fashion." ("Willst du aber Keine von beiden, so wäre es doch am besten, Du bliebst bei der Sonate in G Moll [aber *ohne* Scherzo], weil die doch auch einen Character fasslich entwickelt"; *Brfw* 2:810–11). For discussion of the revisions to the first movement of the G-minor Sonata, see below.

23. Both the titles and the dedications to opp. 18 and 19 suggest the same generic shift. To his friend Henriette Voigt he wrote of "three new compositions [from Vienna] . . . amongst which a *Humoreske*, which is admittedly more melancholy, and a *Blumenstück* and *Arabeske*, which however are not very significant. The titles also say as much." ("drei neue Compositionen [aus Wien] . . . darunter eine Humoreske, die freilich mehr melancholisch, und ein Blumenstück und Arabeske, die aber wenig bedeuten wollen: die Titel besagen es aber ja auch"; *BNF2*, 167).

24. In a letter to Clara during this period, Robert writes ecstatically: "For the past four weeks, I have done almost nothing else but compose, as I wrote to you; it came to me in a constant stream, with me always singing along—and most of it has been successful. I am playing with forms." ("Seit 4 Wochen habe ich fast nichts als componirt, wie ich Dir schon schrieb; es strömte mir zu, ich sang dabei immer mit—und da ist's meistens gelungen. Mit den Formen spiel' ich.") These experimental forms are evident in both op. 17 and op. 21. Similarly, in a letter of 7 September 1838 to his friend Hermann Hirschbach, Schumann enthused, "I no longer think about form when I compose; I simply do it." ("An Form denk' ich nicht mehr beim Componiren; ich mach's eben"; *BNF2*, 137).

25. See the letter to Clara of 24 January 1840, quoted in Boetticher 1942: 320: "In the preceding days I have been working on a *Faschingsschwank* and have finished it here, that is, without the last page, which I will begin a bit later. It will amuse you, and has by the way become rather fleshed out, to nearly thirty pages." ("Die vorigen Tage arbeitete ich an einem *Faschingsschwank* und hab' ihn fertig hier, d.h. ohne die letzte Seite, die ich aber in später Stunde noch anfangen will. Er wird Dich amüsieren, ist übrigens beleibt worden, wohl an die 30 Seiten.")

Most commentators from Jansen forward have assumed that op. 26 is the "grosse romantische Sonate" referred to in the much quoted letter to Simonin de

Sire of 15 March 1839 concerning Schumann's current projects. We should not take this as unambiguously true. The most sonatalike movement of op. 26, the finale, was not yet finished even in January 1840. The first movement is like the large-scale rondo-based movements of opp. 20 and 21; the middle movements are like the smaller character pieces published in opp. 23, 28, and 32. (In fact, movement 4, Intermezzo, was published as a *Beilage* in the *NZfM* of December 1839, where it was announced as "aus bald erscheinenden Nachstücke" [op. 23]). Thus, there is not much reason for Schumann in March 1839 to think of the *Faschingsschwank*, whose title invokes the original title for op. 9, as a sonata. Perhaps in his letter to de Sire Schumann was referring to the never completed F-minor sonata, about which he talks often in letters to Clara of 1838, and which was in an advanced enough state in February 1839 to offer to Breitkopf and Haertel (*BNF2*, 422).

26. As Robert put it in the now famous letter of 5 May 1843 to Carl Kossmaly, who was preparing to write an article on Schumann's works for *AmZ* (discussed below): "Formerly [in the period of the early piano works] it was all the same to me whether one paid attention to me or not. When one has wife and children, then this becomes quite different. One must think of the future; one has to see the fruits of one's work, not the artistic fruits but the prosaic, everyday ones that belong to life. And only greater renown can bring and increase these fruits." ("Sonst galt es mir gleich, ob man sich um mich bekümmere oder nicht—hat man Frau und Kinder, so wird das ganz anders—man muss ja an die Zukunft denken, man will auch die Früchte seiner Arbeit sehen, nicht die Künstlerischen sondern die prosaischen, die zum Leben gehören, und diese bringt und vermehrt nur der grössere Ruf"; *BNF2*, 227). One should note that Robert is not explicitly disavowing the early piano pieces with these words (indeed, he puts the pieces forward "with their warts"), but excusing himself for pushing his own works for journalistic review.

27. I skip over significant early reviews of individual works, such as Fink's of opp. 3–5 (*AmZ* 35/37 [September 1833], 613–17, highly unfavorable); Rellstab's of op. 4 (*Iris im Gebiete der Tonkunst* 5/2 [January 1834], likewise unfavorable); Ignaz v. Seyfried's of op. 5 (*AmZ* 36/37 [September 1834], rhapsodic but vague); Moscheles's of op. 11 (*NZfM* 5/34 [October 1836], largely favorable, recognizing the originality and talent); and Liszt's of opp. 5, 11, 14 (*Revue et Gazette musicale de Paris* 4/46 [November 1837], reprinted in Was 275–79 [App. F], like Moscheles, cautiously favorable).

28. Boetticher, 1941: 355, traces the history of this term in its application to Schumann. Significantly, it disappears from criticism of the music Schumann wrote in the second half of the 1840s.

29. Schumann himself edited one of the most important musical periodicals and felt constrained by conflict of interest from featuring his music there. Gottfried Wilhelm Fink, the editor of the other most important journal from 1827–41, was an avowed enemy. Wasielewski (130) also remarked that the journalistic critics ignored Schumann's early music: *AmZ* was against it; *NZfM* could not touch it; only *Cäcilia*, a journal neither as respected nor as influential as the others, could mention it. Note that Brendel's article appeared only after Schumann had retired from *NZfM*.

30. Ambros, too, comments that the piano technique demanded by Schumann was more "perverse" and demanding than that called for by Czerny, Herz, or

Kalkbrenner, and that Schumann, when he tries to write simple textures (he cites op. 118 and op. 68, beginning), is dull (91). Brendel was surprisingly accurate in his reading of future changes in the concert situation. The serious solo piano concert, as it split off from the more entertainment-oriented diversion typical of the 1830s, would in fact be the venue that opened the way to popularity for Schumann's early piano music, especially as this serious kind of concert took hold over a wide area in the 1850s and 1860s. Clara seems to have led the way in introducing Robert's pieces into the recital repertory, performing op. 22 in Berlin (1840), op. 28 in St. Petersburg (1844), and two years later in Nordeney. In the following decade she brought his op. 13 (Holland, 1853), op. 9 (Vienna, 1856), and op. 16 (Vienna, 1859) into her programs, and in the 1860s added his opp. 18, 20, 21, 23, and 26. The young Carl Tausig gave performances in the 1860s of op. 9 (Vienna, 1862), op. 13 (Berlin, 1865), and opp. 6 and 7 (Leipzig, 1868). Anton Rubinstein played op. 13 in 1869 (Basel), and regularly thereafter, op. 9, plus individual pieces from op. 12, from 82 ("Vogel als Prophet"), and (surprisingly) the *Studien* for Pedal Piano, op. 56. Beginning likewise in the 1860s Hans von Bülow regularly programmed a piece (unspecified) from op. 28, a *Novellette*, and op. 17. Opuses 14 and 26 appear regularly in his programs from 1872 onward. Charles Hallé performed op. 9 in 1864 (London) and op. 20 in 1870 (Paris). (Information drawn from Kehler, which contains representative—but by no means exhaustive—records of programs by major recitalists.)

31. Schumann's own analysis of the situation in the letter to Kossmaly of 5 May 1843 mentioned especially points 1 and 2 in Brendel's analysis. In sending his piano music to Kossmaly for review, Schumann remarked that "these things are little known, for obvious reasons: (1) because of their intrinsic difficulties of form and content, (2) because I am not a virtuoso such as could perform them in public, (3) because I am editor of my periodical, in which I could not mention them, (4) because Fink is editor of the other, and did not want to mention them." ("Diese Sachen sind alle nur wenig bekannt worden, aus natürlichen Gründen: (1) aus inneren der Schwierigkeit in Form und Gehalt, (2) weil ich kein Virtuos bin, der sie öffentlich vortragen könnte, (3) weil ich Redacteur meiner Zeitschrift, in der ich sie nicht erwähnen konnte, (4) weil Fink Redacteur der andern, der sie nicht erwähnen wollte." *BNF* 2, 227).

32. [Riccius] 1850. According to Boetticher, 1941: 371, in his own *Zeitungsstimmen* Schumann identified the author of this unsigned series as [August Ferdinand] Riccius (b. 1819), Leipzig composer and conductor and from 1854 the music director at the Leipzig Stadttheater. The *Zeitungsstimmen* are explained as a source in Boetticher, 1941: 626. Boetticher (1941: 369–75) traces the history of the subjective-objective binary opposition in Schumann criticism from the 1840s onward. In this critical *topos*, Mozart was the "objective" composer, Beethoven the "subjective." Dahlhaus (1982: 78) notes that the "concern for objectivity was an indispensable criterion" for what he calls musical *Realismus*, the musical aesthetic that replaced romanticism in the middle of the century.

33. "Für den grossen Haufen der Dilettanten waren seine Compositionen zu schwierig und zu unverständlich, für die Musiker von Fach zu excentrisch, von dem Gewohnten und nach Kunsttraditionen Geregelten zu sehr abweichend" (Ambros, 60).

34. On the matter of leisurely, solitary reflection: technically demanding music could not be read, reflected upon, and savored by the solitary individual as could

the novel (the explicit aesthetic model for much of Schumann's early music), because it could not be easily called up before the mind. For most dilettantes, the calling up of Schumann's music demanded a highly skilled performer, who presented it to the listener in a fleeting performance, without the possibility of leisurely reflection and savoring. Only recently have recordings made it possible for the solitary amateur to sample Schumann's piano music repeatedly on his or her own, as with favorite passages from a novel.

35. Liszt, in his 1837 review of opp. 5, 11, and 14, comments that the title "Concert" for op. 14 is scarcely appropriate because the style of the piece does not seem designed for public performance (Was, 279–80).

36. See Reich, table on pp. 268–69; and countless letters of the *Brfw* (e. g., 1:112). Liszt in his letter to Wasielewski of 1857 explicitly says that he had given up in private concerts, too.

37. Dahlhaus, 1982: 34 (concerning op. 9).

38. We know next to nothing about the sales or print runs for Schumann's early piano music. One fragment of evidence concerns the proposed transfer of plates and 170 remaining copies of op. 6 to another publisher because of inadequate sales—see *BNF* 2, 434. One might guess from this that 200 to 250 had been printed. In a letter to Clara of 27 October 1839 Robert reported asking Breitkopf and Haertel about the sales of his recent music. They reported sales of 250 to 300 for opp. 9 and 12 and 300 to 350 for op. 15, which last had been out for only six months. Still, publishers did not seem to have viewed Schumann's piano music as a hot item. In a letter to Moscheles of March 1836 (*BNF* 2, 70), Schumann complains that "the publishers pay no attention to me." Even in 1848, Haertel turned down op. 68 (which turned out to be a considerable commercial success), saying "the market for your compositions is, by and large, rather limited—more limited than you could believe. . . . It has now been eleven years since we received the first work from you for publication, which has since been followed by sixteen others. . . . I communicate to you most unwillingly the results of this operation: we have lost through the publication of your work a significant sum and there is at this point no prospect of recovering it." ("Es ist der Vertrieb Ihrer Kompositionen überhaupt ziemlich beschränkt, beschränkter, als Sie glauben mögen. . . . Es sind nunmehr elf Jahre, seitdem wir das erste Werk zum Verlag von Ihnen erhielten, welchem dann bis jetzt 16 andere folgten. . . . Ich teile Ihnen sehr ungern das Resultat dieser Operation mit: wir haben an dem Verlag Ihrer Werke eine bedeutende Summe verloren und es ist bis jetzt keine Aussicht auf Ersatz"; Boetticher, 1968b: 172).

39. See Dadelsen (1957), and the fugue collections mentioned in Abraham (1952: 261) and Boetticher (1941: Appendix 2). No less an authority on Bach than Spitta was of the opinion that Schumann had entered more thoroughly than Mendelssohn into the "mysterious depth of feeling" in Bach's polyphony, and calls Schumann's fugues masterpieces (411a). Indeed, the craggy integrity of, for example, op. 72 no. 1 makes it more memorable than any of Mendelssohn's much smoother op. 35.

40. See Hermann Kretzschmar, "Die Bach-Gesellschaft: Bericht über ihre Thätigkeit," in J. S. Bach, *Werke*, ed. Bach Gesellschaft 46 (1899): xxiv–xl.

41. Related to them but less ambitious are the *Fughettas* of op. 126 and the strangely inept canon in op. 124 (no. 20, not playable by two hands—seemingly a throwaway idea from op. 56, cf., for example, op. 56 no. 6). The audience at

which these imitative studies was aimed is not clear, and apparently was not clear in the 1840s. When C. F. Becker (the author of Becker, 1837–39) reviewed op. 56 for *NZfM* (Bd. 23/49, 16 December 1845), he recommended it as domestic music for piano, three hands. A. G. Ritter, on the other hand, reviewing op. 60 in the same journal (Bd. 26/50, 21 June 1847) found it appropriate only for the organ.

42. "Es ist schlimm, das gerade für die in der deutschen Nationalität am tiefsten eingewurzelten Eigenthümlichkeiten und Begriffe wie für das Gemüthliche (Schwärmerische) und für den Humor, der die glückliche Verschmelzung von Gemüthlich und Witzig ist, keine guten und treffenden Worte in der französischen Sprache vorhanden sind. Es hängt dieses aber mit dem ganzen Character der beiden Nationen zusammen. Kennen Sie nicht Jean Paul, unseren grossen Schriftsteller? von diesem hab' ich mehr Contrapunkt gelernt als von meinem Musiklehrer" (*BNF* 2, 149, letter of 15 March 1839 to Simonin de Sire, who had asked Schumann for his recent compositions). For an explanation of the *Witzig,* see Daverio.

43. See *Tgb* 1:399 (28 May 1832): "Die Papillons schienen mir die Gesellschaft nicht au fait gesetzt zu haben—denn sie sahen sich auffällig an u. konnte die raschen Wechsel nicht fassen." ("Papillons does not seem to have gone down quite right with the public—for they looked at each other with surprise and could not grasp the rapid changes.") Or, *Tgb* 1:407 (9 June 1832): in the *Papillons* "der Wechsel zu rasch, die Farben zu bunt sind und der Zuhörer noch die vorige Seite im Kopfe hat, während der Spieler bald fertig ist." ("The changes are too rapid, the colors too bright, and the listener is still thinking about the previous page, while the performer is almost finished.") In his review of Liszt's attempt to program some of *Carnaval* in Leipzig in 1840, he commented, "mag manches darin den und jenen reizen, so wechseln doch auch die musikalischen Stimmungen zu rasch, als dass ein ganzes Publikum folgen könnte, das nicht alle Minuten aufgescheucht sein will" (*Ges Schr* 1:484). ("Many things in it will charm this or that person, but the musical moods change too quickly for them to be followed by a whole audience that does not want to be shaken up every minute.")

44. Ambros's inspired characterization of Schumann's early pieces—"music stands itself on its head" (88)—in fact recalls contemporary descriptions of Jean Paul's novelistic technique (which was in turn an explicit imitation of Laurence Sterne's in *Tristram Shandy,* widely successful in German translation from the 1770s onward). Spitta in his article on Schumann for the first *Grove's Dictionary* (1883) also notes repeatedly the importance of the influence of Jean Paul on Schumann (385, 405, 408, 411). The point is developed in Newcomb, 1987, and Daverio.

45. Harry Verschuren traces the decline of interest in Jean Paul by the reading public to as early as the beginning of the *Restaurationszeit,* i. e., from ca. 1815 onward. See *Jean Paul's "Hesperus" und das Zeitgenössische Lesepublikum* (Assen, 1980), 120.

46. Late Beethoven, however, is another matter. Many contemporary commentators saw late Beethoven as the predecessor for the quirky, "subjective," early Schumann style. (See the Moscheles 1836 review of the F♯-minor Piano Sonata cited above, n. 27, or Brendel.) Schumann himself seemed to agree—see the letter of 14 June 1839 to E. Krüger: "Only the most exceptional things attract me—almost all Bach, Beethoven especially in his later works." ("Mich nur das

Äusserste reizt, Bach fast durchaus, Beethoven zumeist in seinen späteren Werken"; *BNF* 2, 157).

47. Dahlhaus, 1974, stresses that the musical *Restaurationszeit* (or *Biedermeier*, a term that some commentators reserve for 1815–30, the first part of the *Restaurationszeit*) is not a musical style but a culture, defined not by compositional ideas but by closeness to the contemporary musical institutions. It is significant in this connection that the rubrics under which music was reviewed in *NZfM* changed early in 1850 from those defined by medium (e. g., *für Männerchor, für Klavier u. Violine*) to those defined primarily by institution, or locus of performance (e. g., *Theatermusik, Haus u. Kammermusik, Concertmusik, Kirchenmusik*).

48. See Valentin, Lichtenhahn, and Petrat.

49. Petrat quotes a passage from Richard Wagner's little article "Über Deutsches Musikwesen," written in 1840 while Wagner was living in Paris, as a clear, early statement of the ideal:

> A father and his three sons are seated round a table; two of the sons play the violin, the third the viola, the father the cello. The piece they are playing with such understanding and fervour is a quartet. . . . Among those simple honest souls art, since it is not concerned to entertain a vast heterogeneous public, naturally sheds its gaudy coquettish trappings and reveals the charm of its essential qualities of purity and truth. . . . If the circle is very small then a piano and a couple of string instruments will serve—a sonata is played or a trio or quartet, or one sings a German four-part song. (225; translation from *Wagner Writes from Paris*, ed. and trans. Robert L. Jacobs and Geoffrey Skelton [London, 1973], 38, 40, 42).

50. See Becker, *NZfM* 1837–39. One of these articles is on early keyboard fingerings, from Ammerbach through the early 18th century!

51. Leon Plantinga, 18, puts forward the idea that another important concept in the German musical canon—the concept of a "classic period" in music with Mozart as its central figure—was first formulated during this same period by Amadeus Wendt, a co-founder of *NZfM*, in a book of 1836, *Über den gegenwärtigen Zustand der Musik besonders in Deutschland und wie er geworden*.

52. In fact, the very same C. F. Becker of the original *Hausmusik* articles, in a review of Schumann's *Studien für den Pedalflügel* op. 56, saw even these pieces as *Hausmusik* for three hands, and gave another glimpse into the cultural movement. "But the pedal piano! Will this unformed colossus not forbid entry for these lovely duets into the cute, cosy music room, where the beings reside who uniquely know how to bring such *Tonwesen* to life? Worry not! A simple grand piano, or any piano, is sufficient." ("Aber der Pedalflügel! verwehrt dieser ungestaltete Koloss diesen lieblichen Duetten nicht den Eingang in das niedliche, trauliche Musikzimmer, wo Wesen weilen, die solche Tonwesen einzig nur auszusprechen verstehen? O daran stosse man sich nicht! Ein einfacher Flügel, ja ein Piano ist auch hinreichend"; *NZfM* 23/49, Dec. 1845).

53. See n. 32 above on this oft-cited criterion.

54. From L. Richter, *Lebenserinnerung eines deutschen Malers,* 12th ed. (Frankfurt, 1905), Appendix by H. Richter, p. 6. Quoted from Edler, 189–90. Richter's woodcut is reproduced *ibid.*, Plate 16.

55. One bit of evidence on this matter is given in Fellinger 1970. A draft version of a piece marked "Zum Carnaval" and "XIII" appears in op. 99 no. 5 with the "somewhat disjunct melody" of the last five measures of each part smoothed out. The sketched ideas that later turn up in pieces in op. 124 preserved on a sketch leaf analyzed by Robert Polansky can tell us nothing about this question, since they are not pieces in any sense, but tiny little jottings, just a few notes each, perhaps intended to be reminders of good ideas to return to and work out later.

56. "Nur, glaube ich, sagen Sie mir zu hoch Erhebendes und dies über Jugendarbeiten, wie die Sonaten, deren theilweise Mängel mir nur zu klar sind. In meinen spätern grösseren Arbeiten, wie den Symphonien und Chorcompositionen, möchte eine so wohlwollende Anerkennung" (*BNF* 2, 355–56).

57. See *BNF* 2, 434 and n. 38 above. He hoped—naively, it would seem—that a better distributed edition of the *Davidsbündlertänze* "must easily find favor in amateur circles as well." Perhaps with that goal in mind, he was going to replace the "mystical title [page]," or perhaps supplement it with the title "Twelve Character Pieces" on a new page. Indeed, the idea of changing the fanciful titles of opp. 6 and 16 had been voiced already in a letter to Clara begun on 24 January 1839 (*Brf* 2:368), and the idea of changing the title page of op. 11, removing what the changing Robert called the *romantischen Beisatz*, was voiced already in a letter to Kistner of February 1838 (*BNF* 2, 422–23).

58. "Die Kreisleriana sind stark revidirt. Ich verdarb mir leider in früheren Zeiten meine Sachen so oft, und ganz muthwilliger Weise. Dies ist nun alles ausgemerzt" (*BNF* 2, 464).

59. "Die erste Konzeption ist immer die natürlichste und beste. Der Verstand irrt, das Gefühl nicht." "*Über Ändern in Komposition*: Oft können zwei Lesarten von gleichem Wert sein (Eusebius). Die ursprüngliche ist meist die bessere (Raro)" (*Ges Schr* 1:25, 28).

60. The publisher G. Heinze of Leipzig issued an edition of op. 16 already in 1858 with a list of its variants from the first edition (see Hofmann, 45). In the 1860s Dr. Adolf Schubring published editions of opp. 6, 13, and 14, bringing together in a somewhat unsystematic fashion the variant readings of these pieces (see Hofmann, 17, 35, 39).

61. Linda Correll Roesner, in a review of the early volumes of this edition for the *Journal of the American Musicological Society* 31 (1978): 157–62, comments on the same anomaly.

62. Boetticher, 1968a: 59–70.

63. Boetticher, 1968a: 59–76, questions the accuracy with which the editors pursue this goal, but the variants that he finds are mostly on an extremely detailed level.

64. See the list of such editions in Boetticher, 1968a: 46–47, nn. 4 and 5.

65. Some of the individual pieces from this edition are available as individual issues with slightly more background material in the preface.

66. So far the *Quellenkatalog* has not progressed beyond op. 13, though long ago Boetticher announced that later volumes were about to appear.

67. See Dadelsen, 1961. Cf. also the typically trenchant observation by Carl Dahlhaus: "Ein Widerspruch zwischen dem ursprünglichen Sinn einer Überlieferung und dem Philologendrang, einen einzigen Text zum authentischen zu erklären, kann auch entstehen, wenn das Prinzip der 'Ausgabe letzter Hand' als Norm herrscht, die kein Ausnahme duldet. Gerade wenn man die Autoreninten-

tion als entscheidende Instanz anerkannt, sollte man mit der Möglichkeit rechnen, das ein Komponist, der im Alter ein Jugendwerk redigiert, gleichsam von aussen in einen Text eingreift, dessen ursprünglicher Intention er längst entfremdet ist." ("Philologie und Rezeptionsgeschichte: Bemerkungen zur Theorie der Edition," in *Festschrift Georg von Dadelsen,* ed. Thomas Kohlhase and Volker Scherliess [Stuttgart-Neuhausen, 1978], 51ff). ("A contradiction can also arise between the original meaning of a text and the philologist's compulsion to propose a single text as the authentic one, if the principle of the last edition supervised by the author is taken as a rule that permits no exceptions. Precisely if one recognizes the author's intention as the decisive criterion, one should reckon with the possibility that a composer who revises a work of his youth at a later time is an outside agent intervening in a text to whose original intention he is largely foreign.")

68. Boetticher, 1984: 46, finds evidence of indecision and revision in ordering in the sources for opp. 2, 3, 6, 9, 12, 13, and 15. To this one could add the variation set of op. 14 (see below) and op. 21 (cf. the diary entry of 20 March 1838 (*Tgb* 2:52): "Die Novelletten sind noch zu ordnen." "The *Novellettes* are still to be put in order."). I know of no special study of the situation with respect to op. 16.

69. *Journal of the American Musicological Society* 42 (1989): 191–92.

70. See Kämper, 142–49.

71. "Hast Du die Kinderscenen nun? Wie gefällt Dir denn das? Und steigen Dir liebliche Bilder auf? das 'bittende Kind', das 'Kind im Einschlummern' u. 'der Dichter spricht' nimm nur ja noch einmal so langsam, als Du es bisher genommen. Das ist auch recht arrogant von mir, nicht wahr? aber ich kenne Dich, Klärchen, und Dein Feuer." (*Brfw* 2:447, letter of 17 March 1839). For the original metronome markings, indeed the entire original format of op. 15, see the facsimile of the first edition, ed. Joachim Draheim (Wiesbaden: Breitkopf & Haertel, 1988).

72. See especially the letter to Heinrich Dorn of 5 September 1839, written in reaction to a review of op. 15 by Ludwig Rellstab (*BNF* 2, 170): "[Rellstab] meint wohl, ich stelle mir ein schreiendes Kind hin und suche die Töne dann danach. Umgekehrt ist es. Doch leugne ich nicht, dass mir einige Kinderköpfe vorschwebten beim Componiren; die Ueberschriften entstanden aber natürlich später und sind eigentlich weiter nichts als feinere Fingerzeige für Vortrag und Auffassung." See also the letters to Moscheles of 23 August and 22 September 1837 (*BNF* 2, 92 and 101–2) and the letter to Simonin de Sire of 15 March 1839 (*ibid.,* 148). In the first letter to Moscheles cited above, Schumann also includes the assembly of the pieces into a collection—so presumably the choosing and ordering of the individual pieces—as something that comes later, after composition.

73. Boetticher quotes Clara's letter of 19 January 1840 in response to Robert's of 17 January proposing titles for the individual pieces of op. 23: "Die Nachtstücke hast Du Dir recht schön und sinnig ausgedacht, für uns, die wir Dich ganz verstehen, herrlich! aber für das Publikum! . . . sie wissen nicht, was Du damit willst und stossen sich daran. Ich meine, Du lässt es bei dem allgemeinen Titel 'Nachtstücke'. . . Die Musik darin spricht ja doch vielmehr noch aus" (1942: 320). ("You have thought out the *Nachtstücke* quite beautifully and meaningfully for yourself—fine for us who understand you well, but for the public! . . . They do not know what you intend [by your titles] and are put off by them. I think you should stick to the general title 'Night Pieces.' . . . The music in them expresses a great deal more.")

74. "Diese Benennungen haben zum Theil heftigen Widerspruch erfahren; man sah nicht ein, dass sie nur Resultat der Reflexion über das schon vorhandene Kunstwerk waren, und hielt sie für das vorher vorhandene Schema, nach welchem der Componist arbeitete" (90–91).

75. This would be consonant with his attitude toward programmatic, or verbal, interpretations of music as well—cf., for example, Lippmann on the variety of interpretations he offered for op. 2.

76. See *Quellenkat* 2:207–9 for evidence of the different orderings; see *ibid.*, 219–22, for the additional piece, which had three stars arranged in a triangle as a title, excluded by Schumann from the first published edition, first printed in 1939, and now available in a variety of modern editions of op. 12.

77. Note Clara's constant pressure to simplify, registered in notes 19–20 and 22–23 above, and the similar pressure from reviewers.

78. I am avoiding as beside this point the question of whether the second theme of the published version went back to an original version of before October 1835.

79. This fair copy was first called to my attention by Walker. My examination of the Ms. leads me to wonder whether the date "19/12/38" is the date of Schumann's revisions or that of the publisher's receipt. The hand that has crossed out the title "Dichtungen" and the opus number "16" and replaced them with "Fantasie" and the opus number "17" is not Schumann's and is in the same ink as the date.

80. See *Brfw* 1:126, letter of 16–19 March 1838: "I have also finished a *Phantasie* in three movements, which I had drafted to the detail level in June 1836. The first movement of it is probably my most refined to date—a deep lament about you—the others are weaker, but nothing to be ashamed about." ("Ausserdem habe ich eine Phantasie in drei Sätzen vollendet, die ich im Juni 36 bis auf das Detail entworfen hatte. Der erste Satz davon ist wohl mein Raffiniertestes, was ich je gemacht—eine tiefe Klage um Dich—die anderen sind schwächer, brauchen sich aber nicht gerade zu schämen.")

81. *BNF* 2, 420, to Kistner.

82. See Newcomb, 1984: 246, for a history of the idea in Schumann criticism.

83. *Brfw* 2:532, letter of 23 May 1839. The one passage about which she does inquire seems to be in the middle of the first section of the march. Note that when Clara does think Robert is borrowing from Beethoven, she mentions it directly (letter of 24 November 1839, *Brfw* 2:798). Note, too, that when Robert borrows, from Clara at least, he makes no secret of it (e. g., the beginning of his op. 6, borrowed from her op. 6 no. 5, or the "Stimme aus der Ferne" of op. 21 no. 8, from her *Notturno* op. 6 no. 2).

84. See the letter of 3 April 1838 to Fischhof, where he speaks of "three [sic] volumes of *Novellettes* (rather sizable, interrelated, adventurous narratives)" ("drei Hefte Novelletten [grössere zusammenhängende abenteurliche Geschichten]); *BNF* 2, 118. Or the letter of 30 June 1839 to Hirschbach, where he reports, "Four volumes of *Novellettes* by me have recently appeared, intimately interrelated, and written with great pleasure" ("von mir sind jetzt vier Hefte Novelletten erschienen, innig zusammenhängend, und mit grosser Lust geschrieben"); *BNF* 2, 158.

85. It was the sixth piece that Robert, in a letter of 1 December 1839, advised Clara that she could not play by itself, removed from the entire cycle (*Brfw* 2:809).

Selected Bibliography

Abbreviations

Album	*Briefe und Gedichte aus der Album Robert und Clara Schumanns.* Edited by Wolfgang Boetticher. Leipzig, 1979.
AmZ	*Allgemeine musikalische Zeitung.* Leipzig. 1798–1848.
BNF 2	*Robert Schumanns Briefe. Neue Folge.* 2d, much expanded edition. Edited by F. Gustav Jansen. Leipzig, 1904.
Brfw	Clara and Robert Schumann. *Briefwechsel: Kritische Gesamtausgabe.* 3 volumes. Edited by Eva Weissweiler. Frankfurt, 1984– .
Ges Schr	Robert Schumann. *Gesammelte Schriften über Musik und Musiker.* 5th ed., 2 volumes. Edited by Martin Kreisig. Leipzig, 1914.
NZfM	*Neue Zeitschrift für Musik.* 1834–.
Quellenkat	Wolfgang Boetticher. *Robert Schumanns Klavierwerke: Neue biographische und textkritische Untersuchungen.* Vol. 1, Opus 1–6; vol. 2, Opus 7–13. Quellenkatalog zur Musikgeschichte, Nos. 9 and 10a. Wilhelmshaven, 1976 and 1984.
Tgb	Robert Schumann. *Tagebücher.* Vol. 1, 1827–1838, edited by George Eismann; vol. 2, 1836–1854, edited by Gerd Nauhaus. Leipzig, 1971 and 1987.
Was	Joseph Wilhelm von Wasielewski. *Robert Schumann.* 2d ed. Dresden, 1869 (first ed., 1858).

Abert, Hermann. *Robert Schumann.* Berühmte Musiker, No. 15. 2nd rev. ed. Berlin, 1910.

Abraham, Gerald, ed. *Schumann: A Symposium.* London, 1952.

———. "The Dramatic Music." In Abraham 1952: 260–82 (1952a).

Ambros, August Wilhelm. "Die neu-romantische Musik." In *Culturhistorische Bilder aus dem Musikleben der Gegenwart.* Leipzig, 1860 (citations are from the 2d ed., Leipzig, 1865: 51–96).

Becker. C. F. "Zur Geschichte der Hausmusik in früheren Jahrhunderten." *NZfM* 7–10 (1837–39).

Blackall, Eric A. *The Novels of the German Romantics.* Ithaca, 1983.

Boetticher, Wolfgang. *Robert Schumann: Einführung in Persönlichkeit und Werk.* Berlin, 1941.

———. *Robert Schumann in seinen Schriften und Briefen.* Berlin, 1942.

———. "Neue textkritische Forschungen an R. Schumanns Klavierwerk." *Archiv für Musikwissenschaft* 25 (1968): 46–76 (1968a).

———. "Robert Schumann und sein Verleger." In *Musik und Verlag: Karl Vötterle zum 65. Geburtstag am 12. April 1968,* edited by Richard Baum and Wolfgang Rehm. Kassel, 1968. Pp. 168–74. (1968b)

———. "Robert Schumanns Toccata Op. 7 und ihre unveröffentlichte Frühfassung." In *Musik-Edition-Interpretation: Gedenkschrift Günter Henle,* edited by Martin Bente. Munich, 1980. Pp. 100–11.

———. "Zum Problem einer Gesamtausgabe der Briefe Robert Schumanns." In *Studier och essäer tillägnade Hans Eppstein.* Kungl. Musikaliska Akademiens skriftserie, No. 31. Stockholm, 1981. Pp. 99–104.

————. "Weitere Forschungen an Dokumenten zum Leben und Schaffen Robert Schumanns." In *Robert Schumann—Ein romantisches Erbe in neuer Forschung,* ed. Robert-Schumann-Gesellschaft, Düsseldorf. Mainz, 1984. Pp. 43–55.

Borchard, Beatrix. *Robert Schumann und Clara Wieck.* Ergebnisse der Frauenforschung, No. 4. Weinheim, 1985.

Brendel, Franz. "Robert Schumann mit Rücksicht auf Mendelssohn-Bartholdy, und die Entwicklung der modernen Tonkunst überhaupt." *NZfM* 22 (1845): *passim.*

Dadelsen, Georg von. "Robert Schumann und die Musik Bachs." *Archiv für Musikwissenschaft* 14 (1957): 46–59.

————. "Die 'Fassung letzter Hand' in der Musik." *Acta Musicologica* 33 (1961): 1–14.

Dahlhaus, Carl. "Romantik und Biedermeier: Zur musikgeschichtlichen Charakteristik der Restaurationszeit." *Archiv für Musikwissenschaft* 31 (1974): 22–41.

————. *Musikalischer Realismus.* Munich, 1982.

Dale, Kathleen. "The Piano Music." In Abraham 1952: 12–97.

Daverio, John. "Schumann's 'Im Legendenton' and Friedrich Schlegel's *Arabeske.*" *19th Century Music* 11 (1987): 150–63.

Edler, Arnfried. *Robert Schumann und seine Zeit.* Laaber, 1982.

Erler, Hermann. *Robert Schumanns Leben, aus seinen Briefen geschildert.* 2 vols. Berlin, 1886–87.

Fellinger, Imogen. "Unbekannte Entwürfe zu Robert Schumanns Klavierstücken Op. 99 und Op. 124." In Gesellschaft für Musikforschung, *Bericht über den Internationalen Musikwissenschaftlichen Kongress Leipzig 1966,* edited by Carl Dahlhaus, Reiner Kluge, Ernst H. Meyer, and Walter Wiora. Kassel, 1970. Pp. 313–16.

Finson, Jon W., and Todd, R. Larry, eds. *Mendelssohn and Schumann: Essays on Their Music and Its Context.* Durham, N.C., 1984.

Gertler, Wolfgang. *Robert Schumann in seinen frühen Klavierwerken.* Leipzig, 1931.

Hofmann, Kurt. *Die Erstdrucke der Werke von Robert Schumann.* Tutzing, 1979.

Kämper, Dietrich. "Zur Frage der Metronombezeichnungen Robert Schumanns." *Archiv für Musikwissenschaft* 21 (1964): 141–55.

Kapp, Reinhard. *Studien zum Spätwerk Robert Schumanns.* Tutzing, 1984.

Kehler, George. *The Piano in Concert.* Compiled and annotated by George Kehler. Metuchen, N.J., 1982.

Kossmaly, Carl. "Ueber Robert Schumann's Claviercompositionen." *AmZ* 46 (1844): 1–5, 17–21, 33–37.

Lichtenhahn, Ernst. "Salonmusik: Ein ästhetisches und gesellschaftliches Problem der Schumannzeit." *NZfM* 146/11 (1985): 9–12.

Lippman, Edward A. "Theory and Practice in Schumann's Aesthetics." *Journal of the American Musicological Society* 17 (1964): 310–45.

Litzmann, Berthold. *Clara Schumann: Ein Künstlerleben.* 3 vols. Leipzig, 1902–8 (citations are from the edition of 1920).

Loesser, Arthur. *Men, Women, and Pianos: A Social History.* New York, 1954.

Mayeda, Akio. Transcription of panel discussion in *Schumanns Werke—Text und Interpretation.* Edited by Akio Mayeda and Klaus Wolfgang Niemöller. Mainz, 1987. Pp. 114–19.

Newcomb, Anthony. "Once More 'Between Absolute and Program Music': Schumann's Second Symphony." *19th Century Music* 7 (1984): 233–50.

————. "Schumann and Late Eighteenth-Century Narrative Strategies." *19th Century Music* 11 (1987): 164–74.

Petrat, Nicolai. " 'Hausmusik' um 1840." *Musica* 42 (1988): 255–60.

Plantinga, Leon. "Schumann's Critical Reaction to Mendelssohn." In Finson and Todd, 11–19.

Polansky, Robert. "The Rejected *Kinderscenen* of Robert Schumann's Opus 15." *Journal of the American Musicological Society* 31 (1978): 126–31.

Reich, Nancy B. *Clara Schumann: The Artist and the Woman*. Ithaca, 1985.

[Riccius, August Ferdinand.] "Robert Schumann." *Die Grenzboten*, Jahrgang 9, Quartal 3, weeks 39–40 (1850): 489–97, 521–30.

Roesner, Linda Correll. "The Autograph of Schumann's Piano Sonata in F Minor, Op. 14." *The Musical Quarterly* 41 (1975): 98–130.

————. "Schumann's Revisions in the First Movement of the Piano Sonata in G Minor, Op. 22." *19th Century Music* 1 (1977): 97–109.

————. "The Sources for Schumann's *Davidsbündlertänze*, Op. 6: Composition, Textual Problems, and the Role of the Composer as Editor." In Finson and Todd, 53–70.

Spitta, Philipp. "Robert Schumann." *A Dictionary of Music and Musicians*. Edited by Sir George Grove. London, 1883.

Valentin, Erich. "Hausmusik." *Die Musik in Geschichte und Gegenwart*. Edited by Friedrich Blume. Kassel, 1979. 16:610–15.

Walker, Alan. "Schumann, Liszt and the C major Fantasie, Op. 17: A Declining Relationship." *Music and Letters* 60 (1979): 156–65.

Wasielewski, Josef Wilhelm von. *Robert Schumann*. 3rd ed. Dresden, 1880.

Wiede. *Robert Schumann, Manuskripte, Briefe, Schumanniana*. Musikantiquariat Hans Schneider, Katalog No. 188. Tutzing, 1974.

CHAPTER NINE

Brahms: From Classical to Modern

Walter Frisch

Most of Brahms's original compositions for piano are clustered at the chronological extremes of his career. His earliest surviving work in any medium is the Scherzo op. 4 (1851), which stands at the head of a six-year span of intense productivity that includes three published piano sonatas opp. 1, 2, and 5; four Ballades op. 10; three sets of variations opp. 9 and 21 nos. 1 and 2; and three pairs of baroque-style dances WoO 3–5. In another concentrated span near the very end of his career (1892–93), Brahms composed the four sets of short piano pieces opp. 116, 117, 118, and 119. Across the intervening thirty-five years other works also fall into groups, most notably the four-hand *Schumann* Variations op. 23, *Handel* Variations op. 24, and *Paganini* Variations op. 35 (all from the early 1860s); and the *Klavierstücke* op. 76 and *Rhapsodies* op. 79 (1878–79).

As shown in Table 9.1 (based on McCorkle), these chronological groupings coincide to some extent with generic ones. The early years are dominated by the piano sonatas, which yield after the mid-1850s to independent variation sets. From the later 1870s onward Brahms tends to abandon such large-scale structures in favor of short character pieces.

Not surprisingly, Brahms's early works are dominated by the piano, the instrument on which he (like so many composers of the common-practice period) received his training and made his early career. What is striking, however, is the ambitious scope and serious nature of the first group of published compositions. From the start, Brahms seems intent on repudiating the virtuoso/salon tradition that so dominated the major musical centers of Europe in the 1830s and 1840s. His early recital programs from 1848 and 1849 had included such salon-style works, for example, a Fantasy on Themes of *Don Giovanni* by Thalberg and a Fantasy on "a Favorite Waltz" by Brahms himself (no trace of this work survives). But alongside these pieces the young pianist programmed more sober works like Beethoven's *Waldstein* Sonata. Very soon he chose to align himself

TABLE 9.1. Brahms's Original Works for Piano

Work	Date of Composition	Original Publication	Brahms Collected Works*
Scherzo op. 4	Aug. 1851	Leipzig: Breitkopf & Härtel, 1854	14:1
Sonata op. 2	Nov. 1852	Leipzig: B&H, 1854	13:29
Sonata op. 1	mvt. 2, April 1852; mvts. 1, 3, 4, Spring 1853	Leipzig: B&H, 1853	13:1
Sonata op. 5	October 1853; mvts. 2 & 4 earlier	Leipzig: Bartholf Senff, 1854	13:55
Variations on a Theme of Schumann op. 9	June 1854; vars. 10, 11, Aug. 1854	Leipzig: B&H, 1854	13:87
Ballades op. 10	Summer 1854	Leipzig: B&H, 1856	14:13
Variations on a Hungarian Song op. 21 no. 2	1854?	Bonn: N. Simrock, 1862	13:115
Two Sarabandes WoO 5	no. 1, prob. early 1854; no. 2, Jan.–Feb. 1855	Berlin: Deutsche Brahms-Gesellschaft, 1917	15:57
Two Gigues WoO 4	Jan.–Feb. 1855	——	15:53
Two Gavottes WoO 3	prob. early 1855	Vienna: Doblinger, 1979	——
Variations on an Original Theme op. 21 no. 1	early 1857	Bonn: N. Simrock, 1862	13:103
Theme with Variations (arr. of mvt. 2 of Sextet op. 18)	Sept. 1860	——	15:59
Variations and Fugue on a Theme of Handel op. 24	Sept. 1861	Leipzig: B&H, 1862	13:125
Variations for Piano Four Hands on a Theme by Schumann op. 23	Nov. 1861	Leipzig & Winterthur: J. Rieter-Biedermann, 1863	13:125
51 Exercises WoO 6	prob. 1850s–60s	Berlin: N. Simrock, 1893	15:126
Studies for Piano: Variations on a Theme by Paganini op. 35 (Books I and II)	Winter 1862–63	Leipzig & Winterthur: J. Rieter-Biedermann, 1866	13:147
Sonata for Two Pianos op. 34b	early 1864	Leipzig & Winterthur: J. Rieter-Biedermann, 1871	11:1
Waltzes op. 39,	Jan. 1865	Leipzig & Winterthur: J. Rieter-Biedermann	
Four hands		1866	12:26
Two hands		1867	14:33

TABLE 9.1 *continued*

21 Hungarian Dances for Four Hands WoO 1	I & II: Fall 1868; some earlier	Berlin: N. Simrock, 1869	12:106
	III & IV: March 1880	Berlin: N. Simrock, 1880	12:162
Nos. 1–10 arr. Two Hands		Berlin: N. Simrock, 1872	15:65
18 Liebeslieder for Four Hands op. 52a	Aug. 1869	Berlin: N. Simrock, 1874	12:48
Variations for Two Pianos on a Theme of Haydn op. 56b	Summer 1873	Berlin: N. Simrock, 1873	11:78
15 Neue Liebeslieder for Four Hands op. 65a	most 1874; some earlier	Berlin: N. Simrock, 1877	12:80
Eight Piano Pieces op. 76	Summer 1878; some earlier (no. 1 by 1871)	Berlin: N. Simrock, 1879	14:61
Two Rhapsodies op. 79	Summer 1879	Berlin: N. Simrock, 1880	14:89
Seven Fantasies op. 116	Summer 1892; some earlier	Berlin: N. Simrock, 1892	14:105
Three Intermezzi op. 117	prob. Summer 1892	Berlin: N. Simrock, 1892	14:129
Six Piano Pieces op. 118	prob. Summer 1893	Berlin: N. Simrock, 1893	14:141
Four Piano Pieces op. 119	prob. Summer 1893	Berlin: N. Simrock, 1893	14:163

*Johannes Brahms Sämtliche Werke, ed. Eusebius Mandyczewski and Hans Gál (Leipzig: Breitkopf & Härtel, 1927; rep. Ann Arbor, 1949).

with this high-minded tradition—even to the point of denying contemporary influences.

As has long been observed, both in genre and in certain aspects of thematic style and phrase structure, the E-flat-minor Scherzo op. 4 is indebted to the Scherzos of Chopin (especially to nos. 2 in B-flat minor and 3 in C-sharp minor). In 1853 Brahms apparently denied knowing any of Chopin's music in 1851, when he composed op. 4. (Similarly, although Brahms would express distaste for—and reportedly even fall asleep at—the music of Liszt, the latter clearly influenced the bravura style of much of the Sonata op. 2, as well as certain techniques of thematic transformation throughout the early piano works). Whatever its models, Brahms's op. 4 is a highly original and individual work, displaying many of the most fundamental characteristics of Brahms's style. A great rhythmic and motivic vitality is joined to a powerful piano idiom. Although its overall structure, consisting of a scherzo proper and two independent trios, is by nature sectional, Brahms attempts to impart continuity by means of thematic interrelationships. Thus the descending scale that forms the theme of Trio I derives from the prominent stepwise descent in mm. 17–20 of the Scherzo.

Equally significant for Brahms's own emerging style is his evident skill at continuous thematic development and expansion on a local level. The opening theme (Example 9.1) is built as an essentially traditional eight-measure structure: an antecedent, comprised of two identical statements of a terse four-note motive, which bucks like a horse trying to get out of the starting gate; and a consequent, in which the motive manages to propel itself forward into a stepwise descent through a seventh (C-flat down to D-natural). The counterstatement, far from being a predictable repeat of the first eight measures, is expanded to twenty-three measures. The initial motive now appears *four* times, still hitting up against the original "starting gate" B-flat, then breaking free to rise up to the climactic descent of mm. 17–20. This passage constitutes a thematic and rhythmic transformation of the original descent of mm. 4–8, whose nervous, upbeat-downbeat pattern has become a more assertive dactylic gesture, ♪ ♪ ♪.

EXAMPLE 9.1. Brahms, Scherzo, Op. 4 (mm. 1–32)

EXAMPLE 9.1. *continued*

After the Scherzo (or perhaps simultaneously), Brahms focused his attention on the piano sonata. We know that the three surviving works in this genre, opp. 1, 2 and 5 (1852–53), were preceded by others that the self-critical composer destroyed. The autograph manuscript of the C-major Sonata op. 1 is headed "Fourth Sonata" (*Vierte Sonate*). If by this reckoning op. 2 is the third (it might also be the first or second), then at least two other sonatas no longer survive.

Brahms's concentration on what was by 1850 largely an outmoded genre may be explained in part by Robert Schumann's remarks in the *Neue Zeitschrift für Musik* in 1839:

> It is strange that those who write sonatas are generally un-known; and it is also strange that the older composers still liv-ing among us . . . least of all cultivate this form. It is easy to guess the reason why the components of the former class—usually young artists—write sonatas: there is no better form in which they can introduce themselves to the higher class of crit-ics and please them at the same time. (Schumann, 64–65)

In the case of Brahms we should add to this rationale the desire of an am-bitious young composer to grapple with the most challenging of classical structural models, sonata form.

He appears to have approached this task obliquely, since at least two of his surviving sonatas (opp. 1 and 5), and perhaps the third as well, were composed from the inside out: Brahms wrote the slow movements before the outer ones (see Table 9.1). The slow movements, as well as the first Ballade of op. 10, manifest a significant predilection of the early Brahms: all are based in some way on folk sources. In op. 2 the melody (as Brahms himself admitted to a friend) can be fitted to the words of an old German Minnelied, *Mir ist leide* (Dietrich, 3). The ostensible source for op. 1 is given in the score, where the words "Verstohlen geht der Mond auf" are placed underneath a theme also identified as "an old German Minnelied" (though in fact Brahms took it from a contemporary anthology compiled by August von Kretschmer and August Wilhelm von Zuccalmaglio [Berlin, 1838–40]). The first Ballade of op. 10 is based on the Scottish bal-lad *Edward;* Brahms encountered it in translation in Herder's famous an-thology *Stimmen der Völker.* (The opening melody can even be fitted closely to the first line of the poem.) The Andante of op. 5 is prefaced by three lines from a poem by C. O. Sternau, "Der Abend dämmert, der Mondlicht scheint." The critic Adolf Schubring suggested in 1862 that the melody of the coda in D-flat (*Andante molto*) is based on a folk tune that had become popular at midcentury when fitted to a poem, "Treue Liebe," by Wilhelm Hauff (see Frisch 1984b, and Bozarth).

The slow movements of opp. 1 and 2 are also significant for consti-tuting Brahms's first surviving efforts in variation form, a structure to which he was to return so often in subsequent years. The Andante of op. 1, comprising three variations and a coda, is cautious but imaginative: cautious because Brahms relies mainly on traditional melodic embellish-ment, imaginative because in variation 2 the reinterpretation of a dominant-seventh chord (G^7) as a Neapolitan (D-flat) gives rise to two ethereal interpolations in the upper register, marked *pianissimo molto leggiero.* The Andante of op. 2, which also consists of only three variations, is (like the sonata as a whole) more pianistically elaborate than op. 1. In variation 2 Brahms expands the second part of the theme with considerable freedom, providing a grand (if somewhat overblown) climax in D, the relative major.

In each of the piano sonatas Brahms attempts to link the various movements by means of thematic transformation. Perhaps the earliest, op. 2, is the most thoroughgoing in this regard (Example 9.2). The theme of the slow movement (a) becomes, note for note, that of the following scherzo (b). A closely related figure, consisting of a rising stepwise third followed by a descending leap, is embedded into the main themes of the first movement (c) and (in truncated form) the finale (d). In op. 1 the weighty main theme of the first movement becomes transformed into the fleet and fiery (*con fuoco*) theme of the finale.

EXAMPLE 9.2. Brahms, Piano Sonata in F♯ minor, Op. 2

In op. 5 the network of intermovement relationships is still more complex. There is actually a pair of slow movements separated by the scherzo. The theme of the first, an Andante, becomes transformed in the second, entitled Intermezzo and appropriately subtitled "Rückblick." Both the D-flat-major themes of the Andante (Example 9.3a–b) are closely related to the theme in the same key that dominates the development section in the first movement (Example 9.3c).

EXAMPLE 9.3. Brahms, Piano Sonata in F minor, Op. 5/I and II

a.

b.

c.

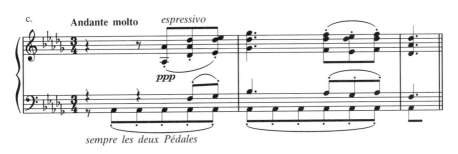

The kind of thematic transformation embodied in these examples is a hallmark of the romantic composers of the period 1820–50, perhaps especially Schubert (e. g., the *Wanderer* Fantasy), Liszt, and Chopin. The contour, rhythmic proportions, and intervallic structure of a theme remain essentially intact, but the tempo, articulation, and mood are strikingly recast. What is especially distinctive about Brahms's sonatas is their attempt to join this kind of transformation to a more dynamic and continuous procedure whereby themes, rather than remaining intact, are broken up into smaller components, which are then manipulated separately. This compositional technique—often called *thematische Arbeit* in German—is less characteristic of the romantics than of the Viennese classicists, especially Haydn, Mozart, and Beethoven. Brahms's sonatas thus emerge as curious but effective hybrids in which a dramatic, developmental style is tempered by romantic transformation. In this way they are genuine embodiments of the often repeated notion that Brahms is "a classicist among romantics."

A fine example is the first movement of op. 5, where Brahms applies the technique of transformation to a motive of a brevity worthy of Beethoven. At the opening the motive is brash and assertive (Example 9.4a). In the succeeding transition the same motive appears, as Brahms himself indicates in the score, "solid and determined" (*fest und bestimmt*: Example 9.4b). In the broad and nocturnelike second theme (Example 9.4c), the motive is now fully lyrical. All these transformations take place within the sonata-form exposition. The D-flat theme of the development constitutes a still further transformation of the inner-voice component of the original motive (compare Gb-F-Eb-F in Example 9.3c with Ab-G-F-G in Example 9.4a).

EXAMPLE 9.4. Brahms, Piano Sonata in F minor, Op. 5/I

The latter relationship is especially striking when we take into account the chronology of op. 5. Since the Andante movement from which this D-flat melody derives *predates* the opening movement, Brahms may have "planted" the theme in the development section before composing the exposition. This probable compositional process provides fascinating evidence for the frequent observation that sonata form in the romantic era is conceived thematically or melodically, whereas classical sonata form tends to be generated by small, open-ended motives. Brahms approached the first movement of op. 5 "romantically," having first conceived a noble melody during the composition of the Andante movement. He then attempted to "classicize" the movement by placing the melody in the development section and abstracting from it a small motif which could then appear to grow toward the melody.

The classic-romantic duality is evident also in another, more private aspect of the sonatas. In each of the autograph manuscripts, the double bars at the end of the individual movements are extended outward to form a "B," for Brahms. But on the final page of opp. 2 and 5 appears the signature "Kreisler jun."; of op. 1, "Joh. Kreisler jun." These inscriptions are the product of a young Brahms steeped in the world of the great romantic writer E. T. A. Hoffmann, the creator of the eccentric but talented Kapellmeister Johannes Kreisler (Brahms's partial namesake; see Kross).

In the manuscript of Brahms's next completed work for piano, the *Variations on a Theme of Schumann* op. 9, the Brahms-Kreisler dichotomy is even more explicit. At the end of certain variations (nos. 5, 6, 9, 12, and 13) the double bar lines are extended outward into a "Kr," for Kreisler; at others (nos. 4, 7, 8, 11,14, and 16) the bar lines are drawn out into a "B" (see Illustration 9.1). Here the inspiration comes more directly from Schumann, who in the original edition of the *Davidsbündlertänze* op. 6 had signed some of the pieces "E," for Eusebius (his contemplative and passive alter ego), and others "Fl," for Florestan (his passionate and impulsive side). In Brahms's op. 9 the Eusebian or reflective variations are signed "B"; the more impassioned ones, "Kr."

The autograph of op. 9 is headed "Little Variations on a theme by him, dedicated to her," the dedicatee being, of course, Clara Schumann. The theme is taken from the first "Albumblatt" (the fourth piece) in Schumann's collection entitled *Bunte Blätter* op. 99. In the preceding year, 1853, Clara herself had composed a set of variations on this theme, which she had presented to Robert on his birthday, June 8. (They were later published as her op. 20.) She played them for Brahms the following May, when Schumann was already in the asylum at Endenich and the twenty-one-year-old composer was living at the Schumann household helping out Clara and her children (soon to number seven, with the birth of Felix on June 11) and, of course, falling ever more deeply in love with her. Brahms's response was to write a set of his own that is perhaps his most intensely personal work, filled with allusions to the two Schumanns with whom his life had become inextricably involved since arriving on their doorstep in September 1853.

The set consisted at first of fourteen variations. At the end of the summer of 1854 Brahms added the present variations 10 and 11 (inscribing them with the phrase, "Rose and heliotrope blossomed"). Variation 10 concludes with a quotation of Clara's *Romance variée* op. 3, a theme which

ILLUSTRATION 9.1. Brahms, *Variations on a Theme of Robert Schumann*, Op. 9. Page 6 of autograph manuscript. Reproduced by permission of the Archive of the Gesellschaft der Musikfreunde, Vienna.

Schumann had also cited in his own *Impromptus on a Theme of Clara Wieck* op. 5. This interpolation enriches the allusion already present in Brahms's final variation (no. 16), where the octaves in the bass recall the bass line with which Schumann had preceded Clara's theme at the beginning and end of his Impromptus.

As recent commentators have suggested, there are numerous other references to Schumann's piano music in Brahms's variations, especially to certain pieces in the *Davidsbündlertänze, Carnaval* op. 9, and the *Études symphoniques* op. 13 (see Floros and Neighbour). More obvious—and yet thoroughly ingenious—is the way Brahms models variation 9 directly on the second "Albumblatt" of Schumann's op. 99, the piece that follows the actual source for the theme. In Schumann's op. 99 the two "Albumblätter" bear no obvious relation to each other, either harmonically or thematically. Brahms retains the key of the second "Albumblatt," B minor, as well as its figuration, but manages nevertheless to create a genuine and easily recognizable variation on the original theme.

As might be suggested by the preceding discussion, the op. 9 Variations interpret the source theme and its bass/harmony with greater freedom than do perhaps any other of Brahms's variation sets. In later years Brahms referred to such treatment as "fantasia-variation" and distinguished it from the stricter procedures derived from the baroque and classical traditions, to which he himself adhered more closely after his early period (Brahms 1909: 7). In this sense, op. 9 represents a kind of culmination of the early, romantic Brahms. Its style and spirit are continued in the four Ballades op. 10, composed in the same summer, and in the very Schumannesque *Variations on an Original Theme* op. 21 no. 2.

Already in the Sarabandes, Gigues, and Gavottes of 1855 (WoO 3–5), we can sense a tempering of the high-flown romanticism of much of the early Brahms. At about the same time Brahms undertook a mutual study of strict counterpoint with Joseph Joachim. In 1858 he composed the two Serenades, which contrast starkly with the early sonatas. All these activities suggest a kind of creative and compositional retrenchment, or what might more properly be considered a *reculer pour mieux sauter*.

The *Variations and Fugue on a Theme of Handel* op. 24 (1861) can be considered the culmination of this neoclassical period: indeed it may stand as Brahms's finest composition to that date. Brahms himself was especially proud of the variations, which he called his "Lieblingswerk" and which (as he told his friend Schubring) he "valued . . . particularly in relation to my other works." It was this work with which Brahms chose to make his Viennese debut as a performer and composer in November 1862, on which occasion the Variations received special praise from the powerful critic Eduard Hanslick (Hanslick, 83). The Variations reportedly prompted even Wagner to express admiration for "what may still be done with the old forms, provided that someone appears who knows how to treat them." In this century the work has attracted commentators as diverse as Heinrich Schenker and Donald Tovey. Schenker accorded it his only extended analysis of a single Brahms work; Tovey ranked it "with the half-dozen greatest sets of variations ever written" (Tovey, 167).

As in two of his most evident models, Bach's *Goldberg* and Beethoven's *Diabelli* Variations, Brahms constructs a monumental edifice upon a theme of the utmost simplicity, here an Air from Handel's Lesson in B-flat in a volume of keyboard suites. (Handel had also written a small, modest set of variations on the Air.) The theme itself makes use of only the most basic diatonic harmonies—the tonic, the dominant, and the subdominant. As the variations unfold, Brahms enriches but never overloads this framework.

As Tovey points out, the fact that the second two-measure phrase of the theme begins as a melodic sequence, a third higher than the first (Example 9.5a), gives rise to many splendid harmonic procedures. In the theme itself both the B-flat of measure 1 and the D of measure 3 are harmonized with the tonic triad. In Variation 2 Brahms already begins to tamper with this design: the addition of a melodic A-flat in measure 3 redefines the tonic as the dominant seventh of the subdominant, which appears on the second beat (Example 9.5b). This nuance gives the first half of the variation a different feeling from the original theme, even though the eventual harmonic goal (the dominant of m. 4) remains the same.

In certain variations (nos. 4, 11, 14, and 19), the D of measure 3 is supported by a D-minor harmony. In Variation 9 Brahms boldly introduces D *major* (Example 9.5c), which lies initially well outside the normal orbit of B-flat, but is then rationalized as V of vi (G minor). In the minor-mode variations (5, 6, 13), the second phrase begins with the analogous third degree, D-flat. In Variation 20, one of the farthest ranging harmonically, Brahms in effect combines the procedure from both modes (Example 9.5d): the variation begins in B-flat major, but the second phrase opens with a D-flat-major triad (in second inversion).

EXAMPLE 9.5. Brahms, *Variations and Fugue on a Theme of Handel*, Op. 24

In the *Handel* Variations such sophisticated techniques are made to blend naturally with older ones derived from a tradition Brahms knew so well. As in many baroque sets, some variations are paired so that the second functions as a "variation" of the first (nos. 5 and 6, 7 and 8, 23 and 24). There are other larger groupings as well, most obviously nos. 14–18, which in Tovey's words "arise one out of the other in a wonderful decrescendo of tone and crescendo of romantic beauty." This "decrescendo" apparently occurred to Brahms relatively late in the compositional process: in the autograph of the Variations, nos. 15 and 16 were set down in reverse order (Jonas; Bernstein).

In contrapuntal technique too the variations draw creatively on the past. Variation 6 is built as a strict canon, which changes after the first double bar into a canon by inversion. The final fugue, in which the subject (derived from the theme) is heard in inversion and augmentation, is a compendium of learned devices. In form, this fugue remains quite close to high baroque models: a series of "entries" (with a countersubject), followed by episodes, and culminating in a passage with a sustained dominant pedal.

From the point of view of piano technique, the *Handel* Variations are clearly the work of a composer with a remarkable (especially for his time) understanding of baroque keyboard idioms, which are adapted without a trace of self-conscious historicism. (In later years Brahms would edit the keyboard works of Couperin and realize continuo parts for Handel chamber duets.) Variations like the Siciliano (no. 19) or the "music box" (no. 22) mingle comfortably with those like the deeply voiced no. 13 and bravura no. 25, which make full use of the resources of the romantic piano. As Tovey observed, the keyboard style of the *Handel* Variations, "though by no means easy, is entirely free from artificiality or makeshift. . . . For pure economy of means [the variations] are as perfect a specimen of the treatment of their instrument as is to be found in art" (Tovey, 172).

The more didactic (but not pedantic) aspect of the *Paganini* Variations op. 35 is suggested by their principal title, *Studies for the Piano*. They were published in two books, each with fourteen numbered variations (followed by unnumbered variation-codas). The apparent inspiration for this monumental double set was Brahms's mutual study, during his first stay in Vienna in 1862 and 1863, of keyboard technique with the renowned pianist Karl Tausig. (Closely linked to the style of the Variations are the *51 Exercises*, WoO 6, which probably originated around this time, but were assembled and published only in 1893.)

Brahms took the theme from Paganini's A-minor Caprice for Violin op. 1 no. 24, itself a set of variations. Schumann had already adapted some of the Caprices for piano (though not no. 24) in his op. 3, published in 1832 with the title (like Brahms's) *Studies for the Piano*. Liszt too arranged a set of *Études d'exécution transcendante d'après Paganini* (published 1840), which included the A-minor Caprice. (The most renowned if also the most sentimental variations on this famous theme are those of Rachmaninoff.)

Brahms was surely acquainted with both works, as well as with Paganini's original, to which he pays direct homage in several of his variations. By comparison with the *Handel* Variations—and, indeed, every other keyboard work of Brahms—these place an emphasis on extreme virtuosity. (Clara Schumann called them "witch variations" and regretted they were beyond her capability.) Among the technical challenges are runs or passagework in thirds (II, 1), sixths (I, 1, 2), and octaves (I, 13); rapid hand-crossing (I, 3; II, 6); stretches across large spans (I, 4); sudden registral shifts (I, 8); athletic contrary motion (II, 8, 11); and fiendish three-against-four cross-rhythms (II, 7).

But as with the études of Schumann, Chopin, Liszt, and Debussy, technique is always allied with genuine and widely ranging musical expression. Only a composer of Brahms's abilities could draw from the harmonic-thematic structure of Paganini's pesky little tune (Example 9.6a) a pianistic snarl as menacing as II, 10 (Example 9.6b) and a melody as broadly radiant as II, 12 (Example 9.6c).

Apart from the variation sets, opp. 24 and 35 (and the four-hand set, op. 23), the early-to-mid 1860s are dominated in Brahms's oeuvre by an impressive series of chamber works, including two piano quartets opp. 25

EXAMPLE 9.6. Brahms, *Variations on a Theme of Paganini,* Op. 35

and 26, the Piano Quintet op. 34 (originally conceived, and later published, as a two-piano sonata op. 34b), the G-Major Sextet op. 36, and the Horn Trio op. 40. Among the important features of these works are the many ingenious ways Brahms finds to enrich and/or obscure the conventional structural divisions of sonata form, the exposition, development, and recapitulation.

This mastery trickles down into the smallest forms in which Brahms was working at the time, including the exuberant set of sixteen Waltzes op. 39, composed in 1865 for piano four hands (and adapted almost immediately for two hands). Dedicated to the critic Hanslick, these waltzes were Brahms's affectionate tribute to the dance form most closely identified with his adopted city, Vienna, where he was to settle permanently in 1872. They were also conceived very much in the spirit of Schubert, whose music Brahms had come to know deeply over the preceding decade. (At about the same time he composed his waltzes, Brahms undertook to edit and arrange Schubert's own dance music; see McCorkle, Anh. Ia, no. 6.)

Almost all Brahms's waltzes are in rounded or "recapitulating" binary form, in which the first half moves to the dominant, the relative major, or some substitute key; the second half begins with a small developmental passage that generally leads back to the main theme and the tonic (though not always simultaneously). As with all normative descriptions, this one hardly does justice to the waltzes of op. 39, whose limited dimensions and thematic scope seem to have stimulated Brahms's compositional ingenuity.

As one example we may offer no. 12 in E major (Example 9.7), which is built essentially from a single idea, a figure of two notes in an upbeat-downbeat pattern. In the expanded consequent phrase, measures 5–12, this idea is modestly varied with the addition of ties and eighth-note diminution. The first half of the piece moves, as expected, from the tonic to the dominant.

The small "development" begins in the tonic minor with a return to the initial thematic idea. In measure 16 the harmony shifts down a third to C major, then, over the sustained C pedal, to an F-major harmony. This chord is one of the remotest harmonies possible in E (the Neapolitan, lying a half-step above the tonic). Its arrival in measure 20 constitutes the still center of the piece, in which harmony and melody, as it were, have been immobilized deep in the bass register. What now follows is the actual *thematic* or rhythmic recapitulation of the opening idea, beginning almost imperceptibly in measure 21 with the inner voice motion F♮-F♯ (the upper voice remains frozen on A), then becoming more recognizable (cf. mm. 21–24 and 1–4).

But although the thematic material has returned home, the *harmony* has not. The C in the bass has dropped to B, which sustains a dominant-seventh harmony across mm. 21–24. Instead of resolving to a root-position E major, this chord leads to another dominant seventh, V^6_5 of IV,

EXAMPLE 9.7. Brahms, Waltz in E major, Op. 39 no. 12

EXAMPLE 9.7. *continued*

on the downbeat of measure 25. Brahms has thus bypassed the expected resolution by turning the tonic into V of the subdominant. This subdominant is sustained as the recapitulation rises upward from the depths. The tonic is confirmed only at the peak of that ascent, in the final measure of the piece.

The whole process of return in the second half of the waltz is so smooth, so continuous that one cannot point to a single moment where the "recapitulation" begins. This compelling mastery of formal, thematic, and harmonic procedures is characteristic of most of the waltzes of op. 39, which in this respect are both miniature embodiments of Brahms's large-scale sonata structures of the 1860s and harbingers of his achievements in the smaller piano pieces of his later years.

From the later 1860s to the end of the next decade Brahms was occupied primarily with large "public" works employing the orchestra, most notably the *German Requiem* (completed in 1868), which made him famous throughout much of Europe, the first two symphonies (1876–77), and the Violin Concerto (1878). It might be said that even when he did turn to the piano medium, one keyboard did not offer sufficient scope for his symphonic impulses—hence the *Haydn* Variations op. 56, composed in 1873 first for two pianos, then arranged for orchestra.

Toward the end of this period Brahms turned his attention once again to the solo piano repertory with the set of Piano Pieces op. 76, containing four Capriccios and four Intermezzos; and the two Rhapsodies op. 79. Apart from the early Scherzo op. 4, the Rhapsodies represent Brahms's largest independent, single-movement works for piano. In this sense they may be seen to comprise "spill-over" from large works of the 1860s and 70s.

Despite the implication of the titles (see below), which might imply rather free or open-ended structures, both Rhapsodies have a clear formal design. On the largest scale, no. 1 has a ternary or *A B A* design, in which the extensive *A* section shows distinct aspects of sonata form and *B* is a recapitulating binary (thus functioning like a trio). In *A* there is a second theme in the relative major (which employs the principal motive of the first theme), a close in that key, and a repeat of the first part. The beginning of the development is distinctive for introducing a new idea, a plaintive *pianissimo* theme in D minor accompanied by arpeggios. It is the third and fourth measures of this theme which become elegantly transformed into the B-major theme of the *B* section of the Rhapsody.

The G-minor Rhapsody, no. 2, has always been the more popular of the two. It begins with one of the most striking (and most analyzed) gestures in all of Brahms, a type of deceptive cadence in which the bass moves properly from V to I, but the tonic G supports an E-flat major, or VI, triad. (The gesture is similar to that at the opening of the D-minor Piano Concerto op. 15, where the tonic root is also harmonized by VI.) As has long been recognized, the structure of the G-minor Rhapsody is that of a full-fledged sonata form. It is distinctive, however, that the second group is not in the relative major, or even the dominant major, but in the dominant minor. This brooding theme constitutes an effective reworking of the opening theme's rhythmic pattern of a quarter-note upbeat followed by three steady quarter notes.

Although they have moments of undeniable power, the Rhapsodies can also strike one as somewhat overblown: there is (for this listener) an uncomfortable disjunction between the immense formal structure and the material with which it is filled. One possible reason for Brahms's subsequent turn toward the smaller forms in his solo piano music was precisely his realization that he could communicate more effectively outside the large-scale "sonata" format. This is not to suggest that he had lost the ability to write larger forms—the last two symphonies and the numerous later chamber works belie that notion—but that the solo piano was to become for him a medium more congenial to intimate, smaller-scale music.

Before we turn to the shorter works, some attention should be given to the titles Brahms assigned his independent piano pieces. Among the thirty-two pieces composing the sets opp. 10, 76, and 116–119 occur the headings Ballade, Intermezzo, Capriccio, Romance, and Rhapsody. In the case of op. 79 Brahms had some trouble deciding just what to name the pieces, and his uncertainty can be taken as symptomatic of his general attitude. The first piece was originally called "Capriccio"; the second was untitled. At the first public performance, in January 1880, both were listed as "Caprices" on the program. In May 1880, two months before publication, Brahms was evidently leaning toward the term "Rhapsody" and wrote to the dedicatee of op. 79, his friend Elisabeth von Herzogenberg, who replied:

> You know I am always most partial to the non-committal word, *Klavierstücke,* just because it is non-committal; but probably that won't do, in which case the name *Rhapsodien* is the best, I expect, although the clearly-defined form of both pieces seems somewhat at variance with one's conception of a rhapsody. But it is practically a characteristic of these various designations that they have lost their true characteristics through application, so that they can be used for this or that at will, without any qualms. (Brahms 1909: 99)

Elisabeth was right: in the nineteenth century titles like those employed by Brahms had lost the more specific or generic associations they had carried in earlier periods. As such, it is probably a mistake for a listener or critic to attach too much meaning to Brahms's titles beyond a general indication of *Stimmung* or mood. "Rhapsody" seems to connote a relatively large-scale and forceful composition, "Ballade" a briefer work in a similar spirit. The name "Capriccio" is attached to shorter energetic, extroverted works, while "Intermezzo" (except for op. 10 no. 3) and "Romance" suggest slower, more reflective pieces.

Only in the case of the Ballades op. 10, the Fantasies op. 116, and the Intermezzi op. 117 did Brahms provide a specific collective title for an entire set; the rest are all designated "Piano Pieces." The title page of the engraver's model for op. 118 also originally bore (in Brahms's hand) the name "Fantasies"; but Brahms crossed it out and replaced it with the "noncommittal" "Klavierstücke" (McCorkle, 473). This alteration may well reflect the attitude revealed by his remarks of the previous year (1892) to his publisher, Fritz Simrock. Apparently Simrock, contented with the "Fantasies" title for op. 116, had asked for something equally evocative for the three pieces of op. 117 (individually entitled Intermezzo), such as Monologues or Improvisations. Brahms resolutely refused, noting that the collection "remains really nothing more than 'Klavierstücke' " (Brahms 1919: 105).

The integrity or unity of the sets does not seem to have been of paramount concern to Brahms, except perhaps in op. 116. As late as a month before publication this set consisted of five rather than seven pieces. (We cannot be sure precisely which five, but a letter to Brahms from Clara Schumann suggests that these included three Intermezzi: A minor no. 2; E major no. 5; and one of the E-major pieces, either no. 4 or 6.) Brahms suggested to his publisher that these five pieces might be issued in one volume rather than two (as in the case of op. 76). If this was not feasible (and Brahms did not insist), then the grouping should be three and two (Brahms 1919: 79). At the last moment Brahms seems to have added two more pieces to the set, which was issued in two volumes (Illustration 9.2).

ILLUSTRATION 9.2. Title page of first edition of Brahms, *Fantasies* for Piano, Op. 116 (Berlin: N. Simrock, 1892).

Despite the two-part format, op. 116 has the strongest case among the late collections for being considered as a coherent whole, for which reason one critic has recently suggested it be taken as a "multi-piece" (Dunsby). The set begins and ends with energetic Capriccios in the same

key, D minor. Of the five inner pieces, the last three (nos. 4, 5, and 6) are
all Intermezzos in E, nos. 4 and 6 in major, no. 5 beginning in minor but
ending in major. Nos. 2 and 3 fall less obviously into any key scheme: no. 2
is in A minor (which can, however, be rationalized as the dominant of the
key of no. 1); no. 3 is in G minor.

The pieces show not only some overall tonal planning but also thematic interrelationships. The most obvious instance is the figure of arpeggiated, descending thirds that opens nos. 3 and 7. Less overtly, but no less
clearly, the upper voice at the opening of no. 1 also spells out descending
thirds. And in m. 15ff. of no. 4, the two-note motive of the right hand has
a counterpoint descending by thirds (see ex. 9.10b).

If we set aside questions of title and grouping, we are left, in opp. 76
and 116–19, with twenty-eight short pieces that by most criteria stand
near the summit of the piano literature of the nineteenth century. As is
often pointed out, they seem to distill or concentrate the most important
compositional techniques developed by Brahms over many years.
Though in some senses "autumnal," the later piano pieces are hardly retrospective. Many passages prefigure significant musical developments in
the century that Brahms did not live to see.

Although less demanding technically than the earlier scherzo, sonatas, and variation sets, the late pieces require perhaps an even higher level
of musicality. This was recognized immediately by Clara Schumann, who
wrote in her diary after receiving from Brahms some of the op. 116 in
manuscript: "As far as demands on the agility of fingers, the Brahms
pieces are, except in a few places, not difficult. But the spiritual [*geistige*]
technique therein demands a delicate understanding. One must entrust
oneself completely to Brahms in order to render these pieces in the way
that he has imagined them" (Litzmann, 3: 563).

The larger form of the late pieces tends to be ternary (especially in
the latest sets), although one also encounters several recapitulating binary
forms with developmental middle sections (as in op. 76 no. 4 or op. 116
no. 1). In the ternary forms the *B* section is on several occasions fashioned
as a stunning transformation of the main theme of *A*. Such procedures are
worthy descendants of the thematic transformation that (as we have seen)
shaped the early piano sonatas. Some of the most elegant instances are
shown in Example 9.8a–c. In each, Brahms retains the basic profile and
rhythmic proportions of the original theme (or motive), but so alters its
mood, figuration, tempo, or tonality that we can genuinely feel we are
hearing a "contrasting" theme.

The mere categorizing of formal types in these late pieces—as in
most of Brahms's works—says nothing about what is most characteristic:
the almost infinite variety of ways in which Brahms reinterprets the standard structural designs, on which he brings to bear the full force of his
thematic, harmonic, and rhythmic-metrical powers.

The B-flat Intermezzo op. 76 no. 4 is one of Brahms's greatest studies in the avoidance or delay of the tonic. The piece has a recapitulating

EXAMPLE 9.8. Thematic Transformation in Brahms's Late Piano Music

a. Capriccio, Op. 76 no. 2 (mm. 7, 46–47)

b. Intermezzo, Op. 117 no. 2 (mm. 1–2, 31–32)

binary form with a repeated first part that moves for its secondary key area to the relative minor, G. The principal theme unfolds over a sustained dominant seventh, which then leads away from rather than toward the tonic. Not until the recapitulation of the secondary material in B-flat is the tonic actually stated.

This Intermezzo offers a very audible example of Brahms's ability to control long-range harmonic motion by means of a stepwise bassline (Example 9.9). Over the course of the first part the bass line moves from F to

EXAMPLE 9.8. *continued*

c. Intermezzo, Op. 119 no. 2 (mm. 1, 36–37)

EXAMPLE 9.9. Brahms, Intermezzo, Op. 76 no. 4, Reduction of Bass Line

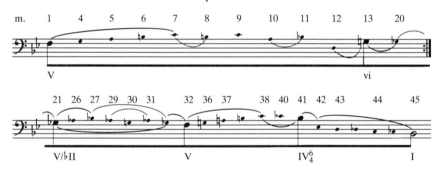

G. Just before the double bar, the G drops to G-flat (harmonizing an E-flat-minor chord), which then underpins the magnificent development section. Here it sustains a G-flat seventh harmony (V of the Neapolitan C-flat), which leads through a series of chromatic harmonies back to the original departure point, an E-flat-minor chord in first inversion. The bass then drops back down to F to begin the recapitulation.

The actual return to B-flat is achieved by a Brahmsian masterstroke. The first deviation from the opening comes at the upbeat to m. 40, where the former B-natural (cf. m. 8) is respelled as C-flat and leads downward to B-flat, instead of upward to C. The tonic note, now in place in the bass, supports not a tonic triad but a subdominant E-flat. At this magical moment we know we are at last home, even though the actual tonic chord arrives only five measures later.

The E-major Intermezzo op. 116 no. 4 demonstrates how remarkably fluid Brahms's conception of form becomes in these late works. Although it has elements of both ternary and recapitulating binary form, the Intermezzo falls squarely into neither category. There are three basic thematic elements, which appear according to the scheme:

A	B	A'	B'	A"	C	A'''	A''''	C'	B"
m. 1	10	15	26	33	37	50	57	60	67

The larger ternary aspect of the design would place the presentation of *C* as the middle section; a binary one would incorporate *C* as a kind of "second" subject in the dominant, which is then recapitulated (*C'*) in the tonic. But as the profusion of prime signs suggests, the material is varied and reinterpreted so thoroughly in this Intermezzo that one is more accurate in speaking of what Schoenberg would call "musical prose," a kind of freely unfolding design that avoids patterned repetition.

A brief consideration of the way *A* is successively transformed can give an idea of this developmental process (Example 9.10a–e). At its two first appearances the theme forms part of a recognizable antecedent-consequent structure. *A* comprises 4 + 5 measures; at *A'* the right-hand part is enhanced, somewhat modestly, by eighth-note diminutions, and the consequent is extended (also modestly) to seven measures. (Only the antecedents are shown in Example 9.10.) At *A"* the changes are more radical: the consequent phrase is omitted, and the antecedent is reharmonized in G-sharp minor. The original right-hand motive, G♯-C♯, appears to be absent here, but a closer look suggests that it has been transferred to the bass, so that it actually *becomes* the bass of the theme. This represents the kind of profound motivic-harmonic reinterpretation for which Brahms has been revered by later generations of composers and analysts. At *A'''* the antecedent is reharmonized yet again, now cadencing in C-sharp major. Only *after* the cadence does the original right-hand motif G♯-C♯ appear, thus again displaced from its original position. The final appearance of the theme, *A''''*, might seem at first to be part of a consequent phrase (and thus not an independent thematic statement), but it also deviates from previous models, now dipping toward the subdominant A major and thus preparing the codalike presentations of *C'* and *B"*.

In Brahms's late works the manipulation of meter becomes a powerful means of development and variation. Indeed, in a work like the C-sharp minor Capriccio op. 76 no. 5 meter is the primary focus of compositional interest. The piece is built from the alternation (and successive variation) of two segments: *A B A' B' A"* Coda (based on *A*). At the opening of *A* two conflicting metrical frameworks are actually superimposed: the notated $\frac{6}{8}$ is supported by the bass, while the melody consistently maintains $\frac{3}{4}$ (Example 9.11a). (The inner voice seems to waver between the two frameworks.) In the *B* section (beginning in E major, then modulating by ascending thirds), Brahms now seems to *alternate* between the two meters: measures 19–20 suggest $\frac{3}{4}$, the following two measures $\frac{6}{8}$ (Example 9.11b). In *B'* Brahms introduces yet another metrical parsing, $\frac{2}{4}$, which then governs the succeeding *A"*.

EXAMPLE 9.10. Brahms, Intermezzo, Op. 116 no. 4 (mm. 1–4, 15–18, 33–36, 50–53, 57–59)

The coda (Example 9.11c) serves as a further metrical variation: the *A* theme returns to its original $\frac{6}{8}$, but that meter is initially overridden by groupings of 5 perceived in a $\frac{5}{8}$ meter. After three such groups Brahms restores the "missing" eighth note (third beat of m. 114). The six-note groupings still fail, however, to coincide with the bar line. Such reconciliation is achieved by the addition of the last three eighth notes in measure 115 (A♯-A♮-A♮), which bring the music into agreement with the bar line just in time for the closing cadential $\frac{6}{4}$ pattern.

While the C-sharp-minor Capriccio perhaps compensates for its metrical complexity by being relatively conventional harmonically, in the C-major Capriccio op. 76 no. 8 an equally (or even more) intricate metrical structure is joined with an unstable harmonic idiom. Despite the notated $\frac{6}{4}$, the opening section unfolds initially with a $\frac{3}{2}$ grouping in both hands (Example 9.12). Across measures 3–4 the harmonic rhythm overrides the $\frac{3}{2}$ with a hemiola that suggests a large measure of $\frac{3}{1}$. Only in measure 8, with a perceptible duple articulation of the measure, does the actual written meter emerge.

The harmonic framework, in which the "notated" tonic C major is nowhere confirmed, is as mobile as the metrical one. As David Lewin has pointed out, the first segment consists mainly of chains of unresolved dominant sevenths, a V^7 of C moving to V^7 of F. The first cadences are made not to the tonic but to F, the subdominant, on the downbeats of measures 3 and 7. The other principal cadential goal in the first segment of the piece is E minor, in measures 9 and 14.

As Lewin suggests, the absent tonic C serves as implied mediator between F major (one step to the flat side) and E minor (one step to the sharp side). By means of proportional temporal reductions, he also demonstrates that the various metrical frameworks function in a way that is analogous or parallel to the main harmonic areas. (He even proposes "tonic," "dominant," and "subdominant" meters.) Such a systematic, or near-systematic, correlation of compositional elements is fully characteristic of the late Brahms and was part of his important legacy to the twentieth century.

One of the most distinctive features of the late piano pieces is their notation. It is perhaps too little appreciated how careful and ingenious Brahms was about capturing graphically the complex musical effects he desired. The late piano pieces feature richly polyphonic textures that, except in a few cases (as in the E-major Intermezzo op. 116 no. 6), fail to conform to conventional three- or four-voiced styles. Brahms's piano polyphony is rather in the tradition of Schumann's, in which voices enter and disappear with great freedom.

In the C-major Capriccio just examined (Example 9.12), for example, Brahms's desire to highlight the tied upbeat as a significant motivic-rhythmic element gives rise to a complex notation whereby the right-hand

EXAMPLE 9.11. Brahms, Capriccio, Op. 76 no. 5 (mm. 1–2, 19–22, 111–117)

EXAMPLE 9.12. Brahms, Capriccio, Op. 76 no. 8 (mm. 1–15)

EXAMPLE 9.12. *continued*

figuration of measure 1 is played by one "voice," that of measure 2 by another. The two parts alternate in closer succession in measure 3. From the point of view of strict independence the notation is ambiguous, since no rests are indicated. And even the two-voice distinction seems to break down in measure 4. Here the E tied over the bar line from measure 3 changes the direction of its stem (and thus its voice?), and a dotted-quarter-note chord appears in the upper register on the second beat. The stemming of the A-C dyad and the following chord (B-G-B) would seem now to suggest *three* voices; but then where are the eighth-note rests above the first solitary B? Clearly this is the wrong question to ask; Brahms does not intend for us to listen or look for traditional polyphonic independence of the voices.

Closely related to these notational idiosyncrasies is the conception of musical "space" in the later piano works of Brahms, where we begin to see a breakdown of the distinction between melody and harmonic support, between "above" and "below." To be sure, Brahms was not alone in initiating such a trend (one could point also to passages in late Beethoven, or in Wagner, such as the Prelude to Act 3 of *Parsifal*). But he surely hastened the process in a work like the F-minor Intermezzo op. 118 no. 4 (Example 9.13a), where both hands play essentially similar musical material in close succession. Here one cannot point to a specifically "melodic" voice or to a "harmonic support." Like so much of Brahms's music this piece is concerned—indeed, obsessed—with imitative counterpoint, which by its very nature tends to imply an equality among parts. Thus, even when the top voice becomes more clearly melodic in the consequent phrase, measure 9, its primacy is challenged by the exact canon unfolding in the tenor.

These procedures are carried even further in the middle section of the Intermezzo (Example 9.13b), which unfolds for forty measures as a strict canon at the octave. The "theme" or subject consists simply of a triad in the treble register followed by a low bass note; the "entries" overlap so that triad is immediately succeeded by triad, bass note by bass note. One could scarcely imagine a more economical mode of discourse, nor one less related to traditional theme-plus-bass texture.

Mirror symmetry provides another way in which the F-minor Intermezzo begins to cloud the up-down distinction. At the opening the triplet figures are freely inverted between the hands, and later on the two hands trade octaves and arpeggios in inversion (Example 9.13c). When combined with such a deliberately restricted rhythmic-motivic language, this tendency toward symmetry points directly ahead to the music of the Second Viennese School some fifteen years later.

In this regard the E-minor Intermezzo op. 116 no. 5 is even more extraordinary. As at the opening of the F-minor piece, there is only one brief "motive," in this case a two-note stepwise figure (Example 9.14). The

EXAMPLE 9.13. Brahms, Intermezzo, Op. 118 no. 4 (mm. 1–4, 52–55, 26–29)

EXAMPLE 9.14. Brahms, Intermezzo, Op. 116 no. 5 (mm. 1–12)

symmetry involves not only horizontally unfolding figures as in op. 118 no. 4 but vertical structures. The chord played by each hand in the first six measures is an exact mirror of the chord in the other. Thus, in the upbeat to measure 1, both hands play octaves that enclose thirds at the outermost extremes and sixths within. None of these symmetrical sonorities is in its own right tonally ambiguous: each forms a harmony analyzable in E minor. But they all appear on *weak* beats and "resolve" in most instances to bare, two-note dissonances on *strong* beats (augmented fourths and diminished sevenths, in mm. 5–6). Thus, Brahms has tampered not only with the vertical/simultaneous dimension of the harmony, but also its horizontal/temporal one, where he reverses the traditional metrical procedures of associating weak-strong with dissonance-consonance. The result is one of the most proleptic pieces not only in Brahms's oeuvre but in the later nineteenth century as a whole.

Symmetry and the blurring of harmonic structure are also evident in one of Brahms's most analyzed late pieces, the B-minor Intermezzo op. 119 no. 1 (see Dunsby, 85–105; Newbould). Here the symmetry is inter-

ILLUSTRATION 9.3. Brahms, Intermezzo, Op. 119 no. 1. From the autograph manuscript. Reproduced from the Collections of The Music Division, Library of Congress, Washington, D.C.

vallic: the opening chord unfolds from the top downward in successive thirds (Illustration 9.3). The ostensible tonic, B minor, is thus embedded in a chord that looks, but cannot be said to function, like an E-minor ninth. The ii triad in measure 2 and the minor v in measure 3 are extended downward by an even longer series of thirds. Only in measure 4 does the texture assume a more normal appearance as it moves toward a cadence. In fact, however, the outer voices—ostensibly "melody" and "bass"— unfold in canon, and the cadence on the downbeat of measure 5 proves deceptive.

"Brahms is everywhere," remarked the critic Walter Niemann in 1912. "None of the more recent piano music is possible without him" (Niemann, 45). An ardent Brahmsian, Niemann of course exaggerates somewhat. But in the decades surrounding 1900 Brahms did cast a long compositional shadow, especially over Austro-Germany. As Niemann points out, the influence was not entirely benign, since the more obvious characteristics of Brahms's piano style—the doubled thirds and sixths, the complicated cross-rhythms, and so forth—"tempt one so readily to partial and superficial imitation, to the surrendering of one's own personality."

Some young composers were only too proud to surrender. Alexander Zemlinsky, who received his training in the Brahms milieu in Vienna and was even given encouragement by the master himself, recalled in later years that "among my colleagues it was considered praiseworthy to compose in as 'Brahmsian' a manner as possible" (Zemlinsky, 70). Even the self-taught Arnold Schoenberg was not immune, as is shown by his Piano Pieces of 1894, composed unmistakably under the influence of the Brahms opp. 116–19 pieces that had been published in the preceding two years.

Even at this early stage in his career, Schoenberg's Brahmsianism could be quite rigorous and sophisticated. The C-sharp-minor *Andantino*, although notated in $\frac{2}{4}$ meter, unfolds from the very beginning as if in $\frac{6}{8}$ (Example 9.15). Both hands fully support the $\frac{6}{8}$ until measures 9–10, where Schoenberg disrupts the pattern. The C-sharp chord in measure 9

EXAMPLE 9.15. Schoenberg, Piano Piece (1894), mm. 1–12. Used by permission of Belmont Music Publishers.

is not followed, as we would expect, by an eighth-note upbeat. Instead, the next phrase begins an eighth note "early" on the notated downbeat of measure 10. Although notated and perceived downbeats coincide here, the $\frac{2}{4}$ meter is not unequivocally restored, since the rhythmic pattern of the melody and accompaniment continues to suggest $\frac{6}{8}$. The last two sixteenth notes of measure 10 hover uneasily in a kind of metrical void: they sound neither like the last beat of a $\frac{2}{4}$ measure (since the preceding rhythmic figure has come to be heard solely in $\frac{6}{8}$) nor the fourth beat of a $\frac{6}{8}$ pattern (since the notes are given no bass support, as we might expect on the strong fourth beat, and as has been the case earlier, for example, on the notated downbeat of m. 2). Such complex metrical procedures derive directly from the world of the late Brahms, especially from works like op. 76 no. 5.

In later years Schoenberg eschewed such overt appropriation of what he came to call the "symptoms" of a composer's style. But he would claim (and attempt to demonstrate) that the more fundamental techniques of a great composer like Brahms could continue to exert influence, even in a very different idiom. There is surely no better example of this than Schoenberg's Three Piano Pieces op. 11 (composed 1909). Although atonal, they are directly indebted to the piano music of Brahms in texture, economy of melodic figures, flexibility of phrase structure, and in the use of constant variation. The proselike processes by which the theme of op. 11 no. 1 unfolds might be profitably compared with those discussed above in Brahms's E-major Intermezzo op. 116 no. 4 (see Example 9.10).

The other major composer of the early twentieth century whose music would be unthinkable without Brahms is Max Reger, whose devotion occasionally took extreme forms. In 1899 he published as op. 24 no. 6 a large Rhapsody for piano, clearly modeled on the identically titled pieces of Brahms's op. 79 and bearing the inscription "To the memory of Johannes Brahms." A more touching and perhaps profound tribute was a short piano piece entitled *Resignation* and subtitled "3. April 1897—J. Brahms†" (the date of Brahms's death). It was published in 1899 as op. 26 no. 5. Although it is fully typical of neither Reger's style nor Brahms's broader influence, *Resignation* forms an appropriate conclusion to this chapter for it shows how thoroughly (and uncannily) a talented composer can absorb—and actually seem to take possession of—Brahms's style.

With its deep bass octaves, polyphonic texture, and harmonic design, the opening theme of *Resignation* (Example 9.16) seems to allude to at least three of the late Brahms Intermezzos: op. 116 nos. 4 and 6, both in E major, and op. 118 no. 2 in A major. Like all three Intermezzi, Reger begins on an upbeat with a root-position tonic chord, which moves on the subsequent downbeat to some kind of pre- or subdominant harmony (here ii⁶). At the approach to the dominant in *Resignation,* measures 6–9, Reger draws upon Brahms's techniques of metrical ambiguity or conflict. As we listen—at least for the first time—measures 5–6 suggest a $\frac{3}{2}$ hemiola superimposed over the notated $\frac{3}{4}$, an effect very characteristic of Brahms. But the downbeat of measure 7 does not, as we might expect, restore the notated meter unequivocally. Instead, the implied $\frac{3}{2}$ measure is, as it were, stretched, as shown in Example 9.16, to accommodate the cadential approach to E through the circle of fifths, C♯-F♯-B-E. Reger now accelerates the harmonic rhythm, so that while the C-sharp lasts a half note, or a full beat in $\frac{3}{2}$, the F-sharp and B are only a quarter note each. The cadential goal, E, thus arrives on the notated last beat of measure 7. The two subsequent measures confirm E with the Phrygian cadence made from F and C, a gesture that owes something to the similar harmonies in op. 118 no. 2 (see mm. 16–17 and 20–21).

This Phrygian passage extends the metrical ambiguity long enough to bring the phrase to a close on the notated second beat of measure 9, thus allowing the varied restatement of the opening to begin in its proper position, on beat 3. The tonic now reappears with another Brahmsian gesture: the A enters a half beat too "early," sounding deep in the bass underneath the prevailing dominant harmony.

EXAMPLE 9.16. Reger, *Resignation,* Op. 26 no. 5 (mm. 1–10)

The elegant procedures in measures 6–9, involving meter, harmony, and phrase structure, make no apparent quotation of, or allusion to, any specific passage in Brahms. Rather Reger shows himself to have gone beyond the "symptoms" to internalize fully some of Brahms's most characteristic compositional techniques. At such moments, Reger's *Resignation*, like the op. 11 Piano Pieces of Schoenberg, manifests the most profound kind of "influence" Brahms's music could generate. It is of the kind where, as Charles Rosen has suggested, no precise model is detectable and the search for one becomes an endeavor of "pure musical analysis."

Selected Bibliography

Bernstein, Jane. "An Autograph of the Brahms 'Handel Variations.'" *Music Review* 34 (1973): 272–81.

Bozarth, George. "Brahms's *Lieder ohne Worte*: the 'Poetic' Andantes of the Piano Sonatas, Ballades, and Intermezzi." In *Brahms Studies: Papers Read at the International Brahms Conference, 5–8 May 1983, Library of Congress*, edited by George Bozarth. Oxford, 1990.

Brahms, Johannes. *The Herzogenberg Correspondence*. Edited by Max Kalbeck. Translated by Hannah Bryant. New York, 1909; repr. ed, New York, 1987.

————. *Briefe an Fritz Simrock*. Edited by Max Kalbeck, vol. 4, Berlin, 1919.

Cadwallader, Allen. "Foreground Motivic Ambiguity: Its Clarification at Middleground Levels in Selected Late Piano Pieces of Johannes Brahms." *Music Analysis* 7 (1988): 59–91.

Cone, Edward. "Three Ways of Reading a Detective Story—or a Brahms Intermezzo." *Georgia Review* 31 (1977): 554–74.

Dietrich, Albert. *Erinnerungen an Johannes Brahms in Briefen besonders aus seiner Jugendzeit*. Leipzig, 1898.

Dunsby, Jonathan. *Structural Ambiguity in Brahms*. Ann Arbor, 1981. Pp. 85–105.

————. "The Multi-Piece in Brahms: *Fantasien* Op. 116." In *Brahms: Biographical, Documentary and Analytical Studies*. Edited by Robert Pascall. Cambridge, 1983. Pp. 167–89.

Floros, Constantin. "Studien zu Brahms' Klaviermusik." *Brahms-Studien* 5 (1983): 25–63.

Frisch, Walter. *Brahms and the Principle of Developing Variation*. Berkeley and Los Angeles, 1984 (1984a).

————. "Brahms and Schubring: Musical Criticism and Politics at Mid-Century." *19th Century Music* 7 (1984): 271–81 (1984b).

Georgii, Walter. *Klaviermusik*. 2d ed. Zurich, 1950. Pp. 388–412, 571–74.

Hanslick, Eduard. *Vienna's Golden Years of Music, 1850–1900*. Translated and edited by Henry Pleasants. London, 1951.

Jonas, Oswald. "Die 'Variationen für eine liebe Freundin' von Johannes Brahms." *Archiv für Musikwissenschaft* 12 (1955): 319–26.

Kirby, Frank E. "Brahms and the Piano Sonata." In *Paul A. Pisk: Essays in His Honor*, edited by John Glowacki. Austin, 1966. Pp. 163–80.

Kraus, Detlef. "Das Andante aus der Sonate op. 5 von Brahms—Versuch einer Interpretation." *Brahms-Studien* 3 (1979): 47–51.

Kross, Siegfried. "Brahms and E. T. A. Hoffman." *19th Century Music* 5 (1982): 193–200.

Lewin, David. "On Harmony and Meter in Brahms's Op. 76, No. 8." *19th Century Music* 4 (1980): 261–65.

Litzmann, Berthold. *Clara Schumann: ein Künstlerleben nach Tagebüchern und Briefen.* 3 vols. Leipzig, 1908.

McCorkle, Margit. *Johannes Brahms: Thematisch-bibliographisches Werkverzeichnis.* Munich, 1984.

Mason, Colin. "Brahms's Piano Sonatas." *Music Review* 5 (1944): 112–18.

Matthews, Denis. *Brahms Piano Music.* London, 1978.

Musgrave, Michael. *The Music of Brahms.* London, 1985.

Neighbour, Oliver. "Brahms and Schumann: Two Opus Nines and Beyond." *19th Century Music* 8 (1984): 266–70.

Newbould, Brian. "A New Analysis of Brahms's Intermezzo in B minor, op. 119, no. 1." *Music Review* 38 (1977): 33–43.

Niemann, Walter. "Johannes Brahms und die neuere Klaviermusik." *Die Musik* 12/1 (1912): 38–45.

Rosen, Charles. "Influence: Plagiarism and Inspiration." *19th Century Music* 4 (1980): 87–100.

Schenker, Heinrich. "Brahms: Variationen und Fuge über ein Thema von Handel, op. 24." *Der Tonwille* 8–9 (1924): 3–46.

Schumann, Robert. *On Music and Musicians.* Edited by Konrad Wolff. Translated by Paul Rosenfeld. Berkeley and Los Angeles, 1983.

Tovey, Donald F. *Essays in Musical Analysis: Chamber Music.* London, 1944. Pp. 167–85.

Zemlinsky, Alexander. "Brahms und die neuere Generation: persönliche Erinnerungen." *Musikblätter des Anbruch* 4 (1922): 69–70.

CHAPTER TEN

Expressive Resonance in Liszt's Piano Music

Dolores Pesce

> I only beg for permission to be allowed to decide upon the forms by the contents. . . . In the end it comes principally to this—*what* the ideas are, and *how* they are carried out and worked up—and that leads us always back to the *feeling* and *invention*, if we would not scramble and struggle in the rut of a mere trade. (Letter to Louis Köhler, 9 July 1856, La Mara [trans. Bache], 1: 273–74)

Liszt's words directly address the central issue in a study of his piano works: their unique structural unfolding and the degree to which their form is dependent on the ideas, both musical and extramusical. From the outset of his compositional career Liszt strove to bring about that union of content and form to which the quotation alludes, at first in isolated cases such as the *Harmonies poétiques et religieuses* of 1833, and *Sposalizio* and *Vallée d'Obermann* from the late 1830s. In the case of *Vallée*, Liszt engaged sonata-form principles in his creative struggle, as he would in much of his later piano music, well into the 1870s. But in all three works, he explored to some degree the principle of thematic change, more commonly known as thematic transformation. Generally employed as a unification device (and as an alternative to traditional techniques of thematic development), thematic transformation was exploited by Liszt as a form-defining agent: in Liszt's music, the transformed theme often assumes a structural importance as great as that traditionally given only to the opening material. The result is a fundamentally different kind of approach to form, characterized by a process of organic growth.

Another sort of structural unfolding finds its roots in the *Dante* Sonata (1839, revised 1849) and *Sonnet 47* (ca. 1850) from Book 2 of the *Années de Pèlerinage*. In the introductions of these pieces, Liszt creates fundamental tonal tensions that govern the tonal and structural design as a whole. In later pieces, particularly in several from Book 3 of the *Années*, we encounter a complete transfer of tonal and thematic impetus to the introduction, which now typically contains some motivic and harmonic gesture that Liszt "resolves" at the end of the piece. The concept of content determining form is here made particularly evident, since Liszt purposefully allows the process of resolution to supersede other structural principles, such as thematic return.

In the last decade of his life, Liszt carried even further the idea of generating and unifying a work with an initial fundamental gesture, but now that gesture tends not to be a melodic motive, but rather raw material such as an augmented triad, a tritone, or a whole-tone progression. Significantly, too, that initial gesture now rarely receives resolution. Recognizing the ambivalent status of these elements within the traditional tonal system, Liszt accordingly allowed their nature to determine the form: open-ended. Although these late pieces differ strikingly from the great bulk of Liszt's tonal piano music, there is a shared compositional aesthetic that rests in their structural reliance on opening materials, which appeared earlier as tonally clad melodic motives and now as ambiguity-ridden abstractions.

We turn to the issue of how much "expressive resonance" Liszt attributed to his musical ideas and their resulting forms.[1] The titles of the late, experimental pieces—*En rêve, La lugubre gondola, Unstern,* and others—suggest emotional states of dreamlike suspension, a distancing sorrow, and unrest fueled by apprehension, all states that lack a sense of defined movement. Thus, Liszt's choice of such tonally ambiguous materials as augmented triads and whole-tone progressions seems appropriate; how he manipulates the materials may have expressive significance as well. In some of the open-ended pieces, we find a textural disintegration, suggesting, perhaps, a loss of hope, a resignation. In others, transformation of themes and their redefinition in more stable forms (in at least one case marked *religioso*) suggest spiritual consolation, even though of a momentary nature.

Throughout Liszt's piano compositions certain programmatic ideas drawn from human experience tend to recur. One dominating theme concerns man's reflections on spiritual existence, in both this life and the hereafter, and his search for spiritual consolation, particularly through religion. This theme is especially evident in the major piano cycles that span the years from 1837 to 1885, beginning with the *Années de Pèlerinage,* Book 1. With the exception of the last cycle, the *Historische ungarische Bildnisse,* the arrangement of titled pieces within the cycles suggests to some degree the relative importance Liszt placed on the human and divine in his search for spiritual comfort. Only in the early cycle *Année 1* does nature play a role, although not a transcendent one.

If we concede that the formal ordering of Liszt's cycles produces expressive resonance, the question of how the designs of their individual pieces contribute to that resonance is less easily answered. In Books 1 and 2 of the *Années de Pèlerinage,* as well as in the cycle *Harmonies poétiques et religieuses,* many pieces are essentially variation structures in which primary thematic material is presented in increasingly elaborate textures. However musically effective these pieces are, their use of variation procedures seems to remain independent of any specific extramusical purpose. These relatively early compositions do not seem far removed from Liszt's celebrated piano improvisations in which he excited audiences with his ability to create ever inventive variations on given themes. As we shall see, Liszt's most expressive use of the variation principle arises when he integrates it within a more complex developmental structure, such as the *Dante* Sonata, thus realizing the romantic's desire for isolated reflective moments. To some degree, this same ideal is conveyed by a cycle of a smaller scale such as the *Consolations,* when each miniature piece has its ideas encapsulated for only the briefest moment, quickly to be superseded by another equally reflective but distinct utterance.

As mentioned earlier, already within Books 1 and 2 of the *Années* we find formal designs that depend on thematic transformation or a link between introduction and coda. Both internal and external evidence suggests that Liszt may have associated the first type of formal evolution with the idea of progressing to spiritual calm. As to the second type, more and more prevalent in Book 3, we find little direct expressive purpose for the structural framing. Instead, Liszt seems more concerned with generating a coherent form through long-range tonal tensions and their resolution.

Liszt's sonata-form movements also raise the issue of the relationship between form and expressive content. In such works as the *Dante* Sonata and the *Grosses Konzertsolo,* Liszt developed an approach to sonata form based on the opposition of unstable and stable materials in the exposition, with a move from a restless first theme to a more secure second theme. In a way, the structural emphasis on the second theme is reminiscent of the treatment of transformed themes in the smaller-scaled pieces mentioned earlier, where extramusical, expressive gestures are frequently implied. Although this structural similarity by itself proves nothing, that Liszt's second themes occasionally draw on melodic shapes from themes that in other contexts carry a specific programmatic meaning does suggest that his approach to sonata form might indeed carry an expressive significance. Regrettably, critical research into this aspect of the piano music is still in an early stage. Interpretations of expressive content have generally been invalidated by uncritical speculations. In the case of the Sonata in B minor, for instance, detailed narrative structures have been adduced, even though the evidence is shaky and Liszt almost never wrote narrative programmatic music. The uniqueness of Liszt's music rests in its ability to convey not the surface of human experience but rather its essence, both spiritual and emotional.

The following discussion of Liszt's piano music, by no means comprehensive, surveys such major categories of composition as the cycles, compositions in sonata form, and a selection of works from Liszt's late period. It also examines the études, rhapsodies, ballades, and dance pieces, which show less obviously individualistic approaches to form than the sonatas, but some of which engage the issues of form and expression in significant ways. For example, the *Hungarian Rhapsodies* reveal how Liszt's concern for structural unity occasionally compromised his attempt to recreate the gypsy improvisational spirit. Similarly, the ostensible *raison d'être* of the études—virtuoso display—was allied to the ideal of creating a mood picture. And, the ballades and dance pieces suggest several levels of interpretation, for example, their relationship to Chopinesque models, and, particularly in the case of the ballades, to literary traditions. In the last group to receive some attention here, the fantasias, Liszt embedded his own interpretation of operas into some of the most challenging and idiomatic works ever created for the piano; Busoni judged one "the almost symbolic significance of a pianistic summit."[2]

The Piano Cycles

Années de Pèlerinage, Première Année, Suisse

The first book of the *Années de Pèlerinage* (*Years of Pilgrimage*) was published in 1855, but its contents relate at least in part to an earlier collection that appeared in 1842, the *Album d'un Voyageur* (*Album of a Traveller*). Their relationship provides a glimpse not only of Liszt's habits of revision but also of his changing concept of the piano cycle, and how the progression of individual, titled movements could assume expressive significance.

The *Album* consists of three parts: *Impressions et poésies,* seven titled pieces that became the core of *Année 1; Fleurs mélodiques des Alpes,* nine untitled pieces based on Swiss folk songs or popular art songs (two reappear in *Année 1*); and *Paraphrases,* three arrangements of Swiss airs. Liszt originally published the *Paraphrases* separately in 1836.

The composition of the *Album* apparently began during Liszt's stay in Switzerland in 1835 and 1836, but many pieces may not have been completed until 1837 or 1838, when he was in Italy.[3] Should both the *Album* and *Année 1* then be viewed as musical reflections of Liszt's experiences during his travels through Switzerland? Is *Année 1,* indeed, "a Romantic traveller's itinerary of Swiss sights and sounds and their associations" (Perényi, 128)?

In the *Album* Liszt directly evoked Swiss locales by using folk songs and airs as the basis of both the *Fleurs mélodiques* and *Paraphrases*. But the *Impressions et poésies* are more difficult to ascribe to particular Swiss sources. Of its seven pieces (see Table 10.1) only two contain musical material distinctly associated with Switzerland: *Chapelle de Guillaume Tell,* an alphorn call, and *Psaume,* a Psalter tune written by the sixteenth-century Genevan composer Louis Bourgeois. On the other hand, the epigraphs that Liszt attaches to several of the pieces do have definite Swiss associations: *Au lac de Wallenstadt* and *Les cloches de G****** carry excerpts from canto 3 of Byron's *Childe Harold's Pilgrimage*, in particular that part where the exile travels near the Rhône in Switzerland. *Vallée d'Obermann* draws on three excerpts from Sénancour's *Obermann*, the 1804 epistolary novel whose main character was exiled to Switzerland. The motto of *Chapelle*— "One for all, all for one"—is, of course, that of the Swiss confederacy.

TABLE 10.1. Contents of the *Album* and *Année 1*

Impressions et poésies from *Album d'un voyageur* (1842)	*Années de Pèlerinage—Suisse* (1855)
Lyon	Chapelle de Guillaume Tell
Au lac de Wallenstadt	Au lac de Wallenstadt
Au bord d'une source	Pastorale
Les cloches de G*****	Au bord d'une source
Vallée d'Obermann	Orage
Chapelle de Guillaume Tell	Vallée d'Obermann
Psaume	Eglogue
	Le mal du pays
	Les cloches de Genève

In the Preface to the *Album* Liszt leaves open the possibility that the impressions recorded in his music are not limited to Switzerland, thus justifying somewhat the inclusion of the otherwise anomalous *Lyon*. It is commonly thought that *Lyon* was inspired by the plight of the exploited workers of Lyon, their uprising in 1834, and the support given them by a man Liszt greatly admired, Félicité de Lamennais (Main, 228–43). In the broadest sense, *Lyon* records Liszt's impressions of an oppressed working class. Not surprisingly, then, he rejected the work for *Année 1* when he decided to group together pieces with Swiss associations.

Table 10.1 compares the order of pieces in the *Album* and *Année 1*. In addition to repositioning individual numbers, Liszt added *Pastorale* and *Le mal du pays,* taken from *Fleurs mélodiques* 3 and 2, respectively, and he composed two new pieces, *Orage* and *Eglogue*. Zoltán Gárdonyi points out that Liszt's new scheme orders the pieces in key relationships a major third apart, while Diether Presser argues that the pieces are grouped according to the intensity of their moods, resulting in two symmetrical groups of four separated by the highly dissonant *Orage*.[4] The organization also seems to rely upon certain types of character pieces. In the first half, *Au lac, Pastorale,* and *Au bord* evoke nature impressions. *Au lac* relies most directly on imitative effects: a gently undulating left-hand accompaniment and a melody emphasizing perfect intervals suggest the lake's stillness and the purity of its source. *Au bord,* though more stylized, presents a similar kind of natural setting. *Pastorale,* on the other hand, evokes the specific genre of the pastoral, with its drones and harmonic stasis, as well as cowherd's songs (*Kühreigen*) from Switzerland's Appenzell region.

Liszt places another pastoral, *Eglogue*, in a symmetrical position within the second half (third from either end). *Le mal du pays,* however, is neither a nature piece nor exclusively an example of the more specific pastoral. Cast in an ABA form, its A sections contain a cowherd's song, as does the *Album* version. The B sections of the two works are different: whereas the *Album* version contains dance music of a light character, the *Année 1* version has a variety of contrasting themes and textures—poignant, two-note sigh figures that give way to a lullabylike phrase and then to another expressive lament. The almost capricious flow of these elements and the ever changing tempo indications in the A sections create a restless effect, in keeping with the idea of nostalgia for home.

Orage, Vallée, and *Eglogue* carry evocative epigraphs from Byron's *Childe Harold,* specifically from stanzas 96, 97, and 98 of canto 3. Liszt's music effectively captures the moods of these stanzas: tempestuousness, weariness, and calm. But Byron's subject in these stanzas is the hero's attempt to find answers in nature to his existential unrest—if not definite answers, than at least solace. If this was also Liszt's purpose, then the placement of *Le mal* as well as of *Les cloches* is telling. After the tranquility of the pastoral *Eglogue, Le mal* juxtaposes natural and human elements, yet unrest remains. The final piece, *Les cloches,* seems to symbolize through its pealing bells a higher faith that offers man ultimate solace and resolution. Indeed, the melody of its new middle section written for *Année 1* begins with almost the exact rhythm (♩♩. ♪ ♩♩) found in the theme of the tumultuous *Orage* (♩♩ ↻ ♪ ♩♩), though it is now clothed in a *cantabile* guise, with "l'accompagnamento dolce, quasi arpa."

Chapelle de Guillaume Tell also has a religious subject. Its primary theme appears in a sketchbook, which Liszt used from 1829 to 1833, with the title *Hymn* (Torkewitz, 27–30); in the *Album* version, the theme is marked *religioso*. What is more, that version carries the motto "One for all, all for one" and the title as they appear in *Année 1*. As early as 1842, then, Liszt patently acknowledged a religious component in a piece dealing with a social issue: unity of the people against oppression. Liszt did remove the marking *religioso* from *Année 1*, yet changed the final cadence from I-vi-I to I-IV-I, that is, to a plagal cadence laden with religious associations.

Liszt also changed the rhythm of the head motive of *Chapelle*, so that in *Année 1*, its rhythm (♩♩.. ♪ ♩.) relates to the head motive of *Orage* and *Les cloches* mentioned above. This is clearly a unifying device, musically as well as programmatically. (Note that the three motivically related pieces are positioned at the beginning, middle, and end of the cycle.) The hero of *Chapelle*, motivated by a religious fervor, is presented in conflict with earthly power. Though the next three pieces focus on the tranquility of nature, the Byronic passages first introduced in *Orage* reveal man in an inner turmoil, seeking and finding respite in nature. The traveler in a state of unrest returns in *Le mal du pays*, after which the work concludes with *Les cloches,* subtitled "Nocturne."[5] If *Les cloches* can be interpreted to symbolize a higher faith, then Liszt's *Année 1* represents more than a travelog of Swiss sights and sounds. Its order and typology of pieces suggest a spiritual journey as well.[6]

TABLE 10.2. Thematic Design of *Vallée d'Obermann*

	Exposition		Development	Recapitulation	Coda
m.	1	75	119	170	204
	initial idea	transformed version	(of basic 3-note motive from initial idea)	transformed version	remnants of initial idea

We cannot leave *Année 1* without looking briefly at its most complex piece, *Vallée d'Obermann*. Table 10.2 demonstrates how thematic transformation is applied within a sonata structure. While this schematic view reveals how the transformed theme assumes structural importance in the recapitulation, it fails to show how volatile even that material remains under Liszt's treatment (for the initial idea and transformed version, see Example 10.1a–b). Symptomatic of Liszt's emphasis on change are the penetration of chromatic pitches into the transformed version only twenty measures after it first sounds, the rhythmic modification in its recapitulation, and its extension at measure 184 by a motive that wavers between E minor and G major.

This treatment is significant for any interpretation that the lighter, *dolcissimo* character of the transformed theme counteracts the gloomy tone of the original idea, as if to suggest a spiritual resolution. Such an argument seems appropriate in another piece, *Harmonies poétiques et religieuses* (1833), where the transformed material is accompanied by the

EXAMPLE 10.1a. Liszt, *Vallée d'Obermann*. Initial idea (mm.1–4)

EXAMPLE 10.1b. Liszt, *Vallée d'Obermann.* Transformed version (mm. 75–78)

words *Andante religioso* and the literary source speaks of the solace that comes to those who pray. In *Vallée,* nothing in the score or literary excerpts justifies August Stradal's view that the transformed theme reveals "the later Liszt, who in all gloomy circumstances designates religion as a shelter" (Stradal, 297). Undeniably, Liszt constantly manipulates mood, for which justification can be found in the two Sénancour fragments and Byron quotation that preface the work. Their essential mood is one of world-weariness, but woven into the existential inquiry of Sénancour's speaker are thoughts of sensual ecstasy and "the allurement of a fantastical world."[7] Thus, the ethereal quality of Liszt's transformed theme emanates from a literary impulse, and one more dimension is added to the spiritual journey embodied in this cycle.[8]

Années de Pèlerinage, Deuxième Année, Italie

Just as Liszt's visit to Switzerland inspired *Année 1,* so his travels to Italy (1837–39) produced several works eventually published in 1858 as part of *Année 2.* The pieces of this collection directly relate to artwork or poetry by Italian masters, including Raphael, Michelangelo, Salvator Rosa, Dante, and Petrarch. Ingres, whom Liszt met during his stay in Rome, idolized Raphael; Liszt, it seems, was particularly intrigued by Raphael's *St. Cecilia.*[9] Michelangelo's painting and sculpture dominate both Rome and Florence, and it was this artist whom Liszt considered "the austere and sublime hero of art."[10] The seventeenth-century painter and poet Salvator Rosa, who led an especially colorful life, was the subject of numerous nineteenth-century operas, by such composers as Rastrelli,

Raimondi, and Sobolewski. A virtual Dante cult flourished in France, spurred by the writings of Chateaubriand and Madame de Staël. As for Petrarch, Liszt was on friendly terms with one of the poet's most ardent admirers in France, the literary critic Sainte-Beuve.

The titles of Liszt's works from 1838 and 1839, including *Année 2*, suggest a preoccupation with two subjects—love and death. Love figures in *Sposalizio,* the *Canzonetta,* and the *Petrarch Sonnets* from *Année 2,* while death plays a role in *Il Penseroso* and the *Dante* Sonata, as well as in two major works sketched in 1839—*Malédiction* and *Totentanz.*

Liszt's concern with the subject of death at the close of the 1830s is noteworthy, since at this time he was intimately involved with Marie d'Agoult. We are reminded that the romantic period idealized love as a transcendent, otherworldly state that could bring one to a higher philosophical or theological truth; so could reflection on death. In *Année 2* Liszt apparently attempted to suggest the relationship between an earthly and transcendent existence. Certainly the framing movements, *Sposalizio* and the *Dante* Sonata, suggest this point of departure. Raphael's *Betrothal of the Virgin* pictures Mary in the most human of actions, yet with a demeanor that has inevitably been described as "celestial" and "divine." The *Dante* Sonata is of course linked to Dante's *Divine Comedy,* though the precise relationship is unclear. Liszt eventually named the Sonata after Victor Hugo's poem "Après une lecture de Dante," which points to the *Inferno*[11] where Dante confronts the hereafter in its most horrible form; the message conveyed is that man's earthly trangressions will be dealt with in the afterlife. But the *Divine Comedy* and, in turn, Liszt's Sonata also suggest the power of love: Dante's Beatrice is an intercessor whose love makes it possible for the poet to experience the true revelation, God. Significantly, the *Dante* Sonata immediately follows the three *Petrarch Sonnets,* the last of which, *I' vidi in terra,* describes the loved one (Petrarch's Laura) as an angelic creature whose sweet words move even heaven. Furthermore, the Sonata contains several ethereal passages that recall the tender love evocations of the Sonnets; one passage (m. 157) even carries the words "con amore."

Il Penseroso, the second piece of the collection, was named after Michelangelo's sculpture before the tomb of Lorenzo de' Medici in Florence. Many have seen in Lorenzo's image a portrayal of existence beyond the grave, of the soul contemplating the supreme truth. Thus, the sources for the outer pieces of *Année 2*—*Sposalizio, Il Penseroso, I' vidi in terra* and the *Dante* Sonata—describe transcendent states of being and love. In contrast, the texts that inspired the middle pieces, the *Canzonetta* and the first two *Petrarch Sonnets,* describe the emotions of physical love and desire. Thus, in *Année 2,* Liszt again orders his pieces according to an expressive purpose; here, the progression emphasizes transcendent experiences that are related to the human experience of love.

The cyclic nature of these pieces is evident by a clear tonal plan:

Sposalizio	*Penseroso*	*Canzonetta*	*Sonnet*			*Dante* Sonata
			47	104	123	
E	c♯	A	D♭	E	A♭	d/D

The first six pieces unfold a descending and ascending series of third relationships. Significantly, for the 1858 publication Liszt altered the keys of
the three Sonnets, originally conceived in 1843–45[12] as songs in A-flat major (in the order nos. 104, 47, 123); this change clearly strengthened the
overall tonal plan. The D tonality of the *Dante* Sonata stands apart in a
tritone relation to the A-flat of *Sonnet 123,* a clear allusion to its infernal
subject matter; yet here too there is a significant musical link: the final
pitch of *Sonnet 123,* A-flat, serves as a reinterpreted leading tone (G-
sharp) to the first pitch of the Sonata, which begins on its dominant A.

Though analyses for several pieces in *Année 2* are available[13]—we
shall return to the *Dante* Sonata later—little attention has been directed to
Sonnet 47, where we can find the incipient use of an introduction to generate a large-scale tonal design. Example 10.2a summarizes how the introductory motif is preceded by a prolongation of an A-major sonority, so
that a third relationship is established with the tonic D-flat. The directional force of this initial gesture is later felt in the climactic appearance of
the pitch A at measure 49 (within a D-major statement of the main theme),
and then in the oscillation between the keys of D-flat and A from measures
69 to 85. Furthermore, the melodic gesture A (B♭♭)-A♭-B♭-A♭ generated
in the opening is later complemented by a linear statement in measure 89
before the final tonic affirmation (Example 10.2a–b). As we shall see, the
introductory gesture becomes more and more critical for the overall design of Liszt's later, tonally more experimental works.

EXAMPLE 10.2a. Liszt, *Sonnet 47*. Introductory materials

EXAMPLE 10.2b. Liszt, *Sonnet 47*. Concluding melodic gesture

Consolations

Composed in the 1840s and published in 1850, the six pieces in this set were evidently grouped under the general title *Consolations* from an 1830 collection of poems by Sainte-Beuve that expresses "themes of hope as yet unfulfilled."[14] Liszt's pieces, cast in diminutive proportions, are lyrical miniatures that stand apart from his other piano music. Each piece is spun from one basic theme or motive; whatever contrasts occur are generally textural or harmonic. The cohesiveness of the set as a whole is ensured by certain tonal emphases and shared melodic gestures. For instance, the melodies of nos. 3 and 4 share a stepwise descending third. Similarly, nos. 5 and 6 begin with the interval G♯-C♯; E is a tonal focus in each case.

Although a lyrical tone pervades the pieces, Liszt imbues them with distinctive characters. The chordal nos. 1 and 4 are the most contemplative and prayerlike (no. 4 actually has the designation *cantabile con divozione*). No. 3 is a nocturne evidently based on Chopin's op. 27 no. 2, also in D-flat major; no. 5 evokes the character of a Schubert impromptu. The final, more ambitiously drawn piece may have been inspired by Sainte-Beuve's twenty-seventh poem, "La Harpe Éolienne"; it is animated almost throughout with rolled chords that create the effect of strumming.

Harmonies poétiques et religieuses

The conception of this cycle dates from 1834, when Liszt said of his new composition *Harmonies poétiques et religieuses*, "I shall first publish it alone, and later I shall write half a dozen."[15] "Later" was not until 1845, when Liszt began to sketch the cycle; many of the pieces, numbering ten, not six, took final form only between 1847 and 1852, and the cycle was published in 1853. Part of its expansion resulted from Liszt's inclusion of four pieces originally conceived for chorus: *Pater noster* and *Ave Maria* of 1846, and *Miserere d'après Palestrina* and *Hymne de l'enfant à son réveil* of about 1847. While the first three are traditional prayers of the Church, *Hymne* draws its text from Lamartine's collection of poems entitled *Harmonies poétiques et religieuses*, the very collection that had attracted Liszt in 1833. In addition to *Hymne, Invocation, Bénédiction de Dieu dans la solitude, Pensée des morts* (the revised version of the 1833 *Harmonies poétiques et religieuses*), and the untitled *Andante lagrimoso* relate to the poems in Lamartine's collection: all but *Pensée* are headed by poetic excerpts. Of the remainder of the cycle, *Funérailles* carries the date October 1849 and was apparently written by Liszt as a funeral tribute to some Hungarian compatriots who had died in the 1848–49 War of Independence.[16] The extramusical associations of the final piece, *Cantique d'amour,* are unclear.

Thus, the 1853 cycle included a mixture of pieces, five of which bore no direct relation to the Lamartine source. In the preface to his volume of poetry Lamartine explained that he wished to depict various emotional states experienced in meditating about God and the wonders of the universe.[17] In the piano cycle, Liszt quoted a part of the preface addressed to the poet's audience, those contemplative souls who turn their entire existence into a prayer and those troubled souls who suffer even as they meditate. The latter, Lamartine desired, would be visited by a Muse, to whose harmonies they would reply, "We pray with thy words, we weep with thy tears, we invoke with thy songs!"[18]

Eleanor Perényi accuses Liszt of misleading this audience since "[t]he piano does not weep or wail" (Perényi, 47). But Liszt was not after mere imitative devices, in which he indulged only rarely. Rather, he attempted to evoke the general emotional states described in Lamartine's preface. The mood of the soul-searcher on the brink of despair is captured in *Pensée des morts* and in *Andante lagrimoso*, whose text begins "Tombez, larmes silencieuses, sur une terre sans pitié." Intensifying this gloomy mood is the presence of two similar pieces before *Andante lagrimoso*, *Funérailles* and *Miserere*. Lamartine's other emotional state, a kind of contemplative ecstasy in which self-awareness is inextricably bound to faith in God, is evoked in Liszt's *Invocation* and *Bénédiction*; the latter has been described as "almost unique among Liszt's works in that it expresses that feeling of mystical contemplation which Beethoven attained in his last period" (Searle, 1954: 55).

Other pieces in the cycle suggest the backdrop of Christian ceremony (*Pater noster*, *Ave Maria*, and *Miserere*) and a longing for the return of childhood faith (*Hymne de l'enfant à son réveil*). The only enigma is the final *Cantique d'amour*. Although Liszt's allusion is ambiguous, the context of the cycle suggests that the intent is love of God, which accords with Lamartine's treatment of love in his cycle of poems.

Several pieces assume large-scale proportions, offering an opportunity to examine Liszt's approach to formal organization during this period (ca. 1845–52). *Invocation*, *Miserere*, and *Cantique* involve multiple presentations of thematic material in gradually expanding textures of sound. In *Bénédiction* and *Funérailles* another sort of structure emerges. Each work contains three thematic elements, each with its distinctive character and tempo; the composite form is A B C A' B' C' where B' and C' signal abbreviated returns and A' signals a more expansive texture. The effect of each piece, however, is quite different.

In *Bénédiction*, A' is self-contained, its sense of closure reinforced by an extended arpeggiation alternating between V and I. Consequently, the subsequent appearance of C' and B' functions more as a coda that lends harmonic confirmation than as a recall of earlier sections. In *Funérailles*, A' appears as a culmination, but Liszt continues onward through a reduced B' to C', the march material whose explosive eight-measure unfolding provides the true culmination. Possibly the prominence of the march theme has expressive significance: triumphant, patriotic expectations despite the recent defeat of the revolution. There may be a musical explanation why these three sections work together as a whole. R. Larry Todd has suggested the fundamental importance of two augmented triads (C-E-A♭ and D♭-F-A) which operate on melodic, harmonic, and tonal levels of the piece. In the A section, the usage is melodic and harmonic; in B, primarily harmonic; and in C, part of the tonal plan of the work (Todd, 1988: 98–101).

Another, fundamentally different construction underlies *Hymne* and *Pensée*; they are essentially bipartite, with a slow section placed in the second position. In *Hymne,* a generative process gradually links the two sections until their fundamental motives, melodic and rhythmic, are blended. In *Pensée des morts* the two major sections contain materials with common contours: thus, the opening A gesture of a stepwise descending third is taken up as a motive in B, and the repeated-note recitation of "De profundis" in section A is echoed in the opening of the B Adagio theme. Only in the coda of the Adagio do we hear actual reminiscences of A's opening texture of repeated chords against stark, stepwise thirds. Liszt strengthens this link by making the reminiscence a harmonic complement of the opening: the third A-G-F♯ is answered by the third E♭-D-C; taken together, they outline the diminished seventh that opens the work and leads to its final pitch, G.

Significantly, the 1833 version of *Pensée* (entitled *Harmonies poétiques et religieuses*) reveals an especially tight bond between the two sections: the theme of its B section, labeled *Andante religioso,* is related to a motive from section A, which Dieter Torkewitz has labeled *Lebewohl,* on account of its resemblance to the opening of Beethoven's *Lebewohl* Sonata op. 81a. In turn, the *Lebewohl* motive is a variant of the *Pendelmotiv* with which the piece begins, so-called because the descending third is mirrored by a symmetrical ascent (Example 10.3a–c gives the three motives).[19] These three motives of *Harmonies* remain distinct even as they are related and thus anticipate Liszt's later, more extensive usage of thematic transformation.

In the final version of *Pensée* Liszt discarded the *Andante religioso* and added an independent Adagio for the B section. Section A now assumed slightly larger proportions through the insertion of a harmonized recitation of Psalm 129 (its superimposed text, "De profundis," recalls Lamartine's poem, *Pensée des morts,* in which God is addressed as the poet reflects on death). Example 10.4a–b shows that Liszt's addition of the psalm facilitates a new harmonic design: the psalm is presented in E-flat major, after which the tonal focus eventually shifts to a B sonority in a coda that recalls the texture and motives of the opening. Liszt's unification of the new tonal plan is striking. In the expanded cadenza leading to the "De profundis," he introduces an augmented triad, emphasized in a thunderous, climactic fashion. The closing phrase of the psalm appears in keys outlining an augmented sonority, E-flat, G, and B. What is more, the tonal areas of the psalm, coda, and Adagio outline the same augmented triad, which also functions conspicuously as a passing chord in the Adagio (m. 141) and

EXAMPLE 10.3. Liszt, *Harmonies poétiques et religieuses* (1833). Related motives (mm. 1–2, 5–6, and 63–67)

then as an accented neighbor chord in its coda (m. 166), where, significantly, it takes the place of the diminished-seventh chord that had previously accompanied the *Pendelmotiv*.

EXAMPLE 10.4a. Liszt, *Harmonies poétiques et religieuses* (1833). Tonal reduction

a.   End of Section A   *Andante religioso*

EXAMPLE 10.4b. Liszt, *Pensée des morts*. Tonal reduction

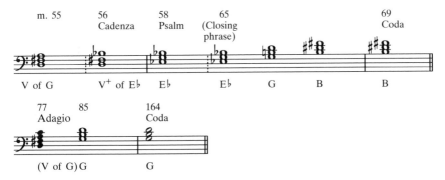

It is not so unusual that Liszt's piano music of the 1840s and 1850s displays prominent third-related tonalities. *Bénédiction*, for example, progresses through the keys F-sharp, D, B-flat, and F-sharp. What is unusual, however, is the coupling of this linear progression with an augmented triad as a basic unifying device, such as in *Pensée des morts*. The extramusical associations of works with noteworthy melodic, harmonic, and structural treatments of augmented triads suggest that Liszt viewed the sonority as a topical symbol, often for death.[20]

Liszt "took greatest pleasure in playing [the cycle *Harmonies*] to his friends in later years, when he had retired from public activity" (Searle, 1954: 55). Certainly its religious tone was in keeping with the spiritual quest that led to Liszt's affiliation with the Church. The same feature may explain, perhaps, why this is the least appreciated of Liszt's cycles: pieces such as *Bénédiction* and *Hymne*, which exude spiritual warmth, are boldly juxtaposed with prayers of the Roman Church, unmistakably stark, chantlike intonations. Subtle overtones become explicit utterances. And we must concede that the cycle is of an inconsistent quality: while *Bénédiction* and *Funérailles* provide examples of Liszt's most exquisite and powerful writing, *Invocation* and *Andante lagrimoso* seem almost perfunctory. Still, Liszt succeeded in creating a musical cycle, not just a collection of pieces with related programmatic associations. Significantly, every piece utilizes in some way a stepwise third: as an essential motive, an accompanimental figure, or, indeed, as a kind of *Urlinie*. In addition, Liszt subjects the third to what Carl Dahlhaus has called *Alternativ-Chroma*, or chromatic alterations (Dahlhaus, 86–87). For example, the motive D-C-B is reworked thus:

Ave Maria	D	C	B♭			
Hymne	D♭	C	B♭			
Miserere	D	C	B			
Cantique	D♯	C♯	B	⟶ D	C♯	B

In short, the cycle is unified not only through the gesture of the third, but more strikingly through Liszt's chromatic manipulation of the gesture.

Années de Pèlerinage, Troisième Année

Liszt composed the third book of the *Années* between 1867 and 1877, the period when he traveled regularly to Rome, Budapest, and Weimar; it was published in 1883. Three of its pieces have titles that refer to the Villa d'Este, a castle in Tivoli where Liszt resided during his sojourns in Rome. In *Les jeux d'eaux à la Villa d'Este* he created a nature impression, just as he had forty years earlier in his *Au lac de Wallenstadt.* The other two works, titled *Aux cyprès de la Villa d'Este*, refer to the ancient cypresses on the Villa's grounds. Subtitled *Thrénodie*, they call forth the tree's ancient association with death and mourning.[21] This association is revived in two other threnodies of the cycle: *Sunt lacrymae rerum*, originally titled *Thrénodie hongroise* in reference to Hungary's defeat in the 1848–49 War of Independence; and *Marche funèbre*, in memory of the slain Mexican emperor Maximilian I. In the *Aeneid* Aeneas utters the phrase "Sunt lacrymae rerum" as he reflects that his struggle to find a homeland for the Trojans is not finished.[22] Clearly, the parallel with Hungary was not lost on Liszt. He again turned to classical poetry for the inscription to the *Marche*: "In magnis et voluisse sat est."[23] Here Propertius muses on his ability to write a paean to Caesar Augustus's victories; Liszt may have attached the sentiment to Maximilian's failed monarchy or to his own musical homage.

The remaining three pieces of the cycle suggest the idea of spiritual reconciliation. The cycle opens with *Angelus! Prière aux anges gardiens* and closes with the *Sursum corda* ("Lift up your hearts"), which opens the Preface to the Mass. The framing of the cycle by these two prayers is complemented by a scriptural quotation that Liszt placed at the center of *Les jeux*, which falls exactly in the middle of the collection: "sed aqua, quam ego dabo ei, fiet in eo fons aquae salientis in vitam aeternam" ("but the water that I shall give him shall be in him a well of water springing up into everlasting life" *John* 4:14). For Liszt, the fountains of the Villa d'Este symbolized spiritual consolation. Thus, we can interpret the entire cycle as a spiritual journey initiated by Liszt's reflections on death and fueled by his belief in God. There is also evidence that his native Hungary played a role in this "year of pilgrimage."[24]

In its style *Année 3* departs considerably from the *Harmonies*. The virtuosic piano writing of the 1840s and 1850s has almost vanished, although the wonderfully atmospheric effects of *Les jeux* make their own considerable technical demands. Declamatory, speechlike passages now occur frequently, in unison or with only sparse accompaniment. Though they can be viewed as illustrative of Liszt's new interest in reduced textures, their typically plaintive tone suggests the composer's preoccupation with the topic of death, for example, in *Sunt lacrymae, Marche funèbre,* and *Aux cyprès 2.*

But in its harmonic and tonal language *Année 3* shows the greatest departure from Liszt's style of the 1850s. An increased use of dissonance is readily apparent, as in *Les jeux,* with its streams of ninth chords that influenced Debussy and other twentieth-century composers, and pungent neighbor chords (Example 10.5a). The opening of *Aux cyprès 2* (Example 10.5b), reminiscent of the Vorspiel to Wagner's *Tristan und Isolde,* demonstrates the hyperchromatic idiom that Liszt habitually explored in his late years. Similarly, pentatonic, whole-tone scales, and other nonmajor/minor scales—occasionally found in Liszt's earlier music—now come to the fore. *Sunt lacrymae* uses both the "Hungarian" ("gypsy") scale and another Hungarian scale known as the *kalindra. Aux cyprès 1* displays a tetrachord that István Szelényi has called "Locrian minor" (semitone-tone-semitone).[25] In each case, the influence of these unusual scalar formations is evident in Liszt's primary motives.

In several pieces of *Année 3* Liszt generates tonal and formal plans from introductory materials, a device he had used in *Année 2.* A good example is *Aux cyprès 2.* This piece opens with the chromatic motive of Example 10.5b (see also Example 10.6), suggesting the tonality of E minor. But at measure 7 the second important tonal focus, A♯ (= B♭), begins to surface, and the conflict between these tritone-related tonalities is thus established already in the introduction. (The two tones are also contained

EXAMPLE 10.5a. Liszt, *Les jeux d'eaux* (mm. 46–49)

EXAMPLE 10.5b. Liszt, *Aux cyprès 2* (mm. 1–2)

within the diminished seventh E-G-B♭-D♭ (= C♯) of measure 26, a core symmetrical structure that unifies the piece.) Example 10.6 shows the melodic movement (B♭-C-D♭, in black notes) that leads to theme A at measure 31, which then mirrors that movement through its sequential presentation in D♭ major, C minor, and B♭ major, the last presented *ff* and *grandioso*. The movement from this B♭ focal point to the ultimate resolution in E major is long delayed, but in the presentation of theme B, E is touched upon during a symmetrical progression, first to C♯ at measure 92, then to E at measure 132, after which there is a tonally ambiguous progression. When theme A reappears, inverted in the bass against tremolos in the treble (m. 162), it is reasserted in the keys of D♭, C minor, and B♭, and B♭ is reemphasized. Thematic return is not accompanied by tonal resolution, but instead a circular motion has in effect taken place: (D♭)-B♭-C♯-E-D♭-B♭, thus perpetuating the tritone relationship.

At measure 192 the material from the introduction returns, leading to the harmonic progression shown in Example 10.6 (cf. mm. 26–29). Note how enharmonic respellings (through an augmented triad) play a role in the subtly changing chromatic progressions. But more significantly, from measure 192 onward, melodic movement at two registral levels leads to the true dominant pitch B-natural in measure 225 (circled half notes, G♯-A-B-C♯-B) and also to E in measure 226 (shown in the rising line of black notes from B♭ to E). Although the tritone B♭-E has thus been "resolved," Liszt toys with an oscillation between E and C♯ minor (the latter the dividing pitch of the tritone) during an appended *piano* statement of the arpeggiated chords that had introduced theme B (m. 226). He concludes in a final master stroke with the opening, unaccompanied motive, now firmly entrenched in its E-major guise. To sum up, what directs this piece is the melodic and tonal development and resolution of the opening motive. Consequently, a new sort of form emerges, in which the coda does not serve, as it traditionally has, to confirm a tonic already established, but instead becomes itself the area of resolution.

With *Sunt lacrymae rerum*, we turn to the most adventuresome of Liszt's experiments in generating long-range tonal tensions from introductory materials. Here Liszt bases the introduction on a *kalindra* scale,

EXAMPLE 10.6. Liszt, *Aux cyprès 2*. Melodic and tonal reduction

identified by its two augmented seconds (Example 10.7a–b). But rather than play upon the scale's two obvious focal points, D and A, he sets up tonal poles at A and C-sharp, using G-sharp as their respective leading tone and dominant. Thus, the passage assumes a tonal uncertainty. The plaintive main theme (m. 10) directly derives from the opening and is stated first on A, then C-sharp, though it now uses the Hungarian scale. C-sharp retains prominence as D-flat when it accompanies in measure 19 a new dancelike figure suggestive of the Hungarian *verbunkos*.[26] Liszt then initiates a chromatic sliding passage followed by entrances of the plaintive main theme (now fragmented) on F-G-A-B-C♯; the passage does not come to rest until measure 57, where he introduces a second theme, related melodically to the *verbunkos* figure, but with a distinctive *cantabile* character (Example 10.7c). Dorothea Redepenning has discovered the same theme in several Liszt works that deal with mourning, lament, and Hungarian topics: she calls it a "heroic-*cantabile* melody type" (Redepenning, 178–79). The second theme appears in A major, though several chromatic pitches tend to weaken its tonal stability.

In measure 101, the motive of the opening (F-E-C♯) reappears in elaborated form, and the A/C♯ dichotomy of the *kalindra* scale is renewed.

EXAMPLE 10.7a. Liszt, *Sunt lacrymae rerum.* Scale forms

EXAMPLE 10.7b. Liszt, *Sunt lacrymae rerum.* Introduction (mm. 1–8)

EXAMPLE 10.7c. Liszt, *Sunt lacrymae rerum*. Second theme (mm. 57–62)

At measure 123, a final unexpected twist: C-sharp octaves are followed by an F-sharp major chord, which then alternates with an A major chord for ten measures; A major is the final sonority heard. But throughout the thirty-three measures of this coda-like section—again the point of resolution—there is no systematic preparation for A major. Nevertheless, that unexpected alternation between F-sharp and A is part of a larger tonal plan for *Année 3*. The elusive A of *Sunt lacrymae* is surrounded by two pieces in F-sharp, *Les jeux* and *Marche funèbre*.

Historische ungarische Bildnisse

More threnodies flooded from Liszt's pen during the final twenty years of his life. His last cycle, *Historical Hungarian Portraits*, comprises seven elegies in homage to various Hungarian statesmen or artists (Table 10.3). Liszt finished the series by 1885, though some of the pieces originated in the early 1870s; the cycle was published only in 1956.

TABLE 10.3. Contents of the *Historische ungarische Bildnisse*[27]

1	*Stephan Széchenyi*	statesman and writer
2	*Joseph Eötvös*	statesman and writer
3	*Michael Vörösmarty*	writer
4	*Ladislaus Teleki*	statesman and writer
5	*Franz Deák*	statesman and writer
6	*Alexander Petöfi*	writer
7	*Michael Mosonyi*	composer

Liszt relied heavily upon Hungarian musical materials in this work. Thus, nos. 1, 5, and 7 all utilize the Hungarian scale on D. In addition, in no. 4, Liszt borrowed a four-note ostinato, used by Michael Mosonyi in a *Funeral Song* (1860) on the death of Széchenyi, that forms a segment of the Hungarian scale on G (Redepenning, 230). Other Hungarian-influenced scale forms common in Liszt's later period include the Aeolian with raised fourth and major with lowered sixth of *Petöfi* (no. 6), and the Locrian tetrachord of *Eötvös* (no. 2, m. 44). In several cases, Liszt exploited these materials to establish tonal ambivalences, both on the local and larger levels. Thus, in the first two-thirds of *Ladislaus Teleki* (no. 4), Liszt maintains tonal ambiguity by sustaining an ostinato derived from a Hungarian scale (Example 10.8), whose unsure leaning toward G is further weakened by a series of counterposed, oscillating chromatic motives. After they culminate in measure 53, the ostinato's final tone, C-sharp, gradually becomes the tonal focus, largely through a technique of repetition.[28] Notwithstanding the key signature, no functional tonal relationship operates in this piece apart from the fifth separating the tones F-sharp and C-sharp within the ostinato (emphasized only toward the end).

EXAMPLE 10.8. Liszt, *Ladislaus Teleki*. Ostinato (mm. 1–5)

In addition to Hungarian scales, Liszt injects into this collection dancelike rhythms, dotted anticipation figures, and a plaintive *cantabile* flavor, all associated with Hungarian music. In four cases (nos. 1, 3, 5, 6), the basic theme appears first in minor, then, after further presentations at different pitch levels, in major.[29] Dorothea Redepenning suggests that Liszt used both the simple themes and their direct minor/major treatment to invoke not only a musical past, but also Hungarian history, which explains his title *Historical Hungarian Portraits*. For Redepenning, each *Portrait* should be experienced as an example of *Erinnerungsmusik*; Liszt frames each piece with "abstract" material, unthematic in character and tonally vague, from which the distinct portrait emerges (Redepenning, 228–29). Thus, the introductory and concluding sections do not structurally determine individual pieces, but rather function to connect and unify them. Her point is well taken if we consider the intervals of the fifth and sixth which appear in a number of the pieces: these bell-like tolling figures of mourning have little to do with the principal melodic contours of the portraits. (Illustration 10.1 shows that Liszt added the introductory eighteen measures to *Vörösmarty* as an afterthought.) Still, we should not summarily dismiss the structural significance of the framing materials. For example, in no. 2, the motive E-F♯-G♯ of the opening section (mm. 1–43)

ILLUSTRATION 10.1. Liszt, *Historische ungarische Bildnisse* No. 3: *Michael Vörös-marty,* Introduction. Autograph, Rosenthal Collection, Music Division, Library of Congress, Washington, D.C.

returns in the closing section (mm. 84–104) with an A-sharp attached, the very tone that forms the melodic climax of the lyrical middle section. Even as these opening and closing sections "frame" Liszt's memory, they are integrally bound to it.

What is more, Liszt carefully manipulates the framing materials to ensure tonal coherence. For example, the final tone of no. 5 (B-flat) is embedded in the opening tetrachord of no. 6 (Example 10.9), thus establish-

EXAMPLE 10.9. Liszt, *Alexander Petöfi*. Opening tetrachords (mm. 1–8)

ing a link between the two, even though that opening has no tonal significance for no. 6.[30] More striking is the ending of no. 3: though this *Portrait* is firmly in b/B throughout, its final eleven measures slide to G, preparing that pitch to become the focus of the ostinato for no. 4. These harmonically nonfunctional, at times tonally ambiguous passages remind us that Liszt continued to explore the limits of his tonal language even as he invoked the spirit of his Hungarian background.

Compositions in Sonata Form

The *Dante* Sonata, *Grosses Konzertsolo,* and Sonata in B Minor exemplify Liszt's contributions to the nineteenth-century piano sonata. They all date from around 1850, the period when Liszt also worked out his approach to sonata form in the symphonic poems,[31] and they share stylistic features not only among themselves but also with the symphonic poems. All three employ sonata principles in some sort of continuous one-movement form. This feature would seem to argue against frequent attempts to claim Schubert's *Wanderer* Fantasy (D. 760) as a primary influence on the Sonata in B minor; the Fantasy uses almost exclusively variation principles. On the other hand, Beethoven's late piano sonatas stretch the limits of sonata form to achieve new unions of form and content, a procedure that Liszt emulated. In fact, in a letter of 2 December 1852 to Wilhelm von Lenz, Liszt described this feature in Beethoven's music; in the letter of 9 July 1856 to Louis Köhler cited at the beginning of this chapter Liszt claimed the union of form and content as his own ideal (La Mara/Bache, 1: 152, 273–74). In the broadest sense, then, the three piano works represent a Beethovenian legacy.

All three works open with relatively unstable melodic material; "idea" thus determines form, for in each case the lack of tonic focus at the outset affects the balance of the resulting form. Since in the exposition the secondary section is thematically more stable than the opening section, Liszt treats the secondary area as the most significant point of arrival in the recapitulation. Hence, in Liszt's approach, the climax occurs later than its traditional location at the end of the development or the onset of the recapitulation.

A second feature of all three works, one partially related to the delay of tonal stability, is the appearance of a slow section or quasi-movement near the midpoints (see Tables 10.4, 10.5, and 10.6). In the *Dante* Sonata (Table 10.4), the Andante section occurs relatively early at measure 115, immediately after the statement of the second theme in F-sharp major. Joan Backus argues that, despite the apparent tonal focus on F-sharp, the Andante contains some points of tonal flux whereby the second theme reaches true tonal stability only with its more tranquil, relatively more diatonic reappearance at measure 136 (*ben marcato il canto*).[32] The first theme, moreover, eventually reappears in a diatonic guise within the Andante (m. 167). Thus, Liszt sustains subtle tonal tensions throughout this section of "reflective thematic variation and metamorphosis" (Backus, 112). The work's subtitle, *Fantasia quasi Sonata*, reinforces the idea that Liszt sought a kind of quasi-improvisatory interlude, or interruption, before the development (see also his direction *quasi improvvisato* at m. 124).

TABLE 10.4. *Dante* Sonata

Exposition			Andante		
tritone motive	chromatic theme 1	unstable theme 2	tritone motive	chromatic theme 1	stable theme 2
modulatory	d	F♯	modulatory	V of F♯	F♯
m. 1	35	103 *fff*	115	124	136

		Development		Recapitulation	
chromatic theme 1	diatonic theme 1	based on tritone motive		chromatic theme 1	stable theme 2
I$^6_4$(F♯)	F♯	modulatory	(A♭)	V of d	D
157	167	181	211	273	306 *fff*

Coda				
tritone motive	chromatic theme 1	diatonic theme 1	chromatic theme 1	tritone motive resolved
modulatory	D⎯			⎯
318	327	339	353	370 *ff*

In the *Konzertsolo* (Table 10.5), Liszt added an *Andante sostenuto* as an afterthought; the section is lacking in the autograph manuscript of the original version (Weimar Liszt Archives; see Searle, 1954: 57). By adding the Andante, Liszt sought to provide contrast, for its melodic content is largely new; in addition, the section reinforces the sense of delayed tonal stability. When theme 2 appears in the mediant key (G) at measure 102, its sense of arrival is quickly deflected by the new Andante material that follows in D-flat major. When theme 2 resumes in G major after the Andante interlude (m. 235), its stability is again undermined by a recall and elaboration of developmental passages heard *before* the earlier G-major statement of measure 102. The tonic E minor is subsequently reestablished, but significantly, the opening thematic group does not return in the "recapitulation"; rather, theme 2, the *grandioso* element in the first part, constitutes the point of reentry. Whereas in the *Dante* Sonata the climactic appearance of theme 2 occurs in the recapitulation, in the *Konzertsolo* it occupies the coda with two texturally expanding statements in E major. And here we encounter a weakness in the *Konzertsolo*: because the earlier appearance of theme 2 in G is not firmly anchored, the extended treat-

TABLE 10.5. *Grosses Konzertsolo*

Exposition			
thematic group 1 = opening motives	theme 2 (*patetico*)	development of opening motives	theme 2 (*grandioso*)
unstable e	e	modulatory	G
m. 1	30	60	102 *ff*

Andante sostenuto			Development	
theme 3	transition (*Allegro agitato assai*)	theme 2	of opening motives (cf. m. 60)	(*stretta*)
D♭	modulatory	G	modulatory	
145	217	235 *f-ff*	252	282

Recapitulation		Coda	
theme 2 *quasi marcia funebre*	theme 3 *sempre cantabile*	theme 2 *Tempo giusto, moderato*	theme 2 *Allegro con bravura*
e	E	E	E
328	351	371 *ff*	388 *ff*

ment the theme undergoes in e/E in the second half is out of balance. The contrasting interruption by the Andante in D-flat does not significantly enhance the overall tonal plan (despite the apparent symmetry of third relationships: D♭-e/E-G).

As Table 10.6 shows, the slow section of the Sonata in B Minor (*Andante sostenuto*) has a different function from the Andante of the *Konzertsolo*. The Andante interrupts the presentation of theme 2; in the Sonata, the *Andante sostenuto* interrupts the course of the development. The use of a relatively static, contrasting section to interrupt the development is characteristic of other works from the period around 1850, including *Ce qu'on entend sur la montagne*, *Les Préludes*, and the *Fantasy and Fugue on "Ad nos, ad salutarem undam."*[33] Liszt's use of substitutions for the developments in these works probably was encouraged by his tendency at this time to disperse the developmental process to transitions and cadential areas. In the case of the Sonata, sequential treatment of motives has already occurred by the beginning of the development proper in measure 205.

TABLE 10.6. Sonata in B Minor

Exposition				*Development 1*
thematic presentation thematic group 1 = motives a, b, c	**tonal presentation** motives b and c		theme 2	motives b and c
unstable g	b		D	modulatory
(a b c) m. (1 8 14)	32		105 *ff*	205

Andante sostenuto = Development 2		*Recapitulation*		
		thematic presentation fugato on motives b and c		**tonal presentation** motives b and c
theme 3 and transformed themes 1 and 2				
F♯ - A - modulatory - F♯		b♭		b
328		460		533

	Coda 1			*Coda 2*	
theme 2	*stretta* motive c	theme 2		theme 3	motives c, b, a
B	modulatory	B		B_____	
					(c b a)
600 *mf*	650	700 *fff*		711	729 737 748

Despite this structural interruption, the effectiveness of the Sonata does depend on the cohesion that typifies this large-scale work. Thematic transformation accounts for this cohesion, as in the *Andante sostenuto* where transformed thematic materials from the exposition are allied with a new theme 3. On another level, the Andante mirrors the Sonata through its incorporation of sonata principles. Winklhofer has shown that in the composing draft of the Sonata Liszt conceived the Andante as a full-fledged sonata movement. When he revised it, he retained the exposition and recapitulation, but significantly curtailed the development, thus mirroring the foreshortened development proper. Other features of the Andante, such as its tonally ambiguous opening, reflect the large-scale plan of the Sonata (Winklhofer, 1980: 158).

Thus, the Andante sections of all three works significantly affect their overall tonal shapes. In the *Dante* Sonata, the Andante subtly extends the tension generated by the tonality of the secondary thematic area, even as it provides a free, improvisatory interlude. In the *Konzertsolo*, the *Andante sostenuto* serves as a decisive point of interruption: its overt tonal and thematic contrast vitiates any strong sense of continuity. Finally, in the Sonata in B minor, the *Andante sostenuto* interrupts an unstable development to provide a sense of tonal stasis; yet by means of thematic transformation, its own inner structure sustains the tensions of that development.

Other distinctive features of the three works concern the use of certain thematic materials as unifying elements in their tonal organization. Both the *Dante* Sonata and the B-minor Sonata have straightforward key schemes (see Tables 10.4 and 10.6), a feature calculated to offset their highly unstable opening motives. In the *Dante* Sonata, a tritone motive (Example 10.10a) opens every section except the recapitulation; the motive retains its instability even after tonal resolution has been achieved with the return of themes 1 and 2 in d/D (m. 273). Example 10.10b shows the overall progress of the motive; when, at the midpoint of the development, an emphasis on A♭ occurs (A♭-E♭, m. 211), a new tritone relationship obtains between A♭ and the tonic key of D minor, thus permitting Liszt to integrate further the fundamental tonal tension of the tritone into the work. Accordingly, the highly dramatic resolution of the tritone in the concluding measures of the coda (A-E♭ to A-D) is the true climax of the piece, superseding even the forceful reentry of theme 2 in D (m. 306).

EXAMPLE 10.10. Liszt, *Dante* Sonata. Tritone motive

The B-minor Sonata also uses unstable opening motives, of which one, the celebrated descending scale (motive a), serves a structural unifying role related to that of the tritone motive in the *Dante* Sonata. Example 10.11a–b shows the first and last appearances of the scale. Tonal resolution is evident to the extent that the modal G flavor of the opening eventually progresses to the tonic B. The scalar form itself has elicited much attention, encouraging some scholars to trace it to various Central European and Near Eastern derivations.[34] István Szelényi shows how the first two scale forms are each generated by a basic tetrachord (tone-tone-semitone and semitone-augmented second-semitone).[35] We can further observe that the final version neatly combines the two (see Example 10.11b). As for appearances of the scale elsewhere in the Sonata, we can interpret them through what Szelényi has termed *Metamorphosen-Motive Technik* (what we have referred to earlier as *Alternativ-Chroma*),[36] in which Liszt experiments with different tetrachord forms to fashion the scale motive. Though the structural use of the scale motive resembles that of the tritone motive in the *Dante* Sonata, lacking in the B-minor Sonata is a final climactic statement. Rather, the resolution of the scale occurs within a quiet epilog (coda 2) that follows a delayed, final emphasis of theme 2 performed *fff* (coda 1 at m. 700).

EXAMPLE 10.11. Liszt, Sonata in B minor. Scale Motive

A discussion of the B-minor Sonata must address the issue of its formal "double-function," a term coined by William S. Newman to describe the work as a sonata in one continuous movement in which various sections function nevertheless as separate quasi-movements (Newman, 373–78). While Searle and Longyear have propounded three-movement schemes,[37] Newman favors a four-movement scheme: the fugato (m. 460) constitutes a scherzo before the finale proper (m. 533). In Newman's interpretation, the Andante and fugato also serve together as the development of a single-movement sonata form.

Several factors argue against a multimovement interpretation. First, "when Liszt wished to compose separate movements, he did so without attempting a one-movement sonata overlay, as in the *Concerto in E-flat* and the *Duo (Sonate)*" (Winklhofer, 1980: 162). Second, as mentioned earlier, an Andante or other contrasting middle section appeared quite often in

Liszt's symphonic sonata schemes, where they serve as substitutes for the development sections. Third, Newman somewhat arbitrarily labels the fugato a scherzo; all of Liszt's fugal subjects from the Weimar period, whether scherzos or not, share such stylistic features as dotted rhythms and heavy accents (Winklhofer, 1980: 162–63). On the other hand, supporting Newman's analysis is the fact that some of Liszt's scherzo themes resemble part of the fugato subject in their use of staccato and triplet upbeat-figures. Such superficial resemblances, however, do not prove that Liszt intended the fugato to be heard as a scherzo. Still, the distinct identity of the fugato cannot be denied: within the recapitulation the fugato offers a thematic presentation quite separate from the subsequent reassertion of the tonic (m. 533), thus balancing a similar treatment in the exposition (see Table 10.6). Fourth, except for the Andante, Newman's other three "movements" do not function as self-contained tonal entities, as we would expect.

Recently, Paul Merrick has argued that Liszt employed the fugue programmatically to stand for struggle and, more specifically, a reaching toward God (Merrick, 267–82). Though this interpretation may be convincing for a number of Liszt's works, its meaning for the Sonata is just as problematic as other programmatic views of the work that have been advanced. Some have considered the work in Faustian terms and have sought to tie themes to Faust, Gretchen, and Mephistopheles; this view rests almost solely on the demonic quality of motives b and c.[38] The course of Merrick's program outlines the Creation, Man's Fall, and Redemption through Christ's Crucifixion (similar to an interpretation offered earlier by Tibor Szász, 1984). We do know that Liszt labeled the opening motive of theme 2 (Example 10.12) the "Cross motive" in its appearance in the oratorio *St. Elisabeth* (Merrick, 284). Furthermore, the same motive can also be found in several other Liszt works concerned with Christian subjects (Winklhofer, 1980: 267, n. 48). Thus, the appearance of the Cross motive in the Sonata may carry a Christian resonance (it is tantalizing to observe that Liszt features this motive in the delayed climax of the work at m. 700). Yet the association of other Sonata materials with specific Biblical characters or events is conjectural, a point emphasized when we read that to one interpreter the Andante suggests the Crucifixion, and to another "Man's devotion to Christ."[39] Until further hard evidence materializes, we would do better to view the thematic manipulations of the B-minor Sonata in purely musical terms.[40]

Études

The set of twelve *Études d'exécution transcendante* (*Transcendental Studies,* published 1852) epitomizes Liszt's command of brilliant, technical writing for the piano. The final form of the studies was largely achieved by 1837 when Liszt's fame as a virtuoso pianist without compare was on the

EXAMPLE 10.12. Liszt, Sonata in B minor. Theme 2 with "Cross motive" (mm. 105–108)

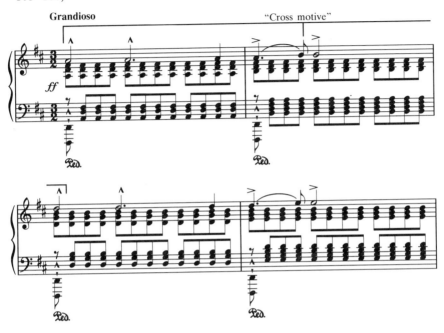

rise. In 1839 he published a version titled *Grandes études* that superseded a version of 1826, *Étude pour le piano en douze exercices,* which, in comparison, is rather straightforward and Czerny-like.[41] When, in 1851, Liszt revised the collection, his purpose was twofold: to title ten studies and to modify some extremely difficult passages that, he feared, rendered the studies unplayable (Perényi, 58).

The *Transcendental Studies* are generally regarded as Liszt's attempt to create a pianistic equivalent of Paganini's brilliant and unprecedented displays for the violin, the celebrated *Caprices* published in 1820. Certainly, this intention is clear enough in Liszt's six *Études d'exécution transcendante d'après Paganini* (composed 1838–39), five of which are transcriptions of Paganini *Caprices.* On the other hand, however far the *Transcendental Studies* stretched the limits of piano technique, Liszt did intend for them to be playable. Indeed, as a whole the studies transcend mere technical display to offer intensely expressive passages, now lyrical, now grandiose, now ominous. When Robert Schumann heard the 1839 version, he commented: "The new version provides a criterion for the artist's present more intense way of thinking and feeling; indeed it affords us a glimpse into his secret intellectual life."[42]

From the beginning, Liszt grouped the studies in pairs of major and relative minor keys: C major, A minor, F major, D minor, and so forth, through the twelfth study in B-flat minor. (Liszt intended to write another twelve studies to complete the circle; that task was eventually accomplished by the Russian pianist Sergey Mikhaylovich Lyapunov at the beginning of this century.) Two studies, *Paysage* (no. 3) and *Ricordanza* (no. 9), perhaps illustrate best how Liszt incorporated poetic ideas into his conception of the étude. If *Paysage* is a demanding study in thirds and chordal passages, it also belongs to the genre of the pastoral, unmistakably exemplified by its harmonic stasis and pedal and drone effects. Liszt's exploration of the keyboard led him to create a novel pianistic effect that reinforces the pastoral image: frequently the melody is surrounded by widely spaced pedal points, suggesting an openness that we associate with nature (Example 10.13).

EXAMPLE 10.13. Liszt, *Paysage* (mm. 31–36)

The melody of *Ricordanza* suggests a nocturne; its *cantabile* quality and graceful turns contribute to a dreamlike, contemplative mood. Its resemblance to Chopin's nocturnes is so strong that many have viewed *Ricordanza* as a reflection of Chopin's influence on Liszt. But Liszt's melody was already more or less determined in the 1826 version, before he met or even knew of Chopin. Apparently each composer was influenced individually by the ever popular *cantabile* style of Italian opera. (One study of Liszt, the untitled no. 10 in F minor, does suggest the influence of Chopin's F minor Étude op. 10 no. 9; their melodic contours, phrasing, and texture are especially similar, as Example 10.14a–b demonstrates.)

Liszt conceived all the titles of the études in 1851 except for *Mazeppa*, which was already affixed to that étude when it appeared separately in 1847. Yet the essential "character" of the études had been determined when they appeared without titles in 1839 as the *Grandes études*: for example, nos. 4 and 7, titled *Mazeppa* and *Eroica* respectively in the 1852 ver-

EXAMPLE 10.14a. Liszt, *Transcendental Study* No. 10 (mm. 22–24)

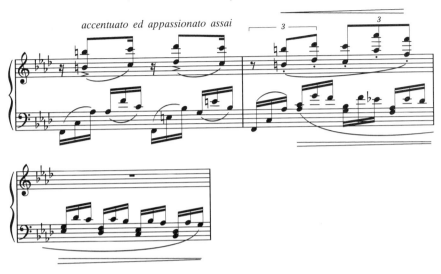

EXAMPLE 10.14b. Chopin, *Étude* Op. 10, no. 9 (mm. 1–4)

sion, displayed in the 1839 version a grand, heroic manner. In the case of *Mazeppa,* Liszt chose to associate that manner with a romantic character from the past, the seventeenth-century Cossack hero Mazeppa, as portrayed in Victor Hugo's poem of the same name. Liszt made his programmatic intentions explicit: the 1852 version ends with the final lines of the poem, "Il tombe enfin . . . et se relève Roi!" Liszt also expanded the coda to include a recitative and a plaintive motive that suggest the near demise of the hero before his triumphant recovery.

The title *Wilde Jagd* (no. 8) refers to the legendary tale of the nocturnal hunt. As in the remaining studies, the music evokes a mood or atmosphere appropriate for the title. *Paysage* (no. 3) and *Vision* (no. 6) are named after odes by Victor Hugo; in *Vision*, the ominous character of the opening captures especially well the poem's chilling description of the Final Judgement. *Chasse-neige* (no. 12) presents one of the most vivid sensual impressions, in Humphrey Searle's words, "the gloomy, rather sinister impression of a whole landscape being slowly and relentlessly covered with snowdrifts" (Searle, 1954: 18). Less tied to clear imagery and close to the mystical evocations of the *Harmonies poétiques et religieuses* is *Harmonies du soir* (no. 11); its main melody has an arching, diatonic contour that recalls the *Bénédiction de Dieu dans la solitude*, while its middle section is melodically restrained and prayerlike. *Harmonies du soir* would seem to bear out Schumann's suggestion that the *Transcendental Studies* reveal Liszt's inner self.

Among Liszt's other études are the *Études d'exécution transcendante d'après Paganini* (1838–39), revised in 1851 under the title *Grandes études de Paganini*, and six concert études. The concert études include one written for the piano method of Fétis and Moscheles (*Morceau de salon, étude de perfectionnement*, published 1841, reworked and published as *Ab irato* in 1852) and two for the method of Lebert and Stark (*Zwei Konzertetüden*, published 1863). Three others appeared in 1849 as *Trois études de concert*. Liszt also completed twelve books of technical studies around 1880 which were not published until after his death. Regrettably, his intention to write a "piano method" was never fulfilled (Walker, 1987: 216–17).

Hungarian Rhapsodies

After a sixteen-year absence, Liszt visited Hungary in 1839 and 1840. Then, from 1840 to 1847, he composed ten volumes of piano pieces based on Hungarian themes: *Magyar dallok*, *Magyar rhapsodiák*, and *Ungarische Nationalmelodien*. These works plus four unpublished ones became the basis for the first fifteen *Hungarian Rhapsodies* which Liszt published between 1851 and 1853; four more Rhapsodies appeared three decades later (1882–86).

Just as Liszt drew musical materials from his Hungarian heritage, he also endeavored to create piano transcriptions of those materials in the style of the indigenous gypsy bands he heard during his Hungarian sojourns. The gypsy musicians especially intrigued him not only with their extraordinary improvisational skills but also with their uncanny ability to depict widely contrasting emotional states, described by Liszt in his 1859 book about the gypsies: "In these melodies the delirium of an extreme joy and the feeble languor of a motionless apathy follow one another quickly, . . . the presumption which overtakes those who are surfeited with the good things of life and the horrible emptiness left by their impotence to satisfy the soul" (*The Gypsy in Music*, 317). Liszt's recognition of the expressive power of gypsy music led him to connect his Hungarian heritage with the older heritage of the ancient Greek rhapsodists whose extraordinary oratorical powers, he thought, had immortalized their race.[43] In his *Hungarian Rhapsodies*, Liszt foresaw something of the same role for himself.

The presumption of Liszt's attitude vexed and angered some later critics, and his claim that the "ancient" melodies of his rhapsodies had been composed and handed down by the gypsies prompted an even greater outcry. In fact, many were popular tunes written by nineteenth-century urban composers such as József Koschovitz, Márk Rózsavölgyi, and Béni Egressy.[44] Notwithstanding Liszt's fundamental misperception, Zoltán Gárdonyi gives a new perspective on the issue by reminding us that in Liszt's time there was little, if any, distinction between "popular" and "national" music; the gypsy music Liszt heard *was* Hungarian music to his mind (Gárdonyi, 1936: 71). Liszt overstated his case by attempting to place the melodies in an ancient tradition.

Most of Liszt's rhapsodies are cast in the sectional design of the nineteenth-century *verbunkos*, a dance popularized by gypsy bands that consists of two or more sections contrasting between the slow *lassu* and the quick *friss*. A straightforward example of the plan is evident in the famous Rhapsody no. 2, which has one extended *lassu* and *friss*. In the *friss*, Liszt captured the erratic quality of the gypsy prototype by constantly interrupting *accelerandos* with abrupt changes of materials. The dizzying effect is further enhanced by appropriate pianistic gymnastics.

A more stylized *lassu/friss* plan occurs in Rhapsody no. 13, on which Liszt brings techniques of Western art music to bear. Specifically, in the opening slow section, which subjects two different melodies to a highly rhapsodic treatment, Liszt develops two motives from the second melody over a chromatically moving bass (m. 72) with the intention of creating a climactic moment. But, effective as the device is in Western art music, here it essentially compromises the nature of the gypsy melodies. As Gárdonyi argues, they enjoy a "static existence" that is not subject to dynamic growth (Gárdonyi, 1936: 82).

For the same reason, Gárdonyi objects to a unifying device Liszt used in some of the rhapsodies, whereby a melodic motive may serve as an introduction, connecting device, and, perhaps, an ending (Gárdonyi, 1936: 81–82). This cyclic thematic treatment offers an alternative to the potpourri of separate melodies that typically make up a rhapsody. Such is the case with Rhapsody no. 14. It opens with a melody marked by a *choriambe* rhythm (long, short, short, long) that frequently appears in Hungarian tunes (Example 10.15a).[45] The somber mood of the melody (*Lento, quasi marcia funebre*) is quickly transformed into the *Allegro eroico* (Example 10.15b), where the same melody is given a heroic cast with its full chords in the tonic major. A second melody (m. 77) marked *a capriccio*, Liszt's designation for a metrically irregular performance style, is twice interrupted by a phrase of the opening theme. Furthermore, the heroic form of that theme acts as a coda to this section, coming on the heels of a third theme that typically serves as a concluding *figura* in *verbunkos* dances (m. 121).[46] Thus, the usually unbridged progression of melodies is arrested several times and the true flavor of the gypsy style lost.

Certainly less compromising transcriptions of the gypsy style occur in some of the rhapsodies. No. 11, for example, is particularly attractive with its opening *lento a capriccio* that mimics *cymbalon* effects. As the music progressively accelerates through three subsequent sections, we hear first

EXAMPLE 10.15a. Liszt, *Hungarian Rhapsody* No. 14. Opening idea (mm. 3–6)

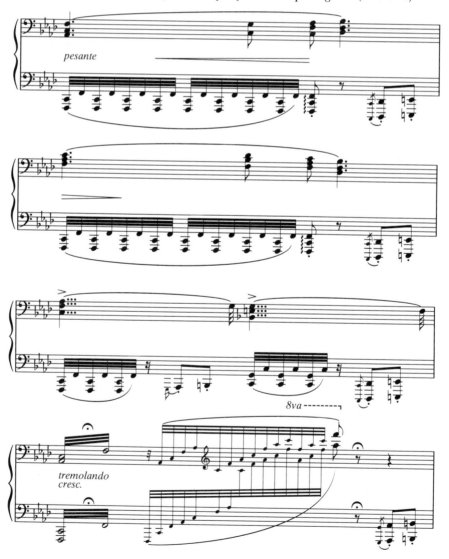

EXAMPLE 10.15b. Liszt, *Hungarian Rhapsody* No. 14. Transformed version (mm. 25–28)

EXAMPLE 10.16. Liszt, *Hungarian Rhapsody* No. 11. *Verbunkos* material (mm. 17–18)

a typical *verbunkos* dance with dotted rhythms and "anticipation" figures (Example 10.16); the last two sections use themes recalling the *csárdás*, the rapid, $\frac{2}{4}$ *perpetuum mobile* dance that developed as a stylized version of the *friss*.

Not surprisingly, a number of the rhapsodies make use of Hungarian scales. In no. 13 (Example 10.17) the Hungarian scale on A is directly

EXAMPLE 10.17. Liszt, *Hungarian Rhapsody* No. 13. Opening idea (mm. 4–7)

ILLUSTRATION 10.2. Liszt, *Hungarian Rhapsody* No. 16, Opening measures. Autograph, Music Division, Library of Congress, Washington, D.C.

incorporated into the melodic material; note how Liszt here allies the raised fourth with a diminished-seventh chord and then an augmented-sixth chord. In the later rhapsodies (e. g., nos. 16 of 1882 and 17 of 1886), Liszt's use of Hungarian scales became more abstract. As in *Sunt lacrymae*, in no. 16, a scalar segment is exploited in a tonally ambiguous way in the introduction, preparing the chromatic inflections that in turn permeate the main melody (Illustration 10.2). No. 17 is framed with material apparently derived from a *kalindra* scale (beginning A-B♭-C♯-D); Liszt manipulates the scale to end on B-flat, thereby obscuring a clear tonal focus. The last four rhapsodies display not only the tonally experimental language of Liszt's later period but also its tendency toward sparse textures; although *cymbalon* effects still abound, the piano rarely attains the thick, quasi-orchestral richness of the earlier rhapsodies.

As a whole the *Hungarian Rhapsodies* attest to Liszt's concerted effort to preserve his Hungarian musical heritage. Though works such as the symphonic poem *Hungaria* and the *Historical Hungarian Portraits* offer more original creations, the rhapsodies retain their historical significance as the first transcriptions of gypsy band performances.

Ballades, Polonaises, Mazurkas, and Other Dances

We have seen how Liszt found in Chopin's piano music models for the D-flat major *Consolation* and the F-minor *Transcendental Study*. The textures of the first and second Concert Études (1849) also suggest Chopin's influence; other examples could be cited as well. But these borrowings are relatively inconsequential in comparison to Liszt's exploration of keyboard genres in which Chopin had excelled, particularly the ballade, polonaise, and mazurka. Their concentrated appearance in Liszt's oeuvre after Chopin's death in 1849 suggests to some that his previous relative neglect of these genres reflected his uneasy relationship with Chopin.[47]

It may be that Liszt intended an homage to Chopin, a view corroborated by the appearance of Liszt's Chopin biography in 1852. The striking resemblance between Liszt's and Chopin's D-flat major *Berceuses* (1854 and 1843–44, respectively) has often been noted. The most substantial debt of Liszt to Chopin, however, occurs in Liszt's first Ballade, completed in 1848 and published in 1849, the year of Chopin's death. Günther Wagner has identified within it elements from four different Chopin works, the first Ballade op. 23, *Grande valse brillante* op. 18, the "Funeral March" from the Sonata in B-flat minor op. 35, and the A-major Polonaise op. 40 no. 1. Furthermore, Liszt's use of four-square, periodic phrasing—rather atypical for him—is a readily acknowledged feature of Chopin's ballades.[48]

Liszt's second Ballade (composed 1853), in sonata form, was written during the period of the B-minor Sonata and the symphonic poems. A technique used in two of the latter, *Ce qu'on entend sur la montagne* and *Mazeppa*, reappears in the Ballade: an exact repetition of material transposed by one-half step. Specifically, the exposition in B minor is repeated in B-flat minor, as though Liszt had in mind an alternative to the traditional literal repeat of the section. Needless to say, Liszt's solution did not spare him from the criticism of being complacent; nevertheless, on closer examination, this unusual tonal shift may actually bear on the overall pitch design.[49] In the ensuing development (m. 70), Liszt presents the main theme (Example 10.18a) at different pitch levels and interjects passages of virtuosic figuration and motivic fragments drawn from the main theme. Midway through the development (m. 143), the second theme (Example 10.18c) reappears, prefaced by the bridge material from the exposition (Example 10.18b), now expanded. At the reprise in B major, the first theme returns marked *cantabile* (m. 254), having assumed momentarily

EXAMPLE 10.18a. Liszt, Ballade No. 2. Main theme—"dramatic" (mm. 3–11)

the lyrical nature of the second theme, which now introduces it: it absorbs the latter's rocking eighth-note motion into its accompaniment. We can speculate that this coalescence of expressive types (as opposed to the three distinct characters identified in Example 10.18) was an essential feature of the Ballade's design. (The labels themselves have been suggested by Günther Wagner, who notes that Goethe considered them the three modes of poetic expression available to a ballade singer.[50]) Illustration 10.3 shows Liszt's revision at measure 225, in which he chooses a more lyrical setting for this expanded bridge material as well.

Following the distinctive treatment of the reprise, Liszt presents a codalike peroration of the main theme, marked *grandioso* (m. 284), to which he adds a brief, final statement of the lyrical second theme. The delay of the final point of arrival is by now familiar to us from Liszt's full-fledged sonata structures, in which second themes become structural goals. In the second Ballade, however, attention is directed in a more traditional fashion to the main theme. Structurally more ambitious than the first Ballade, Liszt's second Ballade thus marks a distinctive contribution that differs considerably from Chopin's pioneering efforts in this genre.[51]

EXAMPLE 10.18b. Liszt, Ballade No. 2. Bridge—"epic" (mm. 17–23)

EXAMPLE 10.18c. Liszt, Ballade No. 2. Second theme—"lyrical" (mm. 24–26)

ILLUSTRATION 10.3. Liszt's revision of the Second Ballade, mm. 225–233. Autograph. Printed with the kind permission of the music publisher B. Schott's Söhne, Mainz.

Liszt's two Polonaises (composed 1850 and 1851) are, in Humphrey Searle's words, "overlong and bombastic, and lack the subtlety of Chopin's works in this form" (Searle, 1954: 57). What Liszt most admired in Chopin's Polonaises was their strength and grandeur: "They harbor the noble sentiments and traditions of ancient Poland, mirroring the firm determination and purposefulness of great men of former times" (paraphrase by Waters, 1961: 185). Liszt's second Polonaise, in particular, captures this martial spirit: its opening is marked *Allegro pomposo con brio*; a second idea (m. 25), *marcatissimo quasi trombe*; and even the contrasting theme of the middle section (m. 67), although labeled *patetico*, is presented *ff* and with the accompanying emphatic polonaise rhythm ♪𝅘𝅥𝅯𝅘𝅥𝅯𝅘𝅥𝅮. This last theme readily brings to mind the middle theme of Chopin's A-major Polonaise op. 40 no. 1, known as the *Militaire* (Example 10.19a–b). Indeed, it seems likely that Liszt may have modeled his Polonaise after Chopin's.

Whereas Chopin's Mazurkas reveal some of his most adventurous and expressive harmonic vocabulary, a feature that Liszt certainly admired, Liszt's own *Mazurka brillante* (1850) reveals a rather straightfor-

EXAMPLE 10.19a. Liszt, Polonaise No. 2. Middle section theme (mm. 66–70)

EXAMPLE 10.19b. Chopin, Polonaise, Op. 40, no. 1. Middle section theme (mm. 25–28)

ward approach to this dance type. The middle section (m. 59) offers a folklike interlude in which four-measure melodic phrases unfold over a drone with the syncopated rhythm ♩ ♩. ♪ .

The other dance form to which Liszt contributed during the 1850s was the waltz, also refined to a high degree by Chopin. Liszt published three waltzes in 1852 or 1853: the *Valse de bravoure*, the *Valse mélancolique*, and the *Valse-Impromptu* (all three had earlier versions). Of the three waltzes, the *Valse-Impromptu* strikes us with its *scherzando* material characterized by piquant harmonic vocabulary and abundant diatonic and chromatic appoggiaturas. The *Valse mélancolique* begins with an introductory section of harmonically unstable arpeggiations. When the main theme appears (m. 76), it too is subjected to frequent modulations; similarly, the second idea is supported by an accompaniment fraught with unstable cross-relationships (mm. 105ff).

Between 1840 and 1883 Liszt wrote marches, of which several were Hungarian tributes, including the *Heroischer Marsch im ungarischen Styl* (1840) and the *Ungarischer Geschwindmarsch-Magyar Gyors induló* (1870). Finally, early in his career, he achieved great success with the ever popular dance, the galop. Liszt's *Grand galop chromatique* (1838) was a virtuosic *tour de force* with which he often ended his public concerts, including the celebrated concert of 4 January 1840 that climaxed his return to Hungary (on that occasion, he added the *Rákóczy March* when the audience failed to stop applauding).[52]

The Piano Transcriptions and Fantasias

Throughout most of his composing career, Liszt turned out an abundant supply of transcriptions and paraphrases or fantasias, that is, semi-original works based on derived material. As early as the mid-1830s, his transcriptions of Berlioz's *Symphonie fantastique*, Beethoven's Fifth, Sixth, and Seventh Symphonies, and Bach's organ preludes and fugues proved remarkably popular. Later, Liszt promoted Wagner's music through the medium of operatic transcriptions.

Space does not permit an extended treatment of this imposing repertory, yet we should remember that for Liszt composition was never far removed from improvisation, and that in the transcriptions and fantasias we come perhaps the closest to an exhibition of his spontaneous, improvisatory style (see Suttoni). But in his operatic fantasias of the 1840s Liszt also demonstrated his ability as a highly original dramatist: among the best known are *Norma*, *La sonnambula*, and *Don Giovanni*. The last, in particular, allows a glimpse of his interpretive spirit. Searle states that "it does summarize three aspects of the story, justice, seduction and carefree enjoyment" (Searle, 1985: 283). The first two are unquestionable: first, Liszt combines the music of the act 2 graveyard scene between the Don and the Commendatore with that of their ultimately climactic meeting; next, he presents the Don's seductive act 1 duet with Zerlina, "Là ci darem la mano." But in Liszt's hands the supposed "carefree" nature of the Don's act 1 aria "Fin ch'han dal vino" is redirected to a different effect—one only hinted at by Mozart. In the middle of Mozart's B-flat major aria, we find a phrase (m. 57) made pungent with a B-flat minor sonority while the Don sings of luring young women into his bed. Liszt takes this phrase with its "dark" suggestion and makes it his point of entry into the aria as well as a significant point of return within it; furthermore, each time he presents the phrase in the key areas B-flat, D, and F-sharp, forming an augmented triad—Liszt's topical symbol for doom and death. In this way, Liszt brings into focus the damned nature of the seductive act.

The Late Period

Macabre, bizarre, dreamlike, and elegiac are adjectives that might be applied to the music of Liszt's late period, which Bence Szabolcsi has labeled the composer's twilight. The piano music of the 1880s, illustrative of Liszt's experimental style at its most extreme, offers the most direct introduction to this final period. What is more, these works are stylistically of a kind and reveal Liszt's preoccupation with certain moods and programmatic subjects. We have already mentioned the *Historical Hungarian Portraits,* the elegiac cycle in honor of Hungarian statesmen and artists. Liszt turned to the elegy again in four works prompted by the death of Wagner: *La lugubre gondola* no. 1 (1882), *La lugubre gondola* no. 2 (1885), *Am Grabe Richard Wagners* (1883), and *R.W.- Venezia* (1883). In view of the numerous elegies composed during the last twenty years of his life,[53] some writers have attributed to Liszt a kind of morbid obsession with death. But Liszt's own words of 19 November 1862, occasioned by deaths of two of his three children, suggest a different point of view: "My soul's tears must, as it were, have lacrymatoria made for them; I must set fires alight for those of my dear ones that are alive, and keep my dear dead in *spiritual and corporeal* urns. This is the aim and object of the *Art task* to me" (letter to Eduard Liszt, La Mara/Bache, 2:39). The elegiac works, even as they expressed sorrow, became vessels of tribute for those who mattered to Liszt, and thus can be viewed in the centuries-old tradition of the *tombeau* or *epitaphe.*

Other piano pieces of the 1880s, including the two nocturnes *En rêve* and *Schlaflos! Frage und Antwort,* and *Unstern* and *Nuages gris,* are highly reflective mood pictures that evoke now pensiveness, now dream-states, and now even quiet resignation. Much of this music suggests an improvisatory flow of materials, as though the composer sought to mimic the discontinuity of thoughts experienced in dreams or intense introspection.

Still another genre of pieces from the 1880s, which Szabolcsi has labeled the "dance phantasy," includes the three *Csárdás,* the four *Valses oubliées,* and the last *Mephisto* Waltzes (in addition to nos. 2, 3, and 4, Liszt conceived another which came to be known as *Bagatelle ohne Tonart*). According to Szabolcsi: "What he [Liszt] is after is a wild shaking-up, a violent revival of an extinct heroic élan, an uncurbed bacchanalia of instincts and impulses, an angry round dance and dangerous dithyramb, a fantastic Doomsday. In truth, what we are witnessing here is the ordeal of a heroless, nay, antiheroic age on behalf of heroes and heroism!" (Szabolcsi, 47). In their own way, these dances share the same visionary, improvisatory impulse of the mood pictures just mentioned. Liszt has thus come full circle in his piano music: just as his performances of the 1830s and 1840s were celebrated for their spontaneous, improvisatory qualities, so too do the compositions from the last decade of his life seem like extemporaneous creations.

In the dances, particularly the *Csárdás,* Liszt achieves the effect of unrelenting spontaneity in part through a rhythmic treatment that allows short, repeated motives to follow closely upon one another, much as in the rhapsodies. In the more reflective pieces (including the elegies), on the other hand, Liszt creates his various moods of dreaminess, unrest, and negating fantasy primarily through tonal manipulation. Not surprisingly, these are the pieces usually cited as examples of how Liszt explored the very limits of tonality, thereby preparing the way for future generations of composers. But examination reveals that Liszt offers no new language, no new system per se.[54]

Instead, he manages to unify these late works with the least directive elements of the traditional tonal system, for example, a whole-tone progression, a tritone, an augmented triad, a diminished triad, or a combination of these.[55] Occasionally, these elements may even supplant the role of melodies or motives. Thus, the aural paradox of these pieces: though they are undoubtedly the most tightly constructed of Liszt's oeuvre, they rarely achieve a sense of tonal closure. Their open-endedness is typically reinforced by a textural design in which an already sparse fabric eventually disintegrates to a single line or a noiselike chord in an extreme register. By design, too, these introspective works contain little idiomatic writing for the keyboard; they seem instrumentally pure.[56] To be sure, Liszt continually turns to his favored instrument for these expressive utterances of his old age, but he no longer calls upon its particular voice: the voice of Liszt the composer stands exposed, now divorced from his persona as a virtuoso performer.

La lugubre gondola nos. 1 and 2 reveal different ways in which Liszt broke with tradition. Liszt composed the first piece in December 1882, "as though it were a presentiment, . . . in Venice six weeks before Wagner's death" (letter of 8 June 1885 to Ferdinand Taborszky, La Mara/Bache, 2:473). The second piece dates from 1885; it survives in two versions, one for piano solo and one for violin and piano. Although nos. 1 and 2 share some melodic material, they represent individual conceptions, not first and second versions.

Example 10.20a shows the opening idea of *La lugubre gondola* no. 1; Example 10.20b shows its subsequent tonal treatment through two descending whole-tone transpositions that are then reversed so that the music regains its initial pitch level. Any suggestion of closure, however, is ruled out by the tonally ambiguous nature of the basic material: both the melody and the ostinato figure of the accompaniment are generated from a tonally elusive augmented triad, A♭-C-E; the implied tonic, F minor, is lacking.

Accompanying this lack of tonal focus is a lack of clear rhythmic impetus; the barcarolle rhythm of the left hand, ♪♪♩ ♪♪♩, is amended every other measure to ♪♪♩ ♪♪♩ , while the even values of the treble melody, mostly dotted quarter notes, are also offset by irregularities. From measure 77 to the end, any impression of defined rhythmic movement disintegrates even further when the left hand takes up a *tremolando* figure that eventually descends to the depths of the piano where it produces a noisy rumble. Thus, Liszt has created in *La lugubre gondola* no. 1 a deconstruction of sorts.[57] Instead of the traditional sense of melodic and harmonic development, we hear mere repetitions of material with no sense of melodic, rhythmic, harmonic, or tonal goal; even the suggestive crescendo that accompanies the return to the original pitch level in measure 95 dies out relatively soon thereafter, leaving us with a *ppp* augmented triad, garbled and barely discernible in its low register.

EXAMPLE 10.20a. Liszt, *La lugubre gondola* No. 1. Opening idea (mm. 1–9)

EXAMPLE 10.20b. Liszt, *La lugubre gondola* No. 1. Subsequent tonal treatment

In his second tribute to Wagner, *La lugubre gondola* no. 2, Liszt created an elegy in which "true melody" and tonal focus again play a role, albeit a nontraditional one. Example 10.21 shows the materials from no. 1 now reworked, with the melody and ostinato possessing a stronger tonal focus on F minor. At measure 69, a bittersweet passage (marked appropriately *dolcissimo, dolente*), consisting of alternating major and minor chords, provides contrast. The original theme returns in measure 109, now *appassionato* and culminating in a *fff* octave passage in measure 121.

EXAMPLE 10.21. Liszt, *La lugubre gondola* No. 2. Main theme (mm. 35–37)

The main theme has taken on a singing quality in contrast to its abstract character in no. 1; it is now a recognizable "mourning song" with accompaniment. And the use of abstract materials is now relegated to an introduction (thirty-four measures) and a codalike counterpart (forty-four measures), largely made up of bare diminished-seventh chords and *recitando* passages also based on that unstable sonority. Liszt's method here reminds us of the *Historical Hungarian Portraits,* in which nonthematic materials frame central portions with clear themes, often dancelike in character. In short, *La lugubre gondola* no. 2 too can be interpreted as an instance of Liszt's *Erinnerungsmusik*[58]; the nostalgic remembrance of Wagner that constitutes the body of the piece emerges from a hazy, undirected image to which Liszt eventually returns. These outer parts suggest disjointed, improvisatory utterances; at the very end, the sense of aimlessness is reinforced by a bare, stripped down fragment of a whole-tone scale. As in *La lugubre gondola* no. 1, we sense here the true welding of form and idea to which Liszt aspired.

Liszt's two late nocturnes—*En rêve* and *Schlaflos! Frage und Antwort*—yield quite different effects from a texture with an expressive treble melody against a broken-chord accompaniment. The title of *Sleepless! Question and Answer,* with its suggestion of uncertainty and subsequent resolution, finds its musical realization through the technique of thematic transformation, including a shift from minor to major (Example 10.22a–b). Liszt's nocturne evokes a highly restless state when, after the tonal clarity of the opening in E minor, chromatic melodic fragments unfold over a tonally inconclusive sonority, F-A-C-E. But at measures 35ff, there surfaces an augmented-sixth sonority, D♯-F-A-C, whose altered tone, D♯, subsequently acts as leading tone to E major, which is securely established in Liszt's "answer" at measure 50.[59]

EXAMPLE 10.22a. Liszt, *Schlaflos! Frage und Antwort*. Opening idea (mm. 1–2)

EXAMPLE 10.22b. Liszt, *Schlaflos! Frage und Antwort*. Transformed version (mm. 50–51)

Whereas *Schlaflos!* is largely bipartite with a movement from ambiguity to clarity, *En rêve* seems almost uniform by virtue of the F-sharp pedal that appears in nearly all of its forty-seven measures. Yet despite the stability that the pedal offers, the music suggests the elusiveness and transience of dream images by the often abrasive insertion of chromatic tones that cause the tonal focus to fade in and out. Whereas in other works Liszt evokes a reflective state by a disjointed succession of ideas, here he cleverly does so with one set of materials.

One of Liszt's late pieces, *Unstern! Sinistre,* is often cited for its ominous tone, yet apparently it was not conceived as an elegy. According to Redepenning's lucid analysis, Liszt designed the piece so that two separately introduced, contrasting elements—diminished and augmented sonorities—eventually fuse in measure 71 into a harsh atonal dissonance (see Example 10.23b), and thus negate the role of a climax as a point of clarifying arrival (this fusion is anticipated earlier in measure 45 by a whole-tone sonority; Redepenning, 256–59).[60] Less attention has been given to the final section of the piece, beginning in measure 84 (Example 10.23c). Clearly this can be viewed as a diatonic, major-mode transformation of the highly volatile material at measure 58 (Example 10.23a). Particularly striking is the character of the transformed material marked *quasi organo*: it now hearkens back to the prayerlike passages of the *Harmonies poétiques* and many other works of a spiritual/religious nature. So it is that a glimmer of optimism and spiritual comfort is evoked, if only momentarily, before the sense of unrest returns, first in the guise of muted chromatic fragments, and eventually of a whole-tone progression against the unresolved dominant seventh of B (Example 10.23d).[61] Perhaps more

EXAMPLE 10.23. Liszt, *Unstern! Sinistre* (mm. 58–60, 71, 84–87, and 139–146)

than any other piece, *Unstern* reflects the philosophical outlook on life that Liszt expressed three years before his death: "Ever since the days of my youth I have considered dying much simpler than living. Even if often there is fearful and protracted suffering before death, yet is death none the less the deliverance from our involuntary yoke of existence. Religion assuages this yoke, yet our heart bleeds under it continually!—'Sursum corda!' " (letter of 22 February 1883 to Lina Ramann, La Mara/Bache, 2:431).

We turn finally to Liszt's dance phantasies, of which the *Csárdás obstinée* (1886) is striking for its progressive chromatic alterations of the four-note motive, A-G-F♯-E, which clashes, at least initially, with its insistent dominant pedal (F♯-A♯-C♯). On the other hand, the earlier *Csárdás macabre* (1881–82) involves a more straightforward alternation of melodic materials that include a theme identical to a widely known Hungarian song[62]; what makes the work stand out is the jarring section beginning at measure 49—long stretches of parallel open fifths, whose unrelenting abrasiveness serves no doubt some programmatic intent. Of the *Mephisto* Waltzes, the third (1883) offers a daring use, both in the framing sections and intermittently throughout, of a sonority composed of fourths, E♯-A♯-D♯. Significantly, another tone, C♯, the lowest in the sonority's linear presentation, becomes through reiteration dominant to the tonic F♯ in which the recurring main melody is presented. Yet, in keeping with his adventurous tonal palette of the 1880s, Liszt does not end the piece conclusively on F♯, but rather with the tonally ambiguous quartal progression, E♯-A♯-D♯.

The angry, violent mood of the third *Mephisto* Waltz conjures up, perhaps, satanic imagery with which Liszt's music was all too frequently associated. Notwithstanding the "Mephistophelean" pieces of the 1880s, including the *Mephisto* Polka (1883) and the other *Mephisto* Waltzes (1880–85), few other works in Liszt's oeuvre fall into this category, if we except, of course, the *Faust Symphony* (1857), *Two Episodes from Lenau's Faust* (1860–61), and the first *Mephisto* Waltz (1859–60). The "diabolical" character attributed to Liszt throughout his lifetime was fostered more by his appearance—particularly his ominous black performance garb, *à la* Paganini—than by any significant representation of such themes in either his compositions or the repertory he performed. On the contrary, excepting the moments of resignation in his final years, he contemplated within his music time and again the positive spiritual values of human existence, in which the strength of his faith and his Hungarian heritage played a principal part. This wellspring of ideas formed the expressive resonance of Liszt's piano music.

Notes

1. Anthony Newcomb describes how certain musical relationships can suggest nonmusical properties and thus produce a "metaphorical" or "expressive resonance." See "Sound and Feeling," *Critical Inquiry* 10 (1984): 625–26. The present study adopts Newcomb's terminology and its conceptual underpinnings.

2. The *Reminiscences of Don Juan*. See *Piano Transcriptions from French and Italian Operas*, iii.

3. This later dating is suggested by Liszt's reference in a letter of October 1837 to his work on the *Album*, by some interpretive markings found in other works completed in 1837–38, and finally, by Liszt's words in the Preface to the *Album*: "As soon as I began to work, my recollections [of sights, sounds, sensations] intensified." See Hughes, 32.

4. Zoltán Gárdonyi, 1969: 190; Diether Presser, "Liszts 'Années de Pèlerinage. Première Année: Suisse' als Dokument der Romantik," in *Liszt Studien* 1 (1977): 143–44.

5. Liszt removed the two quotations of the *Album* version, both of which revealed man absorbed by nature. (One is an excerpt from Byron's *Childe Harold*, canto 3, stanza 72, and the other, a three-line French motto; cf. the *Neue Ausgabe*, I/6, 74.)

6. In a related interpretation Karen Wilson observes that nearly all the pieces in *Année 1* involve the idea of pilgrimage, exile, or refuge. See Wilson, 19.

7. The excerpts are found in the *Neue Ausgabe*, I/6, 30.

8. Márta Grabócz argues for an interpretation of *Vallée* as "der evolutionäre Variationszyklus," in which measures 1, 75, 119, and 170 coincide with particular character variations of the initial idea: (1) speaking, questioning; (2) pastoral-amorous; (3) stormy, heroic, combative; (4) pantheistic-religious. These thematic characters in turn correspond to the mental/emotional states of the hero Obermann, and, beyond, of the heroes in other novels of disillusionment (Grabócz, 1984: 214–15; 1980: 318–19). According to Grabócz, such an "epic model," in which slow, gradual change is more essential than dramatic contrast and development, was adopted by Liszt early on and even underlies many of the nonprogrammatic pieces of the Weimar period, including the Sonata in B minor (Grabócz, 1984: 209ff. See also n. 40).

9. An article attributed to Liszt, "La Sainte Cécile de Raphaël," appeared in the *Revue et Gazette musicale* on 14 April 1839. It is reprinted in Liszt, *Pages romantiques*, 250–56.

10. Letter of 14 October 1877. *The Letters of Franz Liszt to Olga von Meyendorff 1871–1886*, trans. William R. Tyler, introduction and notes by Edward N. Waters (Washington, D.C., 1979), 295.

11. For the evolution of the title, see Winklhofer, 1977: 27–32; the earliest title was *Fragment dantesque*.

12. This dating is a revision of the traditionally accepted one of 1838–39. See Rena Mueller, review of Alan Walker, *Franz Liszt*, vol. 1, *The Virtuoso Years, 1811–1847*, in *Journal of the American Musicological Society* 37 (1984): 190.

13. See Neumeyer, 2–22; Leon Plantinga, *Romantic Music: A History of Musical Style in Nineteenth-Century Europe* (New York, 1984), 186–88; and Howard Cinnamon, "Chromaticism and Tonal Coherence in Liszt's Sonetto 104 del Petrarca," *In Theory Only* 7 (August 1983): 3–19.

14. Harold Nicolson, *Sainte-Beuve* (New York, 1957), 27.

15. Quoted in Merrick, 9.

16. Noting that October 1849 was the month of Chopin's death, Alan Walker draws attention to the resemblance of a passage from *Funérailles* (m. 135) to the central episode of Chopin's A♭-major Polonaise op. 53 and suggests that *Funérailles* may have been a threnody on Chopin's death. See Walker, 1970: 60–61.

17. M. de Lamartine, *Harmonies poétiques et religieuses avec commentaires et poésies diverses* (Paris, 1866), 1–3.

18. Ibid., 3: "Nous prions avec tes paroles, nous pleurons avec tes larmes, nous invoquons avec tes chants!" See also the *Neue Ausgabe*, I/9, 30.

19. Dieter Torkewitz, "Die Erstfassung der 'Harmonies poétiques et religieuses' von Liszt," in *Liszt Studien* 2 (1981): 220–36. Torkewitz goes on to describe how the three motives are subjected to reharmonizations, contractions coupled with sequential presentation, and occasional expansions.

20. See Todd, 1988: 101–103. He notes this association in later pieces, including *Via crucis, La lugubre gondola, Am Grabe Richard Wagners,* and *Nuages gris.*

21. See the entry "Zypresse" in *Lexikon der christlichen Ikonographie,* ed. Engelbert Kirschbaum, Günter Bandmann, *et al.* (Rome, 1968–76) 4:591–94.

22. Book 1: line 462. ("There are tears for human affairs.")

23. Book 2: poem 10, line 6. ("It is sufficient to have aspired toward great things.")

24. The author presents various sorts of evidence to support the interpretation that Liszt may have conceived Book 3 with his native Hungary in mind and, furthermore, that an image cherished by the Hungarian people, the Holy Crown, was its conceptual impulse (Pesce, 1990).

25. Szelényi, "Der unbekannte Liszt," in *Franz Liszt: Beiträge von ungarischen Autoren,* 278.

26. A dance used from about 1780 to 1849 to recruit soldiers for the Hungarian army. It survived into the nineteenth century as a ceremonial dance, and typically consisted of two or more sections, some in the character of a slow introduction *(lassu),* others of a rapid and wild nature *(friss).*

27. In a recent article, Dezsö Legány has proposed a new ordering: *Széchenyi, Deák, Teleki, Eötvös, Vörösmarty, Petöfi, Mosonyi,* according to Liszt's letter of 30 July 1885 to Carolyne Sayn-Wittgenstein. Legány, 80–81.

28. Thus, one can take issue with Sándor Kovács's view that the Hungarian scalar materials by themselves do not play a significant role in the *Portraits:* "Formprinzipien und ungarische Stileigentümlichkeiten in den Spätwerken von Liszt," *Liszt Studien 2* (1981): 121. See further *Mosonyi* (no. 7), where the G♯-A-B♭ segment of the D scale serves as part of the fundamental melodic gesture of the piece.

29. In *Vörösmarty* (no. 3), Liszt takes his theme (m. 19) from the 1843 setting by Béni Egressy of Vörösmarty's poem *Szózat,* which served as a Hungarian national anthem, particularly between 1849 and 1867.

30. Actually the closing of no. 6 involves an *Alternativ-Chroma* manipulation of the opening tetrachords: they appear a half step higher to end the piece. This gesture operates somewhat independently of the treatment of the main theme.

31. Although the *Dante* Sonata was conceived as early as 1839, it was revised in 1849 (publication 1858). The *Grosses Konzertsolo* was probably composed in 1849 (publication 1851); the date of composition generally accepted for the Sonata in B minor is 1852–53 (publication 1854).

32. One can argue that the more stable effect at m. 136 results from the absence of nonharmonic tones generally and not from diatonic versus chromatic content.

33. See Winklhofer, 1980: 155; and R. Larry Todd, "Liszt, Fantasy and Fugue for Organ on 'Ad nos, ad salutarem undam,' " *19th Century Music* 4 (1981): 256.

34. See, for instance, Gárdonyi (1936: 95), who refers specifically to the gypsy minor.

35. "Der unbekannte Liszt," 277.

36. Ibid., 275–82.

37. Searle, 1954: 57, and R. M. Longyear, 202–09. Furthermore, Searle interprets the *Grosses Konzertsolo* in the same light and views it as anticipating the unique form of the *Dante* Sonata.

38. See, for example, Louis Kentner in "Solo Piano Music (1827–61)," in Walker, 1970: 89–91.

39. Merrick, 292–94; Szász, 55.

40. One writer who has given significant attention to the issue of symbolic elements in Liszt's piano music is Márta Grabócz. Aside from some fairly common elements which she labels "Pastoral-pantheistische" and "Makabreske" figures, she explores a number of theme types or "Intonationen" adopted by Liszt from Beethoven and contemporaries such as Donizetti, Bellini, and Chopin. The types include one of a heroic, epic character related to Beethoven's *appassionata, agitato,* or *energico* themes, and one of a traditional Italian bel-canto nature. Grabócz suggests that the appearance of the heroic-epic melody type or of *tempestuoso* and *eroico* passages can be interpreted symbolically even in a nonprogrammatic work such as the Sonata in B minor (1980: 314). Thus, she identifies the very same Cross motive discussed above as belonging to this gestural, heroic-epic type without mention of its possible "Christian" resonance. See also n. 8, above.

41. Folke Augustini compares parts of the various versions in *Die Klavieretüde im 19. Jahrhundert. Studien zu ihrer Entwicklung und Bedeutung* (Duisburg, 1986), 190–97.

42. Robert Schumann, *On Music and Musicians,* trans. Paul Rosenfeld, ed. Konrad Wolff (New York, 1946), 146–47.

43. See, for example, *The Gypsy in Music,* 288–90, 333–38; also, Gárdonyi, 1936: 79–80.

44. See Gárdonyi, "Paralipomena zu den Ungarischen Rhapsodien Franz Liszts," in *Franz Liszt. Beiträge von ungarischen Autoren,* 197–225.

45. Gárdonyi identifies not only the nineteenth-century Hungarian popular song that is the basis for this melody but also the sources for several other melodies in this rhapsody. See ibid., 212.

46. See Lujza Tari, 2–4, for further discussion of the use of such figures.

47. Günther Wagner, 56; and Walker, "Liszt's Musical Background," in Walker, 1970: 60.

48. Wagner, 49–54. Specifically, the four borrowings are: (1) the Neapolitan relationship of the opening recitative, D-D-flat (cf. the opening of Chopin's Ballade op. 23, A-flat to G); (2) the headmotive of Liszt's first theme (cf. the theme of the middle section of Chopin's *Grande valse brillante* op. 18, also in D-flat); (3) the two motives from the central *Tempo di marcia,* mm. 63–64 and 69 (cf. Chopin's Sonata in B-flat minor op. 35, "Funeral March," mm. 3 and 15–16); and (4) the material of mm. 96ff. (cf. the opening theme of Chopin's A-major Polonaise op. 40 no. 1).

49. I am indebted to Fred Maus for bringing this to my attention. Liszt may have designed the second Ballade to bring B-flat (= A-sharp, the leading tone of B) in and out of focus, acting within a nexus that includes the lowered seventh degree, A♮.

50. Wagner, 61 and 46. Wagner offers no proof that either Chopin or Liszt was directly influenced by Goethe's theory.

51. For another view of this work, see Grabócz, 1986: 186–89.

52. For Liszt's recollection of the performance, see Perényi, 215. Liszt later produced a second, simplified version of the composition. Two other galops, the *Galop de bal* and Galop in A minor, date from ca. 1840 and 1841.

53. See, for example, the two *Elegies* of 1874 and 1877, and the *Marche funèbre* in *Année 3,* among others.

54. See, for example, Harold Adams Thompson, "The Evolution of Whole-

Tone Sound in Liszt's Original Piano Works" (Ph.D. diss., Louisiana State University, 1974), 262, where he suggests that Liszt foreshadows twelve-tone technique.

55. Allen Forte (1987) has recently focused attention particularly on Liszt's use of augmented and diminished triads and the more elaborate pitch-class structures of which they form a part, 4–19 and 4–18 respectively. He argues that such nontonal formations appear as linear-harmonic projections even in some of Liszt's works before the "experimental idiom" takes hold in the 1880s, and provide a link to early twentieth-century music.

56. See also John Ogdon, "Solo Piano Music (1861–86)," in Walker, 1970: 152.

57. See also Dorothea Redepenning, 243.

58. Cf. *supra*, 376, and Redepenning, 249.

59. Interestingly enough, the last eleven measures turn to C-sharp minor, ending inconclusively on its dominant tone. But Liszt also writes an *ossia* conclusion in which E major is retained: in this version, the "confirming" nature of the major tonality is allowed to stand.

60. This opening section has engaged a number of writers: see Sándor Kovács, "Formprinzipien und ungarische Stileigentümlichkeiten in den Spätwerken von Liszt," 115–18; Dieter Rexroth, "Zum Spätwerk Franz Liszts—Material und Form in dem Klavierstück 'Unstern,' " *Bericht über den internationalen musikwissenschaftlichen Kongress Bonn 1970*, ed. Carl Dahlhaus *et al.* (Kassel, 1971), 544–47; and Forte, 221–23, who looks at the melodic unfolding of E-G♯-B-C (set 4–19) in measures 1–70.

61. One last observation on the tonal design: the melodic outline of the second half—C♯-F♯—acts as the *Alternativ-Chroma* complement to the two highlighted tones C and F of the opening twenty measures. Liszt continued to use such chromatic gestures as structural links even in the highly experimental language of the 1880s.

62. The composition from the early 1800s, in folk song style, is entitled "Ég a kunyhó, ropog a nád." See *Neue Ausgabe*, I/14, xi–xii.

Selected Bibliography

Editions

Complete Piano Transcriptions from Wagner's Operas, with an introduction by Charles Suttoni. New York, 1981.

Liszt Society Publications. London, 1950– .

Musikalische Werke. Edited by F. Busoni, P. Raabe, *et al.* Leipzig, 1907–36. Reprint London, 1966.

Neue Ausgabe sämtlicher Werke. First series. Edited by Z. Gárdonyi, I. Sulyok and I. Szelényi. Kassel, 1970–.

Piano Transcriptions from French and Italian Operas. Selected and with an introduction by Charles Suttoni. New York, 1982.

Books and Articles

Backus, Joan. "Aspects of Form in the Music of Liszt: The Principle of Developing Idea." Ph.D. dissertation, University of Victoria, 1985.

Dahlhaus, Carl. "Liszt: Mazeppa," *Analyse und Werturteil. Musikpädagogik* 8 (1970): 85–89.

Forte, Allen. "Liszt's Experimental Idiom and Music of the Early Twentieth Century," *19th Century Music* 10 (1987): 209–28.

Franz Liszt: Beiträge von ungarischen Autoren. Edited by Klara Hamburger. Budapest, 1978.

Gárdonyi, Zoltán. *Le Style hongrois de François Liszt.* Budapest, 1936.

――――. "Neue Tonleiter- und Sequenztypen in Liszts Frühwerken (Zur Frage der 'Lisztschen Sequenzen')," *Studia Musicologica* 11 (1969): 169–99.

Grabócz, Márta. "Die Wirkung des Programms auf die Entwicklung der instrumentalen Formen in Liszts Klavierwerken," *Studia Musicologica* 22 (1980): 299–325.

――――. "Renaissance de la forme énumérative, sous l'influence du modèle épique, dans les oeuvres pour piano de Liszt; facteurs de l'analyse structurale et sémantique," *Studia Musicologica* 26 (1984): 199–218.

――――. *Morphologie des oeuvres pour piano de Liszt: Influence du programme sur l'évolution des formes instrumentales.* Budapest, 1986.

Hughes, William H., Jr. "Liszt's *Première Année de Pèlerinage: Suisse*: A Comparative Study of Early and Revised Versions." D.M.A. dissertation, Eastman School of Music, 1985.

Kókai, Rudolf. *Franz Liszt in seinen frühen Klavierwerken.* Freiburg, 1933. Reprint Kassel, 1968.

La Mara, ed. *Franz Liszts Briefe.* 8 vols. Leipzig, 1893–1902. (*Letters of Franz Liszt.* Vols. 1 and 2. Translated by Constance Bache. London, 1894. Reprint New York, 1968.)

Legány, Dezsö. "Hungarian Historical Portraits," *Studia Musicologica* 28 (1986): 79–88.

Liszt, Franz. *Des Bohémiens et de leur musique en Hongrie.* Paris, 1859. (*The Gipsy* [sic] *in Music.* Translated by Edwin Evans. London, n.d.)

――――. *Pages romantiques.* Edited by Jean Chantavoine. Paris, 1912.

Liszt Studien 1. Kongress-Bericht Eisenstadt 1975. Edited by Wolfgang Suppan. Graz, 1977.

Liszt Studien 2. Referate des 2. Europäischen Liszt-Symposions Eisenstadt 1978. Edited by Serge Gut. Munich/Salzburg, 1981.

Longyear, R. M. "Liszt's B Minor Sonata: Precedents for a Structural Analysis," *Music Review* 34 (1973): 198–209.

Main, Alexander. "Liszt's *Lyon*: Music and the Social Conscience," *19th Century Music* 4 (1981): 228–43.

Marget, Arthur W. "Liszt and Parsifal," *Music Review* 14 (1953): 107–24.

Merrick, Paul. *Revolution and Religion in the Music of Liszt.* Cambridge, 1987.

Neumeyer, David. "Liszt's *Sonetto 104 del Petrarca*: The Romantic Spirit and Voiceleading," *Indiana Theory Review* 2 (1979): 2–22.

Newman, William S. *The Sonata since Beethoven.* 3rd ed. New York, 1983.

Perényi, Eleanor. *Liszt: The Artist as Romantic Hero.* Boston, 1974.

Pesce, Dolores. "Liszt's *Années de Pèlerinage*, Book 3: A 'Hungarian' Cycle?" *19th Century Music* 13 (1990): 207–29.

Ramann, Lina. *Franz Liszt als Künstler und Mensch.* 3 vols. Leipzig, 1880–94.

Redepenning, Dorothea. *Das Spätwerk Franz Liszts: Bearbeitungen eigener Kompositionen.* Hamburg, 1984.

Searle, Humphrey. *The Music of Liszt.* London, 1954.

————. "Franz Liszt," *The New Grove Dictionary of Music and Musicians*. London, 1980.

————. "Franz Liszt," *The New Grove Early Romantic Masters 1*. London, 1985. Pp. 237–378.

Stradal, August, "Das 'Album d'un voyageur' und 'La première année de pèlerinage' ('La Suisse') von Franz Liszt," *Neue Musikzeitung* 33 (1912): 41–43, 153–54, 195–96, 214–15, 255–57, 296–98, 355–56, 394–95, 436–37, 476–78.

Suttoni, Charles. "Piano and Opera: A Study of the Piano Fantasies Written on Opera Themes in the Romantic Era." Ph.D. dissertation, New York University, 1974.

Szabolcsi, Bence. *The Twilight of Ferenc Liszt*. Translated by András Deák. Budapest, 1959.

Szász, Tibor. "Liszt's Symbols for the Divine and Diabolical: Their Revelation of a Program in the B Minor Sonata," *Journal of the American Liszt Society* 15 (1984): 39–95.

Tari, Lujza. "Eine instrumentale ungarische Volksmelodie und ihre Beziehungen zu Liszt und Beethoven," *Studia Musicologica* 25 (1983): 61–71.

Todd, R. Larry. The 'Unwelcome Guest' Regaled: Franz Liszt and the Augmented Triad," *19th Century Music* 12 (1988): 93–115.

Torkewitz, Dieter. *Harmonisches Denken im Frühwerk Franz Liszts*. Munich/Salzburg, 1978.

Wagner, Günther. *Die Klavierballade um die Mitte des 19. Jahrhunderts*. Munich/Salzburg, 1976.

Walker, Alan, ed. *Franz Liszt. The Man and His Music*. London, 1970.

————. *Franz Liszt*. Vol. 1, *The Virtuoso Years 1811–1847*. Rev. ed. New York, 1987. Vol. 2, *The Weimar Years 1848–1861*. New York. 1989.

Waters, Edward N. "Chopin by Liszt," *Musical Quarterly* 47 (1961): 170–94.

Wilson, Karen. "A Historical Study and Stylistic Analysis of Franz Liszt's *Années de pèlerinage*." Ph.D. dissertation, University of North Carolina, 1977.

Winklhofer, Sharon. "Liszt, Marie d'Agoult, and the 'Dante' Sonata," *19th Century Music* 1 (1977): 15–32.

————. *Liszt's Sonata in B Minor: A Study of Autograph Sources and Documents*. Ann Arbor, 1980.

Index